BANNED BOOKS

Literature Suppressed on
SEXUAL
GROUNDS

Ken Wachsberger, General Editor

BANNED BOOKS

Literature Suppressed on

SEXUAL GROUNDS

Dawn B. Sova

Introduction by
Ken Wachsberger

Foreword by
David Greene

☑®

Facts On File, Inc.

To my son, Robert Gregor, and to all young
people who will try to make the world they
have inherited a better place.

Banned Books: Literature Suppressed on Sexual Grounds

Facts On File, Inc.
11 Penn Plaza
New York NY 10001

Library of Congress Cataloging-in-Publication Data

Sova, Dawn B.
Banned books : literature suppressed on sexual grounds / Dawn B.
Sova : introduction by Ken Wachsberger.
p.   cm. — (Banned books)
Includes bibliographical references (p.) and index.
ISBN 0-8160-3305-6
1. Erotic literature—Censorship—United States—History—20th
century. 2. Prohibited books—United States—History—20th century.
3. Erotic literature—Censorship—History. 4. Prohibited books—
History. I. Title. II. Series.
PN56.E7S68   1998   97-40369
363.3'1—DC21

Facts On File books are available at special discounts when purchased in bulk
quantities for businesses, associations, institutions, or sales promotions. Please call
our Special Sales Department in New York at 212/967-8800 or 800/322-8755.

You can find Facts On File on the World Wide Web at http://www.factsonfile.com

Text design by Cathy Rincon
Cover design by Whizbang! Studios

Printed in the United States of America

MP FOF 10 9 8 7 6 5 4 3 2 1

This book is printed on acid-free paper.

CONTENTS

*T*here is no freedom either in civil or ecclesiastical
[affairs], but where the liberty of the press is maintained.

—Matthew Tindal

*I*f all mankind minus one were of one opinion, and only
one person were of the contrary opinion, mankind would be
no more justified in silencing that one person, than he, if
he had the power, would be justified in silencing mankind.

—John Stuart Mill

*D*are to think for yourself.

—Voltaire

ACKNOWLEDGMENTS

The long history of censorship has created many heroes, both famous and obscure, authors and publishers who have dared to defy the restrictions of their respective ages in order to reveal truth in their writings. The works of some appear in this volume, but many more were silenced and their works destroyed. To all, however, this book owes both life and purpose. Had they acquiesced to those who challenge, censor and ban books containing ideas or language that displease vocal minorities, our intellectual universe would be significantly smaller.

I am grateful for my association with Bert Holtje of James Peter Associates, Inc., whose support and advice as both literary agent and friend helped me to maintain perspective throughout this lengthy project. His insight and literate commentary helped to resolve seemingly insurmountable problems.

My sincere appreciation also belongs to Facts On File, Inc., editors Gary M. Krebs, who saw potential in the idea and courageously proposed a censorship series, and Drew Silver, who provided substance and direction to the work. Gary gave the project life, and Drew worked with me to form its personality as he guided the work to completion. I also appreciate my collaboration with General Editor Ken Wachsberger, who had the often thankless task of structuring the project and keeping the writers on task.

Actual works were used to create entries in this volume, giving this book an authenticity that the use of mere summaries could not. This often difficult to locate literature would not have been available to me without the efforts of I. Macarthur Nickles, Director of the Garfield (New Jersey) Library, a man whose professional expertise and insight have been invaluable. He has made certain that my sometimes obscure research requests are satisfied and continues to introduce innovations in my hometown library. I am also grateful to reference experts Kathleen Zalenski and Karen Calandriello, who tracked down unusual books and odd quotations, dates and notes, always persevering long after I had given up the chase.

In my personal life, no one has meant more to me than my son, Rob Gregor, who helped me to organize my thoughts, contributed insights on various works and kept me human. I appreciate greatly the continued support of my parents,

Emil and Violet Sova, whose pride in my accomplishments and unwavering confidence in my abilities have always sustained me.

Finally, although I can never meet them, I appreciate the efforts of the many authors over centuries who risked their livelihoods and lives to stand strong against the oppressive efforts of those who would silence all who refuse to conform.

INTRODUCTION

We Americans are proud of our Constitution, especially its Bill of Rights. The First Amendment right to freedom of speech and religion has inspired dissenters and nonconformists everywhere. Censored writers such as Salman Rushdie, Pramoedya Ananta Toer and Aleksandr Solzhenitsyn have looked to our country's example for strength as they battled for their right to express their own thoughts, and that of others to read them, even at the risk of their lives.

Yet censorship has been a major part of American history, from the time of Roger Williams and other early colonial freethinkers. Many of our richest literary works—*The Adventures of Huckleberry Finn, The Color Purple, The Grapes of Wrath, The Jungle, Uncle Tom's Cabin, Tropic of Cancer*—have been censored at one time or another. Even today school boards, local governments, religious fanatics and moral crusaders attempt to restrict our freedom to read. Advancing technology has provided more diverse targets—the record, film and television industries, and the Internet—for the censors and would-be censors to aim for, as they work their strategies to restrict free expression and the freedom to read, watch and listen, dumbing us all down in order to shield their children and you, from original or disturbing thoughts.

Fortunately, our country has a strong tradition of fighting censorship as well. Groups such as the National Coalition Against Censorship, the American Library Association's Office for Intellectual Freedom, People for the American Way, the American Civil Liberties Union and the PEN American Center exist to defend the First Amendment, through legal action and by raising public awareness. They deserve our moral, political and financial support.

The four volumes in this collection add to that rich tradition by spotlighting more than 400 works that have been censored for their political, social, religious or erotic content, in the United States and around the world, from biblical times to the present day. While many of these have been legally "banned"—or prohibited "as by official order"—all indeed have been banned or censored in a broader sense: targeted for removal from school curricula or library shelves, condemned in churches and forbidden to the faithful, rejected or expurgated by publishers, challenged in court, even voluntarily rewritten by their authors. Censored authors have been verbally abused, physically attacked, shunned by their families and communities, excommunicated from their religious congregations and shot, hanged or burned at the stake by their enemies, who thus made them heroes and often enough secured their memory for posterity. Their works include novels, histories, biographies, children's books, religious and philosophical treatises, dictionaries, poems, polemics and every other form of written expression.

It is illuminating to discover in these histories that such cultural landmarks as the Bible, the Koran, the Talmud and the greatest classics of world literature have often been suppressed or censored from the same motives, and by similar forces, as those we see today seeking to censor such books as *Daddy's Roommate* and *Heather Has Two Mommies*. Every American reading these volumes will find in their pages books they love, and will be thankful that their authors' freedom of expression and their own freedom to read, are constitutionally protected. But at the same time, how many will be gratified by the cruel fate of books we detest? Reader-citizens capable of acknowledging their own contradictions will be grateful for the existence of the First Amendment and will thank its guardians, including the authors of this series, for protecting us against our own worst impulses.

To prevent redundancy, works banned for multiple reasons appear in only one volume apiece, based on the judgment of the editor and the volume authors. The alphabetical arrangement provides easy access to titles. Works whose titles appear in SMALL CAPITAL LETTERS within an entry have entries of their own elsewhere in the same volume. Those whose titles appear in *ITALICIZED SMALL CAPITAL LETTERS* have entries in one of the other volumes. In addition, each volume carries complete lists of the works discussed in the other volumes.

—Ken Wachsberger

FOREWORD

Sex and literature have proved a volatile combination for centuries. The erotic content of literary works was chief among the evils that Anthony Comstock, who as inspector with the United States Postal System would become America's foremost censor of the early 20th century, sought to eradicate. Comstock believed that erotic literature was a "trap" designed by Satan expressly to detour pure and decent young people from the path of righteousness to the road of depravity.

In his essay "Traps for the Young," published in 1883, Comstock wrote: "These sure-ruin traps comprise a large variety of half-dime novels, five-and-ten-cent story papers, and low-priced pamphlets for boys and girls. This class includes the silly, insipid tale, the coarse, slangy story in the dialect of the barroom, the blood-and-thunder romance of border life, and the exaggerated details of crimes, real and imaginary." Comstock bemoaned the heroes of these books: young villains who "favor[ed] violation of marriage laws and cheapen[ed] female virtue."

It is easy enough, more than a hundred years later, to dismiss Comstock as merely an overzealous product of a less permissive society. However, American society is still grappling with the culture of moralism that is Comstock's legacy. Our definitions of "offensive," "indecent," "pornographic" and "obscene" have changed since Comstock's time, but the notion that our government, or our society in some other form, can set a national standard of decency and decide the suitability of literacy "erotica" remains with us in full force.

The line separating so-called appropriate from inappropriate literature may have been moved, but that line is still being drawn. As we near the end of the 20th century, art depicting sexual acts and nudity is still stigmatized as "pornography." Since the Internet has opened a library in every computer, the government and the Internet industry have rushed to restrict the sexual content of cyberspace. We enjoy a vibrant freedom of expression, as guaranteed by the First Amendment to the United States Constitution, but we do not enjoy a strong freedom of expression of sexual ideas. The Supreme Court has crafted an exception, a category of expression it has labeled "obscenity," simply because it has determined that such expression is harmful to our national moral fiber. Unlike the other exceptions to the First Amendment created by the Supreme

Court—words likely to provoke serious physical damage to persons and property, defamation and libel—the "obscenity" exception is not an accommodation to the competing freedoms of other persons.

In the fight against censorship of erotic literature, we not only confront the task of defining "obscenity," we must also, as this volume details, respond to the moral pronouncements of "offensive" and "indecent." American society will continue to struggle with where to draw "the line"—including agonizing over what books may be banned—until we stop conceding that it is necessary to draw a line at all. Even those who oppose censorship too frequently defend books on the strength of their "responsibility" message and downplay their feared "immoral" influences. However, in so doing, they tacitly admit that there exists a public morality from which certain books deviate, acknowledging that there is some literature that is so dangerous that individuals should not be able to decide for themselves whether to read it.

We cannot just dismiss the censors as prudes. Their dogma that our society should have a moral standard is a threat to our most basic notions of a free society. There is an unexplainable irony that American culture, which has vigorously nurtured liberty and democracy, has been so reluctant to include erotic expression within the panoply of freedoms we celebrate.

> —David Greene, Program Director
> National Campaign for Freedom
> of Expression
> Washington, D.C.

PREFACE

Changing social mores have moved many books formerly forbidden because of explicit sexual content out of locked cabinets and onto the open shelves in libraries and bookstores. Many such books have also entered high school and college classrooms to be read by students who little realize their notorious pasts.

A changed society has taken literary criticism out of the courts. In 1961, the United States Supreme Court pondered if D. H. Lawrence's *Lady Chatterley's Lover* was lewd or literary. By 1969, the novel was required reading in college literature courses. The same is true of other works, such as James Joyce's *Ulysses*, Vladimir Nabokov's *Lolita*, Henry Miller's *Tropic of Cancer* and Voltaire's *Candide*, all once banned and considered indecent. When did the "obscene" and the "pornographic" become the "erotic" and the "classic?"

Dirty words alone are not enough to make a work erotic, although many books in the 19th and early 20th centuries were banned simply for that reason. Similarly, many books have been banned because they discussed or alluded to such familiar social phenomena as prostitution, unwed pregnancy and adultery, among them Thomas Hardy's *Jude the Obscure* and Nathaniel Hawthorne's *Scarlet Letter*. Neither can reasonably be termed an erotic or pornographic work, yet both books were banned for their sexual content.

In 1957, the U.S. Supreme Court changed its definition of obscenity to refer to works that had sexual content but no "redeeming social importance." This redefinition sent Americans in search of works both erotically interesting and socially redeeming, and thus legally sexually titillating. Anonymous Victorian novels, the underground pornography of their day, joined art books with lavish reproductions of Japanese and Indian erotic painting and sculpture and explicit psychological case studies of sexually "abnormal" behavior as the standard middle-class erotica of the early to mid-20th century. During that time, American courts tried obscenity cases and pondered the literary merits of *Fanny Hill: Memoirs of a Woman of Pleasure*, *Lady Chatterley's Lover*, *Ulysses* and *Tropic of Capricorn*.

By 1970, the barriers were down and the Report of the United States President's Commission on Obscenity noted that "Virtually every English language book thought to be obscene when published, and many similar books translated into English, have been reissued by secondary publishers. The entire stockpile of 'classic erotic literature' (e.g., *The Kama Sutra*, Frank Harris, de Sade, etc.) published over centuries has thus come onto the market."

As formerly banned works gained acceptance, many novels published in the last two decades have benefited and freely include sexual detail and gratuitous sex scenes. Society's view of sex has changed and many books that would once have been condemned as pornographic or obscene now become best-sellers. Even cheaply produced "adult" books that do not pretend to any purpose other than sexual arousal are now easily available to willing buyers through direct mail and retail stores. The legal line between pornography and erotica has disappeared, and the differences are now defined more according to aesthetic appeal than to content.

But, how is "erotic" different from "pornographic?" Nineteenth-century booksellers coined the term *erotica* to describe risqué writing found in such classics as the poems of Catullus, the satires of Juvenal and love manuals such as the *Kama Sutra*, as well as that perennial favorite, *Fanny Hill, Memoirs of a Woman of Pleasure* (1748–49), the subject of the first U.S. obscenity trial in 1821. These early works bore no resemblance to the cheaply produced, and cheap-looking, books of the mid-20th century. The market catered to men of means who could well afford the lavishly illustrated deluxe editions that satisfied what was termed their "curious" tastes. Patrons paid handsomely for their pleasure.

The growth of mass demand for erotica required mass production, and cheaply produced pulp novels with lurid covers and plotless texts appeared in great number. These contrasted strongly in appearance with the lavishly illustrated and expensively produced gentlemen's erotica of the 19th century, but they were identical in purpose. Price was the primary distinguishing factor. The differences became so blurred that the 1970 Report of the United States President's Commission on Obscenity struggled and failed to define what was obscene and pornographic, and thus illegal.

The definitions were no clearer in 1986, when the Attorney General's Commission on Pornography (often called the Meese Commission) revealed that its findings were inconclusive regarding the dangers of pornography. Although the Commission recommended intensified enforcement against child pornography and material showing sexual violence, the Commission members hedged in their recommendations regarding all-text materials. The panel recommended "extraordinary caution" in regard to prosecuting those who distributed materials that contained no photographs, pictures or drawings. "The written word has had and continues to have a special place in this and any other civilization." Designating as among the "least harmful" types of pornography "books consisting of the printed text only," the Commission observed that such text might not always meet its criteria for pornography, that it be "sexually explicit and intended primarily for the purpose of sexual arousal."

The century and a half of obscenity trials regarding literature came to a halt, and the old argument was invalidated. Those who could read could indulge themselves in the provocative power of words that arouse, stimulate and titillate—they were consumers of "erotica." The less literate, more likely to view X-rated videos or picture magazines that arouse, stimulate and titillate, were indulging in "pornography." The appeal of the categories is the same, but their audiences differed as did the assumed consequences.

There are currently no books in print that systematically survey the content of and controversies surrounding specific erotic works. In general, related books currently in print have one of three purposes: (1) to discuss the nature of erotica in one culture or era, (2) to define or to argue the legal aspects of pornography or (3) to anthologize without critical comment (or to promote actively) current or past erotic writings.

Several thematically arranged books discuss erotica in various cultures (i.e., Indian, Chinese and Japanese) and various time periods such as the Victorian era. The intent of these texts is to examine the sociological implications or role of the literature in a particular time period rather than to provide information about specific books.

The goal of this volume of works censored on grounds of sexual content is neither to deride nor defend either the mainstream erotica or the pulp pornography that has been published over the centuries. Instead, it is to illuminate changing cultural attitudes toward the erotic, through a survey of the legal fate of classic and representative works in centuries past as well as in the 20th century.

—Dawn B. Sova, Ph.D

Works Discussed in This Volume

AN AMERICAN TRAGEDY
Theodore Dreiser

THE ARABIAN NIGHTS, or *THE THOUSAND AND ONE NIGHTS*
Sir Richard Burton, trans.

THE ART OF LOVE (ARS AMATORIA)
Ovid (Publius Ovidius Naso)

BESSIE COTTER
Wallace Smith

THE BLUEST EYE
Toni Morrison

BOY
James Hanley

CANDIDE
Voltaire (François Marie Arouet Voltaire)

CANDY
Maxwell Kenton

THE CARPETBAGGERS
Harold Robbins

CASANOVA'S HOMECOMING (CASANOVA'S HEIMFAHRT)
Arthur Schnitzler

THE CHINESE ROOM
Vivian Connell

CHRISTINE
Stephen King

THE 120 DAYS OF SODOM (LES 120 JOURNÉES DE SODOME)
Marquis de Sade

OUR LADY OF THE FLOWERS (NOTRE-DAME DES FLEURS)
Jean Genet

PAMELA, OR VIRTUE REWARDED
Samuel Richardson

PANSIES
D. H. Lawrence

THE PERFUMED GARDEN
Sir Richard Burton, trans.

PEYTON PLACE
Grace Metalious

THE PHILANDERER
Stanley Kauffmann

POEMS AND BALLADS
Algernon Charles Swinburne

POINT COUNTER POINT
Aldous Huxley

RABBIT, RUN
John Updike

THE RAINBOW
D. H. Lawrence

REPLENISHING JESSICA
Max Bodenheim

SANCTUARY
William Faulkner

THE SATYRICON
Gaius Petronius Arbiter

SEPTEMBER IN QUINZE
Vivian Connell

SERENADE
James M. Cain

SEXUS
Henry Miller

TROPIC OF CAPRICORN
Henry Miller

ULYSSES
James Joyce

VENUS AND TANNHAUSER (UNDER THE HILL)
Aubrey Beardsley

THE WILD PALMS
William Faulkner

WOMEN IN LOVE
D. H. Lawrence

A YOUNG GIRL'S DIARY
Anonymous

LITERATURE
SUPPRESSED ON
SEXUAL GROUNDS

AN AMERICAN TRAGEDY

Author: Theodore Dreiser
Original date and place of publication: 1925, United States
Original publisher: Boni & Liveright
Type: Novel

SUMMARY

An American Tragedy is a fictionalized version of the Chester Gillette murder case that was tried in 1906. The story examines the manner in which one man's fate is determined by his background, personality and environmental conditions that lead him to desire luxuries and perquisites beyond his reach. The novel was originally published in two volumes, a first part that recounts events that lead to a death and a second part that relates the story of the murder trial.

Clyde Griffiths is the son of street evangelists whose skid-row mission income cannot provide him with the fine clothes, high social status and sophisticated friends that he craves. As a bellhop in an expensive Kansas City hotel, he comes into contact with wealthy people who have everything that he wishes to possess. He also explores his sexual needs in his infatuation with Hortense Briggs, on whom he spends his salary. After he accidentally kills a pedestrian in an automobile accident, Clyde leaves Kansas City and travels to Lycurgus, New York, where his uncle gives him a job as a supervisor in the family collar factory. Clyde also makes his first visit to a brothel in a scene that describes both the interior of the brothel and the variety of girls available to him. His chosen partner leads him upstairs to a room and "calmly, and before a tall mirror which revealed her fully to herself and him, began to disrobe."

Wishing for a "free pagan girl of his own," Clyde becomes sexually involved with Roberta Alden, a factory worker who believes that he loves her. Although their sexual activity is not graphically described, the reader is clearly aware that their relationship is not platonic as they struggle "in vain against the greater intimacy which each knew that the other was desirous of yielding to, and eventually so yielding, looked forward to the approaching night with an eagerness which was a fever embodying a fear." The affair proceeds, but Clyde becomes infatuated with and hopes to marry the daughter of a wealthy factory owner. When he tries to break off his relationship with Roberta, he learns that she is pregnant. Despite his efforts to arrange an abortion through visits to pharmacists and a doctor, Roberta remains pregnant and insists that Clyde honor his promise to marry her. They take a day trip into the Adirondack mountains, and Roberta drowns in an isolated lake when their boat tips and she tumbles overboard. Clyde fails to save her, and the author leaves unclear whether or not he had even tried. Although Clyde runs away, he is caught and placed on trial. Eventually convicted, he is sentenced to die in the electric chair, but up until his death he remains unsure whether or not he committed a murder.

CENSORSHIP HISTORY

In 1929, *An American Tragedy* was suppressed in Boston after a jury declared New York publisher Donald Friede guilty of violating the Massachusetts antiobscenity statute by selling the novel. In the case of *Commonwealth v. Friede*, Mass. 318, 171 N.E. 472 (1930), the attorney for the Watch and Ward Society read various passages in the courtroom, and neither the judge nor the members of the jury read the entire novel. After reading the passage regarding the scene in the brothel when the girl begins to undress, the prosecuting attorney stated to the all-male jury: "*Well*, perhaps where the gentleman who published this book comes from it is not considered obscene, indecent, and impure for a woman to start disrobing before a man, but it happens to be out in Roxbury where *I* come from."

When Friede's attorney Arthur Garfield Hays and Dreiser asked the court to consider the entire book rather than merely specific passages, the judge refused. The defense also brought in noted trial attorney Clarence Darrow, whose main role consisted of reading passages from the book aloud. Hays had intended to question Dreiser in a way that would allow the author to show that he had never intended to write an indecent or obscene book, but Dreiser was denied that opportunity as the judge excluded all of the defense attorney's questions. Friede was convicted of selling an "impure and obscene" book, although he received no sentence. In May 1930, the publisher appealed the case but the Massachusetts Supreme Court upheld the conviction in *Commonwealth v. Friede*, 271 Mass. 318, 171 N.E. 472, 69 A.L.R. 640 (Sup. Jud. Ct. 1930) and forced Friede to pay a fine of $300. The trial judge refused to allow the entire book to be read in court, ruling that it would have been impractical to read the whole book to the jury and observing that omission of the allegedly obscene passages would have eliminated nothing essential from the novel. The court also overruled the appeal of the bookseller, who had been entrapped into selling the book. The irony is that, while the trial was in progress, the novel was required reading across the Charles River in a Harvard University English course.

The public outcry over *An American Tragedy* motivated the Massachusetts legislature to reform the laws regarding censorship. Of several bills that were proposed, a law that would have required the whole book rather than excerpts to be considered in court was defeated on April 1, 1929, in the Massachusetts Senate in a vote of 15 to 13. The bill was submitted a second time and again defeated, this time with a vote of 20 to 17.

FURTHER READING

Boyer, Paul S. "Boston Book Censorship in the Twenties." *American Quarterly* 15 (Spring 1930): 3–24.

Bullard, F. Lauriston. "Boston's Ban Likely to Live Long." *New York Times* (April 28, 1929): Sec. 3: 1, 7.

Gilloti, Chris F. "Book Censorship in Massachusetts: The Search for a Test of Obscenity." *Boston University Law Review* 42 (Fall 1962): 476–91.

Grant, Sidney S., and S.E. Angoff. "Recent Developments in Censorship." *Boston University Law Review* 10 (November 1930): 488–509.

Markmann, Charles L. *The Noblest Cry: A History of the American Civil Liberties Union.* New York: St. Martin's, 1965.

"More of the Same: Massachusetts Supreme Court and Dreiser's *American Tragedy.*" *Outlook* 155 (June 11, 1930): 214.

Schriftgiesser, Karl. "Boston Stays Pure." *New Republic* 58 (May 8, 1929): 327–29.

THE ARABIAN NIGHTS, or THE THOUSAND AND ONE NIGHTS

Translator: Sir Richard Burton
Original date and place of publication: 1881, England; 1885–88, Switzerland
Original publisher: Worthington Book Company; The Kama Shastra Society
Type: Collected folktales

SUMMARY

Long considered merely children's entertainment, the tales of *The Arabian Nights* were familiar to English readers through such stories as "Sinbad the Sailor," "Aladdin and His Lamp" and "Ali Baba and the Forty Thieves." Of Persian, Indian and Arabic folk origin, the tales were first collected in Cairo around 1450 and known as *The Book of a Thousand and One Nights.* The French translation by Antoine Galland, published privately from 1707 to 1717, brought the tales to the attention of Europeans, and countless adaptations were published in England and the United States in the 18th and 19th centuries.

All editions have followed the same story framework. The storyteller is Shahrazad (Scheherazade in other translations), who begins the tales as a means of staying alive. After ordering beheadings of his queen and 10 favorite concubines who had cuckolded him, the Sultan Shahryar (Schahriah in other translations) marries each night for three years a new wife who is strangled at daybreak. When his country protests the depletion of available young women to become queen for a night, he marries Shahrazad, who asks that her sister Dinarzade remain with her. Shahrazad begins a story for her sister one hour before daybreak on her wedding night. Shahryar also listens and becomes intrigued, but Shahrazad stops midstory at daybreak. Because Shahryar wants to know how the story ends, he spares her life and asks her to continue the story that evening. Cunning Shahrazad continues her story but ends midstory each daybreak for 1,001 nights, by the end of which she has borne three children, told 270 tales, and earned her husband's trust and love.

Edward William Lane published privately the first English translation in 1840 and John Payne's *The Arabian Nights* appeared in 1881, but Sir Richard Burton's translation remains the most complete and alone captures the tone of the original, although it has generally remained unavailable. Lane translated fewer than half of the tales and omitted sexual references. Payne translated substantially more tales and many of the tales lack sexual incidents while other tales contain metaphoric sexual references: "She did off her clothes and I had a lover's privacy of her and found her an unpierced pearl and a filly no man had ridden." Animal-human intercourse is reported and thighs, breasts and buttocks are frequently mentioned.

Burton, whose translation includes even more explicit sexual detail, wrote in his foreword that he translated the tales into language "as the Arab would have written in English." Thus, they are exuberant, earthy and unembarrassed tales of lust, lesbianism, sodomy, bestiality, male transvestism, pederasty, incest and sexual mutilation. His sexually willing slave girls, nubile virgins, omnipresent eunuchs, lecherous old women and wine-induced lust entice the reader. Although most of the descriptions of sexual behavior are tastefully presented with euphemisms, the sexual nature of the actions is clear. One story details a porter's carousing with three ladies who admire and toy with his "prickle" while he teases about "thy slit, thy womb, thy coynte, thy clitoris." Several seductions begin as a man and a woman "warm with wine" embrace with "kisses and murmurs of pleasure and amorous toyings," after which they indulge in "hot lust" before having "abated her maidenhead."

Included in Burton's translation is the lengthy "Terminal Essay," which devotes one-quarter of its 166 pages to analyzing, describing and evaluating on a country-by-country basis the variations of pederasty and sodomy with which he had become familiar in his years of travel. Written in the language of the social anthropologist and quoting the writings of travelers, historians and medical experts, he identifies known homosexual liaisons from history and describes the practices as well as the social roles of pederasts and homosexuals in history and in the 19th century.

CENSORSHIP HISTORY

The Obscene Publications Act was passed in 1857 with the express purpose of suppressing sexually explicit material, and fear of prosecution made Burton cautious. Although he did not expurgate his work, he did modify greatly the manner in which it was published. He had 1,000 copies of the work printed in Benares, India, at his own expense and named the Kama Shastra Society, of which he and fellow author Foster Fitzgerald Arbuthnot were founders and sole members, as the publisher. The first printing was sold to subscribers for the equivalent of $200 in today's currency. The books were financially successful, and Burton made a profit of 10,000 guineas ($25,000 in 1890s currency).

Burton claimed that *The Arabian Nights* was meant only for men and particularly for male scholars who wished to increase their understanding of other cultures. As Rice reports, Burton was denounced in the *Edinburgh Review* as "a man who knows thirty-five languages and dialects, especially that of pornography" and an authority on "all that relates to the bestial element in man." His lengthy work was called by another reviewer "an extraordinary agglomeration of filth."

After Burton's death, abridged forms of his work were published, but the full unexpurgated version remained unavailable to the public—and was banned by U.S. Customs—until after 1931. When Burton died, his wife, Lady Isabel, destroyed all of his private papers, as well as the original notes and manuscript for *The Arabian Nights*. She also entrusted William Coote, secretary of the National Vigilance Association, to burn books and papers after her death to remove all remaining "indecencies."

Payne's translation was one of a number of expensive editions of literary classics, including Boccaccio's DECAMERON, Queen Margaret of Navarre's THE HEPTAMERON, Rabelais's *Gargantua and Pantagruel*, Fielding's HISTORY OF TOM JONES, Rousseau's CONFESSIONS and Ovid's ART OF LOVE (*Ars Amatoria*), involved in the civil case *In re Worthington Company*, 30 N.Y.S. 361(1894). In 1894, the New York Society for the Suppression of Vice, under the zealous leadership of Anthony Comstock, brought civil proceedings against the bankrupt Worthington Book Publishing Company that sought the right to sell off assets. The receiver for the company asked the court to allow sale of the books, expensive volumes of world-renowned literary classics. Comstock appeared in the court record as opposing the sale.

In stating the decision of the court, Judge Morgan J. O'Brien stated that "a seeker after the sensual and degrading parts of a narrative may find in all these works, as in those of other great authors, something to satisfy his pruriency," but he added that to simply condemn an entire literary work because of a few episodes "would compel the exclusion from circulation of a very large proportion of the works of fiction of the most famous writers of the English language." The court decision characterized the specific editions as being "choice editions, both as to the letter-press and the bindings . . . as to prevent their being generally sold or purchased, except by those who would desire them for their literary merit, or for their worth as specimens of fine book-making." In short, even though the text remained the same as that in cheaper editions, Judge O'Brien determined that the "very artistic character, the high qualities of style, the absence of those glaring and crude pictures [set these books] entirely apart from such gross and obscene writings as it is the duty of the public authorities to suppress."

The United States Customs Office continued to ban the import of Burton's unexpurgated translation until 1930, when the Tariff Act removed the ban on acknowledged literary classics.

FURTHER READING

"Anthony Comstock Overruled." *Publishers Weekly* 45 (June 30, 1894): 942–43.
Bercovici, Alfred. *That Blackguard Burton!* Indianapolis, Ind.: Bobbs-Merrill, 1962.
Brodie, Fawn M. *The Devil Drives: A Life of Sir Richard Burton.* New York: Norton, 1967.
Rice, Edward. *Captain Sir Richard Francis Burton.* New York: Scribner's, 1990.
Thomas, Donald. *A Long Time Burning: The History of Literary Censorship in England.* New York: Praeger, 1969.

THE ART OF LOVE (ARS AMATORIA)

Author: Ovid (Publius Ovidius Naso)
Original date and place of publication: c. A.D.1, Rome; 1926, England
Original publisher: John Lane Co. (England)
Type: Poetry collection

SUMMARY

The Art of Love is a guide to attracting and holding a member of the opposite sex, and it is composed in three parts. The first part gives wise advice to men concerning how to win a mistress; the second part advises men how to retain the interest of the mistress and the third part tells women how they can satisfy the sensual desires of men. Ovid provides suggestions regarding the care of the body and the face, the ways of flattery and the advantages of selecting a mature mistress. Critics have noted parallels between advice given by Benjamin Franklin in "Advice on Choosing a Mistress" and passages from *Ars Amatoria*, such as

> Let me see my girl with eyes that confess her excitement;
> Let her, after she comes, want no more for a while.
> What does youth know of delight? Some things ought not to be
>   hurried.
> After some thirty-odd years, lovers begin to learn how.

Ovid also gives women advice regarding how to make the most of their good points, including the ways in which to pose themselves in various situations.

> Lie on your back, if your face and all of your features are
>   pretty.
> If your posterior's cute, better be seen from behind
>   . . . .

If the breasts and thighs are lovely to look at,
Let the man stand and the girl lie on a slant on the bed.

The advice to men is geared toward grooming them to be effective predators, and his advice for women prepares them to be desirable prey.

CENSORSHIP HISTORY

The Art of Love appears to have created difficulties for Ovid in A.D. 8, when Augustus banished Ovid from Rome for political reasons, but historians note that the erotic content of the poems provided a contributing factor. In 1497, in Florence, Italy, *The Art of Love* was burned with the works of Dante for their "immoral" content in Fra. Girolamo Savonarola's Bonfire of the Vanities. In 1564, the work was added to the list of books banned by the Tridentine Index in Rome, for "treating of lascivious or obscene subjects."

In 1892, *The Art of Love* was involved in the litigation of the Worthington Book Publishing Co., which was in financial difficulty. The receiver wanted to sell some of the company stock, including Burton's translation of ARABIAN NIGHTS, Fielding's HISTORY OF TOM JONES, Boccaccio's DECAMERON, Queen Margaret of Navarre's HEPTAMERON, Rabelais's *GARGANTUA AND PANTAGRUEL* and Rousseau's CONFESSIONS to pay off creditors, but Anthony Comstock stepped in to oppose the sales. He demanded of the court that the books be officially burned. (See *Arabian Nights*.)

In 1926, United States Customs officers in San Francisco held up a new English edition of the *Love Books of Ovid*, illustrated by Jean de Bosschere, published by John Lane Company. The edition had been limited to only 300 copies and was already sold out. The work was banned from importation until the passage of the 1930 amendment to the Tariff Act eased restrictions on foreign classics.

FURTHER READING

Craig, Alec. *Suppressed Books: A History of the Conception of Literary Obscenity*. New York: World Publishing, 1963.
Hurewitz, Leon. *Historical Dictionary of Censorship in the United States*. Westport, Conn.: Greenwood, 1985.
Loth, David. *The Erotic in Literature*. New York: Dorset, 1961.

BESSIE COTTER

Author: Wallace Smith
Original date and place of publication: 1935, England
Original publisher: Heinemann
Type: Novel

SUMMARY

Bessie Cotter, praised highly as a literary work when it was first published in January 1935, depicts the life of a prostitute in realistic and unglamorized images. Set in Chicago in the early part of the 20th century, the novel relates the story of Bessie Cotter, who willingly enters the life of prostitution simply because it pays better than factory work. She is not a miserable victim of the streets, nor has she been drugged, tricked or abused into selling her body. Neither is she consciously immoral or evil.

Instead, Bessie is a likable character, basically decent and caring toward others, whose simple philosophy of life is based on survival. She clearly does not like the "sporting life," but life in Miss Myrtle's "parlour house" is warm and secure. Bessie is content that she is fed well and earns $25 each night at Miss Myrtle's. She contrasts these earnings with the $10 per week that she would earn if she worked in a factory, the only other type of work that someone lacking in marketable skills might find. The other "ladies" working at Miss Myrtle's have chosen their line of work for similar reasons.

Although the main action of the book takes place in a house of prostitution, the sexual activity is only suggestive and not overt. In a similar manner, the language of the women and their clients is inoffensive; "obscenities" are used at only one point in the novel, when two waiters are clearing away dishes from the previous night. The fault of the novel, according to its critics, lies in the failure of the author to condemn Bessie and the other ladies of Miss Myrtle's for their lifestyles, or to provide them with punishment for their actions.

CENSORSHIP HISTORY

Bessie Cotter was sold openly for four months before A. F. Winnington-Ingram, the bishop of London and chair of the Public Morality Council, contacted authorities with a complaint that the novel portrayed "an immoral life" without regrets or recriminations. The publisher was charged with selling an "obscene book" with "intent to corrupt" and ordered to appear before the Bow Street magistrate. Attorney General Sir Thomas Inskip made the following opening statement for the crown: "The book deals with what everybody will recognize as an unsavory subject—gratification of sexual appetite." In the relatively short hearing, Heinemann pleaded guilty when accused of "obscenity in publishing" and agreed to pay the fine of £100 and court costs of 100 guineas. The book, which had sold 6,000 copies in four months of sales, was removed from distribution.

FURTHER READING

Craig, Alec. *The Banned Books of England and Other Countries*. London: Allen & Unwin, 1962.
Rolph, Cecil Hewitt. *Books in the Dock*. London: Deutsch, 1961.

THE BLUEST EYE

Author: Toni Morrison
Original date and place of publication: 1970, United States
Original publisher: Holt, Rinehart and Winston
Type: Novel

SUMMARY

The Bluest Eye is a sad and tragic novel that recounts the abuse and destruction of Pecola Breedlove, a young African-American girl whose mother knew that her very dark baby would grow into an unattractive young girl. The novel, which takes place in 1940, is narrated by Claudia MacTeer, two years younger than Pecola and her only friend. Black in a white-dominated world, Pecola begins to believe that life would be prettier and better if she were white, and she views blue eyes as symbolic of whiteness. She watches her father, Cholly Breedlove, become increasingly violent as his shattered dreams and constant humiliations as an African American heighten his frustrations, and her mother, Pauline, escapes into the clean and orderly life of working as a maid in a white family's home.

Pecola is raped by her father one spring afternoon when he returns home drunk and the two are alone. She becomes pregnant after he rapes her a second time. Traumatized by the attacks, she drifts further from reality and visits fraudulent minister Micah Elihue Whitcomb, known commonly as Soaphead Church, to ask him to give her blue eyes. For a fee, Soaphead claims that he can help her, but she must perform a task for him. He has wanted to rid himself of an old, sick dog, so he gives Pecola poisoned meat to feed the dog but tells her only that feeding the dog will result in a sign regarding her wish. Pecola is horrified as she watches the dog stagger around the yard, then die.

The combination of the rapes and this incident drives Pecola mad, leading to her complete loss of touch with reality. Pecola believes that she does have blue eyes and invents an imaginary friend who is always nearby for reassurance that her eyes are the bluest in the world.

CENSORSHIP HISTORY

Several incidents in the book have sparked controversy. The two rapes of Pecola have been criticized for being too graphic in description, and the novel describes the sounds that Pecola hears of her parents having sex in the room next to hers. Another incident that is specifically described is Cholly's first sexual encounter, during which he is surprised by three white hunters who focus a flashlight on the young people and force them to conclude their sexual act.

The Bluest Eye has been challenged in several school districts because of its "vulgar" and "obscene" language as well as for its "graphic sexual description."

In 1994, the novel was removed from the 11th-grade curriculum at Lathrop High School in Fairbanks, Alaska, after parents complained that the language was "obscene" and that it contained explicit sexual episodes. School administrators ordered the book taken off the required reading list and stated as their reasons that "it was a very controversial book; it contains lots of very graphic descriptions and lots of disturbing language."

That same year, the novel was challenged in the West Chester, Pennsylvania, school district and at Morrisville (Pennsylvania) Borough High School. Parents in both districts complained to the school board of education about the "sexual content" of the novel and its "objectionable language." After reviewing the complaint and the book, the boards in both districts rejected the parents' request to remove the book from the school libraries and readings lists.

FURTHER READING

Butler-Evans, Elliott. *Race, Gender and Desire: Narrative Strategies in the Fiction of Toni Cade Bambara and Toni Morrison.* Philadelphia: Temple University Press, 1989.
Kuenz, Jane. "*The Bluest Eye*: Notes on History, Community and Black Female Subjectivity." *African American Review* 27 (Fall 1993): 421–31.
Newsletter on Intellectual Freedom (May 1994): 86; (January 1995): 25; (March 1995): 44–45.
Tirrell, Lynne. "Storytelling and Moral Agency." *Journal of Aesthetics & Art Criticism* 48 (Spring 1990): 115–26.
Weinstein, Philip M. *What Else but Love? The Ordeal of Race in Faulkner and Morrison.* New York: Columbia University Press, 1996.

BOY

Author: James Hanley
Original date and place of publication: 1931, England
Original publisher: Boriswood Ltd.
Type: Novel

SUMMARY

Boy is a novel with social implications, written to expose the abuses that are perpetrated on a young boy who runs away to sea. Only 13 years of age, the working-class boy not only must deal with the usual hardships of work onboard the ship but is also subjected to sexual abuse by several members of the crew while the others simply ignore his plight. Despite his onboard treatment, when the ship docks in Alexandria, another shipmate takes the boy to the brothels to provide him with an introduction to heterosexual intercourse. The boy later contracts syphilis and is murdered by the captain of the vessel, because he is seen to pose a threat to the other sailors.

The aim of Hanley is not to titillate readers. Instead, his book contains a strongly moral tone that offers more of a warning than an invitation to those who might fantasize about a life on the open seas. The sailors are made to speak in the coarse and crude manner that dockers and sailors speak, and the brothel scenes are graphically recounted, without romanticizing the sexual encounters. As evidence of its serious intentions to produce a quality work, the publisher first issued the novel in an expensive limited edition.

CENSORSHIP HISTORY

Soon after it first appeared, *Boy* was expurgated by the publisher and reissued in a less expensive edition than the first. The second edition contained asterisks in the place of certain words spoken by the sailors and in descriptions of sexual activity. In a cheaply printed third edition published in 1934, the publisher replaced the asterisks with euphemisms and omitted certain passages entirely. Police seized copies of this edition in November 1934 from a lending library in Manchester and charged the librarian with distributing an "obscene publication." The directors of Boriswood Ltd. were prosecuted for aiding and abetting in the distribution, and the company was later arraigned as the principal perpetrator. On the advice of attorneys, the publisher pleaded guilty to the charges and paid fines totaling £400.

The action panicked other reputable publishers who became more conservative in signing works to publish. Author E. M. Forster publicly deplored the use of the law to punish the publication of what he called "a novel of much literary merit." His remarks were made in a paper entitled "Liberty in England," presented at the International Congress of Authors in Paris in June 1935.

FURTHER READING

Craig, Alec. *The Banned Books of England and Other Countries.* London: Allen and Unwin, 1962.
Dangerfield, George. "Invisible Censorship." *North American Review* 244 (Winter 1937–38): 334–48.
Forster, E. M. *Abinger Harvest.* New York: Harcourt, Brace, 1936.

CANDIDE

Author: Voltaire (François-Marie Arouet de Voltaire)
Original date and place of publication: 1759, Switzerland
Original publisher: Gabriel and Philibert Cramer
Type: Satire

SUMMARY

Candide, originally *Candide, ou l'optimisme*, is a satire of optimism and of the belief that "the world is the best of all possible worlds and everything in it is a necessary evil," a theory attributed to the philosopher Gottfried Leibniz. Voltaire refused to accept the philosopher's assertion that evil and death are part of a universal harmony, and he structured *Candide* to show the ridiculous nature of such thought. Voltaire hid his identity when publishing the book, noting that it was "translated from the German of Doctor Ralph with the additions which were found in the Doctor's pocket when he died at Minden in the Year of Our Lord 1759."

The work recounts the adventures of Candide, a young man educated by the optimist philosopher Pangloss to believe that the world in which he lives is "the best of all possible worlds." He lives at the castle of Baron Thunder-ten-tronckh and falls in love with the baron's beautiful daughter, Cunegonde. Caught kissing the young woman, Candide is ejected from the castle and begins to roam the world, penniless and hungry. He is witness to natural and social catastrophes, including the great earthquake of Lisbon and the terror of the Inquisition, in which numerous people suffer. On his journey, Candide becomes reacquainted with Cunegonde, who has her own adventures as the favorite of a series of men. Candide becomes, in turn, a captain in the army, a Jesuit priest, a sheepherder in South America and a philosopher in Paris, where he also enjoys a love affair. When he finally finds Cunegonde once again, she has suffered several instances of rape and abuse, and she is now a servant. They settle on a farm with the string of characters who have joined Candide on his journey, but they soon become bored. To their good fortune, the group meets an old man who advises them to find contentment in cultivating their own garden.

CENSORSHIP HISTORY

In 1821, *Candide* was among the works to which Etienne Antoine, bishop of Troyne, referred when he wrote a pastoral letter to all clergy in France in which he reaffirmed all censorship orders previously issued by the clergy of France and the individual orders issued by the archbishops of Paris:

> in which these works were condemned as godless and sacrilegious, and as tending to undermine morals and the States. We prohibit, under canonical law, the printing or sale of these books within the territory of this diocese, and we charge the vicar-generals to enforce this regulation and to see to the carrying out of the necessary penances for all who make confession of disobedience to these regulations.

The authority of the Catholic church in France appears to have been considered sufficient for control of the matter, and no application was made to have the work placed on the Roman Index. Nonetheless, as a means of establishing authority, Pope Pius VII had placed *Candide* on the list of prohibited books of the Roman Index of 1806 and later renewed the prohibition.

In 1893, the American Library Association for the first time offered a 5,000-title book guide for small popular libraries and branches, calling it a collection that "one could recommend to any trustee." Geller observes that no works by Voltaire were included on the list because several of his works might prove to be "offensive" to some readers. Unlike Rousseau, whose biography, but not his works, the ALA at least included in the guide, no mention was made of Voltaire.

Candide was being studied by universities worldwide, was available in libraries and appeared on college reading lists when United States Customs seized a shipment of the imported edition of the novel in 1928 and declared it obscene. The shipment was ordered by a professor of French at Harvard as assigned reading for his students. Relying on a previous ruling, a Customs official in Boston seized the shipment because the edition was unexpurgated. The professor and his Harvard colleagues contacted officials in Washington, demanding an explanation, and were told that Voltaire was on the list of banned works and that the Customs officer had acted correctly in confiscating the shipment. After the intercession of several influential politicians, the shipment was later released for use in the classroom. U.S. Customs recognized, after a major setback in the 1933 litigation of ULYSSES, that a more discriminating appraisal of books was needed. The appointment of Baltimore attorney Huntington Cairns to assess the problems of Customs censorship resulted in new procedures which, by 1937, deprived Customs collectors and their deputies of their decision-making power. This ended the confiscation of accepted literature, such as *Candide*, in most cases, unless the editions contained illustrations that were "too vulgar or erotic," according to Customs bureau standards.

FURTHER READING

Ayer, Alfred Jules. *Voltaire*. New York: Random House, 1986.

Besterman, Theodore. *Voltaire*. New York: Harcourt Brace & World, 1969.

Geller, Evelyn. *Forbidden Books in American Public Libraries, 1876–1939*. Westport, Conn.: Greenwood, 1984.

Paul, James C. N. *Federal Censorship: Obscenity in the Mail*. New York: Free Press, 1961.

Putnam, George Haven. *The Censorship of the Church of Rome and Its Influence upon the Production and Distribution of Literature*. Vol. 2. New York: Putnam, 1906.

CANDY

Author: Maxwell Kenton (pseudonym for Terry Southern and Mason Hoffenberg)

Original date and place of publication: 1958, France; 1964, United States

Original publisher: Olympia Press (France); G. P. Putnam's Sons (United States)

SUMMARY

Candy is a satire that places its nubile and sexually acquiescent heroine, Candy Christian, from Racine, Wisconsin, in a series of adventures that culminate in a case of outrageous incest in a Tibetan temple. A clear spiritual descendant of Voltaire's *Candide*, Candy makes her way through numerous bizarre incidents that allow the authors to satirize social reformers, college professors, the American adoption of Zen mysticism and the medical profession.

Candy is all body and no brains, a witless innocent who professes her virginity even as she is willing to yield to the advances first of her college ethics teacher, Professor Mephisto, who "needs" her, then to those of a Mexican gardener to show him that she considers him her equal. She leaves home and travels to Greenwich Village, where she encounters an inarticulate man with a large hump on his back. Eager to show him that she does like him, and eager for him to like her, Candy invites the man to have dinner with her. His first words to her at her apartment are, "'I want'" as he unbuttons her jeans, "then he swiftly forced his hand across the panty sheen of her rounded tummy and down into the sweet damp . . . his stubby fingers rolling the little clitoris like a marble in oil. Candy leaned back in resignation, her heart too big to deprive him of this if it meant so much." He removes her jeans and panties, then adjusts her legs around his neck, "his mouth very deep inside her honey pot" as Candy continues to think, "It means so much to him." After being told by the hunchback, "I need fuck you!" Candy becomes the aggressor and shrieks, "Give me your hump!" He manipulates his body, "burying his hump between Candy's legs as she hunched wildly."

Candy then finds a gynecologist named Johns and a lecherous mystic named Grindle. She yields her body to both because "it means so much" to them. When he believes that Candy might be pregnant, Grindle, who has been her guru, gives her a one-way ticket to Tibet and tells her that she can achieve her spiritual acme there. Intellectually attracted to a mud- and dung-covered holy man, Candy is surprised to find him following her to a temple that contains a huge statue of Buddha. An earthquake occurs, causing the statue to topple. The holy man is thrown against Candy, the head of the Buddha statue rolls close behind her and its nose "moved slowly into Candy's coyly arched tooky. . . . *the Buddha, too, needed her!*" As she moves rhythmically in "esoteric Exercise Number Four," the movement has "definite effect on the situation in her honey-cloister as well, forcing the holy man's member deeply in and out." The rain washes away the mud and dung from the holy man's face as "the hopeless ecstasy of his huge pent-up spasm began" and Candy realizes: "Good grief—it's Daddy!"

CENSORSHIP HISTORY

Olympia Press publisher Maurice Girodias described his view of *Candy* as "a parody of pornography, rather than the real thing . . . done convincingly enough to satisfy the sex-obsessed whose sense of humor is notoriously blunted." One year after publication in Paris, *Candy* was banned by the Paris police while the publisher still had 2,000 of the original 5,000 printed copies unbound and at the printer. Because Girodias liked the book, he ordered the reprinting of the cover and the first few pages, giving the book the new name *Lollipop* to conceal the identity of the book from the French police. The publisher knew that this simple action would fool the inspectors because the police listed banned titles in alphabetical order and "a policeman's imagination seldom goes beyond the first letter of a word when it is not under orders to go any further."

The book continued to sell steadily and escaped further action until its publication in the United States by Putnam. Girodias recognized in the introduction to *The Olympia Reader* that *Candy* was not defensible on artistic grounds because it "dealt with the offensive subject of sex in such an open and unabashed manner that one would have expected a brutal reaction from the censors. In fact, very little happened, and this in itself is quite remarkable."

In 1964, members of the Illinois chapter of the National Organization for Decent Literature (NODL) issued a formal complaint against sale of the novel in Chicago bookstores. City officials warned booksellers not to sell or advertise *Candy* and told them that police would be watching to make certain that they complied. In light of court victories in recent years that had freed sales of LOLITA, TROPIC OF CANCER and LADY CHATTERLEY'S LOVER, the booksellers organized to protest strict police censorship and threatened court action, charging that "the harassing of reputable book dealers is worse in Chicago than in any other city in the country" and that it had become the "Boston" of America. The NODL complaint was withdrawn and sales of *Candy* were permitted.

In 1966, law enforcement officials in Massachusetts responded to complaints of parents and educators who objected to sales of the novel to individuals under the age of 18. The case went to trial in *Commonwealth v. Corey*, 351 Mass. 331, 221 N.E.2d 222 (1966), and the prosecuting attorneys made clear that they did not seek to totally ban the book from sale. Rather, the question before the court was whether or not booksellers would be required to restrict sales of the book to people age 18 and over. After only brief testimony, during which booksellers did not offer resistance, the court ruled in favor of the prosecution.

FURTHER READING

Cook Bruce. "Candy Comes to Chicago." *Nation* 199 (September 14, 1964): 125–26.
Girodias, Maurice. Introduction, in *The Olympia Reader*. New York: Grove, 1965.
Murray, D. M. "Candy Christian as a Pop-Art Daisy Miller." *Journal of Popular Culture* 5 (1971): 340–48.
Newman, M. W. *The Smut Hunters*. Los Angeles: All American Distributors, 1964.
Podhoretz, Norman, and Brian O'Doherty. "The Present and Future of Pornography." *Show* 4 (June 1964): 54–55+.

Sachs, Ed. "I Want *Candy*." *Focus/Midwest* 3 (February 1964): 11–13, 23–24.
Silva, Edward T. "From *Candide* to *Candy*: Love's Labor Lost." *Journal of Popular Culture* 8 (1974): 783–91.

THE CARPETBAGGERS

Author: Harold Robbins
Original date and place of publication: 1961, United States
Original publisher: Simon & Schuster
Type: Novel

SUMMARY

The Carpetbaggers, a novel containing numerous scenes of sex and of violence, is based loosely on the life of Howard Hughes. One reviewer, who estimated that "there is sex and/or sadism every 17 pages" of the novel, observed that the novel also "inaugurated a new mode of hard-boiled best-sellers." In many sections the novel combines both.

Robbins takes his title from the name given to those Northern opportunists who overran the South after the end of the American Civil War, people who carried all of their worldly possessions in faded, multicolored bags made of remnants of carpet—carpetbags. In the same manner that the original carpet-baggers came to plunder the South, so do the characters in this novel exploit each other and Hollywood in its infancy. The story covers the years 1925 to 1945 in the lives of two men, Jonas Cord, Jr., and Nevada Smith. The scion to the Cord Explosives empire, Jonas is used to having anything and anyone that he wants. Born Max Sand, Nevada Smith is the son of a white man and a Kiowa woman, and he has spent time in prison for murder and robbery. He is hired by old Jonas Cord, Sr., to teach the boy to ride, as well as to become young Jonas's general companion. After the old man's death, young Jonas inherits his father's fortune and pays off his young stepmother, Rina, who tries in vain to convince Nevada to take her with him.

As years pass, the paths of Jones and Rina cross again in Hollywood, where Jonas becomes wealthy by investing in movies, Nevada starts as a stuntman and becomes famous as a cowboy movie star and Rina becomes an actress. Despite Rina's ongoing lesbian relationship, she marries Nevada in a media extrava-ganza, then divorces him soon after and marries again. The three thrive professionally in the growing film industry of the 1930s, but their personal lives are fraught with unhappiness as they drift from one sexual relationship to another. Eventually, Rina dies of encephalitis contracted while filming in Africa, but Jonas and Nevada survive. As the novel ends, Jonas has made the decision to reunite with his wife and daughter and Nevada has found a peaceful home life after the turbulence of his acting career.

Objections to the novel have centered on the explicit sexual descriptions, the frequent instances of adultery that pepper the novel and the several instances of lesbian lovemaking that occur. Such lines as "her breasts rose like twin white moons against my dark, clenched fists" are common in the novel, as are such flowery euphemisms as "the foliage of her pubis" and terms such as "cunt," "fuck" and "bitch." The novel also contains a detailed rape sequence between Rina and her adoptive brother, in which Robbins places heavy emphasis on the specter of incest.

CENSORSHIP HISTORY

The Carpetbaggers was one of the most sensational paperback books of the early 1960s. In 1961, motivated by complaints filed by members of the National Organization for Decent Literature, police in Waterbury and Bridgeport, Connecticut, used informal censorship in asking that local wholesalers and retailers withdraw the book from sale because it was "obscene." The paperback reprinter of the novel, Pocket Books, sued for damages and asked that a permanent injunction be granted, but the local court denied their request. In 1962, similar methods to ban the book were taken in Warwick, Rhode Island; Rochester, New York; and Mesquite, Texas, despite sales in the first two years that topped 2 million copies nationwide.

In 1965, booksellers in New Zealand experienced threats from local law enforcement officials, based on scattered complaints by individuals, that sales of *The Carpetbaggers* would either be banned or severely restricted. The firm of E. J. Hyams and Son Limited, acting on behalf of the publisher, New English Library Limited of London, submitted an application to the Indecent Publications Tribunal for review of the unexpurgated paperback edition of the novel to determine whether it was indecent. Although the counsel for the applicant offered brief submissions in support of the application, the counsel for the Department of the Secretary of Justice made no submissions. In its March 4, 1965, determination that the book "is not indecent within the meaning of the statute," the tribunal stated:

> It is a long story, prolix to the point of tediousness. There are accounts of sexual behaviour but we do not consider the narrative is such as to deprave a reader or to be injurious to the public good. We do not think there is any warrant for holding it to be indecent.

FURTHER READING

Lewis, Felice Flanery. *Literature, Obscenity, & Law*. Carbondale: Southern Illinois University Press, 1976.

Perry, Stuart. *The Indecent Publications Tribunal: A Social Experiment*. London: Whitcombe and Tombs, 1965.

Robbins, Harold. "Master Harold." *Advocate: The National Gay and Lesbian Newsmagazine* (August 22, 1995): 38–43.

CASANOVA'S HOMECOMING (CASANOVA'S HEIMFAHRT)

Author: Arthur Schnitzler
Original date and place of publication: 1918, Germany; 1921, United States
Original publisher: S. Fischer (Germany); Thomas Seltzer (United States)
Type: Novel

SUMMARY

Casanova's Homecoming imaginatively recreates the final conquest of the aged Casanova, who has become disgusting and contemptible to himself and to others. The novel begins with the 53-year-old impoverished Casanova waiting in Mantua to learn if he will be allowed to return to Venice, which he had left many years earlier after escaping from prison. He agrees to visit an old friend named Olivo, who has an attractive young niece visiting him. Remembering his past sexual conquests, among them Olivo's wife and her mother, Casanova becomes sexually aroused by Marcolina, Olivo's niece, whose unresponsiveness and seemingly incorruptible nature only arouse him further. He desires her more than he has desired any previous woman and observes that "Beneath the shimmering folds of her dress he seemed to see her naked body; her firm young breasts allured him."

Casanova deceives both the women with whom he has sex and his male friends, showing no regret for any of his actions. He is also highly disrespectful of the church and its representatives, and he refers to having been involved in an orgy with two nuns. When he learns that the seemingly pure Marcolina is sexually involved with Lieutenant Lorenzi, her young suitor, Casanova first thinks of denouncing her as "a lustful little whore," then decides to take advantage of the situation. He plans to disguise himself one night and take Lorenzi's place in her bed. While he waits for the right moment to approach her, he seduces Olivo's daughter, gloating all the while that he had already seduced the girl's mother and grandmother. When night comes, Casanova enters Marcolina's window at midnight, wearing only the lieutenant's cloak over his nude body. He has sex with Marcolina and compliments himself on his performance: "From Marcolina's sigh of surrender, from the tears of happiness which he kissed from her cheeks, from the ever-renewed warmth with which she received his caresses, he felt sure that she shared his rapture." When she awakens the next morning, Casanova must face reality when Marcolina reacts with horror, showing in her face her disgust for the "old man."

CENSORSHIP HISTORY

Casanova's Homecoming, translated from German by Eden and Cedar Paul, was one of three books published in 1922 by Thomas Seltzer and seized by the New

York Society for the Suppression of Vice. Armed with a warrant, John Sumner led other society members on a raid of the publisher's offices on July 11, 1922, and seized more than 800 copies of *Casanova's Homecoming*, D. H. Lawrence's WOMEN IN LOVE and the anonymously written A YOUNG GIRL'S DIARY. The publisher was also forced to use his own trucks to transport the books to police headquarters. Stock was also taken from the shelves at Brentano's and Womrath's bookstores, resulting in what *Publishers Weekly* labeled "one of the most widely discussed cases in book censorship before the courts." Seltzer hired attorney Jonah J. Goldstein and the two organized a comprehensive defense campaign, including newspaper publicity and letters of praise for the three books from literary figures and psychologists.

When the case went to trial on July 31, 1922, the magistrates' court contained highly respected witnesses for the defense, including Columbia University professor and literary critic Carl Van Doren, psychiatrist Adolph Stern and magazine editors Gilbert Seldes and Dorothea Brand. The defense also argued against using isolated passages as the basis for deeming a book "obscene." Magistrate George W. Simpson dismissed all charges against Seltzer on September 12, 1922, after praising the three novels as "a distinct contribution to the literature of the present day." Simpson also cautioned the society:

> It has been said, with some justice, that the policy of pouncing upon books too frank for contemporary taste, without regard to the motive or purpose for which they were written, or the use to which they are to be put, is objectionable and should be curbed.

In 1923, Sumner succeeded in securing a grand jury indictment against *Casanova's Homecoming* and A YOUNG GIRL'S DIARY. The case never went to trial, and the society dropped the case two years after filing it when Seltzer withdrew the two books from distribution and agreed to destroy the plates. German-speaking Americans in the United States were free to enjoy the novel in its original language while litigation continued over the English-language version.

Simon & Schuster published the novel in 1930, and Sumner once again moved to block sales of the book. Armed with a search warrant and accompanied by a special agent and two police officers, Sumner seized an initial 477 copies of the novel from the publisher's office and served summonses on the firm and its sales staff. The society led by Sumner later seized more than 1,000 additional copies. The financially secure publisher, determined to fight the seizure and the tactics of the society, took the case to court and won a dismissal of charges. To avoid further unsavory maneuvers by Sumner and possibly expensive legal action, publisher Max Schuster traveled with a truck to the society headquarters and retrieved 1,500 confiscated copies of *Casanova's Homecoming*.

FURTHER READING

Boyer, Paul S. *Purity in Print: The Vice-Society Movement and Book Censorship in America.* New York: Scribner's, 1968.

"Censorship Beaten in New York Court." *Publishers Weekly* 102 (September 16, 1922): 801–4.

"The Law and the Censor." *New York Times* (September 14, 1922): 21.

Tanselle, G. Thomas. "The Thomas Seltzer Imprint." *Papers of the Bibliographical Society of America* 58 (Fourth Quarter 1964): 380–416.

THE CHINESE ROOM

Author: Vivian Connell
Original date and place of publication: 1942, United States
Original publisher: The Dial Press
Type: Novel

SUMMARY

The Chinese Room is a psychological thriller that also attempts an indictment of upper-class English life, an approach that one reviewer called a "large part sheer nonsense." The plot focuses on London banker Nicholas Bude, who decides to experiment on his mind by writing anonymous letters to himself. Before he can begin, however, he receives several anonymous letters from someone else. While he attempts to sort out the puzzle, he isolates himself further from his already-estranged wife, Muriel. Long dissatisfied with her marriage, she takes the first of a series of lovers and discovers happiness through her reawakened sexuality. The psychological implications of this discovery are lost in the combined mystery story and attempts at psychological exploration. As a reviewer in *The Nation* observed, "If only because of the prurience of its sexual detail, a novel that might have been in the line of, say, D. H. Lawrence's *Lady Chatterley's Lover* turns out to be in the line of adolescent reverie."

The novel presents a hard-hearted mistress in her slinky oriental silk pajamas, the elderly bank employee who goes home each night to become his version of a Chinese mandarin and the man whose hands have personalities he cannot control, as well as opium smoking and hints of the supernatural. As Bude discovers his true self, he realizes that everyone carries inside a "Chinese room."

The sexual descriptions are suggestive. The village doctor propositions Muriel and twists "his kiss on her mouth as if he were twisting a cork into a bottle." She later begs him to kiss her again, crying out, "I want love so badly!" In their later lovemaking, Muriel discovers "the animal hunger of the woman" and readers learn that "his tongue never got tired." She also enjoys his "sadistic handling" and "felt that love-making, to be healthy, must be something nearer to a fight than a five-finger exercise on the body."

Bude has an affair with his secretary, Sidonie Coleman, a woman who "had as much humanity as a statue." In one scene, Bude "pressed his face into her breasts. . . . he had seized her and taken her into the bedroom." Only then does she exhibit feeling, "then during the fierce, inarticulate conflict of their passion she would grip his shoulder with her teeth and never let go until the end." He later learns that she uses opium and also has a deformed foot, "the hoof of Pan" where her small toe should be.

As Muriel begins to exude sexuality, Bude finds himself attracted, once again, to her. Despite a near-fatal shooting, and after the discovery of the individual who is sending the letters, the Budes reunite and create a truly passionate marriage.

CENSORSHIP HISTORY

The Chinese Room was reprinted by Bantam Books in 1948 as a paperback and sold 2.5 million copies by 1951. In 1950, Middlesex County, New Jersey, prosecutor Matthew Melko collaborated with the local Committee on Objectionable Literature to produce a list of objectional publications, which included *The Chinese Room*. He wrote to a major book distributor in the area, informing the New Brunswick News Dealers Supply Company in Elizabeth, New Jersey, of the list that contained books "of such a nature that they should be withdrawn from circulation."

Viewing the letter as a mandate to remove the books, the company manager, Ben Gelfand, did so immediately. Just as quickly, Bantam asked that the prosecutor review the books listed, which he did, clearing all but *The Chinese Room*. Bantam Books then sued Melko in *Bantam Books v. Melko, Prosecutor of Middlesex County*, 25 N.J. Super. 292, 96 A.2d 47 (1953). In rendering his decision, Judge Sidney Goldman questioned if the prosecutor had the authority to ban the sale of books, if he had issued an order to ban *The Chinese Room*, if the prosecutor should be restrained from further notifying distributors of the novel that it should not be sold in Middlesex County and if Melko had acted illegally and beyond the scope of his authority. Judge Goldman ruled that *The Chinese Room* was not obscene and authorized an injunction against the prosecutor's interference with the sale of the book. He also stated, "I hold that neither the prosecutor nor the committee constituted by him had the authority to proscribe the distribution or sale in Middlesex County of books deemed by them, or by either of them, to be objectionable." In assessing the novel, Goldman stated, "It cuts a rather poor and pale figure in the colorful company of recent "historical" novels of the FOREVER AMBER type, which may be found in almost any public or circulating library, fresh from the best-seller lists." The prosecutor appealed the decision in *Bantam Books v. Melko, Prosecutor of Middlesex County*, 14 N.J. 524, 103 A.2d 256 (1954), but the New Jersey Supreme Court upheld the ruling of the lower court.

In July 1950, in Fall River, Massachusetts, authorities charged two local dealers and two store managers with intent to sell to persons under 18 years of age books that were "indecent, obscene or impure, or manifestly tend to corrupt the morals of youth." The resulting order to refrain from further distribution involved 14 books from six different publishers, including *The Chinese Room* and Charles O. Gorham's GILDED HEARSE. The books were withdrawn from sale and the charges were rescinded.

FURTHER READING

Davis, Kenneth C. *Two-Bit Culture: The Paperbacking of America.* Boston: Houghton Mifflin, 1984.
De Grazia, Edward. *Censorship Landmarks.* New York: Bowker, 1969.
"In Brief: *The Chinese Room.*" *The Nation* 156 (January 9, 1943): 67.
"A Reader's List: *The Chinese Room.*" *New Republic* 107 (November 9, 1942): 618.

CHRISTINE

Author: Stephen King
Original date and place of publication: 1983, United States
Original publisher: The Viking Press
Type: Novel

SUMMARY

Christine is a macabre story of teenage love and tragedy, motivated by an automobile named Christine that has diabolical powers. Scrawny, pimple-faced Arnie Cunningham and his friend Dennis Guilder are two high school students driving home after work one summer afternoon when Arnie abruptly calls for Dennis to stop the car and back up. He has seen what he wants, a wreck of a 1958 Plymouth Fury with a For Sale sign on it. Arnie vehemently refuses to listen to Dennis when told that the car, with its cracked windshield, rusted and dented body, loose parts and puddle of oil beneath, will be expensive to restore. He buys the car from its hate-filled, vulgar owner Rollins LeBay for $250, then finds a lot in which to park and restore the car.

Dennis senses something sinister about the car. That fear is confirmed soon after when LeBay dies "suddenly" and he speaks with LeBay's brother. He learns that LeBay's daughter had choked while riding in the car, then died by the side of the road, and LeBay's wife had committed suicide six months after while seated in the car. Nothing dissuades Arnie from his new obsession, and Christine soon goes on homicidal rampages and kills anyone who hurts Arnie. Dennis realizes that LeBay's spirit has taken control of Arnie, the son of two college professors, and he has rejected college plans for his present work of smuggling liquor and cigarettes across state lines.

In the early stages of ownership, Arnie's life seems to become better as he gains new courage and strength to fight tormentors. His complexion clears and he acquires a girlfriend, Leigh, who also interests Dennis. This leads to several passages that describe her erect nipples or the sexual delirium that Arnie feels, as well as the boys' thoughts of having sex with Leigh. The love triangle soon evolves into Christine, Arnie and Leigh, but Arnie is possessed by the spirit of the vengeful LeBay. Dennis battles furiously to save his friend, but the novel ends tragically with the deaths of not only Arnie's enemies but his parents and himself.

CENSORSHIP HISTORY

The novel has been censored and banned in many schools and libraries because it depicts the explicit sexual thoughts of teenage boys and contains sexual references. While numerous books by King have been banned or censored because of "vulgar language," "filthy" language or other charges of being "obscene," *Christine* joins only a few King books, including *Carrie*, *Firestarter*, *The Shining* and *The Stand*, that have been attacked for containing "explicit sex" and "sexual descriptions." Of these books, *Christine* has been most frequently attacked.

In 1985, parents of students in the Washington County, Alabama, school district complained to their school board that the novel contained "unacceptable language" and that it was "pornographic." After reviewing the novel, the county board of education banned the novel from all county school libraries. In 1987, the West Lyon Community School in Larchwood, Iowa, removed the book from its library, charging that "it does not meet the standards of the community." The book was removed from the Washington Middle School library in Meriden, Connecticut, in 1989, after parents complained that it contained "offensive" passages.

In 1990, parents of students attending the Livingston (Montana) Middle School complained that *Christine* and *The Shining* should be removed from the library because they contained "violence," "explicit sex" and "inappropriate language." The librarian agreed that the books were not "suitable for the intended audience," and the school principal commended the librarian for using "good judgment." In 1991, a school official removed the novel from the curriculum after receiving verbal complaints from parents of high school students in Hazel Park, Michigan, who objected to its use in an American novel class.

In 1992, parents in Peru, Indiana, petitioned the school board to remove from the high school library 12 novels written by Stephen King, claiming that they contained violence and obscenity. The board reviewed the novels and voted 5 to 1 to ban *Christine*, *Cujo* and *The Dead Zone*. *Christine* was also challenged in 1993 with all King novels contained in the Webber Township High School library and in Bismarck, North Dakota, in 1994 with eight other Stephen King novels on the basis of "age appropriateness." Neither challenge was successful.

FURTHER READING

Hohne, Karen A. "The Power of the Spoken Word in the Works of Stephen King." *Journal of Popular Culture* 28 (Fall 1994): 93–103.

King, Stephen. "Banned Books and Other Concerns: The Virginia Beach Lecture." In *The Stephen King Companion.* Ed. by George Beahm. Kansas City, Mo.: Andrews & McMeel, 1989.

Newsletter on Intellectual Freedom (January 1986): 7; (May 1987): 86; (July 1987): 125; (May 1989): 75; (January 1991): 12; (July 1992): 106; (July 1993): 124; (May 1994): 84–85.

THE CLAN OF THE CAVE BEAR

Author: Jean Auel
Original date and place of publication: 1980, United States
Original publisher: Crown Publishing
Type: Novel

SUMMARY

The Clan of the Cave Bear is the story of Ayla, a prehistoric girl orphaned by an earthquake and forced to live for a time by herself in the forest. When a human tribe, the Clan of the Cave Bear, finds her and takes her in, Ayla tries hard to conform to their code despite her obvious differences from them. She is one of the "Others"—taller, blond and blue eyed—and she also has more developed powers of speech than the members of the Clan, who still communicate largely by gesture. Cared for by the Clan medicine woman, Iza, and her brother, Creb, Ayla learns the customs and the language of the Clan, but she frequently violates their expectations because she does not share their racial memories. Ayla becomes adept at the skill of hunting, forbidden to women of the Clan, and her prowess makes an enemy of Broud, the son of the Clan leader. He torments her continuously as they grow up, then rapes her when they are older. His actions are acceptable according to tradition, because any female must submit to a male at his will. The members of the Clan have not yet made the connection between sexual intercourse and reproduction, so they are amazed when Ayla becomes pregnant, more so because they had assumed that her differences would make her incapable of bearing children. She gives birth to a son, but when an earthquake destroys the Clan's cave, Broud, now the leader, blames Ayla. He curses her and expels her from the Clan, but she must leave her son behind.

CENSORSHIP HISTORY

In 1988, parents of students attending Berrien Springs (Michigan) High School challenged the use of the novel in the classroom and asked that it also be removed from the high school library. Their complaints cited the passages of brutish behavior of the male clan members and the physical abuse and rape of Ayla as "vulgar, profane, and sexually explicit."

In 1992, one parent of a student attending Cascade Middle School in Eugene, Oregon, complained that the rape scene in the novel was offensive. The board of education considered the complaint and ordered the book removed from the middle school library and banned from future use.

The novel was challenged in 1993, but later retained on the recommended reading list at Moorpark High School in Sunneyville, California, after parents objected that the novel contained "hard-core graphic sexual content."

FURTHER READING

Newsletter on Intellectual Freedom (January 1989): 28; (July 1992): 107; (January 1994): 14; (March 1994): 70; (May 1994): 99.
Wilcox, Clyde. "The Not-So-Failed Feminism of Jean Auel." *Journal of Popular Culture* 28 (Winter 1994): 63–70.

CONFESSIONS

Author: Jean-Jacques Rousseau
Original date and place of publication: 1884, Switzerland; 1891, England
Original publisher: Waltham (Switzerland); Worthington (England)
Type: Memoir

SUMMARY

Jean-Jacques Rousseau's *Confessions* was published posthumously, but he had completed the work just before his death in 1778. In this extensive journal of his life, Rousseau recreates the age in which he lived and brings to life the politics and society of 18th-century France. He also suffers from what one biographer refers to as "moral exhibitionism" and appears obsessed with revealing "the indecent and puerile details of his sex life." The work deals openly with his relationship with Therese Levasseur, his mistress for 16 years whom he "always treated like a wife." The two had five children, all sent to the foundling hospital. Rousseau admits that he was so disinterested in the children that he did not even keep records of their identities or dates of birth.

Several specific passages in *Confessions* have motivated attempts at censorship. Rousseau traces his sexual development to when he was aged 8 and the 30-year-old baby-sitter, the sister of a parson, spanked his bare bottom. He says that this act had the effect to "determine my tastes, my desires, my passions, my very self, for the rest of my existence . . . these strange tastes which persisted with a depraved and insane intensity." Several passages speak openly of Rousseau's addiction to masturbation, to the point that he risked his health and believed himself to be epileptic, "seduced by the vice which shame and timidity find so convenient . . . I set about destroying my sturdy constitution."

When he resides at a Roman Catholic hospice in Turin, after fleeing Protestant Geneva, the 16-year-old Rousseau condemns the sister converts at the hospice as being "the greatest set of sluttish, abandoned whores that had ever contaminated the Lord's sheepfold." The brother converts are no less lustful, particularly one who "frequently kissed me with an ardour which I found most displeasing. . . . He wanted to come into my bed . . . and finally took the most revolting liberties and, by guiding my hand, tried to make me take the same liberties with him." Rousseau claims to have been ignorant of the other young man's true intent.

Not only is the reader treated to a thorough discussion of Rousseau's sex life, but his prostate problems in later life are also detailed in *Confessions*. As Rousseau advanced in age, he found the need to urinate frequently, but the respected writer and philosopher usually found himself cornered at social events and unable to reach even a convenient corner of a courtyard in which to relieve himself. He relates, "In short, I can usually urinate only in full view of everybody and on some white-stockinged leg."

CENSORSHIP HISTORY

Rousseau's lengthy *Confessions* has been banned mainly for its sexual content and for his open discussion of life with his mistress of 16 years. In 1821, *Confessions* was among the works to which Etienne Antoine, bishop of Troyne, referred when he wrote a pastoral letter to all clergy in France in which he reaffirmed all censorship orders previously issued by the clergy of France and the individual orders issued by the archbishops of Paris:

> in which these works were condemned as godless and sacrilegious, and as tending to undermine morals and the States. We prohibit, under canonical law, the printing or sale of these books within the territory of this diocese, and we charge the vicar-generals to enforce this regulation and to see to the carrying out of the necessary penances for all who make confession of disobedience to these regulations.

The authority of the Catholic church in France appears to have been considered sufficient for control of the matter, and no application was made to have the work placed on the Roman Index. Nonetheless, as a means of establishing authority, Pope Pius VII had placed *Confessions* on the list of prohibited books of the Roman Index of 1806 and later renewed the prohibition because of the sexual adventures that Rousseau recounted.

In 1892, Rousseau's *Confessions* was involved in the litigation of the Worthington Book Publishing Company, which was in financial difficulty. The receiver wanted to sell some of the company stock, including ARABIAN NIGHTS, THE HISTORY OF TOM JONES, THE ART OF LOVE, THE HEPTAMERON,

Gargantua and Pantagruel, Boccaccio's THE DECAMERON, and *Confessions* to pay off creditors, but Anthony Comstock stepped in to oppose the sales. He demanded of the court that the books be officially burned. The court disagreed. (See *Arabian Nights.*)

A year later in 1893, the American Library Association for the first time offered a 5,000-title book guide for small popular libraries and branches, calling it a collection that "one could recommend to any trustee." No works by Rousseau were included on the list, yet a biography of the author was included. Based upon this observation, Geller notes, "This discrepancy between a writer's reputation and the acceptance of his work is a good indicator of censorship: exclusion on grounds other than significance."

United States Customs banned the book from entry in 1929, claiming that it was "injurious to public morals." Customs reversed the ban the following year.

FURTHER READING

Cranston, Maurice. *The Noble Savage: Jean-Jacques Rousseau.* Chicago: University of Chicago, 1991.
Geller, Evelyn. *Forbidden Books in American Public Libraries, 1876–1939.* Westport, Conn.: Greenwood, 1984.
Huizinga, J. H. *Rousseau: The Self-Made Saint.* New York: Grossman, 1976.
Putnam, George Haven. *The Censorship of the Church of Rome and Its Influence upon the Production and Distribution of Literature.* Vol. 2. New York: Putnam, 1906.

THE DECAMERON

Author: Giovanni Boccaccio
Original date and place of publication: 14th century, Italy; 1921, England
Original publisher: Privately printed (Italy); The Navarre Society (England)
Type: Collection of tales

SUMMARY

The Decameron is one of the oldest fictional works to have been charged as "obscene" in the United States. The premise of the collection of tales is that 10 young men and women, secluded for a time to escape the plague, divert themselves by telling stories on a variety of topics. Each must tell one story per day on a specific theme, for a total of 100 tales. Of the total, only eight tales are purely erotic while the remainder deal with social criticism, the outwitting of one person by another and the criticism of nuns and priests.

In some of the tales, references to adultery or fornication are brief or oblique. In others, references are suggestive but not explicit. The stories contain figures of speech that replace explicit sexual description. Breasts and genitalia are spoken of metaphorically, and numerous metaphors are drawn from sowing, plowing and reaping. Thus, a wife complains that her husband has neglected "tilling of my poor field." A lover boards his mate in the way that "the unbridled stallions . . . assail the mares of Parthia." Even common implements such as the mortar and pestle become metaphors for sexual activity, as in the story in which a man complains that "if she will not lend me her mortar, I will not lend my pestle."

Of the eight largely erotic tales, four are based upon a trick or joke. In one, the 10th story told on the ninth day, a priest persuades a man that changing his wife into a mare will help the man in his peddling business. Thus, the wife dutifully strips and stands on all fours, as the priest carefully explains to the husband that putting on the mare's tail is the most difficult part of the process. The wife waits patiently as the priest pretends to turn her various body parts into the body of a mare. He then engages in the sexual act that will make the mare's tail, but it is described through the use of metaphor:

> Ultimately, nothing remaining to do but the tail, he pulled up his shirt and taking the dibble with which he planted men, he thrust it hastily into the furrow made therfor and said, "And be this a fine mare's tail."

The 10th story of the third day contains the lengthiest description of an act of sexual intercourse, and it was rarely translated until recent years. In this story, a friar persuades a naive young girl that she is serving God by submitting to him, because he has a "devil" in him that can only be subdued if he places it into her "hell." Even this story is humorous, for the girl outpaces the friar in showing her enthusiasm in serving God, as she tires the friar with her ardor.

CENSORSHIP HISTORY

The Decameron was first placed on the Roman Index of prohibited books in 1559, by the order of Pope Paul IV, and the prohibition was confirmed in 1564. The objections centered on the "offensive sexual acts" in which clerics, monks, nuns and abbesses in the work engaged. However, due to popular demand, in the form of an "urgent requirement" from the public, the Giunti of Florence, Italy, printed an expurgated edition in 1573, which contained a special authorization from Manrique, grand inquisitor, as well as one from de Pise, inquisitor-general of Florence. Revised under the authority of Pope Gregory VIII, the sexual activity and innuendo remained, but the religious characters were replaced by citizens, nobles and bourgeoisie. Pope Sixtus V did not find the expurgation satisfactory and the book was again placed on the Index, but the demand for copies by readers, ecclesiastics and others was so great that Sixtus authorized another expurgated edition, with orders to remove more of the sexual activity and crude innuendo. This version was printed in 1588, but the new edition did not satisfy Pope Sixtus V, and the book remained on the Index. Yet, it continued to be available in general reading and the authorities closed their eyes to this particular instance of disobedience, mainly because popular demand was so strong.

In a report entitled "How to Make a Town Library Successful," published in 1876, Frederick Beecher Perkins, assistant librarian of the Boston Public Library, recommended censorship of the collection:

> It should exclude such books as Rabelais, *The Decameron*, THE HEPTAMERON, the *Contes drolatiques* (DROLL STORIES) of Balzac, . . . all of which are sold in English translations for money by otherwise respectable American publishers. Few, indeed, are those who will object to this exclusion of ribald and immoral books from public circulating libraries.

In 1892, *The Decameron* was involved in the litigation of the Worthington Book Publishing Compnay, which was in financial difficulty. The receiver wanted to sell some of the company stock, including ARABIAN NIGHTS, THE HISTORY OF TOM JONES, THE ART OF LOVE, *The Heptameron, Gargantua and Pantagruel*, Rousseau's CONFESSIONS and *The Decameron* to pay off creditors, but Anthony Comstock stepped in to oppose the sales. He demanded of the court that the books be officially burned. (See *Arabian Nights*.)

One year later, the American Library Association offered for the first time a 5,000-title book guide for small popular libraries and branches, calling it a collection that "one could recommend to any trustee." No works by Boccaccio were included on the list. When the American Library Association released its *Catalog* in 1904, works by Boccaccio were still excluded, leading Geller to characterize the situation as censorship by omission. In 1894, the U.S. Supreme Court applied the Hicklin rule, imported from England, to rule that standard works of high literary quality were not obscene. The first case involved editions of THE ARABIAN NIGHTS, THE HISTORY OF TOM JONES, *The Decameron*, THE HEPTAMERON and THE ART OF LOVE.

In 1903, the Boston Watch and Ward Society began a campaign of harassment against four area booksellers who were openly advertising and selling *The Decameron* and *Gargantua and Pantagruel* despite the request from the society that they refrain from doing so. Rather than acquiesce as in the past, the four met with other Boston booksellers and with publisher Little, Brown and Company to organize a resistance to this attempt at censorship. Booksellers, including the Old Corner, N. J. Bartlett, George E. Littlefield, Charles E. Goodspeed and six others, joined Little, Brown to raise money for a legal defense fund. The case went to Boston municipal court, and the booksellers won judgment against the society.

The Decameron was declared to be an "obscene, lewd and lascivious book of indecent character" by a jury in Cincinnati, Ohio, in 1906. Edward Stiefel, president and general manager of the Queen City Book Company, was indicted by a grand jury for sending a copy of the book through the mail to Crawfordsville, Indiana. Stiefel gathered a strong defense, calling as witnesses a well-known judge, a member of the Cincinnati Board of Education and a well-respected newspaper editor to testify to the status of the work as a classic. In addition, Stiefel offered into evidence library catalogs, catalogs from booksellers all over the world and catalogs from public auctions of books in New York and Boston, all listing *The Decameron*. Despite the evidence, the jury deliberated only an hour and 15 minutes before finding Stiefel guilty of sending "obscene" materials through the mail. The judge, who appeared less punitive, only fined the defendant $5 and court costs.

In 1927, United States Department of the Treasury officials in Washington, D.C., rendered an opinion that reversed a ruling by New York Customs inspectors and admitted 250 copies of the work, imported by A. & C. Boni, thus ending forever the banning of this classic in the United States.

FURTHER READING

Boyer, Paul S. *Purity in Print: The Vice-Society Movement and Book Censorship in America.* New York: Scribner's, 1968.

Geller, Evelyn. *Forbidden Books in American Public Libraries, 1876–1939.* Westport, Conn.: Greenwood, 1984.

Putnam, George Haven. *The Censorship of the Church of Rome and Its Influence upon the Production and Distribution of Literature.* Vol. 2. New York: Putnam, 1906.

Tebbel, John. *A History of Book Publishing in the United States.* Vol. 2. New York: Bowker, 1975.

THE DEER PARK

Author: Norman Mailer
Original date and place of publication: 1955, United States
Original publisher: G. P. Putnam's Sons
Type: Novel

SUMMARY

The Deer Park was originally subtitled "A Search for the Obscene," and Mailer crossed out but did not remove the subtitle when he first submitted the work. The main title is taken from the Deer Park of Louis XV, where the most beautiful maidens of France were brought as "ladies of pleasure awaiting the pleasure of the king." The title was appropriate for a novel about the fictional Hollywood resort Desert D'Or, "middle aged desperados of corporation land and the suburb" and the venal people in it. It is a setting of decadence, and of "drinking in that atmosphere, I never knew whether it was night or day. . . . afternoon was always passing into night, and drunken nights into the dawn of a desert morning."

The novel relates the story of a liberal movie director, Charles Francis Eitel, who is blacklisted by the studios for refusing to name his Communist friends at a congressional hearing, but who later relents because he needs to work again. Narrated by Sergius O'Shaugnessy, six feet tall, blond haired and blue eyed, movie-star handsome and a fake Irishman who decided in the orphanage to assume that name and ethnic identity, the work concentrates on the mores of stars, starlets, producers, sensualists and panderers. O'Shaugnessy had been a decorated first lieutenant in the United States Army Air Force in World War II, but he had a nervous breakdown when he realized how many thousands of faceless people he had killed. Remembering his victims has left him sexually impotent at the beginning of the novel, but blond and sensuous sex star Lulu, once married to Eitel, restores his prowess. After regaining his potency, O'Shaugnessy becomes a hard-drinking "stud."

The drama shifts from O'Shaugnessy to Eitel, whose depression over his lack of work leads him into an affair with Elena Esposito, an uneducated, sensuous woman and sometime actress who has been humiliated by many men. Their relationship is the main focus of the novel. Eitel considers Elena to be his intellectual and social inferior, but she does anything that Eitel wants, including experimenting sexually with other couples. Sex is a vital presence throughout the novel, and it was the reason that the novel was repeatedly rejected by publishers. One scene that described fellatio between Hollywood power broker Herman Teppis and a call girl named Bobby caused a furor:

> Tentatively, she reached out a hand to caress his hair, and at that moment Herman Teppis opened his legs and let Bobby slip to the floor. At the expression of surprise on her face, he began to laugh. "Just like this, sweetie," he said, and down he looked at that frightened female mouth, facsimile of all those smiling lips he had seen so ready to be nourished at the fount of power and with a shudder he started to talk. "That's a good girlie, that's a good girlie, that's a good girlie," he said in a mild lost little voice, "you're just an angel darling, and I like you, and you understand, you're my darling darling, oh that's the ticket," said Teppis.

The numerous couplings throughout the novel, although less detailed than the specified scene, aroused the "disgust" of potential publishers and later reviewers alike.

CENSORSHIP HISTORY

Mailer had a contract with Rinehart and Company for *The Deer Park*, but publisher Stanley Rinehart was uncomfortable with the book and asked critic John Aldridge to provide an outside opinion. In a careful analysis of the work, Aldridge said that the novel had "no morality," but he said that it was not pornographic. Mailer had avoided explicit language because he recognized the problems that his frank sexuality alone would create. Rinehart remained uncomfortable with the work, and Mailer agreed to rewrite it. When he showed it to Rinehart in May 1954, the publisher stated that he was still unhappy with the work's "sexual frankness. . . . extremely radical for 1954." In November 1954, three months before publication, Rinehart told Mailer that he would have to delete six lines of the fellatio scene. Rinehart claimed that he was "concerned about what his mother [mystery author Mary Roberts Rinehart] would think, since she was on the board of directors."

Once again, Mailer agreed to change words and to rewrite several lines, then changed his mind. A day after Mailer called with his refusal, Stanley Rinehart stopped publication of the book, which was already in galley form, and broke Mailer's contract. Charles "Cy" Rembar, an attorney and Mailer's cousin, challenged Rinehart's assertion that the novel was "obscene" and, as a result, "unpublishable." He offered to "test the issue in a suit for the advance of royalties." Threatened with a lawsuit, Rinehart maintained that the book was "obscene," but he paid the $10,000 advance to Mailer "for the privilege of not publishing his book."

Mailer then took the novel to seven other publishers, all of whom turned it down: Random House, Alfred A. Knopf, Farrar & Giroux, Charles Scribner's Sons, Harper & Row, Simon & Schuster and Harcourt Brace. Lawyers for several of the houses provided lists totaling 100 excerpts that "must be deleted," "must be changed" and "should be changed," but the passage protested by Rinehart did not appear in those lists.

Walter Minton, son of the president of G. P. Putnam's Sons, committed to buy the book sight unseen, convinced that a book turned down by so many other publishers "would sell because of the controversy. . . . It never occurred to me for an instant that there would be any censorship activity." Putnam capitalized on the notoriety with an advertisement that listed all of the negative comments made by reviewers: "Unfair," "Undiscriminating," "Embarrassing," "Unsavory," "Junk," "Moronic Mindlessness," "Nasty," "Disgusting." The book sold 50,000 copies and rose to number six on the best-seller list.

FURTHER READING

Balbert, Peter. "From *Lady Chatterley's Lover* to *The Deer Park*: Lawrence, Mailer, and the Dialectic of Erotic Risk." *Studies in the Novel* 22 (Spring 1990): 67–81.

Manso, Peter. *Mailer: His Life and Times*. New York: Simon & Schuster, 1985.

Mills, Hillary. *Mailer: A Biography*. New York: Empire Books, 1982.

Rembar, Charles. *The End of Obscenity*. New York: Random House, 1968.

Rollyson, Carl. *The Lives of Norman Mailer*. New York: Paragon House, 1991.

THE DEVIL RIDES OUTSIDE

Author: John Howard Griffin
Original date and place of publication: 1952, United States
Original publisher: Smith's Inc.
Type: Novel

SUMMARY

The Devil Rides Outside is an autobiographical novel about a young man, an unnamed war veteran interested in music, who goes to a French monastery to study manuscripts of Gregorian chants. While there, he decides to abandon his sensual life and embark on an ascetic course. The desire is newly born, because he has just left Paris and a mistress before coming to the monastery. The narrator resents the harsh life of the monks at first, until he realizes that those who immerse themselves in the effort to resist worldly pleasures achieve a deep peace and serenity. He becomes a close companion to Father Clement, in whom he confides and who voices the narrator's central problem when he asks: "If only you could say no just once, is that it?"

Throughout the first part of the novel, the narrator desires to return to his mistress in Paris, but he lacks the money to do so. When he suffers a severe attack of malaria during which the monks nurse him back to health, he begins to understand their strength of character, but his sexual desires remain, and he decides to go to the village to satisfy those desires. He encounters Madame Vincent, an attractive, middle-aged visitor, with whom he has a passionate encounter that Griffin describes in sensuous detail. Madame Vincent refuses to meet with him again, but the village women learn of her indiscretion, and she is forced to leave the town. When she returns sometime later, she reveals that she is dying of cancer and wants only to spend her final days near the monastery in spiritual contemplation.

The second part of the novel begins as the narrator moves out of the unheated monastery and into a villa in the town nearby in order to avoid further illness. He continues his efforts to resist his sexual desires, and he deliberately chooses to take his meals with Madame Renee, who holds no attraction for him. An overbearing, middle-aged widow, she is nasty and cunning and soon tries to dominate him and to force him into intimacy with her, despite his feelings of repulsion. He eventually submits to her, but Griffin makes clear to the reader that his narrator is having sex with Madame Renee out of pity rather than desire.

After acceding to her, his descriptions of their encounters are grotesque, including, as they do, visions of her "swollen into a gigantic serpentine voluptuousness . . . grasping, choking . . . suffocating me." When he finds himself actually sexually aroused by her, the possibility disgusts him and he calls upon the Virgin Mary for assistance, even as he struggles physically with Madame Renee. He pulls himself free and slaps the woman, pleased that he has finally become capable of saying no. In essence, even though he has rejected a woman whom he had grown to hate and who repulsed him, he feels that he has achieved mastery over his sensual nature.

CENSORSHIP HISTORY

The Devil Rides Outside is the novel involved in the unanimous Supreme Court decision in *Butler v. Michigan*, 352 U.S. 380 (1957) that declared as unconstitutional the standards for defining obscenity that had been used for more than 70 years by federal and state censors. Before that final case, however, the novel attracted criticism from its first publication for the frank sexuality it portrayed. Reviewing the work in *Saturday Review*, B. R. Redman noted that "Mr. Griffin spares his hero and his readers nothing. He stops at no frontier of good taste—and, indeed, some saints have not—in his fusion of the sacred and the profane." The same reviewer questioned whether Griffin had exaggerated the sexual prowess of his hero and noted that "he errs in another way, and more importantly, when he asks us to believe in the absurd, unendurable, daily relationships of the hero and Madame Renee." Another reviewer stated that Griffin outdid Henry Miller in his frank treatment of sex and stated that interest in the work was "limited to specialists in psychopathia sexualis or mysticism."

The frankness of the sexual imagery resulted in charges that the novel contained "obscene, immoral, lewd, lascivious language." Censors objected to Griffin's lengthy descriptions of sexual activity, such as that between the narrator and Madame Vincent, of which Griffin provided a lengthy description:

> No longer do we kiss with our mouths drinking each other—our arms, our legs, our stomachs join in the kiss. . . . Hands descend the length of warm flesh, till they come to rest in the fleshiness of buttocks, the very feel of which fills us with profound drunkenness. Hands search further into our innermost selves . . . we become slowly united. . . . And the long sigh, unheard, pouring forth from the edges of consummation.

Even in the unwanted couplings with Madame Renee, the narrator exudes a wealth of sensuous detail as he relates "a vision of strong legs, deep navels, bursting milk-white breasts—insatiable, grasping, choking triangles of pubic greyness before my eyes," among other similarly graphic descriptions.

The novel was subject to suppression in Boston from its publication in 1952, but an important legal challenge to its sale occurred in Detroit, Michigan, in 1954, when a bookseller named Alfred E. Butler was found guilty and fined for selling the work to an undercover police officer. The judge in the Detroit trial determined that the sale was in violation of Michigan Penal Code, Section 343, that barred sales of books "containing obscene, immoral, lewd or lascivious language, or . . . descriptions tending to incite minors to violent or depraved or immoral acts, manifestly tending to the corruption of the morals of youth. . . . Butler appealed to the United States Supreme Court, which reversed the decision. Writing the resulting opinion of the unanimous decision, Judge Felix Frankfurter called the statute "unreasonable" and determined that no bookseller should be sent to jail by enforcing such an unreasonable statute. He conceded that juveniles must be protected, but viewed this antiobscenity law as excessive. He wrote the following:

The State insists that, by thus quarantining the general reading public against books not too rugged for grown men and women in order to shield juvenile innocence, it is exercising its power to promote the general welfare. Surely, this is to burn the barn to roast the pig. . . . We have before us legislation not reasonably restricted to the evil with which it is said to deal. The incidence of this enactment is to reduce the adult population of Michigan to reading only what is fit for children.

The decision in *Butler v. Michigan* was significant because it declared the view that whatever corrupted the morals of youth was obscene—a position that had been applied by American judges since the 1868 *Hicklin* ruling in England—to be an undue restriction on the freedom of speech.

FURTHER READING

Campbell, Jeff H. *John Howard Griffin*. Austin, Tex.: Steck-Vaughn, 1970.
Egerton, John. *A Mind to Stay Here: Profiles from the South*. New York: Macmillan, 1970.
Henderson, R. W. "The Devil Rides Outside." *Library Journal* (November 1, 1952): 77.
Kuh, Richard H. *Foolish Figleaves? Pornography In and Out of Court*. New York: Macmillan, 1967.
Paul, James C. N., and Murray Schwartz. *Federal Censorship: Obscenity in the Mail*. Glencoe, N.Y.: Free Press, 1961.
Redman, B. R. "The Devil Rides Outside." *Saturday Review* (November 1, 1952): 16.

THE DIARY OF SAMUEL PEPYS

Author: Samuel Pepys
Original date and place of publication: 1970, United States
Original publisher: University of California Press
Type: Diary

SUMMARY

The Diary of Samuel Pepys is an intimate record of daily life in seventh-century London told with frankness by Pepys, who wrote in shorthand code and included his honest observations and feelings. Although originally written over the years 1660 to 1668, the volumes were willed to Magdalene College, Cambridge, where they remained untouched until 1818. The diaries were deciphered three years later and published in expurgated form at various times until the first fully unexpurgated edition appeared in 1970.

Eberhard Kronhausen and Phyllis Kronhausen view the book to be a masterpiece of erotic realism, and they assert that "Samuel Pepys was a realist in politics and finance, as well as in whoring." The work employs down-to-earth language, "which did not leave out the erotic or excrementitious," and it contains numerous mentions of Pepys's extramarital sexual experiences, his observations of the sexual and hygiene habits of his contemporaries and his often-sexual fantasies. In one usually expurgated passage, Pepys relates that "the Duke of York hath got my Lord Chancellor's daughter with child" but refuses to marry the girl despite promising to do so. The lord chancellor "do make light of it" and tells Pepys one of his father's old sayings: "that he that do get a wench with child and marry her afterwards is as if a man should shit in his hat and then clap it on his head." In another instance, Pepys is sorry to hear that a friend's maid had left service, "for I was in hopes to have had a bout with her before she had gone, she being very pretty."

Pepys speaks of strolling through the streets and trying hard to resist the "pretty strumpets . . . so apt is my nature to evil." He sometimes writes in polyglot, as when he fears that a woman of his acquaintance is pregnant by him. He visits her and is "met with the good news que elle ne est con child [that she is not with child] the fear of which she did give me the other day, had troubled me much." Pepys also has the uncomfortable experience of being caught by his wife while hugging and kissing their maid Deb, a revelation that costs him several nights of sleep and requires of him strong protestations of love for his wife. Soon after, when Deb is dismissed by Mrs. Pepys, he meets the girl in a coach, kisses her and gives her money with directions for future assignations.

CENSORSHIP HISTORY

The Diary of Samuel Pepys was heavily expurgated from its first publication, and the first complete edition did not appear until 1970, when the University of California Press created a new and complete transcription of the 2,500 pages. In 1825, Lord Braybrooke, a college trustee, edited the manuscript and, according to Perrin, omitted "a couple of thousand passages which he regarded as trivial as well as indecent." His first edition contained about half of the original work. When Sir Walter Scott wrote a review of the version, he stated, "something has been kept back, which would have rendered the whole more piquant, though perhaps less instructive." In 1848, Braybrooke admitted the expurgation and promised to produce another edition that would

> insert in its proper place every passage that had been omitted, with the exception of only those entries as were devoid of the slightest interest, and many others of so indelicate a character, that no one with a well-regulated mind will regret their loss; nor could they have been tolerated even in the licentious days to which they relate.

In 1875, Mynors Bright, the new president of Magdalene, published what he said was a more complete version of the diary. While he did add to the text and state that the reader now had the whole work "with the omission of but a few passages," he still left out more than 20 percent of the original. In 1893, Henry Wheatley claimed to have printed the whole diary "with the exception of a few passages which cannot possibly be printed." His omissions amounted to 30 pages, but that percentage was small compared to the original, and his edition contained 99 percent of the original. Until 1970, additional editions of the diary based their text on Wheatley, thus continuing the publication of an expurgated edition. Nearly 150 years passed from the time that the diaries were first deciphered until they were printed in their complete, original form.

FURTHER READING

Bryant, Arthur. *Samuel Pepys: The Man in the Making*. London: Cambridge University Press, 1943.
Craig, Alec. *Suppressed Books: A History of the Conception of Literary Obscenity*. New York: World Publishing, 1963.
Loth, David. *The Erotic in Literature*. New York: Dorset, 1961.
Perrin, Noel. *Dr. Bowdler's Legacy*. Boston: Godine, 1961.

DROLL STORIES

Author: Honoré de Balzac
Original date and place of publication: 1832, France; 1884, England
Original publisher: Madame Louise de Bechet (France); Henry Vizitelly (England)
Type: Short story collection

SUMMARY

Published in France as *Contes drolatiques*, the work is a collection of stories that are written in the bawdy style of Rabelais in which the author gives free rein to his imagination. Balzac wrote the 30 tales in the style of his own interpretation of medieval French, including numerous archaic spellings to reinforce his efforts. He uses the ploy that he collected the tales in the monasteries of Touraine, but most are of his own creation whereas others are based only lightly on rumored misbehaviors among priests, nuns and peasants. He also claims that he edited the tales considerably to avoid offending his readers. In the prologue to the tales, Balzac writes that he had omitted "such old words as, being yet a whit too fresh, might hurt the ear, shock the eye, bring a blush to the cheek and set on edge the teeth of betrousered virgins and of ladies who cultivate true virtue and three lovers."

Viewed as pornographic by his contemporaries, as well as by later critics, the stories were created as entertainment rather than as a means of plumbing the depths of human nature, as he does in the numerous volumes of *La comedie humaine* (*The Human Comedy*). Graham Robb, a recent biographer of Balzac, observes that "to English readers, they are known as the *Droll Stories*, sometimes found lurking on the shelves of second-hand bookshops, with large-breasted women on their cover."

The topics of the stories range from necrophilia, nymphomania and adultery to the bodily functions. In one story, a character is obsessed with "bowel evacuation" as a means of maintaining his health, while several other stories contain characters who urinate, defecate and flatulate. Adultery is commonplace, and entertainment lies in watching the clever means by which the characters escape punishment for their behavior. The opening story, "The Beautiful Imperial," the story of a mistress, was first published in *Revue de Paris* in 1831. After its publication, Louis Veron, the editor, wrote to Balzac, "our subscribers are as prudish as ever, and to be perfectly honest, your writing is giving them erections. . . . Try to do something chaste if you can, if only to show them how versatile you are." In a later story, "The Wife's Appeal," an adulterous wife whose two children were fathered by a young priest is finally caught by her husband while in bed with the priest. As the husband advances with sword drawn, ready to kill both,

> she sprang at her husband with outstretched arms, half-naked, her hair dishev-
> elled, beautiful in shame, but more beautiful still in her love.
>   "Stay, unhappy man!" she cried. "You are about to kill the father of your
> children!"

CENSORSHIP HISTORY

In a report entitled "How to Make a Town Library Successful," published in 1876, Frederick Beecher Perkins, assistant librarian of the Boston Public Library, recommended censorship of the collection:

> It should exclude such books as Rabelais, the DECAMERON, the HEPTAMERON, the *Contes drolatiques* (*Droll Stories*) of Balzac, . . . all of which are sold in English translations for money by otherwise respectable American publishers. Few, indeed, are those who will object to this exclusion of ribald and immoral books from public circulating libraries.

In 1885, Anthony Comstock, secretary of the New York Society for the Suppression of Vice, saw an advertisement placed by the Globe Publishing Company of Paulsborough, New Jersey, for two books that suggested sexuality to him. Using a fictitious name, Comstock sent $2 for a copy of *Droll Stories* to John A. Wilson, who signed the advertisement. After he received the book, he then sent another $2 to purchase THE HEPTAMERON by Queen Margaret of Navarre. Comstock swore out a complaint and, in a case heard before a federal grand jury, obtained two indictments against Wilson for sending obscene literature through the mails. In dealing with the indictment against *Droll Stories*, the defense attorney argued that Balzac was accepted as a classic writer, and well-educated individuals had read and approved of his work, despite the existence of some "objectionable" passages that might also be found in the works of Shakespeare, Fielding and Sterne. The jury refused to listen to this reasoning and delivered a verdict of guilty, leaving Wilson with no grounds to argue the second indictment, to which he pleaded no contest. Wilson was sentenced to two years in the state prison and fined $500 and court costs. The verdict had serious repercussions for publishing and bookselling, leading *Publishers Weekly* to write in the March 12, 1887, issue, "It is, to say the least, preposterous to class these books with the kind of literature intended to be prohibited by law, and if they are to be shut out from the mails on the score of decency it will be hard to say where dictation and persecution in this direction will stop."

In 1944, in New York City, Concord Books issued a sale catalog of 100 books, including *Droll Stories* and Voltaire's CANDIDE. The New York branch of the United States Department of the Post Office informed the publisher that mailing the catalog would violate the statute that banned the mailing of obscene literature, unless the offending titles were blackened out. The publisher complied with the demand.

Droll Stories was banned in Ireland on February 13, 1953. A prohibition order was published in the *Iris Oifigiuil*, "the only official source from which booksellers [and readers] might learn of a new prohibition order," in which all articles blacklisted by the Irish Board of Censors were listed. According to the Censorship of Publications Bill of 1928, "the notice in *Iris Oifigiuil* should be sufficient evidence in the courts of summary jurisdiction as to the character of the publication," despite the acknowledgment by justices quoted in Adams's thorough study of Irish censorship laws that "this gazette is not a publication which booksellers are addicted to reading." The Irish Board of Censors found the collection of stories "obscene" and filled with "indecent passages." The work was officially banned from sale in Ireland until the introduction of the Censorship Publications Bill in 1967 reduced to 12 years the duration of a prohibition order, and the work was among 5,000 titles released from the list of banned books.

FURTHER READING

Adams, Michael. *Censorship: The Irish Experience*. University, Ala.: University of Alabama Press, 1968.

Balzac, Honoré de. *Correspondence*. Ed. by Roger Pierrot. Paris: Barnier, 1969.

Geller, Evelyn. *Forbidden Books in American Public Libraries, 1876–1939*. Westport, Conn.: Greenwood, 1984.

Gerson, Noel B. *The Prodigal Genius*. Garden City, N.Y.: Doubleday, 1972.

Loth, David. *The Erotic in Literature*. New York: Dorset, 1961.

Robb, Graham. *Balzac: A Biography*. New York: Norton, 1994.

Tebbel, John. *A History of Book Publishing in the United States*. Vol. 2. New York: Bowker, 1975.

Zweig, Stefan. *Balzac*. London: Cassell, 1970.

DUBLINERS

Author: James Joyce
Original date and place of publication: 1914, England
Original publisher: Grant Richards
Type: Short story collection

SUMMARY

Dubliners is a short story collection containing 15 stories that deal with incidents in childhood, adolescence, maturity and married life. The characters and scenes are drawn from ordinary Catholic middle-class life, and many of the stories are tragic. Joyce not only created characters, but he also used the names of actual people and places in the stories.

The stories are realistic in setting and character. In "Two Gallants," a young man believes that he could settle down "if he could only come across some good simpleminded girl with a little of the ready" while his friend Corley fears that a girl he meets periodically will "get in the family way." In "The Boarding House," a rather disreputable mother manipulates the situation so that her daughter will trap an older but naive man into marriage. In "The Dead," a husband learns that his wife once loved a young man now dead and realizes that he has never really known her. The same realism pervades the remaining stories.

CENSORSHIP HISTORY

Dubliners was printed in Dublin, Ireland, in 1912 after years of delay and wrangling. Twenty-two publishers and printers had already read the manuscript and refused to publish it. The edition of 1,000 copies was printed then destroyed by the printer John Falconer, who decided that the stories contained objectionable passages. Falconer kept only one copy from the print run. The work was finally published in 1914 by Grant Richards, using the manuscript from the 1912 printing that was destroyed.

FURTHER READING

Johnson, B. S. "Pi Printers." *Censorship* 3 (Summer 1965): 43–45.
Joyce, James. "A Curious History." *Egoist* 1 (January 5, 1914): 26-27.

THE EARTH

See *LA TERRE, ÉMILE ZOLA*

FANNY HILL, OR MEMOIRS OF A WOMAN OF PLEASURE

Author: John Cleland
Original date and place of publication: 1748, England; 1821, United States
Original publisher: G. Fenton (England); Peter Holmes (United States)
Type: Novel

SUMMARY

Fanny Hill, or Memoirs of a Woman of Pleasure was written while John Cleland was incarcerated in a London debtor's prison. The story of an orphaned 15-year-old country girl who moves to London to find employment as a household worker but who instead enters a brothel is primarily composed of descriptions of her sexual experiences and those that she observes. Her first job is with a brothel keeper who trains Fanny for her future profession as a woman of pleasure. Those who have sought to ban the novel over the course of more than two centuries have complained that it contains numerous incidents of heterosexual and lesbian sexual activity, female masturbation, flagellation and voyeurism. Typical of the criticism leveled at the novel is that of United States Supreme Court Justice Thomas C. Clark, who observed in a dissenting opinion in 1966,

> In each of the sexual scenes the exposed bodies of the participants are described in minute and individual detail. The pubic hair is often used for a background to the most vivid and precise descriptions of the response, condition, size, shape, and color of the sexual organs before, during and after orgasms.

Such criticism ignores the many instances in which the language is ornate and metaphorical as Cleland refers to genitalia through such euphemisms as "engine," "champion" and the "machine," as well as "the tender small part framed to receive it," the "pit" and the "wound." Although the novel may be "essentially a guidebook to erotic variations," the author presents them with humor. The author uses none of the "four-letter" words that are usually labeled "obscene," although he does use such candid terms as "maidenhead" and "defloration." The frequent labeling of the novel as priapic is also evident in the fascination that Fanny shows with the male anatomy, as in the scene in which she and her first lover Charles have sex:

> a column of the whitest ivory, beautifully streak'd with blue veins, and carrying, fully uncapt, a head of the liveliest vermilion: no horn could be harder or stiffer; yet no velvet more smooth or delicious to the touch. . . . a pair of roundish balls, that seem'd to pay within, and elude all pressure but the tenderest, from without.

At the end of the novel, after having experienced every variation of sexual intimacy, Fanny leaves her life of sin and marries Charles, providing the reader with her observation that "looking back on the course of vice I had run, and comparing its infamous blandishments with the infinitely superior joys of innocence, I could not help pitying even in point of taste, those who, immers'd in gross sensuality, are insensible to the so delicate charms of VIRTUE."

CENSORSHIP HISTORY

In 1749, less than one year after publication of . . . *The Memoirs of a Woman of Pleasure*, John Cleland was imprisoned on the orders of Lord Newcastle, the British secretary of state, on a charge of "corrupting the King's subjects." The action was taken after high-ranking officials of the Church of England had protested the nature of the book and demanded the arrest of Cleland, his publisher and his printer. The bishop of London had personally contacted Newcastle, asking him to "give proper orders, to stop the progress of this vile Book, which is an open insult upon Religion and good manners, and a reproach to the Honour of the Government, and the Law of the Country."

The trial of *Fanny Hill* in 1821 in Massachusetts was the first obscenity case involving a book to be heard in the United States. The novel had been surreptitiously published in the United States for many years, beginning with several expurgated editions of the novel published by Isaiah Thomas between 1786 and 1814, but not until Peter Holmes published the first edition of the novel in its original form in 1821 did censors take notice. The publisher was convicted for publishing and printing a "lewd and obscene" novel. Holmes appealed to the Massachusetts Supreme Court, claiming that the court had not seen the book and that the jury had only heard the prosecution's description. In delivering a decision on the appeal, Chief Justice Isaac Parker observed that the publisher was "a scandalous and evil disposed person" who had contrived to "debauch and corrupt" the citizens of the commonwealth and "to raise and create in their minds inordinate and lustful desires." Of the novel, he stated that "said printed book is so lewd, wicked and obscene, that the same would be offensive to the court here, and improper to be placed upon the records thereof." In short, Holmes lost his appeal because the judge refused to review the book, to have the jury read the book and to enter passages from the book into the court record for to do so "would be to require that the public itself should give permanency and notoriety to indecency, in order to punish it."

In 1930, while the Massachusetts legislature debated a revision of censorship laws, *Fanny Hill* was among 300 books seized in a raid on a Philadelphia bookshop. The city district attorney led the raid and announced at the same time that Philadelphia officials would undertake an extensive campaign to curb sales of "obscene" literature.

In 1963, G.P. Putnam's Son's announced that it would issue an unexpurgated edition of *Fanny Hill*. New York City prosecutors with city attorney Leo

A. Larkin decided to take legal action against the publisher. Because Putnam had a reputation as a responsible firm with book sales in many of New York City's largest bookstores, the city decided against arrests and criminal charges. Instead, city officials utilized the state injunctive procedure that allowed them to order the listing of inventories and to freeze stocks to prevent further sales until *Larkin v. G.P. Putnam's Sons*, 40 Misc. 2d 25, 243 N.Y.S2d 145 (Sup. Ct. N.Y. Co. 1963) was decided. A further advantage to the prosecution in proving the book was pornographic was that the injunctive procedure required the lesser proof of a civil case rather than the proof beyond a reasonable doubt of a criminal case. Judge Charles Marks issued an order to restrain sales of the novel. The case then went before the state supreme court and was tried without a jury before Justice Arthur G. Klein in *Larkin v. G.P. Putnam's Sons*, 14 N.Y.2d 399, 200 N.E.2d 760 (1964). Expert witnesses argued that the novel portrayed the economic realities of the times and emphasized its literary merit. The reporting of the British Profumo scandal, a sex-and-spy scandal that threatened to topple the British government, occurred while Justice Klein was deliberating. He dissolved the restraining order and dismissed the city's action, asserting that

> if the standards of the community are to be gauged by what it is permitted to read in its daily newspapers, then Fanny Hill's experiences contain little more than the community has already encountered on the front pages of many of its newspapers in the reporting of the recent "Profumo" and other sensational cases involving sex.

The prosecution appealed the decision in 1964, and in a 3 to 2 split decision in *Larkin v. G.P. Putnam's Sons*, 20 A.D.2d 702, case no. 2, 247 N.Y.S.2d 275 (1st Dep't 1964) the New York State intermediate appeals court reversed Justice Klein's action and ordered Putnam to refrain from selling the novel in the state of New York. Putnam then took the case to the New York Court of Appeals, which in a 4 to 3 decision reversed the decision of the lower court and granted final judicial amnesty to *Fanny Hill* in New York.

In 1963 the United States Supreme Court considered the validity of a Massachusetts Supreme Judicial Court decision that the novel was "pornographic" in *A Book Named "John Cleland's Memoirs of a Woman of Pleasure" v. Massachusetts*, 383 U.S. 413 (1966). The court cleared *Fanny Hill* of obscenity charges in a conditional decision. Justice William J. Brennan stated in the majority decision that historical importance is a factor and "the circumstances of production, sale and publicity are relevant in determining whether or not the publication and distribution of the book is constitutionally protected."

In London in 1963, the publication of unexpurgated paperback versions of the novel motivated the director of public prosecutions to secure a seizure order for all copies of the novel that were currently displayed in the window of a small Soho bookstore. The store proudly proclaimed on a sign in the window that the novel was "Banned in America." The trial was held early in 1964; after four days of testimony, the novel was determined to be obscene and the seized copies were ordered to be destroyed.

In 1965, Paul's Book Arcade of Auckland, New Zealand, sought to avoid censorship and applied to the Indecent Publications Tribunal for a determination regarding the expurgated paperback edition of the novel, published by Mayflower Books Limited of London in 1964. In a decision rendered on May 20, 1965, the tribunal ruled:

> The book has no substance other than to relate the experiences of a prostitute and we think that it might arouse interest in the one form of perversion it describes. . . . We accordingly make a ruling which the statute permits classifying it as indecent in the hands of persons under eighteen years of age, though we feel considerable doubt as to how far, if at all, such a classification will have the effect sought.

FURTHER READING

Cooper, Morton. "Fanny Hill vs. the Constitution." *Pageant* 14 (June 1964): 14–20.

Foxon, David F. "John Cleland and the Publication of *Memoirs of a Woman of Pleasure*." *Book Collector* 12 (Winter 1963): 476–87.

Kuh, Richard H. *Foolish Figleaves? Pornography In and Out of Court*. New York: Macmillan, 1967.

Rembar, Charles. *The End of Obscenity: The Trials of "Lady Chatterley's Lover," "Tropic of Cancer" & "Fanny Hill" by the Lawyer Who Defended Them*. New York: Random House, 1968.

Rolph, Cecil Hewitt. *Book in the Dock*. London: Deutsch, 1961.

Sebastian, Raymond F. "Obscenity and the Supreme Court: Nine Years of Confusion." *Stanford Law Review* 19 (November 1966): 167–89.

Stuart, Perry. *The Indecent Publications Tribunal: A Social Experiment*. Christchurch, New Zealand: Whitcombe and Tombs, 1965.

Wald, Emil W. "Obscene Literature Standards Re-Examined." *South Carolina Law Review* 18 (Spring 1966): 497–503.

THE FIFTEEN PLAGUES OF A MAIDENHEAD

Author: Anonymous
Original date and place of publication: 1707, England
Original publisher: James Reade and Angell Carter
Type: Poetical bagatelles

SUMMARY

The Fifteen Plagues of a Maidenhood catalogs the troubles or "plagues" faced by young women still in possession of their maidenheads, making them burdens whose loss is to be desired. Each bagatelle offers encouragement to the virgin and often repetitive instructions by which she might accomplish this loss. The book represents what Loth has characterized as "a typical example of the new commercial smut." An excellent example of the character of the book lies in the middle bagatelle, the "Eighth Plague":

Now I am young; blind Cupid me bewitches.
I scratch my belly for it always itches,
And what it itches for I've told before:
Tis either to be wife or be a whore.
Nay, any thing indeed, would poor I
E'er maidenhead upon my hands should lie
Which till I lose, I'm sure my wat'ry eye
Will pay to love so great a sacrifice
That my carcass soon will weep out all its juice
Till grown so dry as fit for no man's use.

CENSORSHIP HISTORY

The Fifteen Plagues of a Maidenhead, John Garfield's *The Wandering Whore* (1660) and Edmund Curll's *Venus in the Cloyster* (1728) were involved in cases that helped to develop the legal concept of "obscene libel" in the 18th century. The move meant a change in the direction of censorship from a major emphasis upon controlling sedition, blasphemy and heresy—issues with which the censorship courts were more familiar—to the effort to control published "obscenity." The responsibility for controlling obscenity also moved from the ecclesiastical to the secular courts, although creating the actual laws for these courts to enforce lagged behind the movement of jurisdiction.

In 1707, James Reade and Angell Carter were prosecuted for publishing *The Fifteen Plagues of a Maidenhead*. The defendants were brought before the king's bench and charged with "obscene libel," but they were acquitted after the defense counsel asserted that the court had no right to try the case because the defendants were not guilty of breaking any existing law. Lord Chief Justice Sir John Holt, one of the masters of English common law, admitted that he disliked the tone and the content of the book, calling it "bawdy." He also acknowledged in his ruling in *Rex v. Reade* that no common law or statute existed that "could warrant an indictment against even the filthiest book."

FURTHER READING

Foxon, David. *Libertine Literature in England, 1600–1745*. New Hyde Park, N.Y.: University Books, 1965.
Gerber, Albert B. *Sex, Pornography and Justice*. New Jersey: Lyle Stuart, 1965.
Kearney, Patrick J. *A History of Erotic Literature*. Hong Kong: Parragon, 1982.

FLOWERS FOR ALGERNON

Author: Daniel Keyes
Original date and place of publication: 1966, United States
Original publisher: Harcourt Brace Jovanovich
Type: Novel

SUMMARY

Flowers for Algernon is a novel about a daring human experiment that transforms a mentally retarded man with an IQ of 68 into a genius with an IQ of 185, thus forcing him to cope with the adult world. The experimental surgery that makes Charlie Gordon "normal" is only temporary, and he must suffer the growing realization that he will lose all that he has achieved and, once again, lapse into mental retardation.

Related as a series of progress reports written by Charlie, the novel shows his early inadequacies through the writing in the halting manner of expression, the considerable misspellings and the lack of grammar skills of the reports. As his abilities increase, so does the quality of the reports. Thirty-two-year-old Charlie has worked at a bakery for 17 years, after being "rescued" by his boss, Mr. Donner, from the Warren State Home where his mother had committed him. Charlie attends classes three nights a week at the Beekman College Center for Retarded Adults, where he joins others in practicing speaking and writing skills. He has no memory of his family or other details from his past, only nightmarish flashes of his mother yelling at him and slapping him, and his father saying, "He can't help it if he gets an erection. It's normal."

After the surgery, which had also been performed on a mouse named Algernon who remains under study in the laboratory, Charlie works hard to obtain the needed skills to utilize his new intelligence, and his former teacher, Alice Kinnian, works with him. His rapidly developing mind can process great amounts of information and he soon begins to trade ideas with experts in various fields, as he also enjoys artistic experiences. Newspaper accounts refer to him as the "moron-genius."

As he develops mentally, Charlie also develops emotionally and falls in love with Alice, who is attracted to him but urges him to become acquainted with other women. Charlie finds that he is haunted by the specter of the younger, retarded boy that he once was. He finally overcomes his fear by drinking a little too much and having sex with his neighbor, the bohemian painter Fay.

Through his scientific studies, Charlie learns that his improvement is only temporary and the deterioration will begin quickly. This fear is confirmed by abrupt changes in Algernon's behavior and the death of the mouse. Before the end, Charlie and Alice spend a long night making love and holding each other, fearing the inevitable. At the end of the novel, Charlie is living in the Warren State Home, his deterioration nearly complete.

CENSORSHIP HISTORY

The novel was banned from the public schools in Plant City, Florida, in 1976 because of its "references to sex" as well as for the sexual encounter between Charlie and his teacher. In 1977, the novel was removed from use in the 11th-grade classrooms in the Cameron County School District after parents protested to the district board of education. They complained that the book was "sexually oriented trash" and that it had no place in a high school classroom. The board agreed and ordered that all copies of the book be removed from the classrooms and that teachers no longer include references to the work in the curriculum.

In 1981, the novel was banned from the Glen Rose (Arkansas) High School library because parents complained about Charlie's first sexual encounter, claiming that it was too detailed and "explicit." In 1983, the novel was challenged for the same reason as a suggested reading at the Oberlin (Ohio) High School.

In 1984, parents of students at the Glenrock (Wyoming) High School challenged use of the novel as a required reading, claiming that several "explicit love scenes were distasteful." In 1986, the novel was removed from a 10th-grade supplemental reading list in the Charlotte-Mecklenburg (North Carolina) school district after parents protested its use and charged that the book was "pornographic."

FURTHER READING

Lambert, Robert. "Charley: Metamorphosis by Media." *Media and Methods* 5 (February 1969): 29–31.

Newsletter on Intellectual Freedom (July 1976): 85; (May 1977): 73; (July 1981): 91; (January 1984): 26; (July 1984): 122; (January 1987): 12; (March 1987): 54; (May 1987): 103; (July 1987): 150.

Shugert, Diane P. "Rationales for Commonly 'Challenged' Taught Books." *Connecticut English Journal* 15 (Fall 1983): 145–46.

THE FLOWERS OF EVIL (LES FLEURS DU MAL)

Author: Charles Baudelaire
Original date and place of publication: 1857, France; 1909, England
Original publisher: August Poulet-Malassis (France); Constable and Company (England)
Type: Poetry collection

SUMMARY

First published as *Les Fleurs du Mal*, the collection contained 100 poems grouped under the following headings: Spleen and Ideal, Parisian Scenes,

Wine, Flowers of Evil, Rebellion and Death. The sole collection of Baudelaire's poems to be published in his lifetime, the volume became notorious for its themes of eroticism, lesbianism, morbidity, perversity and rebellion. His observations of and emphasis upon subjective experiences among prostitutes, drug users, the poor and other images of Parisian ruin vie with images of unexpected beauty that he discerned beneath the perversity and corruption of modern civilization. To Baudelaire's contemporaries, the modernity of his rendering of the antithesis of good and evil was too great a deviation from contemporary work.

Although critics halfheartedly protested Baudelaire's "religious immorality" in such poems as "Saint Peter's Denial," "Abel and Cain" and "Satan's Litanies," the greater criticism was launched at his glorification of physical pleasures. Particular objections were raised against such lines as "Like a poor profligate who sucks and bites the withered breast of some well-seasoned trull" ("To the Reader") and adoration of a lover's body in "Jewels," in which the poet glories in "the sleek thighs shifting, shiny as oil, the belly, the breasts—the fruit on my vine." When the book, author and publisher were placed on trial in 1857 for "immorality," the prosecuting attorney made a point of quoting lines from "Jewels" and "Lethe" ("the reek of you that permeates your skirts. . . . those entrancing pointed breasts"). He also declared that "the most intimate habits of lesbian woman" were depicted in "Lesbos," "Damned Women" and "Metamorphoses of the Vampire."

CENSORSHIP HISTORY

The Flowers of Evil was published in an edition of 1,100 copies in 1857 and immediately motivated an uproar among critics for the startling imagery and daring metaphors of the poems. Baudelaire had expected that his poems would offend readers, but he counted on the recent acquittal in the trial of MADAME BOVARY and the preoccupation of the government with elections to protect his work from prosecution. In a letter to his mother dated July 9, 1857, the poet stated, "People have been spreading the rumour that I am going to be prosecuted, but it won't happen. A government with the terrible Paris elections on its hands won't have time to prosecute a lunatic." He was wrong, for attacks on several poems had already begun in the form of articles in the satiric publication *Figaro*, which drew the attention of the courts to Baudelaire's work. On July 5, 1857, his publisher, Poulet-Malassis, received a letter from the Paris distributor stating that the rumor abroad, "especially in high society," was that *Les Fleurs du Mal* was going to be seized.

The minister of the interior declared *Les Fleurs du Mal* to be "one of those unhealthy and profoundly immoral works destined to have a *succes de scandale*, and he apprised the office of the public prosecutor of his opinion that the book was "an outrage of public morality." Police were sent to seize all copies of the work from the offices of the publisher and the printer. On August 20, 1857,

Baudelaire appeared before the Sixth Criminal Court, faced by Deputy Imperial Prosecutor Ernest Pinard, a future minister of the interior. Pinard identified "Saint Peter's Denial," "Abel and Cain," "Litanies of Satan" and "The
Murderer's Wine" as breaches of religious morality but did not press the point,
so the court dropped the charge of blasphemy. Instead, the emphasis was placed
upon the "immoral passages" of other poems, lines from which Pinard eagerly
read, including "Jewels," "Lesbos," "Lethe," "Against Her Levity," "Metamorphoses of the Vampire" and two poems entitled "Damned Women." Baudelaire's defense attorney, Chaix d'Est-Ange, pleaded that the poet's work
depicted vice in a way that made it odious to the reader, but the court was not
convinced and ruled that the book contained "obscene and immoral passages
or expressions." The poet was fined 300 francs and the publisher and printer
were each fined 100 francs. All three were also deprived of their right to vote.
Further, the court ordered the first five "immoral" poems named above and
the version of "Damned Women" subtitled "Delphine and Hippolyta" deleted
from future editions of *Les Fleurs du Mal*. The ban on the poems in France
remained until May 31, 1949, when the French Appeals Court declared that
the poems contained no words either obscene or vulgar, "though certain
descriptions may, by their originality, have alarmed certain minds at the time."

FURTHER READING

Bergeron, Katherine. "The Echo, the Cry, the Death of Lovers." *Nineteenth Century
    Music* 18 (Fall 1994): 136–51.
Cohen, Emily Jane. "Mud into Gold: Baudelaire and the Alchemy of Public Hygiene."
    Romanic Review 87 (March 1996): 239–55.
Morgan, Edwin. *Flowers of Evil: A Life of Charles Baudelaire*. Freeport, N. Y.: Books for
    Libraries Press, 1943.
Pichois, Claude. *Baudelaire*. London: Hamish Hamilton, 1989.
Ramazani, Vaheed K. "Writing in Pain: Baudelaire, Benjamin, Haussmann." *Boundary
    2* 23 (Summer 1996): 199–224.

FOREVER

Author: Judy Blume
Original date and place of publication: 1975, United States
Original publisher: Bradbury Press
Type: Young adult novel

SUMMARY

Forever is a novel about first love and the chaotic feelings that accompany the
romance and the sexual desire of teenagers Katherine and Michael. After
meeting at a New Year's Eve party, the two date for several weeks, becoming
closer and more sexually aroused each time that they meet. Katherine is a virgin

and hesitant to "lose control," but Michael's passionate overtures eventually overcome her doubts. Their first few times having sex are unremarkable for Katherine because Michael reaches orgasm before she is completely aroused. After they finally synchronize their desire, Katherine becomes an enthusiastic aggressor, enjoying their lovemaking and seeking times to be alone with Michael. They pledge to love each other "forever," and for her 18th birthday, Michael gives Katherine a silver necklace on which her name is inscribed on one side of a disk with the words "forever, Michael" inscribed on the other.

Both partners act in a responsible manner, discussing their concerns regarding birth control and the prevention of sexually transmitted diseases and substituting mutual masturbation for sexual intercourse until birth control is available. Their encounters are detailed for the reader who can trace the growing intensity of their desire from Michael's sensitive exploration of Katherine's breasts to their later frequent and varied lovemaking. Sexual activity is also integral to the subplots involving several friends. Sibyl who "has a genius I.Q. and has been laid by at least six different guys" has a baby whose father she cannot identify. Erica seeks to help talented high school actor Artie determine if he is gay or not by having sex with him, but her efforts push him to attempt suicide.

Concerned that Katherine is too young to make a lifetime commitment to Michael, her parents urge her to date others and eventually demand that she work at a summer camp several hundred miles away to test the relationship. When her grandfather dies, Katherine rushes into the arms of fellow counselor Theo, who wisely tells her he wants her but "not with death for an excuse." This makes Katherine realize that she really will not love Michael "forever." When they next meet, she breaks off the relationship, leaving Michael angry and embittered.

CENSORSHIP HISTORY

Forever has been repeatedly challenged and banned in schools and libraries because of the detailed sexual descriptions and the perceived frequency of the sexual activity in the novel. In 1982, the parents of students attending Midvalley Junior-Senior High School in Scranton, Pennsylvania, challenged the book, charging that it contained "four-letter words and talked about masturbation, birth control, and disobedience to parents." It was also challenged that year in the Orlando, Florida, schools and at the Park Hill (Missouri) South Junior High School library where librarians were required by the school board to place the book on the "restricted" shelves. In 1983, parents called for the removal of the book from the Akron, Ohio, school district libraries and from the Howard-Suamico (Wisconsin) High School library because "it demoralizes marital sex." In 1984, challenges to the book by parents resulted in its removal from the Holdredge (Nebraska) Public Library young adult section to the adult section because of claims that the "book is pornographic and does not promote the sanctity of family life." That same year, parents challenged inclusion of the book in the Cedar Rapids (Iowa) Public Library because it was "pornography and explores areas God didn't intend to explore outside of marriage."

The Patrick County (Virginia) School Board, responding to parent complaints in 1986, ordered the novel placed on a "restricted" shelf in the high school library, and challenges were raised against its inclusion in the Campbell County (Wyoming) school libraries because it is "pornographic" and would encourage young readers "to experiment with sexual encounters." Parents of students in the Moreno Valley (California) Unified School District sought to remove the novel from the school libraries in 1987 and claimed that it "contains profanity, sexual situations, and themes that allegedly encourage disrespectful behavior." In 1987, charging that the "book does not paint a responsible role of parents," that its "cast of sex-minded teenagers is not typical of high schoolers today" and that the "pornographic sexual exploits are unsuitable for junior high school role models," parents of students attending Marshwood Junior High School in Eliot, Maine, demanded its removal from the classroom library. In 1988, the principal of West Hernando (Florida) Middle School yielded to parents' complaints that the novel was "inappropriate" and asked that it be removed from the school library shelves.

The challenges to *Forever* continued in the 1990s. In 1992, the novel was placed on the "reserve" shelf at the Herrin (Illinois) Junior High School library because it was "sexually provocative reading," and students could only check out the book if they had written permission from their parents. In 1993, the novel was removed from the Frost Junior High School library in Schaumberg, Illinois, after parents charged that "it's basically a sexual 'how-to-do' book for junior high students. It glamorizes sex and puts ideas into their heads." Also in 1993, the superintendent of schools in Rib Lake, Wisconsin, filed a "request for reconsideration" of the book after determining that it was "sexually explicit." The novel was placed on the "parental permission shelf," then later confiscated by the high school principal. A high school guidance counselor who spoke out against the district book policy and criticized the actions of the principal in restricting student access to the novel was not rehired for the following academic year. He sued the school district and a federal jury in Madison, Wisconsin, awarded him $394,560 in damages and lost wages. In 1994, school officials in Mediapolis, Iowa, responded to parent complaints about the novel and removed it from the school libraries because it "does not promote abstinence and monogamous relationships and lacks any aesthetic, literary, or social value." The book was returned a month later, but only to the high school library.

FURTHER READING

Forman, Jack. "Young Adult Books: 'Watch Out for #1.'" *Horn Book* 61 (January-February 1985): 85.

Maynard, Joyce. "Coming of Age with Judy Blume." *New York Times Magazine* (December 3, 1978): 80+.

Newsletter on Intellectual Freedom (July 1982): 124, 142; (May 1982): 84; (May 1983): 85–86; (March 1984): 39; (May 1984): 69; (March 1985): 59; (September 1985): 167; (March 1986): 39; (March 1987): 66–67; (July 1987): 125; (November 1987): 239; (March 1988): 45; (May 1992): 80; (May 1993): 70; (July 1993): 98, 104–05; (September 1993): 146–47; (May 1994): 83, 86; (July 1994): 109; (March 1995): 56.

Thompson, Susan. "Images of Adolescence: Part I." *Signal* 34 (1981): 57–59.

FOREVER AMBER

Author: Kathleen Winsor
Original date and place of publication: 1944, United States
Original publisher: The Macmillan Company
Type: Novel

SUMMARY

Forever Amber relates the career of Amber, an illegitimate child born of noble lineage in 1644, from her rustic upbringing through her adventures in London when she becomes a duchess and the mistress of Charles II. She has numerous lovers and gives birth to three children by three different lovers. She does marry four times, but only her first marriage is legal, and she fails to marry one man whom she truly loves.

The novel contains historically accurate detailed descriptions of the Restoration period, including Newgate Prison, the Great Plague and the Great Fire in London, as well as numerous notable Restoration figures. The author achieves accuracy in recreating the court of Charles II, as well as the costumes and the stage of the period. Amber loves forever Bruce, the first man who seduces her, but she is proud to become the mistress of King Charles II, assuring herself after their first encounter, "I'm somebody now! I've lain with the King!" After being moved into the palace, where she bears the king several children, she also makes several advantageous marriages, one to the older Lord Radclyffe whose grown son she also seduces. Throughout the novel, Amber uses her sexuality to achieve her aims, actions befiting the times as portrayed in the novel in which most of the characters ignore traditional morality and use any means to achieve their ambitions.

Despite the disapproval of critics, anatomical references are limited to descriptions of Amber's breasts, as "full and pointed, and upward tilting," and the sexual scenes are presented in general terms. Typical of such vague description is Amber's first seduction:

> At last his arm reached out, went around her waist, and drew her slowly toward him; Amber, tipping her head to meet his mouth, slid both her arms about him.

The restraint he had shown thus far now vanished swiftly, giving way to a passion that was savage, violent, ruthlessly selfish. Amber, inexperienced but not innocent, returned his kisses eagerly. Spurred by the caressing of his mouth and hands, her desire mounted apace with his. . . .

Amber, crying, half-mad with passion and terror, suddenly let herself relax.

CENSORSHIP HISTORY

Literary critics generally condemned the value of the novel; and the condemnation by *Atlantic* reviewer Frances Woodward that *Forever Amber* was "without any literary distinction" was typical. In 1946, the United States Department of the Post Office declared *Forever Amber* "obscene" and banned it from the mails, in theory until 1957, when the ban was officially lifted. The ruling had no significant effect upon sales of the book because mail distribution did not represent an important means of sales, although suggestive advertising materials sent through the mail had motivated the banning.

Forever Amber had been in print for four years, with 1.3 million copies sold in the United States and more than 100,000 copies in England, when it became the target of censors in the Commonwealth of Massachusetts in 1948. The case went to the highest court in the state as a civil rather than a criminal action under a new law that provided that whenever there was reasonable cause to believe that a book was "obscene, indecent or impure" the attorney general or any district attorney could ask a justice of the Superior Court to rule on the book. State Attorney General George Rowell charged that the book contained "70 references to sexual intercourse; 39 to illegitimate pregnancies; 7 to abortions; 10 descriptions of women undressing, dressing or bathing in the presence of men; 5 references to incest; 13 references ridiculing marriage; and 49 miscellaneous objectionable passages." The decision in *Attorney General v. Book Named "Forever Amber"*, 323 Mass. 302, 81 N.E.2d 663 (Sup. Jud. Ct. 1948) went against Rowell. Judge Donahue of the Massachusetts Supreme Court acknowledged the historical accuracy of the novel and stated that "these matters indicate a certain amount of study and research . . . that *Forever Amber* is sufficiently accurate for the purpose of representing a portrait of the period and its customs and morals; that it does not exaggerate or falsify any traits of the Restoration." The judge also noted that "sexual episodes abound to the point of tedium" and observed that they "are lacking in realistic detail, although some are coarse." Judge Donahue noted in closing statements that the book was "a soporific rather than an aphrodisiac" and noted that "while the novel was conducive to sleep, it was not conducive to a desire to sleep with a member of the opposite sex."

In 1952, the novel was banned in New Zealand after the Honourable Walter Nash, Minister of Customs, reviewed a copy seized by Customs officers. Applying powers granted him by the Customs Act of 1913, Nash acted as censor and made the final decision banning further importation of the novel. Perry notes that the law also allowed for the importer to "dispute the forfeiture, for the Attorney-General to lay an information against the importer for the condemnation of the book, to which the importer would file a defence . . . I can, however, find no record in the *New Zealand Law Reports* of a case relating to books prohibited on grounds of indecency having been dealt with in this way." Only the Dunedin members of the New Zealand Library Association Fiction Committee raised a protest against the censoring of *Forever Amber*. Although they criticized the novel as "trivial and naive," they found the way in which the Minister of Customs had dealt with the work to be objectionable and they made the public statement that "the operation of censorship in New Zealand was 'casual, arbitrary and ill informed'." Their views had no effect on the ban.

FURTHER READING

Ernst, Morris L., and Alan U. Schwartz. *Censorship: The Search for the Obscene.* New York: Macmillan, 1964.

Gillotti, Chris F. "Book Censorship in Massachusetts: The Search for a Test of Obscenity." *Boston University Law Review* 42 (Fall 1962): 476–91.

Morse, J. M. "*Forever Amber*: Defendant at Trial in Suffolk County Superior Court, Boston." *New Republic* (January 6, 1947): 39–40.

Paul, James C. N., and Murray L. Schwartz. *Federal Censorship: Obscenity in the Mail.* New York: Free Press, 1961.

Perry, Stuart. *The Indecent Publications Tribunal: A Social Experiment.* London: Whitcombe and Tombs, 1965.

Woodward, Frances. "*Forever Amber*." *Atlantic* (December 1944): 137.

FROM HERE TO ETERNITY

Author: James Jones
Original date and place of publication: 1951, United States
Original publisher: Charles Scribner's Sons
Type: Novel

SUMMARY

From Here to Eternity is a lengthy novel that chronicles the experiences of American soldiers stationed in Hawaii in the months preceding the Japanese attack on Pearl Harbor on December 7, 1941. Jones relates the daily lives of the men and the women whom they meet and love on the tropical beaches, in the cities and in the numerous bars where soldiers yearning for girls back home meet women to temporarily quell their loneliness.

The soldiers speak in a realistic manner, and the descriptions of the bar girls and prostitutes they meet are described bluntly. At the New Congress Hotel and the Black Cat, the men hope to spend their money on the Chinese girls with their thin breastless side view and the startlingly curved front view, the Japanese girls with their stockiness of heavier breasts, shorter legs, and more voluptuous hips, but best of all the hapa-Portagee girls with their hot smoking, cat clawing sexiness, everywhere women, women, women, and them cockily feeling their load.

The novel focuses attention upon several characters. The principal character is Robert E. Lee Prewitt, said to be the great-grandson of Confederate Robert E. Lee. Always on the side of the underdog, he rescues a "meek, frightened-faced little bundle of nerves" of a dog who is being held by two soldiers while they encourage a German Shepherd to mount her, then gets into a fight that lands him in the stockade. While there, he murders a man, then deserts. Prewitt is killed when he runs away from two military policemen after returning to camp.

The novel also focuses on the love affair that occurs between Sergeant Milton Warden and Karen Holmes, wife of Captain Dana Holmes. Karen has trouble dealing with the hysterectomy that she had to undergo several years earlier, after being infected with gonorrhea by her husband. She is bitter about the betrayal and bitter that she can no longer have children. As their love affair continues, Warden breaks through her defenses and their love scenes are tenderly portrayed. The sergeant is also inspired to become a commissioned officer, which he does near the end of the novel. The affair motivates several scenes of adultery, more suggested than explicit, and detailed discussions of Captain Holmes's infidelity and the result of the gonorrhea. As the novel ends, the war with Japan has begun and Karen Holmes is on a ship with her son, going home and leaving Warden behind.

CENSORSHIP HISTORY

From Here to Eternity was the object of several attempts to censor it. In 1953, two years after the novel won the National Book Award, the police chief of Jersey City, New Jersey, "suggested" to booksellers and newsstand dealers that they remove the paperback edition of the book from their racks. The majority of book dealers complied with the "suggestion." The book was released for sale after a representative of the American Book Publishers Council informed the Jersey City legal authorities that this action violated earlier court decisions in the state.

The novel was banned from the mails in 1955 by the New York City post office four years after it had become a best-seller. A carton of paperback copies broke open in a large mailing station, and one of the clerks happened to observe some "dirty words" on several pages. After the publisher entered a protest, the ban was reversed.

In 1956, the prosecuting attorney in Port Huron, St. Clair County, Michigan, ordered booksellers and distributors to cease displaying and selling all books that appeared on the disapproved list of the National Organization for Decent Literature, a Catholic censorship group founded in 1938. The books were identified as "objectionable," and the complaining organization cited the few erotic passages in each novel as the basis for identifying as objectionable *From Here to Eternity*, and other novels such as John O'Hara's TEN NORTH FREDERICK, Bud Schulberg's *On the Waterfront*, Ernest Hemingway's *To Have and Have Not* and John Steinbeck's *THE WAYWARD BUS*. The ban on all of the books was lifted after New American Library, paperback publisher of *From Here to Eternity*, joined with other publishers and obtained a federal district court injunction against the prosecution for "going beyond legal authority."

FURTHER READING

Champion, Laurie. "Jones's *From Here to Eternity*." *Explicator* 54 (Summer 1996): 242–44.

Davis, Kenneth C. *Two-Bit Culture: The Paperbacking of America*. Boston: Houghton Mifflin, 1984.

Hempl, William J., and Patrick M. Wall. "Extralegal Censorship of Literature." In *Issues of Our Time*, ed. by Herbert W. Hildebrandt. New York: Macmillan, 1963.

Oboler, Eli M. *The Fear of the Word: Censorship and Sex*. Metuchen, N.J.: Scarecrow, 1974.

Paul, James C. N., and Murray L. Schwartz. *Federal Censorship: Obscenity in the Mail*. New York: Free Press, 1961.

Tuttleton, James. *The Novel of Manners in America*. New York: Norton, 1972.

THE GENIUS

Author: Theodore Dreiser
Original date and place of publication: 1915, United States
Original publisher: John Lane Company
Type: Novel

SUMMARY

The Genius, the most thoroughly autobiographical of Dreiser's novels, relates the stormy history of artist Eugene Witla as he attempts to reconcile the twin drives of his life, a career in art and his powerful sexuality. Growing up in the last years of the 19th century in the United States, Witla faces a society in transition, in which the outward morality of a seemingly Victorian society clashes with new freedoms and increasingly flexible social and moral standards. These differing standards are emphasized by Witla's move from a small Illinois town to Chicago and, eventually, to New York City, as well as in his erratic love affairs in each setting.

Witla yearns for bohemian freedom and appears to have met a woman who allows him freedom while fulfilling his sexual desires when he becomes the lover of artists' model Ruby Kenny. Emotionally unsatisfied by their liaison, he becomes seriously involved with Angela Blue, a physically beautiful but emotionally distant school teacher. While courting Angela, Witla conducts brief sexual affairs with other women, who tempt him with their beauty or intellect, as he tries to penetrate Angela's sexual reserve. One evening after one more unsuccessful attempt at seduction, Witla asks Angela to marry him but she puts him off. He leaves to make his mark as an artist in New York City, where "he must enter and do battle," but continues to think of Angela. When the incompatible young people eventually do marry, Witla's tribulations increase as do his infidelities. Even when he tries to create a more stable life as the art editor for a huge publishing conglomerate, Witla becomes infatuated with and seduces Suzanne Dale, the daughter of a close friend of his employer. The seduction is revealed, and Witla is dismissed from his job right after learning that Angela is pregnant. Her pregnancy is difficult and she dies in childbirth, leaving Witla with a daughter, "Angela junior," to raise. As he determines to rebuild his life and to provide his daughter with a good future, Witla feverishly begins to paint and dreams of the lost Suzanne, not of his dead wife.

CENSORSHIP HISTORY

In 1916, eight months after publication of *The Genius* and after sales of about 8,000 copies of the book, the novel caught the attention of John Sumner, secretary of the New York Society for the Suppression of Vice. Sumner had received an unmarked envelope containing pages torn from a copy of the novel, as well as word from the Western Society for the Suppression of Vice in Cincinnati that a local clergyman had seen a young girl borrowing the novel from the local circulating library. Sumner warned the John Lane Company to withdraw the novel from circulation or face charges of distributing a lewd and profane novel, and he demanded that the publisher destroy the book's plates as well. He complained that the novel contained "seventeen profane and seventy-five lewd passages," and he expressed the view that it was "wholly conceivable that the reading of the book by a young woman could be very harmful." Many of the scenes to which he alluded depicted Witla as feeling passion, but there is little explicit sexual material in the novel. Alerted by Sumner to the moral danger posed by the novel, two postal inspectors also visited the publisher and expressed doubts about the novel.

In the initial contract with Lane, Dreiser had guaranteed the publisher that the novel contained "nothing of a scandalous, immoral, or libelous nature." After the New York Society for the Suppression of Vice threatened to prosecute Lane for violating the laws of the state against obscene literature, Lane withdrew the book from sale and discontinued its publication. Dreiser then bought the plates from Lane before suing the company, claiming that the publisher's refusal to continue sales of *The Genius* constituted a breach of the contract to which Lane had agreed if the sale, advertisement or publication of the book did not constitute a violation of the law. Dreiser and the publisher took the matter to the Appellate Division of the New York State Supreme Court as a submitted controversy, a move that took the case directly to the body without previous adjudication. The publisher included in the brief the text of the threat of prosecution made by the society and asserted that he had withdrawn the novel from sale because of the threat. Dreiser declared his book to be fit and proper for general sale, and backing him were such prominent writers as H. L. Mencken, Robert Frost, Sinclair Lewis, Amy Lowell, Willa Cather and Edwin Arlington Robinson. The Appellate Division ruled that determining if a publication was "objectionable" was a question of fact "to be decided as such in the proper manner," that is, in a criminal proceeding and not by the court as a matter of law, and it dismissed the case. No further litigation occurred because no charge of obscenity had formally been lodged, but the novel remained unpublished.

In 1923, Boni & Liveright reissued the novel. The power of the censors had lessened considerably by this time, and distribution of the novel was not again challenged. Although Dreiser appeared to have lost in the dismissal, his effort to fight the censors served to ease the way for a new generation of writers, including Sherwood Anderson, William Faulkner and Ernest Hemingway.

FURTHER READING

Auerbach, Joseph S. "Authorship and Liberty." *North American Review* 207 (July 1918): 902–17.

Boyer, Paul S. *Purity in Print: The Vice-Society Movement and Book Censorship in America.* New York: Scribner's, 1968.

Brooks, Van Wyck. *The Confident Years: 1885–1915.* New York: Dutton, 1952.

De Grazia, Edward. *Girls Lean Back Everywhere: The Law of Obscenity and the Assault on Genius.* New York: Random House, 1992.

Dudley, Dorothy. *Forgotten Frontiers: Dreiser and the Land of the Free.* New York: Smith & Haas, 1932.

Durham, Frank M. "Mencken as Missionary." *American Literature* 29 (January 1958): 478–83.

Gilmer, Walker. *Horace Liveright: Publisher of the Twenties.* New York: Lewis Publishing, 1970.

Tjader, Marguerite. *Theodore Dreiser: A New Dimension.* Norwalk, Conn.: Silvermine Publishers, 1965.

THE GILDED HEARSE

Author: Charles O. Gorham
Original date and place of publication: 1948, United States
Original publisher: Creative Age Press
Type: Novel

SUMMARY

The Gilded Hearse takes place on a single day in September 1938 in the lives of Richard Stiles Eliot and his wife Mary, who have reached a crisis in their marriage. Richard, the publicity director of a large New York publishing firm, is insecure in his professional and personal lives, partly because Mary, a fabric designer for the firm of Golding and Jack, makes more money than he does. During the course of the day, they quarrel, review the sexual affairs that both have had, attempt to advance themselves economically and socially and decide to reconcile. As they consider newspaper accounts of the Munich Conference and of Mr. Chamberlain's promise of peace with honor, they recognize the truth of Mary's statement, "most of us gave up our honor a long time ago. We'd settle for the peace without the honor."

Early in the novel, as Richard and Mary quarrel, the frustrated husband lashes out, "You dirty pig-Irish bitch. I suppose you're not screwing that Jew bastard, Golding, huh? I suppose you're not getting your nuccy from him?" In another part of the novel, a neurotic young society widow in whom Richard is romantically interested tells her roommate, "If I decide to copulate, I'll copulate."

In the incident that aroused the censors to action, Mary recalls accidentally meeting Monroe Golding on a train. The two retire to his train compartment and

> she pulled her dress up over her head. . . . there were Monroe's hands at her underclothes, helping her to undress, and then they stood together in the dark, without any clothes. . . . She felt panic and moaned and tried to turn away, but then there was the fruity, sweet taste of the brandy mixed with the taste of his kiss as he bent her backward across the berth, and a lifeless giving-in at first as he took her . . . she lost her grip on time and place and let herself go coursing through to the end, through the waves and the breakers and the blinding lights.

Worried because she has a physical response to a man to whom she has no emotional attachment, Mary consults a doctor who reassures her with the following observations:

> An orgasm . . . is produced by suitable irritation of the clitoris, the walls of the vagina, and other parts of the body. I guess love helps, but it ain't necessary. Even women who have been mass raped have experienced automatic orgasm.

CENSORSHIP HISTORY

The Gilded Hearse was one of several novels published after World War II, including *MEMOIRS OF HECATE COUNTY* and *END AS A MAN*, that contained language that would have banned a book in the years preceding the war. The language of the main couple's quarrels and the description of Mary's intimacy with her employer's son, Monroe Golding, provided the basis for complaints and resulted in legal difficulties for the publisher. The incident in which the doctor explains in clearly clinical terms how an orgasm occurs drew criticism, but the unemotional presentation and the absence of anatomical detail deprived it of erotic content.

In 1948, a private citizen named Harry Kahan complained to the New York Society for the Suppression of Vice that the novel was "obscene." Acting in Kahan's interests, John Sumner, secretary of the society, brought an action against Creative Age Press, publisher of the novel. When the case went to court in *People v. Creative Age Press, Inc.*, 192 Misc. 188, 79 N.Y.S.2d 198 (1948), the magistrate in the case agreed to review favorable reviews of the book but not letters from "prominent members of the community" to attest to the author's character and intent in writing the book. Magistrate Strong stated the following regarding Gorham's purpose:

> The author testified that his primary purpose in writing the book was to express his conception that, at any given time, the condition of national morality is reflected by the then current condition of individual morality and that national policies of compromise at the expense of principle occur when it has become common practice for individual moral standards to be disregarded for the sake of material advantage.

Strong dismissed the action against Creative Age Press, stating that the two passages dealing with sexual relations "contain little anatomical detail" and that "neither husband nor wife derives any satisfaction from their infidelity."

FURTHER READING

De Grazia, Edward. *Censorship Landmarks*. New York: Bowker, 1969.
Lewis, Felice Flanery. *Literature, Obscenity & Law*. Carbondale: Southern Illinois University Press, 1976.
Smith, Harrison. "Practitioners of Culture." *Saturday Review of Literature* (February 28, 1948): 13.

THE GINGER MAN

Author: J. P. Donleavy
Original date and place of publication: 1955, France; 1956, England; 1965, United States
Original publisher: Olympia Press (France); Neville Spearman (England); Seymour Lawrence (United States)
Type: Novel

SUMMARY

The Ginger Man is a comic study of life in Dublin as seen through the eyes of Sebastian Dangerfield, an American. Married and with a child, Dangerfield goes to Dublin to read law at Trinity College and to live out his particular philosophy of life that is far different from his former expectations of bourgeois respectability. Often broke and on the fringe of starvation, Dangerfield drinks heavily, becomes involved in brawls and generally sabotages his dreams of becoming a lawyer, although he professes to hope for success in that field.

Moody and difficult with those around him, Dangerfield lives a lunatic existence, as he moves from one pub to another and comes to know the alleyways of Dublin better than the legal reading rooms. He also has several affairs, one with a nurse named Chris in a prolonged scene that describes her act of undressing in minute detail until "she pressed her breasts together . . . swung her chest and flesh . . . and said she was ready." In another sequence, his friend Kenneth O'Keefe writes that he has "abandoned homosexuality for it has only succeeded in complicating my life further. I have been satisfying myself by hand as usual but find it very boring."

When Dangerfield's wife finally has enough of his behavior and leaves him, he decides to go to England but must first dodge his landlord Egbert Skully, to whom he owes months of back rent. In a funny scene, Dangerfield seduces the prim and straitlaced, aptly named Miss Frost, who complacently allows him to sleep on the floor of her room and charitably allows him into her bed, then wails, "It's a mortal sin which I have to confess to the priest and it's adultery as well." Once in England, Dangerfield finds Mary, a seemingly dewy-eyed innocent whose sexually insatiable nature matches his own and who, as the novel ends, seems to promise him happiness at last.

CENSORSHIP HISTORY

The Ginger Man was published in unexpurgated form by Olympia Press in 1955, but the novel was not publishable in England, Ireland or the United States. Donleavy submitted the manuscript for consideration to Charles Scribner's Sons in New York in 1954 but, as he states in a letter to Maurice Girodias of Olympia Press on September 7, 1954, "Although impressed by it they felt they could not publish it because of obscenity. The obscenity is very much a part of this novel and its removal would detract from it." After deciding to publish the novel, Girodias stated in a letter dated January 7, 1955, that he believed the novel more than likely would be "banned in the U.K. and U.S." and noted that "the publicity created by banning often favours sales." The novel was published as part of "The Traveller's Companion Series" with the words "special volume" following the title listing. To Donleavy, this designation, meant by the publisher to set it apart from other titles, "could also be interpreted to mean in such context that *The Ginger Man* was a particularly raunchy variety of dirty book."

Publisher Neville Armstrong of Neville Spearman Ltd. required that Donleavy heavily censor the novel before publishing it in hardcover in England in 1956. In their initial meeting, Armstrong warned Donleavy,

> I think one must warn that as the book stands, it could also land the author and publisher in legal difficulties if not prison and involve the printer in the same plight. It's [sic] being an offense, as I am sure you know, to publish indecent books and to deprave and corrupt those into whose hands such publications may fall. If I am allowed to make some judicious cuts in the Paris edition and perhaps have an introduction written drawing attention to the work's literary merit, this will help allay a printer's misgivings and avoid the book's being prosecuted as an obscene publication.

In 1965, Seymour Lawrence launched his imprint with Houghton Mifflin of Boston by publishing the complete and unexpurgated edition of *The Ginger Man*.

FURTHER READING

Clancy, Ambrose. "Wild Irish Rogue." *Gentleman's Quarterly* 61 (June 1991): 60–68.
Donleavy, J. P. *The History of the Ginger Man*. Boston: Houghton-Mifflin, 1994.

GOD'S LITTLE ACRE

Author: Erskine Caldwell
Original date and place of publication: 1933, United States
Original publisher: Grosset & Dunlop
Type: Novel

SUMMARY

God's Little Acre relates the story of a poor, illiterate Georgia farmer, Ty Ty Walden and his family. They struggle to survive on a rundown farm that barely provides a living while Ty Ty and his two sons, Buck and Shaw, dig holes all over the farm in search of gold, after hearing that nearly 15 years earlier gold nuggets had been found in the area. A pious man, Ty Ty once dedicated one acre of the farm to God, promising that all proceeds from that acre would go to the church, but he changes the site of the dedicated acre as he searches for gold to avoid discovering gold on God's acre. Because he never works the promised acre, whatever its location, the church receives nothing. In their search for gold, Ty Ty and his sons neglect farming, leaving the raising of cotton to two sharecroppers.

The sexual activities of his daughters Rosamund and Darling Jill, his sons, son-in-law Will and daughter-in-law Griselda exist as a matter of course in the novel, as they become involved in numerous sexual relationships that lead to quarrels and violence. Even Ty Ty, who declares himself too old to be sexually active, is aroused by Buck's wife, Griselda, who has "the finest pair of rising beauties a man can ever hope to see." At one point, he tells her, "The first time I saw you, . . . I felt like getting right down there and then licking something." References to cunnilingus are made at other points in the novel. When Rosamund's husband, Will, decides that he will "take" Griselda, he tears off her clothes and refers to Ty Ty's earlier statement:

> He said you were so God damn pretty, a man would have to get down on his hands and knees and lick something when he saw you like you are now. Didn't he? Yes, so help me God, he did! And after all this time I've got you at last, too. And I'm going to do what I've been wanting to do ever since the first time I saw you. You know what it is, don't you, Griselda? You know what I want. And you're going to give it to me. . . . And I'm going to lick you, Griselda.

After the episode, Griselda tells Ty Ty that "after a woman has that done to her once, Pa, she's never the same again."

The family members generally have a casual attitude toward sex. Pluto, a millworker who is dating Darling Jill, complains to her father that she has been "fooling around with a lot of men," and Ty Ty expresses approval of her behavior and tells Pluto that "It's up to you to satisfy her." Darling Jill is caught in bed with Will, after enthusiastically having sex with him and screaming out her approval, but Rosamund only strikes Will and spanks Darling Jill with no further repercussions in the family. Ty Ty chances upon Darling Jill and the albino Dave Dawson having sex in the dark outside the Walden home, and he secretly watches them.

Near the end of the novel, Buck kills his brother, whom he believes tried to take Griselda from him. He then leaves the farm with a shotgun, leading the reader to assume that he will commit suicide. The novel ends as the father sees the dissension in his family and realizes that his attempts to keep peace among family members have failed. He despairs over the "blood on my land!" and resumes digging for gold.

CENSORSHIP HISTORY

In 1933, John Sumner, secretary of the New York Society for the Suppression of Vice, brought a complaint of "obscenity" against Viking Press, publisher of *God's Little Acre*, and against Helen Schiller, a clerk employed by the publishers who sold the book to an agent of the society. The complaint cited specific passages from the book in the court complaint and maintained that it violated section 1141 of the Penal Law, making the book within the meaning of that statute, "obscene, lewd, lascivious, filthy, indecent or disgusting." In hearing *People v. Viking Press*, 147 Misc. 813, 264 N.Y.S. 534 (1933), City Magistrate Benjamin Greenspan observed that, to sustain the prosecution, "the court must find that the tendency of the book as a whole, and indeed its main purpose, is to excite lustful desire and what has been rather fancifully called 'impure imaginations.'" In defense, the publisher collected testimonials from literary critics, social workers and educators, as well as literary reviews that supported the claim of high literary merit. After a careful reading, Judge Greenspan concluded that the book did not treat vice and lewdness as virtues nor would it "incite lustful desires in normal minds." The court ruled against Sumner, stating,

> The court declines to believe that so large and representative a group of people would rally to the support of a book which they did not genuinely believe to be of importance and literary merit. The court is of the opinion, moreover, that this group of people, collectively, has a better capacity to judge of the value of a literary production than one who is more apt to search for obscene passages in a book than to regard the book as a whole.

Although the complaint against the publisher was dismissed, *God's Little Acre* suffered repeated prosecution for the next two decades. In 1934, faculty members at Columbia University complained that the novel was "indecent and tending to corrupt" and compelled its removal from the Teachers College library, even though the book was a required reading in several university English courses. In 1946, officials in St. Paul, Minnesota, banned sales of the book after a citizens group signed a complaint stating that the novel was "obscene" and "lewd." In 1947, officials in Denver, Colorado, banned the novel for similar reasons.

In 1948, *God's Little Acre* was among 25 books condemned as obscene by a Philadelphia fundamentalist minister who complained to the police that obscene books were being sold in the city. A police officer purchased the identified books, and nine were determined to be "obscene." Criminal proceedings were brought against five booksellers who were charged with possessing and intending to sell the following allegedly obscene novels: James Farrell's STUDS LONIGAN TRILOGY (*Young Lonigan, The Young Manhood of Studs Lonigan* and *Judgment Day*), Farrell's *A World I Never Made*, William Faulkner's SANCTUARY and WILD PALMS, Calder Willingham's *End as a Man*, Harold Robbins's *Never Love a Stranger* and *God's Little Acre*.

The case, *Commonwealth v. Gordon et al.*, 66 Pa. Dist. & Co R. 101 (1949) went to trial without a jury in the Court of Quarter Sessions in Philadelphia County, Pennsylvania, presided over by Judge Curtis Bok, who read the books "with thoughtful care." He wrote the first carefully reasoned judicial opinion to interpret the limitations that First Amendment guarantees should exert upon obscenity proceedings. He determined that obscenity is an indeterminate term, "that it is not constitutionally indictable unless it takes the form of sexual impurity, i.e., "dirt for dirt's sake" and can be traced to actual criminal behavior, either actual or demonstrably imminent." Judge Bok based his judgment on the books as a whole and upon their place in the arts. He discussed at length the concern whether in censoring obscenity the courts were contravening the principles of freedom of speech and of the press. Of *God's Little Acre*, Judge Bok observed, "It is a frank and turbulent story, but it is an obvious effort to be faithful to the locality and its people." He concluded, "I hold that the books before me are not sexually impure and pornographic, and are therefore not obscene, lewd, lascivious, filthy, indecent, or disgusting." This judgment was later sustained in the Superior and Supreme Courts of Pennsylvania.

The decision had important implications in later obscenity trials, and Judge Bok's exoneration of *God's Little Acre* and the other books in the case because they did not contain "dirt for dirt's sake" was used in the defense of other works. The questions raised in the *Commonwealth v. Gordon* case regarding the constitutionality of the statutes censoring obscenity were raised again in the *United States v. Roth* (1957), and defendants cited the case in subsequent trials of LADY CHATTERLEY'S LOVER, TROPIC OF CANCER and FANNY HILL.

In 1950, despite earlier exoneration in two major court cases, the book was banned from the state of Massachusetts in the case of *Attorney General v. Book Named "God's Little Acre"*, 93 N.E. 2d 819 (1950). The Watch and Ward Society of Boston initially brought a complaint that the novel was "obscene and pornographic" against the book in the city of Boston, but the case was dismissed. The lower court judge conceded that the novel contained "racy, off-color or suggestive paragraphs," but stated the opinion that it did not have "a substantial tendency to deprave or corrupt its readers by inciting lascivious thoughts or arousing lustful desires." The society then took its case to the Supreme Judicial Court of Massachusetts, where the state attorney general argued that "the book abounds in sexual episodes and some are portrayed with an abundance of realistic detail. In some instances the author's treatment of sexual relations descends to outright pornography."

Despite evidence as to the literary merit of the book, Justice Spalding determined that evidence of the literary, cultural and educational character of the work "does not change the substantive law as to what is obscene, indecent, or impure." Moreover, the judge stated that a discussion of the decisions in *People v. Viking Press, Inc.* (1933) and *Commonwealth v. Gordon* (1949) "would not be profitable" because "the interpretations placed on the statutes there involved differ materially from that which this court has placed on our statute." Judge Spalding also dismissed the contention that the rights of freedom of the press were at stake, claiming that such a concern "requires no discussion." The court reversed the lower court ruling and entered a new decree "adjudicating that the book in question is obscene, indecent, and impure."

FURTHER READING

Caldwell, Erskine. "My Twenty-Five Years of Censorship." *Esquire* 50 (October 1958): 176–78.

———. "Protest Against Columbia University's Ban on *Tobacco Road* and *God's Little Acre*." *New Republic* 79 (June 27, 1934): 184–85.

DeVoto, Bernard. "The Easy Chair: Liberal Decisions in Massachusetts." *Harper's Magazine* 199 (July 1949): 62–65.

Kauffman, Stanley. "God's Belittled Acre." *New Republic* 138 (June 30, 1958): 21.

Klevar, Harvey L. *Erskine Caldwell: A Biography*. Knoxville, Tenn.: University of Tennessee Press, 1993.

St. John-Stevas, Norman. "Art, Morality and Censorship." *Ramparts* 2 (May 1963): 40–48.

Watson, Jay. "The Rhetoric of Exhaustion and the Exhaustion of Rhetoric: Erskine Caldwell in the Thirties." *Mississippi Quarterly* 46 (Spring 1993): 215–29.

"Worcester Library Directors Support Their Librarian." *Library Journal* 74 (April 15, 1949): 649.

THE GROUP

Author: Mary McCarthy
Original date and place of publication: 1963, United States
Original publisher: Harcourt, Brace & World
Type: Novel

SUMMARY

The Group relates the story of eight women, graduates of the Vassar College class of 1933, who formed a clique while undergraduates. Six of the group are from wealthy Eastern families, one of the remaining two is the daughter of a wealthy self-made man whereas the other is of middle-class background and raised in the West. All members of the group are determined to make their mark in the world and to have careers that will give them lives far different from those of their mothers. Inspired by the progressive thinking that they enjoyed at Vassar, the young women approach life with enthusiasm and with the expectations of those who have experienced privileged educations.

Comic and ironic at turns, the novel begins a week after commencement, as the group gathers to celebrate the first wedding of one of their numbers, Kay Strong, who had daringly lived with Harald [sic] beforehand. As the other members of the group, whose nicknames include "Pokey," "Lakey" and "Priss" as well as Dottie, Libby, Polly and Helena, assess the possible success of the marriage, they reveal their shallow personalities and equally shallow values. In the 10 years that follow, the group members dabble in "Trotskyite" politics, join the bohemian theater world, engage in numerous love affairs and deal with abusive boyfriends and husbands. Lakey spends years in Europe, later bringing home her lesbian lover, the baroness, whose demeanor leaves the others insecure that "Lakey would now look down on them for not being Lesbians."

The novel ends with the funeral of Kay, said to have lost her balance and fallen from a window on the 20th floor of the Vassar Club in New York City while airplane-spotting only a few weeks before the United States enters World

War II. Mrs. Davison, an older Vassar graduate present in the lounge when the incident occurs, refutes suggestions of suicide. She claims that Kay appeared to be in good spirits and "had left a cigarette burning in the ashtray by her bedside. She states that "'no young woman who was going to kill herself would do it in the middle of a cigarette.'"

References to sexual situations and graphic descriptions of the group's affairs aroused criticism when the novel was published. Later, the following passage was labeled "disgusting" in the 1970 President's Committee Report on Obscenity and Pornography:

> Down there, she felt a quick new tremor. Her lips parted. Dick smiled. "You feel something?" he said. Dottie nodded. "You'd like it again?" he said, assaying her with his hand. Dottie stiffened; she pressed her thighs together. She was ashamed of the violent sensation his exploring fingers had discovered. But he held his hand there, between her clasped thighs, and grasped her right hand in his other, guiding it . . . over that part of himself, which was soft and limp, rather sweet, really, all curled up on itself like a fat worm. Sitting beside her, he looked into her face as he stroked her down there and tightened her hand on him. "There's a little ridge there," he whispered. "Run your fingers up and down it." Dottie obeyed, wonderingly. She felt his organ stiffen a little, which gave her a strange sense of power.

CENSORSHIP HISTORY

The Group was banned in Ireland on January 21, 1964. A prohibition order was published in the *Iris Oifigiuil*, "the only official source from which booksellers [and readers] might learn of a new prohibition order," in which all articles blacklisted by the Irish Board of Censors were listed. According to the Censorship of Publications Bill of 1928, "the notice in *Iris Oifigiuil* should be sufficient evidence in the courts of summary jurisdiction as to the character of the publication," despite the acknowledgment by justices quoted in Adams's thorough study of Irish censorship laws that "this gazette is not a publication which booksellers are addicted to reading." The Irish Board of Censors found the work "obscene" and "indecent," objecting particularly to the author's handling of the characters' sexuality, suggestions of homosexuality and "promiscuity." The work was officially banned from sale in Ireland until the introduction of the Censorship Publications Bill in 1967 reduced to 12 years the duration of a prohibition order, and the work was among 5,000 titles released from the list of banned books.

In March 1964, New Zealand Customs placed the novel on its "Publications Restricted or Prohibited" list, classifying it under Category VI, reserved for "publications which, if imported, should be detained and copies referred for decision." The principal distributors' associations in New Zealand as well as the New Zealand Library Association quickly expressed their disapproval of the censorship. On May 20, 1964, the New Zealand Library Association wrote to the Ministry of Justice, reminding officials that the novel had been freely circulating for months and asking the Justice Department to refer the work to the Indecent Publications Tribunal for a decision rather than to allow the Customs department to have the final word. Newspaper reports ridiculed the Wellington Customs department's claim that they had delayed referring the work to the tribunal until they could obtain copies of the book, because libraries had received copies the previous year and the books were still being sold in bookstores. Faced with public disapproval, the comptroller of Customs announced on June 24, 1964, that the book would neither be referred to the tribunal nor would future imports of the book be detained.

FURTHER READING

Adams, Michael. *Censorship: The Irish Experience.* University: University of Alabama Press, 1968.
Brightman, Carol. *Writing Dangerously: Mary McCarthy and Her World.* New York: Clarkson Potter, 1992.
Gelderman, Carol. *Mary McCarthy: A Life.* New York: St. Martin's, 1988.
Perry, Stuart. *The Indecent Publications Tribunal: A Social Experiment.* London: Whitcombe and Tombs, 1965.
United States President's Commission on Obscenity and Pornography. *The Report of the Commission on Obscenity and Pornography.* New York: Random House, 1970.

HAGAR REVELLY

Author: Daniel Carson Goodman
Original date and place of publication: 1913, United States
Original publisher: Mitchell Kennerley
Type: Novel

SUMMARY

Hagar Revelly is a naturalistic novel that deals with the problems that two poverty-stricken sisters, Thatah and Hagar Revelly, face in New York City. Thatah appears to voice the author's views about sex in her statements that "virtue is not an affair of the body, it's an affair of the mind. . . . Nowadays it is only hypocrisy that the world calls virtue." In contrast, the naive Hagar is led astray, seduced by her employer, a department store manager. Unwilling to become the manager's mistress, she turns for comfort to a seemingly honest laborer, a man who later leaves her pregnant. The desperate young woman is tempted to become a prostitute to support herself but rejects that life. She decides, instead, to accept her former employer's long-standing offer to become his mistress, viewing this choice as morally superior to prostitution.

The daring subject matter of the novel is subtly presented, and the sexuality is only suggestive throughout. One of the most criticized passages of the novel describes Hagar's first drink of liquor and her ruin:

> For only a moment did Greenfield watch the drooping lashes, the quivering lips, the tremulous pulsation of her bosom. Then he lifted her into his arms, and despite a moment of slight resistance—carried her into the next room.

CENSORSHIP HISTORY

Hagar Revelly presented a significant challenge to the 1868 Hicklin test, which permitted juries to convict if even a single passage in an otherwise clean publication was judged obscene, when it was placed on trial for being "obscene." In 1913, Anthony Comstock, secretary of the New York Society for the Suppression of Vice, made an unannounced raid on the offices of publisher Mitchell Kennerley and arrested the publisher and his clerk on a federal writ. Boyer reports that reviews of the book had been generally favorable, and publications such as the *Review of Reviews* praised the "high plane" of Goodman's prose. The society seized the plates and all copies of *Hagar Revelly*, including the 2,000 being processed at the bindery. Comstock provided Judge Learned Hand with a copy of the novel, with specific passages underlined, but the judge reminded him that the book could only be assessed if the passages were read within the context of the entire book.

Judge Hand dismissed a demurrer filed by the publisher and expressed the opinion that popular ideas regarding the discussion of matters related to sex must be modified in order that the problems they involved may be seriously analyzed. He also stated that only a jury could determine whether the content of a book was obscene and refused to make a determination from the bench. Hand condemned those individuals who professed that they were shocked by passages that were "honestly relevant to the adequate expression of innocent ideas" and stated that legal obscenity must be defined simply as "the present critical point in the compromise between candor and shame at which the community may have arrived here and now" rather than as moral corruption.

When the case went to trial in the Criminal Branch of the United States District Court in *United States v. Kennerley*, 209 F. 119 (S.D.N.Y. 1913), the presiding judge ordered that all members of the jury be given copies of the novel, and they were told to read it in its entirety. In giving the jury its instructions, the judge cautioned jury members that finding Kennerley not guilty would set a dangerous precedent, and he directed them that their task was to determine if the book "might be injurious to the morals of any person. If it would then it is obscene under the statute. The defense attorney stressed the reformist intent of the author, a 30-year-old St. Louis physician and social hygienist who had written the book with the desire to teach "the innocent youth of the land . . . the wiles of vice. After five-and-a-half hours of deliberation, and a first ballot in which they had stood 6 to 6 for conviction, the jury announced a not guilty verdict." This loss was the last major case initiated by Anthony Comstock, who died a year later.

FURTHER READING

Boyer, Paul S. *Purity in Print: The Vice-Society Movement and Book Censorship in America*. New York: Scribner's, 1968.
De Grazia, Edward. *Censorship Landmarks*. New York: Bowker, 1969.
Ernest, Morris L., and Alan U. Schwartz. *Censorship: The Search for the Obscene*. New York: Macmillan, 1964.
Lockhart, William B., and Robert C. McClure. "Literature, the Law of Obscenity, and the Constitution." *Minnesota Law Review* 38 (March 1934): 320–34.

THE HANDMAID'S TALE

Author: Margaret Atwood
Original date and place of publication: 1986, United States
Original publisher: Fawcett
Type: Novel

SUMMARY

The Handmaid's Tale provides a view of a frightening future in which racism and homophobia run rampant, personal freedom is lost, sexual practices are ritualized and the earth has become polluted beyond reclamation. The satire depicts a postrevolutionary world run by religious and political conservatives who deport Jews to Israel, execute homosexuals and resettle African Americans in North Dakota. Critics reviewing the novel have noted that these characteristics reflect real-world abuses, such as Romania's anti-birth-control edicts, the religious fanaticism of Iran's government and the stringent rules of Puritan society in colonial New England.

Set in a thinly disguised Cambridge, Massachusetts, the novel is framed as a taped interview with narrator Offred, who is a Handmaid and one of the few remaining women who have not been made sterile by nuclear disasters and toxic waste. Her narrative poignantly alternates between her present mechanized life and a past when she was a young working woman with a loving husband and a child. All women have become enslaved, but the fertile Handmaids exist solely to be made pregnant by the Commanders (referred to throughout with the capital *c*) and whose babies will be raised by the Commanders' Wives (referred to throughout with a capital *w*).

The novel contains numerous sexual scenes resulting from the fertilizations, encounters in brothels patronized by the high-ranking Commanders and the secret sexual liaisons that spring up in this totalitarian state, yet their effect is more apocalyptic than erotic. The brothels are staffed by women who wear such prerevolutionary costumes as Playboy Bunny outfits and other fetish-related items. Working in one such brothel is Moira, a pre-revolutionary lesbian friend of Offred's and a strong and rebellious character. Atwood not only depicts the excesses of conservatism but also presents the results of militant feminism gone awry. Pornography of all sorts has been outlawed, women shun all makeup and clothing that hints of sex appeal and the Handmaids kill any man accused of rape. No one can be trusted, and even after Offred falls in love with Nick, the chauffeur of a Commander, she is uncertain if he will keep his promise to spirit her out of the United States into Canada or England.

CENSORSHIP HISTORY

In 1990, the novel was challenged as a reading assignment in a 12th-grade English class at Rancho Cotati High School in Rohnert Park, California, for being "sexually explicit" and "profane." A local minister asked that the book be withdrawn from the curriculum because the main character of the novel was a woman and young men were unable to relate to her. In a campaign to have the book removed from the schools, one parent circulated a letter to local residents stating, "If you as parents do not rise up and go to your schools over issues such as these, we will continue to educate our kids for the gutter." The school board formed a committee to review the novel, and the work was subsequently retained.

In 1992, parents in Waterloo, Iowa, challenged the use of the book as an optional reading in 12-grade English classes because of "profanity," "lurid passages about sex," "themes of despair" and statements that they claimed were defamatory to minorities, women, God and the disabled. The school board rejected the complaints of the protestors by a vote of 6 to 1 and one member stated, "The objectors are trying to take away the rights of others to read the books." The protestors appealed to the Iowa Department of Education, which informed them that school districts determined the content of the reading lists.

The novel was removed from the Chicopee (Massachusetts) High School reading list in 1993 because parents complained that it contained "profanity" and "sex."

FURTHER READING

Benhuniak-Long, Susan. "Feminism and Reproductive Technology." *Choice* 29 (October 1991): 243.

Cooper, Pamela. "Sexual Surveillance and Medical Authority in Two Versions of *The Handmaid's Tale*." *Journal of Popular Culture* 28 (Spring 1995): 49–66.

Ferns, Chris. "The Values of Dystopia: *The Handmaid's Tale* and the Anti-Utopian Tradition." *Dalhousie Review* 69 (Fall 1989): 373–82.

Newsletter on Intellectual Freedom (January 1991): 15; (July 1992): 126; (May 1993): 73.

"School's Purchase of Four Books Ignites a Furor in Waterloo." *Des Moines Register* (April 15, 1992): M2.

Stein, Karen. "Margaret Atwood's Modest Proposal: *The Handmaid's Tale.*" *Canadian Literature* 23 (Spring 1996): 57–73.

Tait, Sue, and Christy Tyson. "Paperbacks for Young Adults." *Emergency Librarian* 16 (October 1988): 53–54.

Wilson, Sharon Rose. *Margaret Atwood's Fairy-Tale Sexual Politics.* Jackson: University of Mississippi, 1993.

THE HEPTAMERON (L'HEPTAMERON, OU HISTOIRE DES AMANTES FORTUNES)

Author: Marguerite d'Angoulême, Queen (Margaret) of Navarre
Original date and place of publication: 1558, France; 1884, England
Original publisher: Privately published (France); Worthington (England)
Type: Collection of tales

SUMMARY

The Heptameron is a French classic of pornography and one of the few famous erotic works written by a woman, in this case a woman who was also a queen. The work is a frank imitation of Giovanni Boccaccio's DECAMERON, but the device used is that the 10 storytellers are trapped by a flood and must each day create stories that illustrate a subject that is newly assigned daily. Unlike THE DECAMERON, the majority of the assigned subjects relate to sexual topics and the percentage of illicit affairs and fornicating clergy is higher in *The Heptameron.* The subject assigned on the first day is "the bad turns done by women to men and by men to women," while the eighth day requires that stories deal with "the most lecherous cases that can be conceived."

The work contains only 72 stories because Queen Marguerite died before reaching her goal. As in THE DECAMERON, the stories contain many uncomplimentary portrayals of members of religious orders and sexual indiscretions of husbands and wives. Two major differences, however, are that *The Heptameron* contains stories of incest, not found in the earlier work, and a greater extent of emetic material. Overall, the stories also contain a greater amount of cruelty and manipulation of the opposite sex than appear in Boccaccio's work. The first story relates the adventures of a wife who takes a bishop for her lover because he pays her, and a young military officer for her lover because he gives her pleasure. When the officer protests and jilts her, she tells her husband, who kills the officer. Later, she learns that her husband is plotting to kill her, so she turns him in to the authorities. Afterward, "the wife, when her husband was removed, sinned more wickedly than before, and so died miserably."

Bizarre occurrences appear in other stories: one monk commits several murders in pursuit of a woman, another monk rapes a young girl as a form of chastisement, a husband kills his unfaithful wife and a woman is soiled by feces in a monastery privy. In general, the stories in *The Heptameron* are not as playful and mischievous as those of Boccaccio, and the reason may lie in Queen Marguerite's stated intention to restrict her stories to true incidents.

CENSORSHIP HISTORY

The Heptameron was published posthumously in 1558 in a highly expurgated version. The complete version, clandestinely printed by private individuals, remained an underground work until late in the 19th century.

In a report entitled "How to Make a Town Library Successful," published in 1876, Frederick Beecher Perkins, assistant librarian of the Boston Public Library, recommended the following approach to censorship of the collection:

> It should exclude such books as Rabelais, the DECAMERON, the *Heptameron,* THE CONTES DROLATIQUES (DROLL STORIES) of Balzac, . . . all of which are sold in English translations for money by otherwise respectable American publishers. Few, indeed, are those who will object to this exclusion of ribald and immoral books from public circulating libraries.

In 1885, Anthony Comstock, secretary of the New York Society for the Suppression of Vice, saw an advertisement for the Globe Publishing Company of Paulsborough, New Jersey, which contained two books that would become his targets. Using a fictitious name, Comstock sent $2 for a copy of DROLL STORIES by Honoré de Balzac to John A. Wilson, who signed the advertisement. After he received the book, he then sent another $2 to purchase *The Heptameron.* Comstock then took his evidence to court and attained two federal grand jury indictments against Wilson for sending obscene literature through the mail. (See *Droll Stories.*)

The Heptameron was involved in the 1892 litigation of the Worthington Book Publishing Co., which was in financial difficulty. The receiver wanted to sell some of the company stock, including ARABIAN NIGHTS, THE HISTORY OF TOM JONES, THE ART OF LOVE, THE DECAMERON, *Gargantua and Pantagruel,* Rousseau's CONFESSIONS and *The Heptameron* to pay off creditors, but Anthony Comstock stepped in to oppose the sales. He demanded of the court that the books be officially burned. The court disagreed. (See *Arabian Nights.*)

In 1900, a bookseller who had sold copies of the work was tried for obscene libel at the central criminal court in London in *Reg. v. Thomson,* 64 U.P. 456. The court record stated that Isabel Florence Thomson,

> then being a person of wicked and depraved disposition, and unlawfully and wickedly devising, contriving, and intending as much as in her lay to vitiate and corrupt the morals of the people of this kingdom unlawfully, wickedly, and wilfully did publish, sell, and utter a certain lewd, wicked, bawdy, and obscene libel in the form of a book entitled *The Heptameron of Margaret Queen of Navarre.*

The defense read extracts about the book from the Encyclopedia Britannica and the *Edinburgh Review* and stated that proceedings should never have been brought against the classic. The defense in this case also observed that

> in the Middle Ages things were discussed which if put forward now for the reading of the general public would never be tolerated. In towns buried from the corrupt times of the Roman Empire, now disinterred or in the course of being disinterred, there are discovered pictures of the most lewd and filthy character. Nobody would think of destroying those pictures, but to sell photographs in the streets of London would be an indictable offense.

The jury returned a not-guilty verdict.

FURTHER READING

Geller, Evelyn. *Forbidden Books in American Public Libraries, 1876–1939*. Westport, Conn.: Greenwood, 1984.

Green, Virginia M. *Heroic Virtue, Comic Infidelity: Reassessing Marguerite de Navarre's Heptameron*. Amherst, Mass.: Hestia Press, 1993.

Rigolet, François. "Magdalen's Skull: Allegory and Iconography in *The Heptameron*." *Renaissance Quarterly* 47 (Spring 1994): 57–73.

Tebbel, John. *A History of Book Publishing in the United States*. Vol. 2. New York: Bowker, 1975.

Thomas, Donald. *A Long Time Burning: The History of Literary Censorship in England*. New York: Praeger, 1969.

THE HISTORY OF TOM JONES, A FOUNDLING

Author: Henry Fielding
Original date and place of publication: 1749, England; 1931, United States
Original publisher: Andrew Millar (England); Brown House (United States)
Type: Novel

SUMMARY

The History of Tom Jones, A Foundling is a road novel that relates the adventures of the sexually impulsive young protagonist, from his illegitimate birth through his marriage to the beautiful and virtuous Sophia Western. Found as a baby in Squire Allworthy's bed, Tom is raised in the household and treated like a family member. Although he falls in love with Sophia, he cannot resist the sexual charms of the gamekeeper's daughter, Molly Seagrim, who becomes pregnant with what he thinks is his child. He confesses his indiscretion to Allworthy, then goes to Molly to give her money, but he finds her in bed with another man. Chastened, Tom decides to concentrate on winning Sophia's love, but her father, Squire Western, refuses to let her marry a foundling and tries to arrange a marriage to Allworthy's nephew Blifil. Squire Allworthy becomes very ill, then recovers, and Tom becomes drunk celebrating the recovery, but conspirators in the household claim that he was celebrating the squire's impending death and his supposed inheritance, so the squire banishes Tom.

While on the road, Tom has an affair with Mrs. Waters, whom he rescued from attack by a surly soldier named Northerton. He later meets Lady Bellaston who, having heard of his attractiveness, seeks him out and seduces him. This affair gave the most offense when the novel first appeared, because he not only has the affair but also becomes her short-term gigolo. After Tom ends the affair, he receives a letter from Sophia, telling him that she knows about the two women and never wants to see him again. Further adventures occur, and a series of coincidences reveal that Tom is the illegitimate child of Squire Allworthy's late sister Bridget. Now that he is an Allworthy heir, Squire Western welcomes Tom as his son-in-law, although Sophia pretends reluctance. The two finally marry, and the novel ends happily as Squire Western gives them his estate.

Despite the lack of actual sexual material in the book, the numerous references to illegitimacy, references to Tom's numerous sexual liaisons and explicit anatomical references made the book a target of censors. In several scenes, female characters suffer having their upper clothing torn from their bodies as they fight to preserve their virtue. In the incident in which Tom rescues Mrs. Waters,

> he had not entered far into the wood before he beheld a most shocking sight indeed, a woman stripped half naked, under the hands of a ruffian. . . . her clothes being torn from all the upper part of her body, her breasts, which were well formed and extremely white, attracted the eyes of her deliverer.

Although he loves Sophia, Tom continues to satisfy his desire for other women, more in the manner of boyish high spirits than in immorality. He views sex much as he views any challenge and "held it as much incumbent on him to accept a challenge to love as if it had been a challenge to fight." In addition to sexual references, Fielding's use of such taboo terms as *bitch*, *slut*, *hussy*, *harlot* and *arse* also incited complaints.

CENSORSHIP HISTORY

The History of Tom Jones was attacked as "vulgar," "low," "indecent" and "devoid of moral sense" from its first publication. Critics claimed that Fielding had written "an enticement to moral corruption." Soon after the novel was published, *Gentleman's Magazine* observed that the "loose images" of the novel "perhaps invite to vice more than the contrast figures alarm us into virtue." In 1750, Bishop of London Thomas Sherlock warned that the novel had been written merely as an excuse to include "the most inexecrable Scenes of Lewdness." In 1772, Reverend Jonathan Edwards denounced *The History of Tom Jones* and warned the young against reading it.

Writing in 1879 regarding those works that should be contained in the well-stocked library, Samuel Green, librarian in Worcester, Massachusetts, pointed out that he:

> would place certain restrictions on the use of the novels of Smollett and Fielding, because while in many respects works of the first order, it is best that the young should read only such books as preserve a certain reticence in regard to subjects freely talked and written about in the last century.

In 1892, *The History of Tom Jones* was involved in the litigation of the Worthington Book Publishing Co., which was in financial difficulty. The receiver wanted to sell some of the company stock, including ARABIAN NIGHTS, THE DECAMERON, THE ART OF LOVE, THE HEPTAMERON, *Gargantua and Pantagruel*, Rousseau's CONFESSIONS and *The History of Tom Jones* to pay off creditors, but Anthony Comstock stepped in to oppose the sales. He demanded of the court that the books be officially burned. The court disagreed. (See *Arabian Nights*.)

In New York City in 1894, the Astor library removed all works by Fielding from its regular collection and placed them in the reference collection, after several patrons noted the "vulgar activities" depicted in the novel.

City and county officials in Dubuque, Iowa, staged a sudden raid on the public library in 1951. Under the authority of a warrant, they seized numerous books that were judged to be "obscene," including works of Rabelais, Boccaccio's DECAMERON and *The History of Tom Jones*.

FURTHER READING

Geller, Evelyn. *Forbidden Books in American Public Libraries, 1876–1939*. Westport, Conn.: Greenwood, 1984.

Green, Samuel S. "Sensational Fiction in Public Libraries." *Library Journal* 4 (September–October 1879): 349–52.

Rolph, Cecil Hewitt. *Books in the Dock*. London: Deutsch, 1961.

Thomas, Donald. *Henry Fielding: A Life*. New York: St. Martin's, 1990.

HOMO SAPIENS

Author: Stanley Przybyskzewski
Original date and place of publication: 1898, Germany; 1915, United States
Original publisher: Hansson (Germany); Alfred A. Knopf (United States)
Type: Novel

SUMMARY

Homo Sapiens is an intense and introspective work written and first published in Germany by the Polish-born writer, then translated and published in the United States. The author's best-known novel uses ornate language to trace the dissolution of the hedonistic artist Erik Falk through alcohol and destructive eroticism, as he searches for something that will fill the emptiness he feels.

Falk embodies Przybyskzewski's theories of a "libidinal unconscious" that drives him to engage in numerous affairs even as he protests that he loves his wife. "But at the same time, he loves his wife unqualifiedly. And he loves her so much that there can be no doubt of the reality of his love. In a word he loves both the one and the other." The protagonist, possessed of "an exceptional personality," is a close relative to Nietzsche's superman, aloof from the common herd yet conscious of the restraints of his existence.

Censors in the United States objected to the manner in which Falk expressed his uniqueness in relation to ordinary individuals in sexual terms:

> "I have never suffered on account of a woman," boasts an old rake, Iltis.
> "Because your organism is very tough, a peasant's organism, my dear Iltis. Your sensibilities have not yet reached the stage of dependence upon the brain. You are like a hydromedusa which suddenly parts with its feelers stocked with sexual organs and sends them off to seek the female, and then does not bother about them any more."

For Falk, the sexual instinct functions as the primary force in life, but his search for sexual union is part of the greater goal to find in woman the miraculous expression of his most intimate, "most precious I." Thus, even his dreams are imbued with sexuality. In one, Falk dreams of two elks fighting violently, one driving "his horns into the other's breast. He drove them in deeper and deeper, tore ferociously at his flesh and entrails. The blood spurted." As the two fight, near them "a female elk was pasturing unmindful of the savage struggle of the passion-mad males."

CENSORSHIP HISTORY

Homo Sapiens was praised when it was first published in Germany in 1898, and advance copies of the American publication of the book received praise in 1915. Writing in *The Little Review*, Alexander S. Kaun called the novel "the book of the age." Other reviewers agreed with the assessment, one stating that "Przybyskzewski compels you to co-operate with him in analysing psychological phenomena." Praise did not save the novel from banning, for preoccupation with "the sex-problem" was unsettling to American censors in 1915.

On December 23, 1915, 23-year-old Alfred A. Knopf, publisher of *Homo Sapiens* and only one year out of Columbia University, appeared before Magistrate Simms in Jefferson Market Court on charges brought by John

Sumner and the New York Society for the Suppression of Vice. The society charged that the novel was obscene and should be removed from distribution. In the brief hearing, Knopf provided evidence that the book had received favorable reviews and sold openly as a work of art. Knopf's attorney requested an adjournment to allow the presiding magistrate to read the book, but Assistant District Attorney Van Castile protested, "His Honor should not be subjected to such cruel punishment. The book is utterly stupid as well as indecent."

Despite the protest, an adjournment was granted and Knopf's wealthy father called in Wilson E. Tipple, his lawyer and a director of the vice society, to speak with young Knopf and convince him to change his mind. At a later meeting between young Knopf and Sumner, the publisher completely reversed his position, promising to withdraw the novel from sale and to melt down the plates. In return, Sumner withdrew the complaint. As Boyer relates, Knopf explained his actions in a letter to *Publishers Weekly*, dated January 22, 1916, in which he stated that the book had been "smirched" and that he did not "deign to satisfy the prurient demand which had been created."

FURTHER READING

Boyer, Paul S. *Purity in Print: The Vice-Society Movement and Book Censorship in America.* New York: Scribner's, 1968.
"*Homo Sapiens*: A Review." *The Little Review* 2 (December 1915): 25–27.
Kaun, Alexander S. "The Ecstasy of Pain." *The Little Review* 2 (December 1915): 16–23.
"Publishing's Past Fifty Years, A Balance Sheet—II." *Saturday Review* 47 (November 28, 1964): 17–19, 69.

IF IT DIE (SI LE GRAIN NE MEURT)

Author: André Gide
Original date and place of publication: 1920, France; 1935, United States
Original publisher: Privately published (France); Modern Library (United States)
Type: Autobiography

SUMMARY

If It Die, titled *Si le grain ne meurt* when originally published, is Andre Gide's attempt to "give form to a confused inner agitation." Recounting his childhood through young manhood, the work contains his early revelation of a homosexual orientation, shown in one episode where the child Gide cries in his mother's arms and declares that he "is unlike the other schoolboys." The work is divided into two parts: Part one describes Gide's childhood and growth to young manhood, and a shorter part two describes his awareness of homosexual feelings and his adventures in acting on those feelings.

Gide relates adolescent incidents of masturbation and homoerotic desire in part one. He describes taking toys under the dining room table on the pretext of playing with a friend, but "we amused ourselves otherwise, beside each other but not with each other: we had what I afterwards learnt are called 'bad habits.'" As an adolescent at the École Alsacienne, he meets another boy for whom he "conceived an absolute passion," and later he meets another young man named Abel who makes Gide an "offer of his heart." With Lionel, he "made regular lovers' trysts, to which we hastened with beating hearts and agitated thoughts," and with Louis he feels "a kind of lover-like bashfulness . . . a sort of boiling agitation . . . a kind of passionate stammer."

In part two, which begins when Gide turns 20, the stirrings of sexual desire become reality. He and a friend travel to Tunisia and Algiers, where Gide has his first sexual experience with Ali, their young Tunisian guide. Ali undresses for their encounter and "he emerged naked as a god. . . . Though his body was perhaps burning, it felt as cool and refreshing to my hands as shade."

In Algiers, he meets Mohammed, who also thrills him and dominates his mind even though the two do not become intimate until later. Still, when Gide has sex with a native girl, he can only bear doing so "because I shut my eyes and imagined I was holding Mohammed in my arms." A short time later, when Oscar Wilde visits and arranges a sexual liaison for Gide with Mohammed, Gide is enthralled by his experience with "the perfect little body, so wild, so ardent, so lascivious" and brags that he "achieved pleasure five times with him" that one night.

Throughout, even as he relates his sexual adventures, Gide expresses feelings of guilt. The autobiography ends with Gide speaking of betrothal to his cousin Emmeline as a cure for his homosexual desires.

CENSORSHIP HISTORY

In 1935, a New York City policeman acting as an agent of the New York Society for the Suppression of Vice purchased a copy of *If It Die* from the Gotham Book Mart. Acting under orders from society secretary John Sumner, who considered passages in the book obscene, the officer then arrested the book mart owner for allegedly violating the New York Obscenity Statute. When the owner was placed on trial in *People on Complaint of Savery v. Gotham Book Mart Inc.*, in the City Magistrate's Court of New York City, Seventh District, Borough of Manhattan, on January 24, 1936, Sumner served as the prosecutor for the people. He directed his attack at 76 pages (20 percent) of the book, and only specific paragraphs contained in 22 of those pages, in the attempt to apply the Hicklin rule, which determined that paragraphs could be taken out of context and the test of obscenity of the entire work would be judged by assessing if the offending paragraphs had the tendency "to deprave the minds of those open to such influences and into whose hands a publication of this character might come."

Judge Nathan D. Perlman presided over the case and refused to grant Sumner the right to apply the Hicklin rule. Instead, in making a determination the judge cited the Woolsey decision in *United States v. One Book Entitled "Ulysses,"* in which the presiding judge emphasized consideration of the entire book and pondered the question: "Is the book dirt for dirt's sake?"Acknowledging that the book "contains a few paragraphs dealing with isolated instances of inversion, which, taken by themselves, are undoubtedly vulgar and indecent," Judge Perlman stated that they were, nonetheless, vital in "forming an essential part of the main theme." He asserted that these scenes were necessary for the author to present a truthful and accurate picture of his life: "It is as an entire creature we must study him, omitting nothing." Based on this assessment, the court ruled that *If It Die* "is not obscene, lewd, lascivious, or indecent within the meaning of the statute." He dismissed the complaint and discharged the owner of the Gotham Book Mart.

In 1938, after Gide publicly announced his disillusionment with communism, the Soviet Union banned all of his works, including *If It Die*. Soviet authorities in the occupation of East Berlin in 1954 banned all of Gide's works from East Germany.

In 1952, the work was placed on the Index Librorum Prohibitorum in Rome, on which it remained until the late 1960s. The Irish Board of Censors banned the work in 1953 for its blatant descriptions of Gide's homosexual relations, and the ban was not lifted until the relaxing of restraints in the 1970s.

FURTHER READING

Katz, Jonathan. *Gay/Lesbian Almanac*. New York: Carroll & Graf, 1994.

Kilpatrick, James J. *The Smut Peddlers*. New York: Doubleday & Company, 1960.

Lucey, Michael. "The Consequences of Being Explicit: Watching Sex in Gide's *Si le grain ne meurt*." *Yale Journal of Criticism* 4 (1990): 174–92.

Weightman, John. "Andre Gide and the Homosexual Debate." *American Scholar* 59 (Autumn 1990): 591–601.

ISLE OF PINES

Author: Henry Neville
Original date and place of publication: 1668, England
Original publisher: Allen Banks and Charles Harper at the Flower-Deluice near Cripplegate Church
Type: Fictional journal

SUMMARY

Isle of Pines is a brief work that holds importance because it was the object of the sole censorship action of the colonial period involving erotica in a time when charges of blasphemy were common. The first part of the work is purported to be the account of a man named George Pine, who writes of his journey from England to being shipwrecked on an island in uncharted waters near the coast of Madagascar. With him are three free women and a female African slave, all of whom become his sexual partners after a few months as "idleness and fulness of every thing begot in me a desire of enjoying the Women."

Between descriptions of the topography and vegetation of the island, Pine recounts the gradual development of sexual intimacy on the island as they begin "to grow more familiar" and he persuades two of the women to let him "lie with them." Pine at first enjoys sexual intimacies in private, with each woman individually. After a time, "custom taking away the flame (there being none but us) we did it more openly, as our Lust gave us liberty; afterwards my Masters [sic] Daughter was content also to do as we did." He observes that the thought that they might never return home lessened their inhibitions and "made us thus bold."

Pine only hesitates regarding the slave, "none remaining but my *Negro*, who seeing what we did, longed also for her share." He waits until she makes the move one night when he is asleep, crawling onto his grass mat close to him, "to beguile me." Pine awakes and "feeling her, and perceiving who it was, yet willing to try the difference, satisfied myself with her."

Although no indication is given of Pine's age at the beginning of the account, he provides an accounting when he turns 60. Over the years, the women had reproduced repeatedly and their children had similarly reproduced, to the point that Pine counted that he had 565 children, grandchildren and great-grandchildren.

The second, briefer part of the work is purported to be the work of a Dutch sea captain who supposedly lands on the island 98 years after Pine's first appearance. While there, he obtains the manuscript from one of Pine's descendants and it later reaches the hands of Henry Neville. The story was translated into several European languages and viewed as a true account.

CENSORSHIP HISTORY

The Isle of Pines was banned the year of its publication after authorities in the Massachusetts colony discovered it while searching for unlicensed material on the premises of the only two printers in the colony. Printer Marmaduke Johnson received a fine of £5 for possession of the pamphlet, but the fine was rescinded after he expressed penitence for possessing the suggestive material.

In 1711, Massachusetts passed a statute entitled "An Act against Intemperance, Immorality, and Profaneness, and for Reformation of Manners" that specifically decreed that no material considered obscene would be tolerated. The comprehensive act was directed toward anyone guilty of "composing, writing, printing or publishing of any filthy, obscene, or profane song, pamphlet, libel or mock sermon, in imitation or in mimicking of preaching, or any other preaching, or any other part of divine worship." Under this statute, suggestive literature like *The Isle of Pines* was banned.

FURTHER READING

Acts and Laws, Passed by the Great and General Court or Assembly of the Province of the Massachusetts-Bay in New-England, from 1692 to 1719. London: John Baskett, 1724.

Ford, Worthington Chauncey. *The Isle of Pines 1668: An Essay in Bibliography*. Boston: The Club of Odd Volumes, 1920.

JANET MARCH

Author: Floyd Dell
Original date and place of publication: 1923, United States
Original publisher: Alfred A. Knopf
Type: Novel

SUMMARY

Janet March represented, in the words of author Floyd Dell, "an attempt to present a characteristic modern girl truly against her social-historical background." The novel stirred controversy throughout the United States for its frank account of the sexual coming of age of the female protagonist, a smart but vaguely discontented child of a successful Midwestern family. Dell hoped to make Janet his representative of the generation of young American adults, young people who had grown up in an America that had lost its earlier patriarchal framework but which had failed to create a new social order.

The novel is divided into four parts: Book One—"Once Upon a Time"; Book Two—"Janet Herself"; Book Three-"Roger"; and Book Four—"Janet and Roger." The novel is a psychological study of a young girl's growing awareness of the world, and sex is at the heart of Janet's struggle for maturity. Her adventures include numerous impersonal sexual encounters with "respectable" boys as well as illicit love affairs, one of which leads to pregnancy and an abortion. Although unsettled by the experience, Janet refuses to feel guilty and, instead, she replays happily in her mind the afternoon of lovemaking that led to her pregnancy. In that passage, Janet recalls their sex as

> a rite that took one back out of civilization into some earlier world, it was a solemn and sacred ceremonial worship of nature. And it was the satisfying of some deep impersonal need, like hunger, like thirst, like the wish for sleep; it was rest, healing, quietness after tumult . . . soaring into perilous heights of ecstasy, alone.

She continues to have affairs, engaging in relationships that reveal the confused mix of loneliness, adventurousness, innocence and curiosity that characterize her discovery of life. When she becomes pregnant a second time, the father of her baby is Roger Leland, a man nearly twice her age whom she wants to marry.

CENSORSHIP HISTORY

Janet March shocked readers and reviewers in 1923 with its open depiction of abortion, free love and sexual searching. In an incident that upset Dell, his literary hero and friend Upton Sinclair reviled the book in an article that appeared nationwide in Hearst newspapers. Calling the book "scandalous," Sinclair charged Dell with being too sympathetic in his portrayal of Janet's sexual curiosity and with failing to mention the possibility of disease in her sexual adventuring. Such criticism drove sales of the book up to 15,000 copies in only two months.

Soon after its publication in October 1923, the novel was banned in Boston under the "gentleman's agreement" that existed between the Watch and Ward Society and the Board of Trade of Boston Book Merchants. The two groups formed a joint committee to review works that had raised objections. When the representatives of both groups on the committee agreed that a particular book was in violation of the obscenity statutes, the board of trade warned its members. Anxious to avoid negative publicity, many dealers simply withdrew the book from sale, and newspapers in Boston also cooperated by refusing to advertise or to review such books.

In December 1923, John Sumner and the New York Society for the Suppression of Vice lodged a formal complaint with the New York City district attorney, charging that the book was "obscene." The office of the district attorney then informed publisher Alfred A. Knopf that steps might soon be taken to ban the book and to prosecute Knopf for publishing *Janet March*. Instead of fighting the threat, Knopf promised to cease printing further copies of the book and withdrew the book. The publisher also issued a statement that the action had been taken "rather than have it attain a large sale through a possible censorship court action." The author initially accepted the seemingly high-minded action, but he stated in his 1933 autobiography, *Homecoming*, that the publisher had let him down badly. Knopf claimed that this was its only recourse because Sumner's seeming omnipotence in the 1920s "made surrender the only feasible course," but the low number of convictions in cases brought by the vice society and the strong defeat of the "Clean Books" campaign of 1923–25 contradicted that fear. Advised by lawyers that various items in the original novel might be grounds for a jail sentence, Dell reluctantly acquiesced, later revising the novel, which was reissued by George Doran in its expurgated version.

FURTHER READING

Boyer, Paul S. *Purity in Print: The Vice-Society Movement and Book Censorship in America.* New York: Scribner's, 1968.

Clayton, Douglas. *Floyd Dell: The Life and Times of an American Rebel.* Chicago: Ivan R. Dee, 1994.

"The Editor Recommends—." *The Bookman* 57 (February 1924): 459.

Hart, John E. *Floyd Dell.* New York: Twayne, 1971.

JUDE THE OBSCURE

Author: Thomas Hardy
Original date and place of publication: 1895, England; 1895, United States
Original publisher: Osgood, McIlvaine (England); Harper (United States)
Type: Novel

SUMMARY

Jude the Obscure is the story of a man whose ambition and desire for prestige war with his personal desires. Jude Fawley, a restless young man whose wanderings reflect his unsatisfied longings, works painfully to educate himself and to learn the classics and theology after his schoolmaster, Richard Phillotson, leaves for the great university town of Christminster. To earn his living, he becomes a stonemason and leaves Wessex for Christminster, where he hopes to advance his education as he works. His relationships with two significantly different women impede his progress.

Jude meets Arabella Donn, the daughter of a pig farmer, before he reaches Christminster. She and other young women are washing pig parts after slaughtering, and she captures Jude's attention by throwing a pig's "pizzle" (penis) at his head. Attracted by her appearance, Jude returns the missile of cold flesh to her and the two engage in a romantic dalliance while the "pizzle" lies draped over the nearby bridge railing. A short while later, Arabella seduces Jude and they marry. Unsuited for each other beyond their initial physical passion, the two eventually separate, though not before having a child.

Free again to pursue his goal of education, Jude goes to Christminster and meets his cousin, Sue Bridehead, an androgynous woman whose intellect and efforts for women's rights and the equality of the sexes make her a "new woman." Although the two are in love, Sue chooses to marry Jude's old schoolmaster, Phillotson. The marriage is not happy and, after Sue leaves Phillotson, she and Jude live together. They have two children who are murdered by Father Time, Jude's child with Arabella, and Father Time then commits suicide. When Sue leaves Jude, he returns to Arabella but does not live for long. Jude dies at the age of 30, wasting away within sight of the college that he had so desperately wanted to attend but which had rejected him. After discovering his dead body, Arabella decides to wait until the next morning to tell anyone, in order to enjoy a night at the festival with Jude's friends.

CENSORSHIP HISTORY

Hardy consented to the bowdlerization of several of his works before they reached the public, thus removing much of the potential controversy. Malcolm Cowley writes that because Hardy "adapted himself to the public" he became "a scandal even in academic circles." *Jude the Obscure* was serialized by *Harper's New Monthly* magazine in the United States but only after the author was willing to make changes in the novel. Pinion records that editor H. M. Alden reminded Hardy that "the Magazine must contain nothing which could not be read aloud in any family circle." Before the monthly installments were published, Hardy had to change the title to *Hearts Insurgent* and present as adopted orphans the two children who are born outside of marriage to Jude and Sue.

The excised material was restored when the novel was published in 1895, and *Jude the Obscure* was more savagely attacked by reviewers than any of Hardy's other works. Martin Seymour-Smith noted that reviewers called it a "grimy story" that was "steeped in sex" and accused Hardy of "wallowing in the mire." The London *World* labeled him "Hardy the Degenerate," and the *Guardian* condemned the novel as "a shameful nightmare to be forgotten as soon as possible." Novelist Mrs. Oliphant wrote in *Blackwood* that *Jude the Obscure* was "foul in detail" and claimed never to "have read a more disgusting book." Bishop How of Wakefield professed that he burned his copy of the novel and urged others throughout England to do the same. The bishop objected to the "crude image" of Arabella's means of introducing herself to Jude, as well as the hanging suicide of little Father Time. How was also successful in having the novel withdrawn from W. H. Smith's circulating library. The popular circulating libraries had significant influence on book sales during the second half of the 19th century. Novels were expensive and authors made little money in sales unless the circulating libraries accepted their books.

In 1903, Hardy revised the novel before it was published by his new English publishers, Macmillan and Company. The scene of the thrown pig pizzle was greatly modified out of fear for future sales. The references to the "clammy flesh" of the pizzle are deleted, as are references to it as the "indecent thing," "the lump of offal," "the fragment of pig" and "the limp object." He also toned down Arabella's seductive behavior and sensual nature.

Although Hardy lived for 33 years after *Jude the Obscure* was first published, it was his final novel. He lost heart when Bishop How burned the book, "the experience completely curing me of further interest in novel-writing." He acknowledges in the 1890 essay "Candour in Fiction" that presenting morally imperfect characters who work out their destinies in a natural manner might result in a novel that contains cruelty, envy or other evils, but that is merely reality. That such writing might have a negative influence on the weak minded is also reality. As Hardy wrote in "Candour in Fiction":

> Of the effects of such sincere presentation on weak minds, when the courses of the characters are not exemplary, and the rewards and punishments ill adjusted to deserts, it is not our duty to consider too closely. A novel which does moral injury to a dozen imbeciles, and has bracing results upon a thousand intellects of normal vigor, can justify its existence; and probably a novel was never written by the purest-minded author for which there could not be found some moral invalid or other whom it was capable of harming.

He also blames the libraries and the magazines for censorship, because they claimed that their readers were younger members of the family and felt it necessary to take precautions that would not be needed for adults. Inevitably, he concedes that satisfying "the prudery of censorship" is "the fearful price" that he has to pay "for the privilege of writing in the English language—no less a price than the complete extinction, in the mind of every mature and penetrating reader, of sympathetic belief in his personages."

FURTHER READING

Cowley, Malcolm. *After the Genteel Tradition*. Rev. ed. Carbondale: Southern Illinois University, 1964.

Hardy, Thomas. "Candour in Fiction." In *Thomas Hardy's Personal Writings: Prefaces, Literary Opinions, Reminiscences*, edited by Harold Orel. Lawrence: University of Kansas Press, 1966.

Pinion, F. B. *Thomas Hardy: His Life and Friends*. New York: St. Martin's, 1992.

Seymour-Smith, Martin. *Hardy: A Biography*. New York: St. Martin's, 1994.

Yevish, I. A. "Attack on *Jude the Obscure*: A Reappraisal Some Seventy Years After." *Journal of General Education* 18 (January 1967): 239–48.

JURGEN: A COMEDY OF JUSTICE

Author: James Branch Cabell
Original date and place of publication: 1919, United States
Original publisher: Robert M. McBride & Co.
Type: Novel

SUMMARY

Jurgen is an exercise in double entendre that resembles THE DECAMERON in its view of the human preoccupation with sex, as well as in its subtle humor and reliance on fantasy and suggestion to ridicule human pretensions. The novel portrays the gods as vain, dense and inept, while it depicts the concept of the ideal woman as merely a fantasy of man's imagination.

The title character is a poetry-writing pawnbroker who is given the opportunity to journey through dream kingdoms in the body of a young man while his mind remains mature. He is on a Faustian quest to satisfy his yearning for perfect love, beauty and holiness, as well as to locate his aging wife, Lisa, whom he had wished would go to the devil and who was spirited away by the god-devil Koshchei. During his quest, Jurgen experiences numerous romantic adventures, both with women whom he once loved and with mythical women, such as Guenevere, Arthur's queen. His sexual encounters are often described, as in his experience with Guenevere: "He remembered always the feel of that warm and slender and yielding body, naked under the thin shift, as his arms first went about her."

The suggestive technique of the language is best illustrated in the episode with Guenevere during which Jurgen captures the magic sword Caliburn, used by the author as a phallic symbol throughout the novel. When Jurgen later meets Queen Sylvia Fereu, he offers her protection and praises its merits.

> "It is undoubtedly a very large sword," said Queen Sylvia. "There is some-thing in what you advance."
> "There is a great deal in what I advance, I can assure you. It is the most natural and most penetrating kind of logic; and I wish merely to discharge a duty."

He is involved in a more erotic mythical encounter on the isle of Cocaigne with Anaitis, the daughter of the Sun. Before his marriage to her, Jurgen is given a ceremonial bath by four girls, who caress him throughout "with the tongue, the hair, the fingernails, and the tips of the breasts." For the marriage ceremony, Anaitis wears a tunic that "had twenty-two openings, so as to admit all imaginable caresses."

The novel uses symbolism, wit and humor to provide discussions of philosophy. Jurgen visits Hell but leaves because it is too democratic. He finds Heaven too autocratic and concludes that there is no justice in Heaven because all is love. After his numerous sexually stimulating experiences, he happily welcomes back his wife, Lisa.

CENSORSHIP HISTORY

Jurgen was the subject of the first celebrated censorship case of the 1920s, and its author was the first prominent American author to have his works tested in court on charges of obscenity. The novel was highly praised by the literary community when it first appeared on September 17, 1919, and it was in its third edition after selling 4,000 copies when a letter to the editor published in the New York *Tribune* on January 3, 1920, drew attention to the sensual possibili-ties of the novel. The writer, Walter J. Kinsley, observed that Cabell "has said everything about the mechanics of passion and said it prettily" and cautioned that "once the trick of transposing the key is mastered—i.e., substituting sex words for poetic words—you can see the extreme sensuality that runs through the book."

Cabell had scattered double entendres throughout the novel in an attempt to get the work by the censors, and he even agreed to censor *Jurgen* before its first publication after his publisher warned him that many sexual references were still too easily perceived. Thus, in a pre-publication letter to Burton Rascoe, Cabell noted that he had made 30 additional changes that resulted in "no real loss to literature."

John Sumner, secretary of the New York Society for the Suppression of Vice, saw a clipping of the letter and on January 14, 1920, sent society representatives with a warrant to the publisher's office, where they seized all plates and copies of the book. At a formal hearing held on January 23, 1920,

Cabell's editor at McBride, Guy Holt, was charged with violating the antiob-scenity provisions of the New York State Penal Code, and the court listened to a formal charge containing a long list of page numbers but heard no lines quoted from the novel for to have done so would have been "offensive to the court" and "improper to be placed in the court records." Authors and publishers then signed and circulated a letter of protest to exhibit their approval and support of the novel. *Jurgen* remained officially out of circulation for two years while the publisher waited for the case to go to trial. When the case went to court on October 16, 1922, Judge Charles C. Nott directed the jury to return a verdict of acquittal. In the decision, Judge Nott indicated that the nonrealistic character of the novel supported the argument against the obscenity charge:

> The most that can be said against the book is that certain passages therein may be considered in a veiled and subtle way of immorality, but such suggestions are delicately conveyed and the whole atmosphere of the story is of such an unreal and supernatural nature that even these suggestions are free from the evils accompanying suggestiveness in more realistic works.

The judge also referred in his ruling to medieval legends discussed in Cabell's preface as proof of the serious and artistic nature of the work. The irony is that the preface was facetious, and the author had only pretended to trace the "Jurgen legends" that he had made up to lend an aura of respectability to the book. Sumner eventually had the dismissal reversed, but Cabell's literary reputation became widespread, and the notoriety made his novel a best-seller.

FURTHER READING

"Again the Literary Censor." *Nation* 3 (September 25, 1920): 343.
Barlow, Samuel L. M. "The Censor of Art." *North American Review* 213 (March 1921): 346–50.
Boyer, Paul S. *Purity in Print: The Vice-Society Movement and Book Censorship in America.* New York: Scribner's, 1968.
Colum, Padraic, and Margaret Freeman Cabell, eds. *Between Friends: Letters of James Branch Cabell and Others.* New York: Harcourt, Brace & World, 1962.
Holt, Guy, ed. *Jurgen and the Law: A Statement with Exhibits, Including the Court's Opinion and the Brief of the Defendants on Motion to Direct an Acquittal.* New York: McBride, 1923.
Kallen, Horace M. "Protean Censorship." *Freeman* 3 (June 29, 1921): 370–72.

JUSTINE, OR THE MISFORTUNES OF VIRTUE

Author: Marquis de Sade
Original date and place of publication: 1797, France; 1965, United States
Original publisher: En Hollande (France); Grove Press (United States)
Type: Novel

JULIETTE, HER SISTER, OR THE PROSPERITIES OF VICE

Author: Marquis de Sade
Original date and place of publication: 1930, France; 1965, United States
Original publisher: Maurice Heine (France); Grove Press (United States)
Type: Novel

SUMMARY

The two interrelated works, created as opposites, form one of the most ambitious and outrageous works of literature ever written. *Justine*, written in 1787, while de Sade was imprisoned in the Bastille, first appeared in print in 1791, published privately in Paris. In 1797, the two works were published as a 10-volume set, four volumes of *Justine* and six volumes of *Juliette*. While Justine is virtue personified, Juliette is the embodiment of evil. The greater the crime, the more depraved the debauchery, the greater Juliette's pleasure. Her crimes include rape, incest, murder and even the defilement of Pope Pius VI, who is not permitted to enjoy her sexual favors until he has performed a black mass in St. Peter's Basilica. De Sade also pairs her with numerous major and minor personages of his time, including the French politician Saint Fond, Queen Caroline of England and King Ferdinand of Naples.

The basic story of the combined works is that sisters Justine and Juliette are brought up at the Panthemont, where "for many a long year the prettiest and most libertine women gracing Paris have regularly emerged from that convent." The nuns in that convent regularly speak of "frigging" and utter such interjections as "O fuck!" The 13-year-old Juliette and her slightly younger sister soon learn about dildoes, sexual excesses and strange rituals involving defecation and urination. Priests and bishops break their vows of celibacy with great frequency, and the nuns procure the most attractive of the young novices to please these men.

The sisters are forced to leave the convent when their parents die, and they make their way in an evil and corrupt world peopled by cross-dressing aristocrats, lords who sexually abuse their valets and men who seek to prey upon the young women. In this world where murder is an aphrodisiac, every possible debauchery occurs, even bestiality with pecking geese, but de Sade punctuates the long passages of sexual activity with equally long digressions on the existence of God and the nature of man. Juliette thrives on evil and prospers, but Justine becomes the victim of everyone with whom she has contact. Despite increased violence against her, she remains unwilling to conform to the vice-ridden world, which makes her appear incorrigible. At the end, Justine dies when she is struck by a bolt of lightning that enters her mouth and exits through her vagina. Four libertines sexually desecrate the corpse while her sister Juliette watches and masturbates.

CENSORSHIP HISTORY

The 10 volumes telling the combined stories of Justine and Juliette were available freely in major bookstores in Paris for about a year after their publication in 1797. Then orders were issued by the French government to seize all copies and to prosecute any bookseller found dealing with the work. For nearly a century and a half afterward, the work was banned in France, although it circulated clandestinely in private editions.

In 1930, Maurice Heine in Paris issued a new edition of the combined novels, limited to 475 copies that were sold with discretion. Authorities under the Fourth Republic in France prosecuted the publisher and convicted him of committing an "outrage to public morals." In an essay that was included in this edition, Guillaume Apollinaire wrote that de Sade was "the freest spirit that ever lived," and he asserted that de Sade chose women as the protagonists of his novels as a means of professing his views that women should be as free as men. He wrote,

> Justine is woman as she has formerly been, enslaved, miserable, and less than human; her opposite, Juliette, represents the woman whose advent he antici-pated, as a being of whom minds have yet no conception, who is arising out of humanity, who shall have wings and who shall renew the world.

Justine alone has also been subject to several instances of censorship. In Ireland, on January 21, 1936, a prohibition order was published in the *Iris Oifigiuil*, "the only official source from which booksellers [and readers] might learn of a new prohibition order," in which all articles blacklisted by the Irish Board of Censors were listed. According to the Censorship of Publications Bill of 1928, "the notice in *Iris Oifigiuil* should be sufficient evidence in the courts of summary jurisdiction as to the character of the publication," despite the acknowledgment by justices quoted in Adams's thorough study of Irish censorship laws that "this gazette is not a publication which booksellers are addicted to reading." The Irish Board of Censors found de Sade's novel "obscene" and filled with "illicit sex behavior." The work was officially banned from sale in Ireland until the introduction of the Censorship Publications Bill in 1967 reduced to 12 years the duration of a prohibition order, and the work was among 5,000 titles released from the list of banned books.

In 1964, New Zealand Customs officers seized *Justine* and two works by Guillaume Apollinaire, MEMOIRS OF A YOUNG RAKEHELL and *The Debauched Hospodar*, originally published in one volume by Olympia Press in 1962. The importer, a Mr. D. W. Cheer of Christchurch, disputed the seizure, and the matter went before a magistrate, who issued an order prohibiting the publica-tion of the titles of the books. The Indecent Publications Tribunal did not continue this order but did refuse to allow citations in the court records of passages that the defense counsel read in court. In testimony, the comptroller of Customs claimed that the books had been detained under the provisions of the Customs Act of 1913 as "Prohibited Imports," because they were indecent. As required by Section 12 of the Indecent Publications Act of 1963, proceedings for the condemnation were instituted by the comptroller before a magistrate who, in turn, was required to turn the matter over to the Indecent Publications Tribunal to determine the manner in which the books might be viewed as "indecent":

> whether the books were indecent within the meaning of the Act, or indecent in the hands of persons under a specified age, or indecent unless circulation was restricted to specified persons or classes of persons.

The counsel for the defense argued that even if a general ban were to be levied on the books, the importer should be free of restriction because he was a "serious collector of all sorts of books," with a library of from 5,000 to 6,000 volumes. Called to testify, the importer expressed his view "of the value of the books to a student of literature."

The tribunal placed *Justine* into an entirely different category than Apollinaire's novels, noting that it was "a well-known work written about 1787 whilst the author was in the Bastille." Acknowledging that the novel related "many sexual excesses and cruelties," they justified the work as being "a representation of de Sade's own character as depicting his disgust at conditions prevailing." Thus, on March 4, 1965, the tribunal concluded that the novel was "a seriously written work, somewhat philosophic in nature" and asserted that "though the episodes related are revolting the language used to describe them is not foul or offensive." Although the work was declared "indecent" as a narrative, "its circulation is restricted to psychologists or psychiatrists or any adult bona fide student of literature or philosophy."

FURTHER READING

Adams, Michael. *Censorship: The Irish Experience*. University: University of Alabama Press, 1968.

Ciardi, John. "The Marquis de Sade II." *Saturday Review* 48 (October 2, 1965): 36.

Lever, Maurice. *Marquis de Sade: A Biography*. New York: HarperCollins, 1993.

Perry, Stuart. *The Indecent Publications Tribunal: A Social Experiment*. London: Whitcombe and Tombs, 1965.

Thomas, Donald Serrell. *The Marquis de Sade*. Boston: New York Graphic Society, 1976.

Wainhouse, Austryn. "Foreword." *The Marquis de Sade: Juliette*. New York: Grove, 1968.

THE *KAMA SUTRA* OF VATSAYANA

Author: Vatsayana (translated by Richard F. Burton and F. F. Arbuthnot)
Original date and place of publication: 1883, Switzerland; 1962, United States

Original publisher: Kama Shastra Society (Switzerland); E. P. Dutton (United States)
Type: Marriage manual

SUMMARY

The *Kama Sutra* of Vatsayana is a Sanskrit classic written in India, circa 300 B.C., and it was well known among the educated classes. English traveler and adventurer Sir Richard Burton translated the work into English in 1883, but the nature of the work limited publication to private editions.

The origin of the work is complicated. Also known as the *Kama Shastra* and the *Ananga Ranga*, the work is an Indian marriage manual. The manuscript used by Burton for translation was actually written by a 16th-century poet named Kalyana Malla, who drew much of his material on erotic subjects from earlier writers, particularly the sage Vatsayana, who was largely credited as being the ancient author of the *Kama Sutra*. In the Indian vernacular, *Kama* was the love god, and Vatsayana's writings were contained in a text known as the *Kama Sutra*, or "Love Verses," a manual of erotic instruction.

Burton had corresponded with Foster Fitzgerald Arbuthnot, who had possession of a copy of the work and had decided to have the erotic classic translated into English. They hired an Indian scholar named Bhagvanlal Indraji to create a rough draft in English, then Burton polished the text and imposed his own view of how a man must treat a woman. As Rice observe, "Thus, many sections of the English version of the *Kama Shastra* come not from Kalyana Malla's Sanskrit but from Burton's fertile brain, developing and improving upon a text that some Western scholars believe is poorer and more pedantic than its translation."

The work contains charts of how and where the man is to touch the woman, from forehead to big toe (the latter assuming the symbolic role of the clitoris) to provide "the touches by which passion is satisfied." The manual also contains significant use of scratching, biting, kissing and chewing, actions that Burton justified by pointing out that the marriages in India often took place between children, so such "play" occurred in the process of becoming familiar with each other.

The following passage from the *Kama Sutra* has been cited by critics as being "a startlingly apparent" example of material that results in psychological disintegration:

> On the occasion of a "high congress" the Mrigi (Deer) woman should lie down in such a way as to widen her yoni, while in a "low congress" the Hastini (Elephant) woman should lie down so as to contract hers. But in an "equal congress" they should lie down in the natural position. What is said above concerning the Mrigi and the Hastini applies also to the Vadawa (Mare) woman. In a "low congress" the woman should particularly make use of medicine, to cause her desire to be satisfied quickly.
>
> The Deer-woman has the following three ways of lying down:

The widely opened position.
The yawning position.
The position of the wife of Indra.
When she lowers her head and raises her middle parts, it is called the "widely opened position." At such a time, the man should apply some unguent, so as to make the entrance easy.

In addition to providing instructions for various sexual positions, of which Burton commented that "one has to be an athlete to engage in," the work also provides women with instructions in how they may use men. The final sections relate "On the Means of Getting Money" and "Subjugating the Hearts of Others."

CENSORSHIP HISTORY

Burton and his collaborators in the Kama Shastra Society anticipated attempts of censorship as they approached the publication of the *Kama Sutra*. Their pretense was that the book was printed outside of England and that it was intended for scholars who wished to study "the great unknown literature of the East." Furthermore, by pricing the books at the equivalent in today's money of $200 each, the publishers also guaranteed that their readers had to be wealthy. The cover contained the words "For Private Circulation Only," and the place of publication was listed as Benares. After their problems in 1875, when the English printers refused to complete production of the book, Burton and his partners used two different printers to prevent confiscation of all copies should the authorities stage a raid. Soon after the first copies appeared in 1883, pirated copies appeared in Paris, Brussels and the English Midlands.

The *Kama Sutra* was not sold openly in England, but pirated copies did appear in the United States. After spending 60 days in jail in 1930 for distributing unexpurgated copies of ULYSSES, Samuel Roth turned to more profitable publications and produced editions of the *Kama Sutra* and THE PERFUMED GARDEN. Agents of the New York Society for the Suppression of Vice brought complaint against Roth, who was prosecuted and sentenced to 90 days in jail for selling those books.

In hearings before the Subcommittee on Postal Operations of the Committee on Post Office and Civil Service in 1962, Robert W. Edwards, Deputy Collector of Customs, United States Customs Mail Division in Boston, testified that the *Kama Sutra* "bears the dubious distinction of being the filthiest book published today. . . . In my opinion, the human mind is scarcely able to withstand the impact of the overwhelming obscenity and sexually based desire for torture in the *Kama Sutra*." The President's Commission on Obscenity and Pornography recommended that books of its sort be "banned from the mails."

THE KREUTZER SONATA

FURTHER READING

Lockhart, William B., and Robert C. McClure. "Censorship of Obscenity: The Developing Constitutional Standards." *Minnesota Law Review* 45 (November 1960): 19.
Rice, Edward. *Captain Sir Richard Francis Burton*. New York: Scribner's, 1990.
Thomas, Donald. *A Long Time Burning: The History of Literary Censorship in England*. New York: Praeger, 1969.
United States President's Commission on Obscenity and Pornography. *The Report of the Commission on Obscenity and Pornography*. New York: Random House, 1970.

THE KREUTZER SONATA

Author: Leo Tolstoy
Original date and place of publication: 1889, Russia; 1890, United States (translation)
Original publisher: Private (Russia); Pollard Publishing Co. (United States)
Type: Novel

SUMMARY

The Kreutzer Sonata is a novella that begins on a train on which the protagonist Posdnicheff tells his fellow travelers that he has killed his wife, whom he suspected of adultery. He slowly builds his case by blaming social conventions that he views as false and disastrous, beginning with an attack on romantic love. On the one hand, Posdnicheff claims that men feel lust, not love, and that, for them, a lifetime of love is impossible: "Every man feels what you call love, whenever he meets a pretty girl." As he rants, he blames doctors and others who encourage unmarried men to seek out prostitutes "for health's sake" and asserts that the lack of emotional involvement with and responsibility for one's partner in "voluptuousness without love" is immoral. The narrator has not always existed on so high a moral plain and admits having earlier been a "drunkard and a libertine."

> I did not consider, then, that debauchery did not consist in physical acts alone, but that the real wrong was in the relaxing of the laws of morality with the woman with whom one has carnal relations. I even looked upon this loosening of moral ties as a thing to be proud of.

Tolstoy claims that "woman has forged for herself, out of her charms, a weapon so powerful that no man, whether young or old, can resist her." He criticizes women for using sex as a weapon and contends that they deliberately appeal to man's sensual nature and regard men as mere sex objects; he includes in his criticism mothers who raise their daughters to marry rich men at any cost. Although Posdnicheff recognizes the efforts that society has made to liberate women, "they emancipate women in universities and in law courts, but continue to regard her as an object of enjoyment." He also observes that a woman, educated or otherwise, "is happy and attains all she can desire when she has bewitched man."

Marriage fails to produce moral behavior, and Posdnicheff claims that many "people marry regarding marriage as nothing but copulation. . . . the husband and wife merely deceive people by pretending to be monogamists, while living polygamously." He claims that he and his wife had experienced "excessive sensuality" early in their marriage, leaving them "disenchanted, like two selfish beings." Thus, he was moved to physically kill his wife as he had killed her spiritually long before.

CENSORSHIP HISTORY

The Kreutzer Sonata was among the first contemporary works by foreign writers to be involved in litigation in the United States. The novel had been banned from sale soon after publication in Russia by Czar Nicholas II for "immoral content." Tolstoy's wife appealed personally to the czar, and he relented in 1891 to allow the novel to appear in an expensive-to-produce compendium of the author's works.

In 1890, the postmaster general banned the work from general distribution and mailing through second- and third-class mail in the United States after an assistant attorney general declared it to be "of an obscene character." The impetus for the banning was a complaint initiated by Anthony Comstock, secretary of the New York Society for the Suppression of Vice, which charged Tolstoy's diatribe against promiscuity as being "pornographic" and "obscene," because it spoke of prostitution, sensuality, adultery and lust. Yet, the work contains no erotic scenes and speaks in condemnatory tones of lust and debauchery. The post office department in New York would only permit the work to be sent if it were placed in a sealed package and stamped with first-class postage. An editorial in the *American Law Review* observed that publicity generated by Civil Service commissioner Theodore Roosevelt calling Tolstoy a "sexual and moral pervert" and others who spoke out loudly against the book "resulted in the very object which it was intended to prevent, in giving enormous circulation to the book." The work received support from critics, who defended the book as one of literary importance. The question posed by Horace Traubel was echoed by many: "With Tolstoy in danger, who is exempt?"

As soon as the ban was enacted, street vendors in New York loaded pushcarts with copies and large signs stating "Suppressed." When they were arrested by police and their total stock of 240 books was confiscated, the vendors revealed that the Pollard Publishing Company had provided expurgated copies that contained none of the original offensive material. Publisher Walter Pollard confirmed their story and proved to the court that the books were bowdlerized copies. The judge dropped charges but insisted that the vendors remove the signs.

Later that year, a Philadelphia vendor was indicted for selling a translation of the novel and taken to court. When the case went to trial in *In re Arentsen*, 26 W.N.C. 359 (Q.S. Ct. Phil., 1890), the prosecutor pointed out that both the U.S. Post Office and the Russian government had censored the book. Despite the earlier judgments, Judge M. Russell Thayer, president judge of Common Pleas Court No. 4, declared it "not obscene," and he wrote in the court decision that neither the post office officials nor the Russian czar had "ever been recognized in this country as a binding authority in questions of either law or literature." Instead, the judge pointed to both the content of the work and Tolstoy's preface, noting that the author's purpose appeared to encourage chastity:

> There is nothing in this book which can by any possibility be said to commend licentiousness or to make it in any respect attractive, or to tempt any one to its commission. On the contrary, all his teachings paint lewdness and immorality in the most revolting colors.

In his decision, Thayer declared the novel to possess "very little dramatic interest or literary merit" and acknowledged as bizarre Tolstoy's recommendation of complete celibacy for all people, married or otherwise, but he also stated that "it cannot, on that account, be called an obscene libel."

FURTHER READING

Flower, Benjamin O. "Conservatism and Sensualism: An Unhallowed Alliance." *Arena* 3 (December 1890): 126–28.

———. "The Postmaster-General and the Censorship of Morals." *Arena* 2 (October 1890): 540–52.

Gustafson, Richard F. *Leo Tolstoy, Resident and Stranger: A Study in Fiction and Theology.* Princeton, N.J.: Princeton University Press, 1986.

"Kreutzer Sonata." *American Law Review* 25 (January-February 1891): 102-4.

Traubel, Horace L. "Freedom to Write and to Print." *Poet-Lore* 2 (October 1890): 529–31.

LADIES IN THE PARLOR

Author: Jim Tully
Original date and place of publication: 1935, United States
Original publisher: Greenberg
Type: Novel

SUMMARY

Ladies in the Parlor recounts the story of Leora Blair, a poverty-stricken young girl from the American Midwest, who enters a life of prostitution to escape her bleak early existence. The novel presents affecting details of her life in the small railroad town on the Ohio River, where she does everything possible to help her overburdened mother and suffering brothers and sisters, as well as to escape her brutal father. Tully also paints a sympathetic portrait of the prostitutes in the Chicago brothel where Leora eventually works, showing the women to be human beings who, although mercenary, are often the victims of their clients.

Leora has her first sexual experience at the age of 15 with Dr. Jonas Farway, whose seduction she encourages. Although she desires his affection and feels sexually attracted to him, she is also conscious that he has the means to help her family and to lessen their dire economic circumstances. After they are alone and he holds her close, "Her curiosity was stronger than his desire. An hour later they rose. Her body glowed. She forgot the slightest hurt he had caused." When they have sex a second time, "he was more patient. She responded slowly with the rhythm of her body. He crushed her to him, exclaiming, 'My God, my God.'"

Despite Farway's desire for her, Leora leaves for Chicago, where she enters a brothel owned by Mother Rosenbloom, a woman of many eccentricities. The prostitutes are friendly to Leora, and their language in describing customers and their past experiences is suggestive, containing anatomical references and the frequent use of "whore." Leora falls in love with powerful political boss Judge Slattery, an old friend of Mother Rosenbloom, and they enjoy one night together.

> She then removed her clothes and lay quiet, expectant, beside him.
> His touch burned her body.
> She half swooned under his embrace.
> Moments of wild delirium followed. Every particle of her body responded in ecstatic rhythm.
> When it was over, she held him close for a long time.

But her happiness is brief. By morning, the judge is dead and Leora is, once again, left to make her way in the world alone.

CENSORSHIP HISTORY

Ladies in the Parlor was one of eight American-authored works that became the subject of obscenity cases between 1934 and 1944, after the ban against importation of erotic classics was eased by the 1930 amendment of the Tariff Act and censors turned their attention to American works. Other works that suffered in this period were Lillian Hellman's *The Children's Hour*, Erskine Caldwell's TRAGIC GROUND, James T. Farrell's *A WORLD I NEVER MADE*,

William Faulkner's THE WILD PALMS, James M. Cain's SERENADE, Lillian Smith's *STRANGE FRUIT* and Kathleen Winsor's FOREVER AMBER.Three of these novels—TRAGIC GROUND, STRANGE FRUIT and FOREVER AMBER—became best-sellers after their challenges in court.

The sexual encounter between the 15-year-old Leona and the middle-aged Dr. Jonas Farway was one of two incidents in the book that led to its condemnation, even though it is more suggestive than explicit. The subdued description of the sexual encounter between the prostitute Leona and Judge Slattery was the second incident identified in complaints.

Defenders of the book suggested that, because the material in *Ladies in the Parlor* was far less explicit than many books that the New York courts had previously cleared, the real reason for its ban may have been its nonliterary style, the concern with the characters and events in a house of prostitution or its failure to make a moral judgment against prostitutes. Whatever the reasons, in 1935, a New York Court of Special Sessions heard the complaint that had been brought against the firm of Greenberg Publishers by a representative of the New York Society for the Suppression of Vice. Although the court declared the novel obscene in a 2 to 1 decision and the publisher was fined $50, Judge Frederick L. Hackenberg warned against such censorship. In his dissenting opinion, published in the *New York Times*, he wrote,

> The daring attitude of yesterday may be considered quite reactionary tomorrow. The function of literary effort reaches beyond a bedtime story with an obligatory happy ending. Enforced silence about disturbing facts does not clear the air. Even vulgar language is one of the acknowledged mediums of literary effort.

FURTHER READING

"Court Bans Tully Book." *New York Times* (November 1, 1935): 19.
Tully, Jim. *A Dozen and One*. Hollywood: Murray & Gee, 1943.

LADY CHATTERLEY'S LOVER

Author: D. H. Lawrence
Original date and place of publication: 1928, Italy; 1959, United States
Original publisher: Orioli (Italy); Grove Press (United States)
Type: Novel

SUMMARY

Lady Chatterley's Lover conveys Lawrence's bitter and deep dissatisfaction with the stultifying effects of industrialization and modern sterile society upon the natural life of all English classes. In general, he portrays the manner in which the upper classes have become devitalized and the lower classes debased by the increasing artificiality of their emotional and physical relationships. The novel relates the experiences of a young woman named Connie Chatterley, married to a baronet who is paralyzed from the waist down after severe injuries incurred fighting in World War I. She is sexually frustrated and becomes increasingly dissatisfied with the artificial and sterile nature of the society in which she lives. A brief affair with a man within her husband Clifford's social circle proves to be unsatisfying and leaves her even more restless and unhappy.

Repelled by her husband's suggestion that she become pregnant by another man and produce a child whom he might make his heir, Connie turns further away from him. Instead, she feels attracted to their gamekeeper, Mellors, Lawrence's example of the "natural man," whom society has neither devitalized nor debased. His coarse exterior and verbal expression mask a highly developed spiritual and intellectual independence, and the two become lovers. Their affair is deeply passionate and their lovemaking extremely tender, as Mellors gradually leads Connie to abandon her preconceived views of propriety and inhibitions. A number of passages contain detailed and candid descriptions of their sexual pleasures and their uncensored utterances and descriptions of both genitals and bodily functions.

"Th'art good cunt, though, aren't ter? Best bit o'cunt left on earth. When ter likes! When tha'rt willin'!"

"What is cunt?" she asked.

"An' doesn't ter know? Cunt! It's thee down theer; an' what I get when I'm i'side thee; it's a' as it is, all on't."

"All on't," she teased. " Cunt! It's like fuck then."

"Nay, nay! Fuck's only what you do. Animals fuck. But, cunt's a lot more than that. It's thee, dost see: an' tha'rt a lot besides an animal, aren't ter? even ter fuck! Cunt! Eh, that's the beauty o' thee, lass."

Such passages, although relevant to the plot and to the development of the characters, became the basis for numerous attempts to ban the novel.

At the end of the novel, Connie is pregnant with Mellors's child and plans to marry him after obtaining a divorce from Clifford.

CENSORSHIP HISTORY

Lady Chatterley's Lover was suppressed long before the case of *Grove Press v. Christenberry* went to trial in 1959. The decision was made to publish the novel in Italy in 1928, then to send copies to subscribers in England to avoid censors. Publishing in this way made it impossible for Lawrence to obtain an international copyright, so the author lost substantial money through the appearance of numerous pirated editions. The United States government had declared the novel obscene in 1929, and the post office ruled the novel barred from the mails. Travelers returning from Europe with copies of the novel faced having the book confiscated by United States Customs. Objections to the novel arose over both the explicit sexual description in the novel and the language used by the characters. As Charles Rembar, the lawyer who defended the novel in the 1959 trial, observed in his account of the case,

> not only did the Lawrence novel devote more of its pages to the act of sex and deal with it in greater detail than anything ever before sold over the counter; it had language that had never been seen in a book openly circulated, except when used for tangential and occasional purposes, and not often then. . . . *Lady Chatterley's Lover* presented the forbidden acts in forbidden detail, and described them in forbidden language.

In 1929, John Sumner, secretary of the New York Society for the Suppression of Vice, alerted officials at the Boston Watch and Ward Society that bibliophile and former Yale librarian James A. DeLacey, now proprietor of Dunster House Bookshop, had ordered five copies of the novel. An agent went to the bookstore to purchase the book and, after repeated refusals, finally obtained a copy. The society then instituted legal proceedings against DeLacey and his clerk, Joseph Sullivan, who were found guilty on November 25, 1929, by Judge Arthur P. Stone in Cambridge district court. DeLacey was fined $800 and sentenced to four months in jail, and Sullivan was fined $200 and sentenced to two weeks in jail. The convictions were appealed, but, despite strong community support for the two men and attestations to their character, on December 20, 1929, Judge Frederick W. Fosdick upheld the lower court conviction. The case was then taken to the state supreme court.

A year later, the novel was the key element of the "Decency Debates" that raged in the United States Senate between Senator Bronson Cutting of New Mexico and Senator Reed Smoot of Utah. Cutting worked to modify the censorship laws while Smoot opposed reform ("Senator Smoot Smites Smut," read one newspaper headline). That same year, a Philadelphia prosecutor authorized a raid on a bookshop and the seizure of 300 books, among them *Lady Chatterley's Lover*, FANNY HILL and THE PERFUMED GARDEN, marking the beginning of an extensive campaign to eliminate the sale of "obscene literature" in that city. Also in 1930, the Massachusetts supreme court affirmed Delacey's conviction, and he was sentenced to four months in jail.

In 1944, John Sumner, acting in the name of the New York Society for the Suppression of Vice, seized copies of *The First Lady Chatterley*, and the book remained on the blacklist of the National Organization for Decent Literature until 1953.

The novel had appeared in expurgated form over the 30 years since it had first appeared, but the Grove Press edition was the full edition with all of the "four-letter words" and sex scenes created by Lawrence. As soon as the novel was published by Grove, Postmaster General Christenberry issued an order to ban the novel from the mails. The publisher went to court and *Grove Press Inc. v. Christenberry*, 175 F. Supp. 488 (S.D.N.Y. 1959) was heard in federal district court by Judge Frederick van Pelt Bryan, who agreed with the publisher and lifted the ban. He stated in his opinion that the application of a rule of contemporary community standards to the case signals acceptance of the book throughout the country:

> the broadening of freedom of expression and of the frankness with which sex and sex relations are dealt with at the present time require no discussion. In one best selling novel after another frank descriptions of the sex act and "four-letter" words appear with frequency. These trends appear in all media of public expression, in the kind of language used and the subjects discussed in polite society, in pictures, advertisements and dress, and in other ways familiar to all. Much of what is now accepted would have shocked the community to the core a generation ago. Today such things are generally tolerated whether we approve or not.
> I hold that at this stage in the development of our society, this major English novel does not exceed the outer limits of tolerance which the community as a whole gives to writing about sex and sex relations.

In *Grove Press Inc. v. Christenberry*, 276 F.2d 433 (2d Cir. 1960), the circuit court of appeals agreed with Judge Bryan's decision.

In 1959, Postmaster General Summerfield made the decision to continue to suppress copies of *Lady Chatterley's Lover* from the mail, declaring that the book was filled with "filthy," "smutty," "degrading," "offensive" and "disgusting" words, as well as with descriptions of sexual acts. He claimed that such "filthy words and passages" outweighed any literary merit that the book might have.

In England in 1960, the director of public prosecutions brought a criminal action against Penguin Books, Ltd., when the publisher announced its intention to openly publish the first unexpurgated British edition of *Lady Chatterley's Lover*. The prosecutor, Senior Treasury Counsel Mervyn Griffith-Jones, asked jurors to test the obscenity of the book themselves by answering these two questions: "Is it a book that you would have lying around your house? Is it a book that you would even wish your wife *or your servants* to read?" The defense attorneys argued that the novel as a whole was not obscene, despite language and sexual content in various passages. Thirty-five defense experts stressed the literary merit of the work, and the jury deliberated for three days before acquitting Penguin Books of all charges. Kuh relates that when the House of Lords debated the trial that cleared the novel, with its sexual episodes between a lady and her gamekeeper, a peer who agreed with the decision was asked, "Would you want your wife to read it?" He replied, "I would not object to my wife reading it, but I don't know about my gamekeeper."

In 1965, the Indecent Publications Tribunal of New Zealand reviewed the paperback edition of *Lady Chatterley's Lover* to determine if it was indecent, despite an earlier decision that no action would be taken regarding the import or sale of the cloth-bound edition of the novel. At the time, the cloth-bound edition sold in New Zealand for 16 shillings and the paperback edition for 5 shillings. The tribunal acknowledged that the novel "is a seriously written work by an author who has an established place in the field of English literature" and that "the text of the story is in the case of each identical; there is no difference between the two editions save in regard to the preface of the one and the introduction of the other and the form of each respectively."

Nonetheless, tribunal members considered if the novel should be kept out of the hands of persons under 18 years of age, and the issue became the difference in cost between the cloth-bound and the paperback editions, the low price of the paperback making it easily available to minors. This consideration motivated dissent among the members of the tribunal, two of whom asserted that "the sale of the Penguin [paperback] edition should be restricted to persons of seventeen years or over. . . . They think it is a matter for regret that the free circulation of the hardcover edition should have prejudiced the issue, embarrassed the Tribunal and made it virtually impossible in a particularly clear instance to invoke the provisions of the statute." The other three tribunal members felt that, given the unrestricted circulation of the hardcover edition, "it would be futile to classify the paperback edition as indecent in the hands of juveniles." Viewing any restrictive action against the paperback edition as futile, the majority view of the tribunal determined on April 7, 1965, that "the paperback edition of *Lady Chatterley's Lover* published by Penguin Books is not indecent within the meaning of the Indecent Publications Act of 1963."

FURTHER READING

Boyer, Paul S. *Purity in Print: The Vice-Society Movement and Book Censorship in America.* New York: Scribner's, 1968.

Grant, Sidney S., and S. E. Angoff. "Censorship in Boston." *Boston University Law Review* 10 (January 1930): 36–60.

———. "Recent Developments in Censorship." *Boston University Law Review* 10 (November 1930): 488–509.

Maddox, Brenda. *D. H. Lawrence: The Story of a Marriage.* New York: Simon & Schuster, 1993.

Paul, James C. N., and Murray L. Schwartz. *Federal Censorship: Obscenity in the Mail.* New York: Free Press, 1961.

Perry, Stuart. *The Indecent Publications Tribunal: A Social Experiment.* London: Whitcombe and Tombs, 1965.

Rembar, Charles. *The End of Obscenity: The Trials of Lady Chatterley's Lover, Tropic of Cancer & Fanny Hill by the Lawyer Who Defended Them.* New York: Random House, 1968.

Roeburt, John. *The Wicked and the Banned.* New York: Macfadden Books, 1963.

United States President's Commission on Obscenity and Pornography. *The Report of the Commission on Obscenity and Pornography.* New York: Random House, 1970.

LA TERRE (THE EARTH)

Author: Émile Zola
Original date and place of publication: 1887, France; 1889, England; 1955, United States
Original publisher: Charpentier (France); Henry Vizitelly & Co., (England); Grove Press (United States)
Type: Novel

SUMMARY

La Terre (in English, *The Earth*) is the 15th in a 20-novel series entitled *Les Rougon-Macquart*, which traces the fortunes of two families, the Rougons and the Macquarts, as well as their expansion into the modern world and into all classes. Not merely the work of imagination, the novels were based on documented evidence obtained through books, newspaper clippings and first-person investigations to ensure historical, social and political accuracy. As for each volume in the series, Zola had a specific stated objective for this novel: "I want to write the living poem of the earth, but in its human rather than symbolic aspect." *La Terre* presents a horrifying view of French peasantry before the Franco-Prussian War and is characterized by a lack of idealism, for which Zola was widely criticized.

The setting of the novel is La Beauce, a rich agricultural area of France just before the 1870 Franco-Prussian War. The land breeds passion and obsession in the peasants, and their greed for land destroys their feelings of humanity. When old Fouan grows too old to farm, he divides his land among his three children, his daughter, Fanny, his younger son, Buteau and his older son, Hyacinthe, also called "Jesus-Christ." In return for their shares of the land, Fougan expects that they will take care of him and his wife, Rose, and feed them until their death. He lives with each of his children in turn, but they victimize him and feel that he asks too much of them in return for his land.

Many incidents in the novel angered critics. The first pages of the novel describe a bull inseminating a cow as a boy and girl who are tending the animals look on with indifference. The character nicknamed "Jesus-Christ" prides himself on his flatulence, and his skill is that he "bombarded his enemies, bombarded the marshall who came to impound his possessions. . . . he could in turn fire at will." Old Fouan's niece Lise is pregnant by Buteau, who lives with her but refuses to marry her and, instead, pursues her younger sister, Françoise, who marries and becomes pregnant by Jean Macquart. Lise and Françoise each have their own land, willed to them at the death of their father, Old Mouche. Buteau is greedy and wants not only his land and the land inherited by Lise, but Françoise's parcel as well, and he tries to drive Jean Macquart away. Fearful that Françoise's land will revert to Jean, Buteau rapes Françoise with Lise's assistance, hoping to produce a child to bind them. The jealous Lise later pushes Françoise against a scythe in the field, piercing her abdomen with the blade. Even as she is dying, Françoise refuses to will her land to Jean, viewing him as an outsider, and Jean is evicted.

Greedy to have all the land and fearful that Fouan might have seen the murder, Lise and Buteau smother the old man with a pillow, then set fire to his bed. Jean Macquart leaves to become a soldier, to defend the earth of France even if he cannot cultivate it.

CENSORSHIP HISTORY

The novel was first published as installments in the newspaper *Le Gil Blas*. Matthew Josephson relates that when the first installment appeared, writer Anatole France was outraged and accused Zola of having created "a heap of filth" and making "an effort to vilify humanity, to insult every aspect of beauty and love, to deny all that is good and decent." He further condemned Zola for portraying the peasants as "rolling about the fields, fornicating."

On the same day that Zola completed the final chapter, a lengthy denunciation of the book appeared in *Le Figaro*, a manifesto signed by five young novelists: Paul Bonnetain, Lucien Descaves, Gustave Guiches, Paul Margueritte and J. H. Rosny-aine. The novelists accused Zola of having deserted the cause of truth and of showing less of a desire to present reality and more of "a violent bias towards obscenity." They speculated that this tendency may have been due to a discovery by Zola that "the profits of pornography were greater than those earned by serious literature" or possibly to some "affection [*sic*] of the writer's lower organs, the nasty habits of a solitary monk, which inclined him to dwell on filth and lechery in his fictional writing." Calling for Zola to withdraw the novel, the writers of the manifesto asserted that *La Terre* contained characters who "are in general simply human animals in rut." They accused him of sinking to a new low with his novel, stating that "in no other of his books does Zola accumulate so many scenes of goatish copulation, frustrated rape, actual rape, incest and sadistic murder."

In 1888, Zola's English publisher, Henry Vizitelly, came under attack by the National Vigilance Association (NVA), a group composed mainly of clergymen founded in 1886 to continue the work of the Society for the Suppression of Vice, which had ceased operations a few years before. All of Zola's works, translated from French into English by the publisher's son, were specifically cited, as were works by Flaubert, Goncourt, Maupassant, Daudet and Bourget. The NVA gained the attention of Samuel Smith, M.P., who spoke in the House of Commons in May 1888 against Vizitelly, "the chief culprit in the spread of pernicious literature." Citing Zola's works as an example of "obscene publications," Smith asserted that "nothing more diabolical had ever been written by the pen of man; they are only fit for swine, and those who read them must turn their minds into cesspools." The House passed a motion that "the law against obscene publications and indecent pictures and prints should be vigorously enforced and, if necessary, strengthened." The government would leave the initiation of proceedings to private individuals.

Other politicians and the newspapers joined the campaign against pornography, widening the scope of the battle to include other works, but Zola remained the focus. In his account of his father's ordeal as the English publisher of Zola's works, Ernest Vizitelly reported that the Roman Catholic newspaper, the *Tablet*, attacked the author as "a pornographer," the *Globe* charged that Zola "sapped the foundations of manhood and womanhood" and the *Whitehall Review* demanded immediate action against his books. The law firm of Collette & Collette, retained by the NVA, obtained a summons on August 10, 1888, against Henry Vizitelly for publishing three "obscene" novels by Zola: *The Earth* (*La Terre*), *Piping Hot* (*Pot-bouille*) and *Nana*. Henry Asquith, prosecutor for the Crown, referred to these novels as "the three most immoral books ever published." The defense argued that Vizitelly had carefully expurgated the books while translating them into English and pointed out that the unexpurgated French versions were being freely circulated and sold in England at the same time. The prosecution declared the fact irrelevant, and the publisher went to trial at the Old Baily in October 1888. Vizitelly was sentenced to four months in Holloway Prison and ordered not to publish any more of Zola's works. The court further agreed that all of Zola's works must be withdrawn from circulation in England, making Zola the only writer to have his works outlawed in England in the 19th century.

All of Zola's novels were banned at once in 1894 when they were placed on the Index Librorum Prohibitorum in Rome, in 1929 when Yugoslavia banned all of his works and in 1953 when Ireland did the same. The major complaints centered on Zola's open portrayal of his characters' sexuality and their reflection of the often sordid sexuality of his society.

FURTHER READING

Hemmings, F. W. J. *The Life and Times of Emile Zola*. New York: Scribner's, 1977.
Josephson, Matthew. *Zola and His Time*. Garden City, New York: Garden City Publishers, 1928.
Schom, Alan, *Emile Zola: A Biography*. New York: Holt, 1987.
Vizitelly, Ernest A. *Emile Zola, Novelist and Reformer: An Account of His Life and Work*. London: Lane, 1904.

LOLITA

Author: Vladimir Nabokov
Original date and place of publication: 1955, France; 1959, England; 1958, United States

Original publisher: Olympia Press (France); Weidenfeld and Nicholson (England); G. P. Putnam's Sons (United States)
Literary form: Novel

SUMMARY

Lolita is structured as a psychiatric case study of the pedophiliac protagonist, Humbert Humbert, the middle-aged lover of 12-year-old Lolita. The book traces Humbert's sexual obsession with young girls, his marriage to Lolita's mother, Charlotte, and the long cross-country trip that he takes with Lolita after her mother's death. Near the end of the novel, the nymphet, now 16, married, pregnant and physically worn out, writes and asks for money. Still obsessed with the image of the young Lolita, Humbert hysterically begs her to leave with him but she refuses. In desperation, he offers her a check for $3,600 and $400 in cash if she will reveal the name of the man with whom she ran off. That man is Quilty, a friend of her late mother's and Lolita's old lover from the time when Humbert was still ogling and desiring the 12-year-old. Revenge is his aim, and Humbert is later incarcerated for shooting and killing Quilty.

Humbert's obsession dominates his adult life as he sees every attractive adolescent as a seductress. As he intellectualizes his lust, Humbert places the blame for his obsession on the girls whom he feels lead him on deliberately. Sitting in parks, he "throbs with excitement," "pulses with anticipation," struggles to control the feelings that make him "race with all speed toward my lone gratification." Before meeting 12-year-old Dolores ("Lolita") Haze and her mother, Humbert has had three breakdowns and confinements in sanitariums. He refers to adventures with a succession of girllike prostitutes and relates that he frequents brothels looking for young girls.

The initial meeting with Lolita is sexually charged as Humbert notes each sensuous detail of the childlike body, then becomes obsessed with determining how to appease his sexual desire. In one early scene, he teases Lolita by taking her apple as she sits beside him on the couch. Humbert experiences "a glowing tingle" that develops into a "deep hot sweetness" that he can barely control. He feels that "the nerves of pleasure had been laid bare" and "the least pressure would suffice to set all paradise loose." As he sits "suspended on the brink of that voluptuous abyss," he moves his hand up Lolita's leg "as far as the shadow of decency would allow."

After Humbert marries Charlotte, with the aim of having freer access to Lolita, he daydreams of "administering a powerful sleeping potion to both mother and daughter so as to fondle the latter through the night with perfect impunity." Charlotte dies when she runs into traffic after reading Humbert's secret diary that details his fantasies, and Humbert tries out his sleeping pill scheme when he retrieves the orphaned Lolita from camp. The pills don't make her comatose as he had planned, but he seduces her anyway. That begins their two years of travel, posing as father and daughter as they go from motel to motel, encountering the seedy side of the American landscape. After Lolita runs away, Humbert once again has a breakdown and enters a sanitarium, which he later leaves with the intent of finding Lolita and avenging his loss.

CENSORSHIP HISTORY

Lolita was denounced as "filth" and "sheer unrestrained pornography" when it was first published. Author Nabokov claimed that *Lolita* was a comedy and disagreed with those who considered it erotic writing, yet he argued strenuously to have the novel published anonymously in order to protect his career as a professor at Cornell University. American publishers were similarly reticent about an association with the topic, and the novel was promptly refused by many when Nabokov's agent circulated it in 1954. Pascal Covici of Viking Press and Wallace Brockway of Simon and Schuster thought it would strike readers as "pornographic." James Laughlin of New Directions refused the book because "we are worried about possible repercussions both for the publisher and the author" and suggested publication in France. Before giving up, Nabokov sent the manuscript to Roger Straus of Farrar, Straus & Young and to Jason Epstein of Doubleday, who also rejected the manuscript. When the novel failed to find a publisher in the United States, Nabokov's agent took it to Olympia Press in Paris, which published it in two volumes.

After Olympia Press published *Lolita* in English in 1955, France banned the book in December 1956. The publisher, Maurice Girodias, asked Nabokov for help in fighting the ban, but the author replied, "My moral defense of the book is the book itself." He also wrote an essay entitled "On a Book Entitled Lolita" that was a lengthy justification, later attached to the American edition, in which he claimed that readers who thought the work erotic were misreading his intentions. Rather, Nabokov stated, "That my novel does contain various allusions to the physiological urges of a pervert is quite true. But after all we are not children, not illiterate juvenile delinquents, not English public school boys who after a night of homosexual romps have to endure the paradox of reading the Ancients in expurgated versions."

Olympia Press won its case in 1957 in the Administrative Tribunal of Paris, and the novel was back on sale in January 1958. When the Fourth Republic fell in May 1958 and General Charles de Gaulle assumed power, the French minister of the interior appealed to the Conseil d'Etat, the highest court in France. By December of that year, the book was again banned in France after the government successfully appealed the initial judgment. No appeal was possible, but the publication of the novel in French by the prestigious French publisher Gallimard in April 1959 gave Olympia Press foundation for a suit. The publisher sued the French government on the basis that the legal principle of equality between French citizens had been violated by the banning of the Olympia Press edition of *Lolita* and not the Gallimard edition. The English version was placed back on the market in France in September 1959.

British Customs banned the book in 1955, the same year that Graham Greene, in the *Sunday Times*, nominated *Lolita* as one of his three favorite books of the year. Greene's article led John Gordon to remark in the *Sunday Express*: "Without doubt it is the filthiest book I have ever read. Sheer unrestrained pornography." Several British publishers were eager to bid for the rights to the novel, but they waited for the enactment of the Obscene Publications Bill in 1959, which would permit literary merit to be taken into account should the book be placed on trial. They expected prosecution because reviewers were already waging a war against the novel, several stating that the novel should be suppressed in England if it could be proven that "even a single little girl was likely to be seduced as a result of its publication." Conservatives in Parliament urged Nigel Nicholson, a member of Parliament as well as a publisher, not to publish the book, claiming that it would be detrimental to the party image. He lost his next bid for reelection, partly because of *Lolita*.

In contrast, United States Customs determined in February 1957 that the book was not objectionable and could be admitted into the country. Therefore, the book could not be legally exported from France, but people who smuggled the book out could import it legally into the United States. Despite its admissibility by Customs, United States publishers refused to publish *Lolita* until G. P. Putnam's Sons took the chance in 1958. A year later, the bans in England and France were lifted and the book was published openly in those countries. In the United States, however, the Cincinnati Public Library banned the book from its shelves after the director observed that "the theme of perversion seems to me obscene."

The novel was also banned in 1959 in Argentina, where government censors claimed that the book reflected moral disintegration. In 1960, the minister of commons in New Zealand banned import of the novel under the Customs Act of 1913 that prohibited importing books deemed "indecent" within the meaning of the Indecent Publications Act of 1910. To fight the ban, the New Zealand Council of Civil Liberties imported six copies of the book and successfully challenged the Supreme Court. Mr. Justice Hutchin delivered the judgment, noting that the book had been written with no pornographic intent and for the educated reader. Basing his decision on the recommendation of a ministry advisory committee that individual orders should be permitted, the justice observed that New Zealand Customs did admit certain books addressed to authorized individuals or intended to be sold to restricted classes. The ban on *Lolita* in South Africa, instituted in 1974 because of the "perversion theme" of the novel, was lifted in 1982, and the South African Directorate of Publications gave permission for its publication in paperback form.

FURTHER READING

Baker, George. "*Lolita*: Literature or Pornography." *Saturday Review* 40 (June 22, 1957): 18.

Centerwall, Brandon S. "Hiding in Plain Sight: Nabokov and Pedophilia." *Texas Studies in Literature & Language* 32 (Fall 1990): 468–84.
Dupee, F. W. "*Lolita* in America." *Encounter* 12 (February 1959): 30–35.
Feeney, Ann. "*Lolita* and Censorship: A Case Study. *References Services Review* 21 (Winter 1993): 67–74, 90.
Hicks, Granville. "Lolita and Her Problems." *Saturday Review* 41 (August 16, 1958): 12, 38.
Levin, Bernard. "Why All the Fuss?" *Spectator* 202 (January 9, 1959): 32–33.
"Lolita in the Dock." *New Zealand Libraries* 23 (August 1960): 180–83.
Patnoe, Elizabeth. "Lolita Misrepresented, Lolita Reclaimed: Disclosing the Doubles." *College Literature* 22 (June 1995): 81–104.
Roeburt, John. *The Wicked and the Banned.* New York: Macfadden Books, 1963.
Scott, W. J. "The *Lolita* Case." *Landfall* 58 (June 1961): 134–38.

THE LUSTFUL TURK

Author: Anonymous
Original date and place of publication: 1828, England
Original publisher: J. B. Brookes
Type: Novel

SUMMARY

The Lustful Turk, viewed by Kronhausen and Kronhausen as "an instance of the juncture of literature and pornography," is an epistolary novel in which Emily Barlow uses letters to reveal her adventures to her friend, Silvia Carey. The long central letter details her capture by Moorish pirates whose "renegade English" captain presents Emily as a gift to the dey of Algiers. She relates graphically her defloration by the dey:

> I quickly felt his finger again introducing the head of that terrible engine I had before felt, and which now felt like a pillar of ivory to me. . . . sucking my lips and breasts with fury, he unrelentingly rooted up all obstacles to my virginity.

She becomes a willing victim in ensuing sexual episodes, and the deflorations of other harem members follow the same description as Emily's.

Silvia derides her friend's apparent acceptance of the imprisonment and writes that she is disgusted by Emily's "account of the libidinous scenes acted between you and the beast whose infamous and lustful acts you so particularly describe." The dey reads the letter and orders his men to abduct Silvia.

The book contains the subplot of two dishonest clerics, Father Angelo and Pedro, the abbot of St. Francis, who run a white-slave trade between France and North Africa. The only connection to Emily is that they supply women to the dey.

As the end of the book nears, the now-pregnant Emily jealously attempts to learn the identity of the Englishwoman rumored to be the dey's new sexual interest. With the help of a friendly eunuch, she enters the dey's private apartments and catches him with the woman. "The first object that met my eyes was a naked female half reclining on a table, and the Dey with his noble shaft plunged up to the hilt in her."

Emily faints, then is revived, after which she learns that the new woman is her friend Silvia, captured by the dey's men and deflowered by him. The two women decide to share him, but his sexual obsessions lead to disaster. A Greek girl, newly recruited to the harem, refuses to engage in anal sex ("buggery") with the dey and partially cuts off his penis. The dey orders a doctor to finish the job. He then pickles the testicles in "spirits of wine in glass vases" and gives Emily and Silvia one each before releasing them to return to England.

CENSORSHIP HISTORY

Such furtively circulated erotica as *The Lustful Turk* was frequently the target of societies for the prevention of vice in both England and the United States in the 19th century. In most cases, shipments of the book were simply confiscated and destroyed without protest by the publishers or distributors who simply churned out new and cheaply printed copies. The novel was advertised in catalogs with other such pornographic pulp as *The Battles of Venus*, *The Bed-Fellows, or the Young Misses Manual*, *The Confessions of a Young Lady*, *The Ups and Downs of Life* and *The Victims of Lust*, in which catalog copy promised "every stretch of voluptuous imagination is here fully depicted, rogering, ramming, one unbounded scene of lust, lechery and licentiousness." The nature of the works meant that they were freely pirated, so numerous editions emerged containing embellishments that varied from one edition to another.

William Dugdale, dubbed by erotica collector Henry Ashbee as "one of the most prolific publishers of filthy books," included *The Lustful Turk* among his stock. By 1857, he had been prosecuted nine times for his publications and suffered the seizure and loss of large amounts of his stock. In 1857, in response to complaints lodged by the Society for the Suppression of Vice, Dugdale appeared in court before Lord Chief Justice Campbell. The justice declared obscene the books seized, including *The Lustful Turk*. After referring to Dugdale as "London's most notorious pornographer," the justice sentenced him to a year in jail. An incensed Dugdale threatened the justice with a penknife, but the sentence was carried out. That same year, Chief Justice Campbell proposed the creation of the Obscene Publications Act of 1857 and worked to make it law, citing *The Lustful Turk* as among the works that the act would outlaw.

In the United States, *The Lustful Turk* was deemed pornography, and the work was automatically confiscated and destroyed in numerous raids on booksellers by Anthony Comstock and the New York Society for the Suppression of Vice. The book never went to trial because, as in England, publishers and distributors simply printed new copies of the pirated book and sold them furtively.

FURTHER READING

Boyer, Paul S. *Purity in Print: The Vice-Society Movement and Book Censorship in America.* New York: Scribner's, 1968.

Broun, Heywood, and Margaret Leech. *Anthony Comstock.* New York: Albert & Charles Boni, 1927.

Kearney, Patrick J. *A History of Erotic Literature.* Hong Kong: Parragon, 1982.

Kronhausen, Eberhard, and Phyllis Kronhausen. *Pornography and the Law: The Psychology of Erotic Realism.* New York: Ballantine, 1959.

Perkins, Michael. *The Secret Record: Modern Erotic Literature.* New York: William Morrow, 1976.

MADAME BOVARY

Author: Gustave Flaubert
Original date and place of publication: 1857, France; 1888, England
Original publisher: Michel Levy (France); Henry Vizitelly (England)
Type: Novel

SUMMARY

Madame Bovary relates the story of Emma Roualt, a young French woman married to hardworking doctor Charles Bovary, and the manner in which she allows impossible romantic ideals to destroy her marriage and her life. Despite her husband's infatuation with her, Emma feels little for him and, instead, seeks the passionate love she has read about in romance novels. When the couple attends a fancy dress ball at the estate of a marquis, Emma dances with royalty and mingles with the rich, then leaves believing that this was the life she was born to lead.

She becomes extremely unhappy, and Charles decides that she needs a change of scenery. As they move from Tostes to Yonville, Emma learns that she is pregnant. This knowledge and the attentions of notary clerk Leon, who shares her interests in art and literature, distract her at least until the baby is born. Having hoped for a boy, Emma is disappointed when a daughter is born, and she begins to borrow money from dry goods merchant Lheureux to buy luxury items that she believes she deserves.

As Emma becomes increasingly unhappy, she gravitates toward Leon and the two profess their love but do not begin an affair. Instead, to avoid temptation, Leon moves to Paris. Emma, however, begins an affair with a patient of her husband's, the wealthy Rodolphe Boulanger, who wants only to add her to his list of conquests. Emma obsessively rushes to Boulanger's estate each morning where the two make passionate love and meets him some evenings after Charles is asleep.

After the novelty wears off and Boulanger ends the affair, Emma sinks into a deep depression, staying in bed for two months. When she recovers, Charles

113

takes her to Rouen to enjoy the opera, but she secretly meets Leon and they begin an affair. She lies to Charles, telling him that she will take weekly piano lessons in Rouen, but she meets Leon in a hotel room each week to continue their affair.

At the same time, her debt to Lheureux increases, and she begins to borrow money elsewhere to pay him back. She becomes desperate when he confronts her and threatens to confiscate all of her property unless she immediately pays him 8,000 francs. Unable to raise the money, Emma commits suicide by ingesting arsenic after writing a letter of explanation to Charles. Her death weakens Charles, who dies soon after, leaving their daughter Berthe to work in a cotton mill to earn her living.

CENSORSHIP HISTORY

Madame Bovary was censored before publication as a novel, when it appeared in installments in *Revue de Paris*, a literary publication run by Flaubert's friend, Maxime DuCamp. Before agreeing to publish the work, DuCamp asked to excise a single passage about a page and a half in length near the end of the novel. The passage relates Emma's extended tryst with Leon behind the closed curtains of a cab, and DuCamp felt that getting it past the censors would be "impossible." Flaubert agreed, but he was not prepared for the following editorial note inserted by the editors in place of the passage: "Here the editors found it necessary to suppress a passage unsuitable to the policies of the *Revue de Paris*; we hereby acknowledge this to the author." The editors later requested that cuts be made in the sixth and final installment of the novel, a move that Flaubert first fought, then reluctantly accepted and to which he added his own disclaimer regarding the quality of the now-fragmented work.

The omission of the offensive passages did not prevent government action being taken against *Madame Bovary*, a move that Flaubert felt was aimed more at the overly liberal *Revue* than his novel. *Madame Bovary* went on trial on January 29, 1857, in highly formal court proceedings in which Imperial Advocate Ernest Pinard admitted that the language of the law of 1819 was "a little vague, a little elastic." He also asserted that the prosecution faced "peculiar difficulty" because reading the entire novel to the jury would be too time consuming, but reading only the "accused passages" would be too restrictive. To solve the problem, Pinard summarized the novel in detail and read verbatim the offending passages. When his version reached the appropriate point in the narrative, Pinard called upon the jury to apply "limits and standards" and noted, "Yes, Mr. Flaubert knows how to embellish his pictures with all the resources of art, but without art's restraints. No gauze for him, no veils—he gives us nature in all her nudity and crudity!"

In defense, Flaubert's lawyer portrayed the novel as a handbook of bourgeois respectability, noting that it taught the consequences of straying from moral behavior. The jury, which waited a week to deliver a verdict, acquitted the author, publisher and printer without costs on the basis that their guilt had been "insufficiently established." In essence, the jury asserted that Flaubert "committed the wrong of occasionally neglecting the rules which no self-respecting writer should transgress, and of forgetting that literature, like art, must be chaste and pure not only in its form but also in its expression, in order to accomplish the good effects it is called upon to produce." A few months later, the novel was published in its entirety, all cuts restored, and sold 15,000 copies in two months.

In 1888, Flaubert's English publisher, Vizitelly, came under attack by the National Vigilance Association (NVA), a group composed mainly of clergymen founded in 1886 to continue the work of the Society for the Suppression of Vice, which had ceased operations a few years before. *Madame Bovary*, translated from French into English by the publisher's son, was specifically cited, as were works by Zola, Goncourt, Maupassant, Daudet and Bourget. The NVA gained the attention of House of Commons member Samuel Smith, M.P., who spoke in May 1888 against Vizitelly, "the chief culprit in the spread of pernicious literature." The House passed a motion that "the law against obscene publications and indecent pictures and prints should be vigorously enforced and, if necessary, strengthened." The government would leave the initiation of proceedings to private individuals.

Other politicians and the newspapers joined the campaign against pornography, widening the scope of the battle. The Roman Catholic newspaper *Tablet* attacked him as a "pornographer." The law firm Collette & Collette, retained by the NVA, obtained a summons on August 10, 1888, against Henry Vizitelly. The defense argued that Vizitelly had carefully expurgated the books while translating them into English and pointed out that the unexpurgated French versions were being freely circulated and sold in England at the same time. The prosecution declared the fact irrelevant, and the publisher went to trial at the Old Bailey in October 1888 where a jury charged him with "uttering and publishing certain obscene libels." Vizitelly was fined and ordered to desist publishing the offensive works. When he repeated the offense in 1889, the publisher received a four-month prison sentence, despite impaired health.

In 1893, the American Library Association for the first time offered a 5,000-title book guide for small popular libraries and branches, calling it a collection that "one could recommend to any trustee." No works by Flaubert were included in the list.

FURTHER READING

Elliott, Desmond. "The Book That Shocked Paris: The Strange Story of *Madame Bovary*." *Books and Bookmen* 5 (June 1960): 11, 46.
Geller, Evelyn. *Forbidden Books in American Public Libraries, 1876–1939*. Westport, Conn.: Greenwood, 1984.
Kendrick, Walter. *The Secret Museum*. New York: Viking, 1987.

Mancuso, Ludwig. *The Obscene: The History of an Indignation*. London: MacGibbon & Key, 1965.

Steegmuller, Francis. *Flaubert and Madame Bovary*. Boston: Houghton Mifflin, 1970.

MADELEINE

Author: Anonymous
Original date and place of publication: 1919, United States
Original publisher: Harper & Brothers
Type: Autobiographical novel

SUMMARY

Madeleine is the anonymous autobiographical novel written by a purportedly reformed prostitute and madam of a house of prostitution. The work provides painstakingly recounted domestic details of life within a bordello, but the references to sexual activity are subtle and infrequent. The reader learns the routine of the establishment, including areas of responsibility for upkeep and the details of running the business.

Despite its sometimes jaded cynicism, such as in the author's comment that the only difference between wives and prostitutes is that prostitutes "do not cheat in the delivery of the merchandise for which they are paid," the book makes an effort to deliver a moral message. Although Madeleine does not encourage others to follow her path, she does distinguish between her own entry into "the life" and those of contemporary young girls, noting that prostitutes in her youth were relatively moral when compared with those of her present. At one point, the author observes that, in her day, "no 'decent' house . . . would have tolerated some of the styles . . . on the streets today." She also condemns the "present-day craze for rag-time."

CENSORSHIP HISTORY

Madeleine was one of the books that emerged from the anti-prostitution movement of New York City in the 1890s, despite its publication in the postwar period. Reviewers who were fully familiar with the "white-slave" investigations were not scandalized and neither were readers who were familiar with the vice commission reports. Still, John Sumner and the New York Society for the Suppression of Vice filed charges against Harper & Brothers in January 1920. Clinton T. Brainard, the president of Harper & Brothers, was convicted in the court of special sessions and fined $1,000. Although the vice society claimed to find *Madeleine* offensive to public morals and Sumner labeled the book "one of the worst and most dangerous books that has come to our attention in a long time," other factors appear to have been behind the charges.

Brainard had been secretary of a grand jury charged with investigating municipal scandals in the administration of John Hylan, New York mayor and a protégé of William Randolph Hearst. The Hearst publication *New York American* launched a campaign against *Madeleine* as soon as it appeared, and the publication pointedly mentioned Brainard in each article. In reporting the conviction, Hearst publications emphasized that Brainard had been "finger-printed like any other common law-breaker." Brainard appealed, and lawyers for the publisher stressed the reformist intent. On July 9, 1920, the appellate court of New York reversed the lower-court conviction, and *Madeleine* was vindicated in *People v. Brainard*, 192 App. Div. 816, 183 N.Y.S. 452. In its ruling, the court stated that "no one can read this book and truthfully say it contains a single word or picture which tends to excite lustful or lecherous desire."

FURTHER READING

Broun, Heywood. "Heywood Broun Comes to the Rescue of Immoral Books." *Current Opinion* 67 (December 1919): 315–16.
Ernst, Morris L., and Alexander Lindey. "The Censor Marches On . . . " *Esquire* 11 (June 1939): 174–77.
Loth, David. *The Erotic in Literature*. New York: Dorset, 1961.
Pringle, Henry F. "Comstock the Less." *The American Mercury* 10 (January 1927): 56–63.

MADEMOISELLE DE MAUPIN

Author: Théophile Gautier
Original date and place of publication: 1835, France; 1887, England; 1900, United States
Original publisher: Ariel (France); Henry Vizitelly (England); C. T. Brainard Publishing Co. (United States)
Type: Novel

SUMMARY

Gautier begins *Mademoiselle de Maupin* with a preface that expresses his view of censors. Written in the voice of his narrator, Chevalier D'Albert, it characterizes the "great affectation of morality" of his era as "one of the greatest burlesques of the glorious epoch at which we have the good fortune to live." He observes that many who seek to censor or to ban art and literature ignore the beauty and value of the whole work and, instead, "if there is any nakedness in a picture or book they go straight to it like swine to the mire."

Mademoiselle du Maupin consists of letters, written to a friend by the 22-year-old Chevalier D'Albert, that satirize virtue and praise sensuality, adultery and fornication. Relating his desires for certain women, D'Albert describes their physical attributes, then provides details of the scenes that lead to their sexual intimacy. He believes that being a gentleman demands that he have a mistress, and he accepts adultery as a social reality.

The first part of the novel details the young man's experiences with his first mistress, Rosette, who yields to all of his desires. D'Albert states, "I caress her as much as I like; I have her nude or dressed, in town or in country." He also claims that she arouses "the brute" in him and "in her society, vulgar and ignoble thoughts alone occur in me."

The second part of the novel describes the adventures of Magdalene de Maupin, who often masquerades as a man. She is also interested in Rosette, and a number of their scenes in which Rosette believes Magdalene to be a man named Theodore include highly sensual and passionate embraces. Magdalene relates one incident:

> I felt her breasts, half bare and excited, heaving against my bosom, while her clasped fingers clutched my hair. A thrill went through me and my bosoms swelled. Rosette did not let go of my mouth. Her lips sucked in my lips, her teeth touched my teeth, our breaths mingled. I drew back for a moment, and two or three times turned my head to avoid her kisses, but an invincible attraction made me turn again, and I kissed her in return almost as ardently as she had kissed me.

At one point Magdalene states that their kisses "agitated me to the highest degree, although they were those of a woman . . . which made me forget that after all I was not a man."

Later in the novel, Magdalene, still disguised as Theodore, seeks to save her landlady's 15-year-old daughter, Ninon, from becoming the mistress of a predatory chevalier and charms Ninon into becoming her mistress. Professing only altruistic intentions, Magdalene writes that "her body was a little marvel of delicacy" and concludes that "only a woman could love her with sufficient delicacy and tenderness." Her growing passion for Ninon leads to Magdalene's realization that "I belong to a third, distinct sex, which as yet has not a name."

Magdalene locates Rosette, now the mistress of D'Albert, who perceives that Theodore is really a woman. Eager for sexual experience, Magdalene invites D'Albert into her bedroom where, after a detailed description of her undressing, the two make love. Late the next day, Magdalene leaves D'Albert for Rosette's bedroom, which she does not leave until noon of the following day. The reader does not learn what occurs between Rosette and Magdalene, only that the maid found the bed in disarray with the imprint of two bodies and two pearls from Magdalene's hair in the sheets. Magdalene departs and asks only that Rosette and D'Albert kiss each other occasionally with her in mind.

CENSORSHIP HISTORY

The novel was severely criticized for its explicitly erotic scenes when it was first published, but the outcry that it should be suppressed because of its "lewdness" and "indecency" strengthened sales, and Gautier reaped a handsome financial profit. At the same time, he experienced a critical backlash when the French Academy voted to bar him from membership.

In 1917, the prosecution of *Mademoiselle de Maupin* in the United States made legal history for the publishing world. John Sumner, the secretary of the New York Society for the Suppression of Vice, saw a copy of the English translation of *Mademoiselle de Maupin* displayed in the window of booksellers McDevitt-Wilson opened to what he perceived to be a "corrupting" illustration. He purchased a copy of the book from store clerk Raymond Halsey, then brought a charge against Halsey for violating section 1141 of the New York Penal Code, the obscenity statute. Halsey was arrested and brought to trial and acquitted in the Court of Special Session. The clerk then sued the society for malicious prosecution and won in a trial by jury. The society appealed and the Appellate Division affirmed the original decision. The society then took the case to the Court of Appeals, where *Halsey v. New York Society for the Suppression of Vice*, 234 N.Y. 1, 136 N.E. 219 (1922) was decided in favor of Halsey in a 5 to 2 decision. Halsey was awarded $2,500 and accrued interest in damages from the society. The court took the following points into consideration in reaching a decision: the reputation of the author, the regard in which the novel had been held by eminent critics since first publication; the whole work, not simply specific passages; the nature of the language that was "not of the street" and the effect that translation from the French might have.

The significance of the case went beyond the victory of one bookseller. Although the presiding Court of Appeals Judge William S. Andrews acknowledged that the novel "contains many paragraphs, however, which taken by themselves are undoubtedly vulgar and indecent," he based his decision on the "whole book" concept and provided more specific criteria to strengthen the defense:

> No work may be judged from a selection of paragraphs alone. Printed by themselves they might, as a matter of law, come within the prohibition of the statute. So might a similar selection from Aristophanes or Chaucer or Boccaccio or even from the Bible. The book, however, must be considered broadly as a whole.

Dissenting Judges J. Crane and J. Hogan wrote that the book "counsels vice" and attempts "to impress upon the readers that vice and voluptuousness are natural to society, are not wrongs but proper practices to be indulged in by the young." They noted that if the activities in the book were expressed in the "language of the street, there would be no doubt in the minds of anybody that the work would be lewd, vicious and indecent." Moreover, the "polished style with exquisite settings and perfumed words makes it all the more dangerous and insidious and none the less obscene and lascivious."

FURTHER READING

Cusseres, Benjamin de. "Case of Prudery against Literature: Attack on Gautier's Novel Brings to Mind Many Historical Examples of Law's Moral Censorship of Books." *New York Times* (May 23, 1920): Sec.7:3.
Marchand, Henry. *The French Pornographers: Including a History of French Erotic Literature*. New York: Book Awards, 1965.
Nelson, Hilda. "Theophile Gautier: The Invisible and Impalpable World." *French Review* 45 (June 1972): 819–30.

THE MAID OF ORLEANS (LA PUCELLE)

Author: François -Marie Arouet Voltaire
Original date and place of publication: 1759, France; 1901, United States
Original publisher: Privately printed (France); E. R. Du Mont (United States)
Type: Satire

SUMMARY

The Maid of Orleans, translated sometimes as *The Virgin of Orleans*, is a highly suggestive work that relates stories of King Charles dallying with his mistress Agnes Sorel while the threat of an English attack looms. The disgusted nobleman St. Denis vows that "every wrong is righted by its opposite" and he looks for a virgin who can lead France to victory, despite the skepticism of other nobles who doubt that any virgins remain in France. When he finds Joan of Arc, many comment that "the key to France's salvation lies under her skirt," and many attempt to violate her chastity. She does come close to surrendering to Dunois, but she stops their lovemaking just in time to prevent defloration:

> "Beloved bastard," she cried, "do stop. Now is not the right time. Heaven knows of our love, so let us not ruin our future. To you alone I pledge my groth. I swear that you shall have my flower. But let us wait until your avenging arm has conquered the Briton and driven out the usurper. Then we shall lie together under our laurels."

After victory on the battlefield, Joan keeps her promise to Dunois.
Voltaire allows Joan her chastity, but the other characters in the satire show distinctly immoral behavior. The king's mistress is licentious, and her charms are described in detail. Voltaire ecstatically observes,

> Below a neck whiter than alabaster were two separate mounds, shapely, stirring and throbbing, rounded by Eros, and tipped with little buttons of rose. Oh, charming, palpitating breasts, you invited the hand to squeeze, the eye to marvel, and the mouth to kiss.

At one point, King Charles surprises Agnes with the naked young page, Monrose, who is described as having "displayed a rear like that which Caesar in his youth shamelessly proffered to Nicodemus, that portion of the anatomy for which valiant warriors, alas, have such a weakness."

The author makes other graphic observations. He states that Robert d'Abriselle liked to lie "between two big-bottomed nuns, to caress four chubby hemispheres and fondle an equal number of breasts, and all that without sinning." In other incidents, an English chaplain sexually assaults Agnes Sorel, and the English king turns over a "mother and daughter to his soldiers."

CENSORSHIP HISTORY

The Maid of Orleans became the object of a legal action in 1909 when a man who had ordered the 42-volume set of Voltaire's works refused to honor the contract and pay $200 for the set. Peter J. Quinn claimed that *The Maid of Orleans* and the *Philosophical Dictionary* were immoral, making this the first case in which a person buying the book for his personal use became a litigant in a literary obscenity case. The case went before the New York Municipal Court, which ruled that the books were immoral and the contract was illegal.

In an appeal to the Supreme Court of New York, the decision was reversed in *St. Hubert Guild v. Quinn*, 64 Misc. 336, 118 N.Y.S. 582 (Sup. Ct. 1909). In his decision, Judge J. Seabury, with Judges Gildersleeve and Geigerich concurring, asserted, "The rule against the sale of immoral publications cannot be invoked against those works which have been generally recognized as literary classics." Seabury added that "the question in a given case is not simply whether the publication be immoral, but whether it is sufficiently so to enable the criminal law to punish it as such." In ruling on *The Maid of Orleans*, he decided that the book in question was sufficiently immoral.

FURTHER READING

De Grazia, Edward. *Censorship Landmarks.* New York: Bowker, 1969.
Lewis, Felice Flanery. *Literature, Obscenity, & Law.* Carbondale: Southern Illinois University, 1976.
Wellek, Rene, and Austin Warren. *Theory of Literature.* 3d ed. New York: Harcourt, Brace & World, 1956.

MEMOIRES

Author: Giovanni Casanova de Seingalt
Original date and place of publication: 1826, Germany; 1922, England
Original publisher: Brockhaus (Germany); The Casanova Society (England)
Type: Autobiography

SUMMARY

Casanova's *Memoires*, originally titled *Memoires: Ecrites par lui-meme*, comprise the world's most famous erotic autobiography. As researchers of sexual behavior Eberhard and Phyllis Kronhausen point out, the work also provides "one of the most important sources for the cultural historian, and especially for the student of sexual customs, the psychologist, and the sexologist."

Throughout the work, Casanova reports in detail a wide and varied range of sexual experiences, and he also reveals important social information regarding contraception and the sexual customs of different classes. In one incident, Casanova and an agent who has procured the sexual services of three beautiful young girls have dinner and drink champagne, then settle down to an amorous evening. The agent takes from his pocket a condom, "this admirable preservative from an accident which might give rise to a terrible and fruitless repentance." The girls are familiar with the item, and "they laughed heartily to see the shape these articles took when they were blown out." In another incident, Casanova not only describes contraceptives but also provides a detailed description of an ejaculation and its "abundant flow of liquid." He relates experiences in which various girls undress completely, allowing him to rhapsodize in detail about their naked bodies, particularly their breasts and buttocks, then make his "bliss complete by presenting me with their maidenheads."

In one instance, Casanova meets a nun who has recently given birth in secret and who joins him in "exhausting all imaginable kinds of pleasure, exciting each other's desires, and only wishing to prolong our enjoyment." Remembering her earlier pregnancy, the next time they engage in sexual intercourse Casanova uses "a little article of transparent skin, about eight inches long, with one opening, which was ornamented with a red rosette . . . this preventive sheath." In another instance, he reports unlacing the corset of a young novice, "and affixing my lips to one of the blossoms of her breasts I sucked it with a voluptuous pleasure which is beyond all description." Afterward, he expresses the great pleasure that he has enjoyed, and she responds that it is no sin for her for it "will easily be wiped out with a little holy water. At all events we can swear that there has been no kissing between us."

Defenders of the work point out that beyond documenting the sexual adventures of a libertine, *Memoires* relates his attraction to a highly pregnant woman and gives details regarding the delivery of a baby and other realistic, antierotic material "which any pornographer worthy of the name would never introduce into his story."

CENSORSHIP HISTORY

Casanova's *Memoires* were published in highly expurgated form in 1826, but the complete work did not appear until 1922. The manuscript remained in the safe of the publisher until the moral climate appeared to have changed sufficiently to allow publication of the entire work. Even in expurgated form, the work created controversy. In 1834, the entire 12-volume set of the expurgated *Memoires* was placed on the Index Librorum Prohibitorum in Rome, where it remained until the dissolution of the Index in the 1960s. In 1863, the French government banned sales of the work without protest from booksellers or distributors. In 1929, United States Customs confiscated a shipment of books containing *Memoires* and other erotic classics, but the court refused to hear the case, so the books were released.

On September 20, 1932, a prohibition order was published in the *Iris Oifigiuil*, "the only official source from which booksellers [and readers] might learn of a new prohibition order," in which all articles blacklisted by the Irish Board of Censors were listed. According to the Censorship of Publications Bill of 1928, "the notice in *Iris Oifigiuil* should be sufficient evidence in the courts of summary jurisdiction as to the character of the publication," despite the acknowledgment by justices quoted in Adams's thorough study of Irish censorship laws that "this gazette is not a publication which booksellers are addicted to reading." The Irish Board of Censors found Casanova's memoirs "obscene" and filled with "illicit sex behavior." The work was officially banned from sale in Ireland until the introduction of the Censorship Publications Bill in 1967 reduced to 12 years the duration of a prohibition order, and the work was among 5,000 titles released from the list of banned books.

FURTHER READING

Adams, Michael. *Censorship: The Irish Experience*. University: University of Alabama Press, 1968.
Kronhausen, Eberhard, and Phyllis Kronhausen. *Pornography and the Law: The Psychology of Erotic Realism*. New York: Ballantine, 1959.
Marchand, Henry L. *The French Pornographers*. New York: Book Awards, 1965.

MEMOIRS OF A YOUNG RAKEHELL

Author: Guillaume Apollinaire
Original date and place of publication: 1962, France; 1969, United States
Original publisher: Olympia Press (France); Grove Press (United States)
Type: Novel

SUMMARY

The Memoirs of a Young Rakehell provides a brief narrative of a young boy's sexual awakening. Master Roger spies on his sister, then attempts to seduce the family maid, before finally becoming sexually involved with the pregnant wife of the bailiff. The work is written from the perspective of the adolescent Roger and notes with details his preoccupation with the "swelling nipples" and his "burning desire to know just what it was that women carried beneath their skirts which was so precious that they were always frantic to hide it." As he observes the women around him more closely, he finds opportunities to see one "fleshly triangular mound" after another.

The author describes Roger's frequent masturbation and fascination with the length, circumference and firmness of his penis. His thoughts focus on sex, and he takes every opportunity to observe the breasts, buttocks or vaginal areas of women, to the point of humor as he hides in various locations to spy on women in their private moments. Eventually, Roger and his sister experiment with sexual intercourse; then he seduces several of the maids. Each incident is fully described, from his initial bumbling forays under their skirts—"slipping my hand beneath her skirts, I discovered a very hairy mound"—to the point where he has one after another "trembling beneath her flimsy clothing" as he fondles breasts, buttocks and thighs. He repeatedly "stands erect" and reaches "voluptuous climax," providing explicit description of each thrust.

In addition to the graphic details, the book contains numerous uses of the terms *fuck* and *prick* and descriptions of breasts and buttocks of all types. For the most part, the brief work consists of a series of adolescent sexual adventures that end with the narrator impregnating his aunt and two maids, then serving as the godfather to all three children. This is all done as part of his fulfillment of "patriotic duty, that of increasing my country's population."

CENSORSHIP HISTORY

In 1964, New Zealand Customs officers seized *Memoirs of a Young Rakehell* and *The Debauched Hospodar*, works by Apollinaire originally published in one volume by Olympia Press in 1962, and the Marquis de Sade's JUSTINE. The importer, a Mr. D. W. Cheer of Christchurch, disputed the seizure, and the matter went before a magistrate, who issued an order prohibiting the publication of the titles of the books. The Indecent Publications Tribunal did not continue this order but did refuse to allow citations in the court records of passages that the defense counsel read in court. In testimony, the comptroller of Customs claimed that the books had been detained under the provisions of the Customs Act of 1913 as "Prohibited Imports," because they were indecent. As required by Section 12 of the Indecent Publications Act of 1963, proceedings for the condemnation were instituted by the comptroller before a magistrate who, in turn, was required to turn the matter over to the Indecent Publications Tribunal to determine the manner in which the books might be viewed as "indecent":

> whether the books were indecent within the meaning of the Act, or indecent in the hands of persons under a specified age, or indecent unless circulation was restricted to specified persons or classes of persons.

The counsel for the defense argued that even if a general ban were to be levied on the books, the importer should be free of restriction because he was a "serious collector of all sorts of books" with a library of from 5,000 to 6,000 volumes. Called to testify, the importer expressed his view "of the value of the books to a student of literature."

In its decision, rendered on March 4, 1965, the tribunal asserted that the content of the two novels was "vile and revolting both to the episodes related and the language used to describe them." Although they acknowledged that Apollinaire had been viewed as a literary "bright light," their judgment was that the books were obscene and should not be circulated generally. However, the tribunal did find the books to be useful in the study of abnormal psychology and concluded that "we classify the translation of the two novels written by Guillaume Apollinaire as indecent unless circulation is restricted to persons professionally engaged in the study of abnormal psychology, who desire to use them for that purpose."

FURTHER READING

Perkins, Michael. *The Secret Record: Modern Erotic Literature.* New York: Morrow, 1976.
Perry, Stuart. *The Indecent Publications Tribunal: A Social Experiment.* London: Whitcombe and Tombs, 1965.

MEMOIRS OF HECATE COUNTY

Author: Edmund Wilson
Original date and place of publication: 1946, United States
Original publisher: Doubleday & Co.
Type: Collection of short stories

SUMMARY

Memoirs of Hecate County consists of six interconnected stories that relate the lives of the well-to-do residents of a New York suburb. All of the short stories—"The Man Who Shot Snapping Turtles," "Ellen Terhune," "Glimpses of Wilbur Flick," "The Milhollands and Their Damned Soul," "Mr. and Mrs. Blackburn at Home"—and the novella entitled "The Princess with the Golden Hair" are related by an unnamed male narrator, but only the novella contains candid accounts of sexual relations.

"The Princess with the Golden Hair" relates the narrator's experiences with two women: the "princess" of the title, Imogen Loomis, the beautiful, sheltered wife of a wealthy advertising magnate, and Anna Lenihan, a young working-class woman of immigrant background who is separated from her emotionally unstable husband. He relates through diary entries his efforts to seduce Imogen while he conducts a satisfying sexual relationship with Anna.

Using frank language, the narrator describes how he "liberated one little breast" of Anna's and relates that she becomes "so responsive to my kissing her breasts that I can make her have a climax in that way." After he contracts gonorrhea from Anna, the narrator sees a doctor and renews his efforts to seduce Imogen.

When the narrator and Imogen finally have an assignation, he learns that she wears a brace on her back. She claims to have tuberculosis of the spine, but the narrator later learns that her ailment is only in her imagination. Nonetheless, their sexual encounter is described at length. In a prolonged passage, the narrator describes Imogen's thighs and genitals:

> all that lay between them was impressively beautiful, too, with an ideal aesthetic value that I had never found there before. The mount was of classical femininity: round and smooth and plump; the fleece, if not quite golden, was blond and curly and soft; and the portals were a deep tender rose.

She does "something special and gentle" to him, then has an orgasm, "a self-excited tremor . . . brimming of female fluid."

The narrator visits Anna, who is hospitalized to undergo surgery to correct the damage of the gonorrhea to her reproductive system. While she is at home recuperating, he urges her to marry another man whom she does not love. The novella ends as the narrator receives a letter from Anna telling him that she has taken his advice, and he now realizes that he will "never make love again."

CENSORSHIP HISTORY

The literary merit of *Memoirs of Hecate County* was established before the work was taken to court and found "obscene" in both California and New York. The *New York Times Book Review* called it "a good, distinguished book," and *Time* magazine named it "the first event of the year which can be described as 'literary.'" A further unusual aspect of the litigation is that the book was ruled "obscene" based only on one of the six stories, despite the increasing agreement of legal authorities to judge a work in its entirety and not according to specific sections that have been determined to be obscene. Wilson's fellow writers asserted that the sexual descriptions were boring rather than arousing. Raymond Chandler observed that Wilson had "made fornication as dull as a railroad time table," while Malcolm Cowley described the sex scenes as "zoological."

In 1946, booksellers in San Francisco and New York City were arrested for selling the work and taken to trial. That same year, copies of the book were confiscated in Philadelphia and the publishers ceased shipment to Massachusetts because of its censorship laws. In San Francisco, a bookseller was charged with selling an "obscene" book, but the first trial was dismissed because it resulted in a hung jury. In the second trial of *People v. Wepplo*, 78 Cal. App. 2d 959, 178 P.2d 853 (1947), the jury acquitted the bookseller.

In New York City, the New York Society for the Improvement of Morals, formerly the New York Society for the Suppression of Vice, brought suit against Doubleday & Co. for violating section 1141 of the New York State Obscenity Statute. Police confiscated 130 copies of the work from four Doubleday bookstores after society secretary John Sumner charged that the book was the "most salacious and lascivious work issued for indiscriminate circulation." The next day, major bookstores such as Brentano's, Scribner's and Hearn's had removed all copies from their shelves. Since its publication a few months earlier, 50,000 copies of the book had been sold. The publisher went to court and was convicted of obscenity for publishing *Memoirs of Hecate County* in *People v. Doubleday & Co., Inc.*, 272 App. Div. 799, 71 N.Y.S.2d 736 (1st Dep't). Literature professor and critic Lionel Trilling testified at the New York trial at the Court of Special Sessions and emphasized that the stories are related and constitute a study of good and evil. He also observed that the sexually frank passages contribute heavily to the "very moral" theme of the book. The district attorney, Frank Hogan, countered with evidence that the book contained "the most intensive concentration of sex episodes, with nothing omitted in the way of bare-skinned description." He asserted in the brief that

> There are 20 separate acts of sexual intercourse. . . . These take place between the protagonist and four different women. Eighteen of the acts occur in the space of an hour or two with two different women. Three of the acts occur with two married women.

The brief cited specific pages on which these acts occur and detailed further attempts at sexual intercourse, nocturnal dreams of intercourse, daydreams of intercourse and "filthy conversations about sex" in the book. The decision was affirmed by the State Supreme Court Appellate Division in *People v. Doubleday & Co., Inc.*, 297 N.Y. 687, 77 N.E.2d 6 (1947) and the publisher was fined $1,000. The state district attorney also warned that booksellers who sold the book would be sentenced to a year in prison. Writing about the decision, *Time* magazine observed that "the decision made thousands of citizens more impatient than ever to get their morals ruined. It also proved again that finding a yardstick for proving a serious book indecent is as difficult as weighing a pound of waltzing mice."

In 1948, the case then went to the United States Supreme Court, which refused to overturn the decision of the lower court and, instead, rendered a 4 to 4 curiam decision that the book was obscene after Justice Felix Frankfurter chose to not participate. The conviction remained but the 4 to 4 decision meant that no opinion was written in *Doubleday & Co. v. New York*, 335 U.S. 848 (1948).

The book was not published in England until 1951 because publisher Frederic Warburg knew of the case against Doubleday & Co. in the United States and wanted to avoid the same action. He tried to have the text set in

England but could not find a willing printer, so he begged Wilson to edit the text. Wilson refused, so the work was not published until 1951 by W. H. Allen.

In 1961, New American Library published the paperback edition of the work with the following legend on its cover: "Not for Sale in New York State." When Ballantine Books issued a paperback edition in 1966, the book was described on the cover as "authentic and unexpurgated" as well as "still banned in the State of New York."

FURTHER READING

Bates, Ralph. "Mr. Wilson's Visit to Suburbia." *New York Times Book Review* (March 31, 1946): 7,16.
"Evil in Our Time." *Time* 48 (March 25, 1946): 102.
Lockhart, William B., and Robert C. McClure. "Literature, the Law of Obscenity, and the Constitution." *Minnesota Law Review* 38 (March 1954): 295–395.
Moskin, Morton. "Inadequacy of Present Tests as to What Constitutes Obscene Literature." *Cornell Law Quarterly* 34 (Spring 1949): 442–47.
"Pound of Waltzing Mice." *Time* 48 (December 9, 1946): 24–25.

THE MERRY MUSES OF CALEDONIA

Author: Robert Burns
Original date and place of publication: 1800, Scotland; 1907, United States
Original publisher: Peter Hill (Scotland); Privately printed for members of the Caledonia Society (United States)
Type: Collection of bawdy poems and songs

SUMMARY

The Merry Muses of Caledonia is a collection of 85 poems and songs compiled by Robert Burns, many of which were selected for use as a private songbook by the drinking club to which Burns had belonged, the Crochallan Fencibles. The group gave the collection its name in 1800, four years after Burns's death, for he had left it untitled. The poet collected ancient and modern folk songs, leaving some as they were and adding his own bawdy endings to others, and he also wrote at least 20 new songs to complete the collection. Many of the songs first appeared in letters sent by the poet to his friends.

The complete collection that Burns commissioned to be printed disappeared after his death and did not resurface until 1815, when Allan Cunningham obtained Burns's own manuscript from a banker's son who claimed that the poet had presented the manuscript to the banker. Editions published before that contained 30 to 40 of the songs, as did many later editions, because the entire collection remained unavailable. Even Cunningham selected only 42 "suitable" items from the manuscript, bowdlerizing and eliminating as he chose. Included among song titles are "Nine Inch Will Please a Lady," "How

Can I Keep My Maidenhead?" and "Nae Hair On't," as well as such lines as "Meg had a muff, and it was rough" and a plethora of such terms as "c – – t," "f – – – – g," "f – – – s" and a – – e" presented with dashes, as well as euphemisms for sexual intercourse such as "mowing."

CENSORSHIP HISTORY

The Merry Muses of Caledonia collection was not published in an unexpurgated edition in Scotland until 1959, when the passage of the Obscene Publications Act liberated the material for publication, and distinguished scholarly editors James Barke and Sydney Goodsir issued privately a complete edition of the collection in Edinburgh. Twenty-nine earlier editions contained largely bowdlerized versions of the songs and poems. A 30th, the 1800 edition, was not expurgated but it was incomplete, because the Crochallan Fencibles did not have Burns's complete manuscript, only selections that he had sent members individually. When Allan Cunningham obtained the complete collection in 1815, he took the liberty of selecting the least "offensive" songs and making changes in them, expurgating them, to make them publishable. He noted the following in his preface:

> In several places small but necessary liberties have been taken with the language. It would have been unwise to omit verses so characteristic, and they would have offended many had they appeared as they stand in the original.

Until the complete text of the songs was published for public consumption in 1959, the only copy was kept in the Private Case of the British Museum Library with other risque literature. Not only was the material expurgated but, as Perrin points out, Burns's biographers effectively expurgated his life by omitting mention of licentious songs to avoid tempting readers into seeking the material. Editors chose to ignore the existence of the songs in so-called standard, or complete, collections of the poet's works. As George Legman observes,

> Annandale of the Standard Edition pretended that there was no *Merry Muses*, as did President Eliot of Harvard (who gave Burns one of the fifty volumes of the Five-Foot Shelf [of the Harvard Classics] to himself). So did J. Logie Robertson, editing *The Poetical Works of Robert Burns* ("the text is presented entire") for Oxford University Press in 1910.

Other editors admitted to the existence of the *Merry Muses* and hinted at their contents but, like American editor James Hunter, who edited *The Complete Works of Robert Burns* in 1886, believed, "To reproduce such pieces in a work dedicated to the genius of Scotland's bard would be sacrilege."

FURTHER READING

Craig, Alec. *Suppressed Books: A History of the Conception of Literary Obscenity*. New York: World Publishing, 1963.

Legman, George, ed. "Introduction." *The Merry Muses of Caledonia: Collected and Written in Part by Robert Burns*. New Hyde Park, N.Y.: University Books, 1965.

Perrin, Noel. *Dr. Bowdler's Legacy: A History of Expurgated Books in England and America*. Boston: Godine, 1992.

Thomas, Donald. *A Long Time Burning: The History of Literary Censorship in England*. New York: Praeger, 1969.

MOLL FLANDERS

Author: Daniel Defoe
Original date and place of publication: 1722, England
Original publisher: Privately printed
Type: Novel

SUMMARY

Moll Flanders is subtitled "The Fortunes and Misfortunes of the Famous Moll Flanders, who was born in Newgate, and during a Life of continu'd Variety, for Threescore Years, besides her Childhood, was Twelve Year a *Whore*, five times a *Wife* (whereof once to her own Brother), Twelve Year a *Thief*, Eight Year a Transported *Felon* in *Virginia*, at last grew *Rich*, liv'd *Honest*, and died a *Penitent*." The author, thus, aptly summarizes his book and provides readers with advance warning about the heroine they will encounter.

The author relates in the Preface that this is "a private history . . . where the names and other circumstances of the person are concealed." Taking the charade farther, Defoe seeks to appease potential critics by acknowledging that the story of a woman so "debauched" and "wicked" makes it difficult "to wrap it up so clean as not to give room, especially for vicious readers, to turn it to his disadvantage." Still, Defoe warns that, to be a true lesson in morality, "the wicked part should be made as wicked as the real history of it will bear."

In this spirit, Moll's adventures and philosophy are presented. She "kept true to this notion, that a woman should never be kept for a mistress that had money to make herself a wife," a state that she enters repeatedly. Sexual relationships are Moll's means to marriage. She is widowed in several instances, and marries her brother in one; thus, nothing is left for "a poor desolate girl without friends" but to try again. When the novel ends, Moll appears comfortable and ready to enjoy a secure old age.

CENSORSHIP HISTORY

Moll Flanders was popular when it first appeared, running to three editions in the first year and another edition annually for the next 60 years. The book then disappeared from publication as a single entity until 1896, when it resurfaced in an edition published in Holland. Perrin states, "It was not expurgated; it was also not reviewed." The highly popular novel was, thus, informally banned by acts of omission, but wealthy fans of the work were able to obtain copies if they were willing to buy expensive entire sets of Defoe's works. This strategy was used by the Victorians to allow "wealthy 'strong' readers" to read forbidden works. Thus, both *Moll Flanders* and the similarly racy *Roxana* (1724) were included unexpurgated in several sets of Defoe's works during the 19th century. Buyers of these volumes secondhand would find one or both novels missing for, as Desmond MacCarthy stated in *Criticism*, "When I was a boy, it [*Moll Flanders*] was not an easy book to come by. . . . From second-hand sets of Defoe's worlds that volume was frequently missing."

In 1892, when Viking Portables decided to issue an anthology entitled *Selections from Defoe's Minor Novels*, meaning everything but Robinson Crusoe, editor George Saintsbury expurgated *Moll Flanders* freely. Perrin describes the expurgation:

> But first he got out his gelding knife. Having picked a group of the blander scenes, he lopped out all racy paragraphs. . . . Then he went through again, cutting out individual sentences. . . . Finally he poked through word by word—and fell abruptly to the ranks of the lower-grade bowdlerists.

Even Defoe's subtitle created consternation among Victorians. In his comprehensive 1878 *Dictionary of English Literature*, W. Davenport Adams summarizes the subtitle as follows: "The title of a novel written by Daniel Defoe; the heroine of which is a female of questionable reputation, who afterwards becomes religious." As Perrin observes, "The one thing Moll's reputation isn't, of course, is questionable."

Through the first three decades of the 20th century, *Roxana* and *Moll Flanders* were among books regularly seized by local United States Customs inspectors for being "obscene," the last time in 1929 in New York City. The ban was lifted when the passage of the 1930 amendment to the Tariff Act eased restrictions on the importation of classics.

FURTHER READING

Alkon, Paul. *Defoe and Fictional Time*. Athens: University of Georgia Press, 1979.

MacCarthy, Desmond. *Criticism*. London: J. Dent, 1932.

Moore, John R. *Daniel Defoe: Citizen of the Modern World*. Chicago: University of Chicago Press, 1958.

Perrin, Noel. *Dr. Bowdler's Legacy*. New York: Atheneum, 1969.

Sutherland, James. *Defoe*. Philadelphia: Lippincott, 1938.
"Defoe's Works Banned." *Publishers Weekly* 116 (October 19, 1929): 1,938.

MY LIFE AND LOVES

Author: Frank Harris
Original date and place of publication: 1925, France; 1926, United States
Original publisher: Privately printed (France); Up-to-Date Printing Co. (United States)
Type: Autobiography

SUMMARY

In the foreword to *My Life and Loves*, Harris claims that he intends to reveal all that life has taught him, and to especially "begin at the A.B.C. of love." He also aims "to warn the young and impressionable against the shoals and hidden reefs of life's ocean . . . . [as well as] to teach youths how to use their magazine gun of sex so that it may last for years." Harris observes in the foreword that an additional goal is to encourage other writers to develop characters evenly by including "the sex side of characters" and thus bringing them fully to life. In short, he claims that "it is the first book ever written to glorify the body and its passionate desires and the soul as well and its sacred, climbing sympathies."

The four volumes of Harris's autobiography present his extraordinary observations of public figures and public and literary events across decades and continents. The work also relates in detail his even more extraordinary sex life, from young childhood through old age, during a life that afforded him the opportunity and the drive for variegated experience. These frankly presented descriptions of his sexual experiences have evoked criticism of the book from its first publication.

Harris gives little attention to his first four years of life, during which his mother died, but moves quickly to relate that he caught the nursery maid in bed with a man and soon learned that he could use this knowledge to blackmail her to give him more sugar on his bread. Sent to a girls' boarding school after his mother's death, he repeatedly drops his pencils to the ground, then crawls under tables, ostensibly to retrieve his pencil. He actually moves closer to the girls' legs, once even touching a calf and experiencing "my first taste of Paradise and the forbidden fruit—authentic heaven!" He claims that he records this incident "because it proves that sex-feeling may show itself in early childhood." From these early experiences, Harris progresses to adulthood and numerous adult sexual experiences, including his initiation by an experienced Greek woman into the ways of cunnilingus, which he dubbed "mouth-worship."

Blended with Harris's accounts of events and figures of his day are other stories of his successes and failures with women, ranging across continents, nationalities and races. He trades stories of sexual prowess with French writer

Guy de Maupassant, chronicles meetings with philosophers such as Maeterlinck, comments on Asian culture while describing the passion and sexual skills of his Japanese mistress and criticizes the United States government for its handling of conscientious objectors during World War I. The work is a valuable social and historical document, despite its notoriety and the candid descriptions of Harris's sexual exploits.

CENSORSHIP HISTORY

My Life and Loves appeared in Paris in 1925 in plain brown wrappers that were also used when the book was shipped into England. Some copies were seized by British Customs officials, but many copies of the book made it to Soho bookshops. After police received complaints from private English citizens, they confiscated and destroyed copies of the work by magisterial order or by virtue of "disclaimers" signed by prudent booksellers. In essence, the police "disclaimer" form was a system developed by the London Metropolitan Police that enabled them to destroy books that no one would care to defend in court. The form of the disclaimer said, in essence, that the bookshop owner disclaimed ownership to specific items seized from the bookstore on a given day, thus indicating that he or she would not dispute the seizures and giving the police freedom to destroy it. The practice saved time because no summons was issued or served and no hearing before or examination of documents by a magistrate occurred. The police simply obtained a signed disclaimer and destroyed the books that they had judged to be indecent, thus making the police the determiners of public morality. Should a bookseller dispute the proceeding, a lengthy and expensive legal battle was certain to ensue.

In 1926 at the urging of the New York Society for the Suppression of Vice, the New York City police raided the Up-to-Date Printing Company, which was printing the American edition of the book, and seized about 300 copies of Volume 2. They also arrested the president of Up-to-Date, Norman Pomerantz, and two employees, as well as Esar Levine, Harris's United States agent. In leading the campaign, John Sumner proclaimed the work to be "the most obscene book published in the present century." He led a raid on the bindery, confiscated an additional 680 copies of the book and arrested Jacob Sidowsky and Harry J. Lebovit.

When the case went to trial, Lebovit and Pomerantz received fines totaling $750, and Levine received a workhouse sentence of 90 days. In its report of the case, *Publishers Weekly* supported the censors and declared *My Life and Loves* to be "unfit for publication under the standards of any country." At the same time, the book received the lead review in the February 14, 1926, issue of the *Saturday Review of Literature*. In an attempt to circumvent the censors, Harris and his supporters quickly organized the Frank Harris Publishing Co. and published a bowdlerized version of the book, which was also challenged but survived.

FURTHER READING

Harris, Frank. Foreword, in *My Life and Loves*. New York: Grove, 1963.

Kronhausen, Eberhard, and Phyllis Kronhausen. *Pornography and the Law: The Psychology of Erotic Realism*. New York: Ballantine, 1959.

"My Life and Loves Unfit." *Publishers Weekly* 109 (March 27, 1926): 1,136.

Rolph, Cecil Hewitt. *Books in the Dock*. London: Deutsch, 1961.

Tobin, A. I., and Elmer Gertz. *Frank Harris: A Study in Black and White*. Chicago: Mendelsohn, 1931.

A NIGHT IN A MOORISH HAREM

Author: Anonymous
Original date and place of publication: 1854, England
Original publisher: Privately published
Type: Novel

SUMMARY

A Night in a Moorish Harem is one of the most famous of the underground pornographic classics that circulated freely in Victorian England. Purported to be the account of "Lord George Herbert," who is described in the preface as "the handsomest man in the English nobility," the first-person narrative relates one night in a Moroccan harem containing nine women, each representing a different Mediterranean nationality. Herbert had anchored his ship, the *Antler*, off the coast of Morocco and gone for a swim to cool his sexual frustrations that had built up after months without one of "the beautiful women of London and the favours which some of them had granted me." After the swim, he fell asleep in a small boat that was initially attached to the ship but which slipped free and floated away from the ship. When he awakened, he was near shore and under the wall of a large building from which nine women of the pasha's harem were watching him. They tied their shawls together and Herbert pulled himself up to their rooms using the shawl rope.

Once Herbert is inside, the women strip him of his wet clothes and then begin to strip themselves. Their pasha is away for the night, and they all are endlessly ardent and eager to gratify Herbert's desires. In between his sexual performances, with each woman in turn, Herbert listens to the stories of their sex lives, including various sexual adventures that include lesbian interludes and one that details a mating with a stallion.

The requisite responses are assigned to each girl, as they "swoon," "groan with pleasure," "undulate" or move "sinuously." For his part, Herbert exhibits great prowess, and his often "rigid shaft" or "swollen shaft" is said to "gush" great quantities of semen. The women, in turn, are all "tight and elastic and hot and juicy." At one point, the women all decide to measure Herbert and, one at a time, each takes her bracelet and "clasped it around my shaft. But the clasp would not fasten. The bracelet was not large enough." He turns the tables on the women and measures their thighs, breasts, and "the length of their slits."

The story ends as the dawn approaches, and Herbert weakly tells the women that he must return to his ship. They help him to dress and lower him safely to his waiting boat below their window; and he returns to his ship while they await the return of the pasha.

CENSORSHIP HISTORY

A Night in a Moorish Harem was a popular underground pornographic classic in Victorian England long before it crossed the Atlantic Ocean and appeared in the United States. The book was published privately, or by overnight presses, and no established publishing house made it part of the backlist. In December 1923, Maurice Inman and Max Gottschalk, two New York booksellers, were arrested for selling three underground literary classics: *A Night in a Moorish Harem*, *Only a Boy* and FANNY HILL. The purchaser was Charles J. Bamberger, a longtime agent of the New York Society for the Suppression of Vice whose specialty in erotica made him a valuable aid to society secretaries Anthony Comstock and John Sumner for more than 40 years. The booksellers appeared in special sessions court in New York City in March 1924, convicted for selling "obscene" material and fined $25 each. *Publishers Weekly* applauded the convictions and observed that the suppression of "such admittedly obscene books" was "a salutary measure of which the book trade may well approve."

In 1931, the vice society brought charges against bookseller Frances Steloff for selling *Hsi Men Ching* and *A Night in a Moorish Harem*, but the court dismissed the charges.

Two years earlier, Reverend Philip Yarrow, leader of the Illinois Vigilance Association, launched a campaign against Chicago booksellers and used entrapment to obtain his evidence. Walter Shaver, owner of a chain of Chicago bookstores, was charged with selling Yarrow a copy of *A Night in a Moorish Harem*. Tried in municipal court in January 1930, Shaver testified that an agent of Yarrow's had badgered him into ordering a copy of the book and argued that his was a case of entrapment. The jury agreed and returned a verdict of not guilty. In retaliation, Shaver instructed his lawyer to file a damage suit against Yarrow, and the vice crusader fought back through his newspaper, *Vigilance*, claiming that "classical smut has no more standing under the law than low-down smut." He was supported by the *Christian Century*, which praised Yarrow for his "moral policing of the beasts who specialized in distributing moral sewage." The *Chicago Evening Post* exposed Yarrow's entrapment methods and published photographs of checks that Yarrow had received as informant fees in obscenity convictions. While the trial progressed, Shaver's business sank into bankruptcy, thus inflaming public opinion further against Yarrow. In April 1931, a Chicago superior court jury awarded Shaver $5,000 in damages, a judgment that was reversed on appeal a year later.

FURTHER READING

"Battling the Wolves." *Christian Century* 48 (April 8, 1931): 470–71.

Boyer, Paul S. *Purity in Print: The Vice Society Movement and Book Censorship in America*. New York: Scribner's, 1968.

"Chicago Bookseller Wins Case." *Publishers Weekly* 119 (April 4, 1931): 1,790.

Farriman, Milton. "Bookseller Victorious in Chicago Reformer's Campaign." *Publishers Weekly* 117 (February 1, 1930): 566–68.

"Gottschalk Fined for Obscene Book Sale." *Publishers Weekly* 111 (March 8, 1924): 834.

Marcus, Stephen. *The Other Victorians*. New York: Basic Books, 1966.

"Neither Censorship nor Puritanism Involved." *Christian Century* 47 (March 19, 1930): 357–58.

"Two Booksellers Arrested on Sumner Complaint." *Publishers Weekly* 110 (December 23, 1923): 1,974.

NOVEMBER (NOVEMBRE)

Author: Gustave Flaubert
Original date and place of publication: 1914, France; 1921, United States
Original publisher: Editions du Seiul (France); Roman Press (United States)
Type: Novel

SUMMARY

The sexual encounters in *November* were based on an actual relationship that the 18-year-old Flaubert had experienced with a 35-year-old woman named Eulalie Foucaud, the daughter of a hotel-keeper named Delanglade, in Marseilles. Never certain if she were widowed or still married, the young author spent four passionate days with her then left, fearful that she would encroach on his private life. They wrote for eight months but never met again.

The novel is divided into three sections. The first two sections present a young man at age 15, then at age 18. In the first section, the young protagonist first becomes sexually aware. He expresses feelings about women in the abstract, relating how he watches the prostitutes and mingles with them on the streets. He also watches the women who entertain at the fairgrounds and becomes "tormented" as he dreams of "those strangely formed thighs so firmly encased in pink tights, those supple arms wreathed in bangles." At 15, he exhibits an inexperienced sensuality and yearns for the women, asserting that "there is no age at which we do not dream of women: as children we squeeze the breasts of the big girls who kiss us and hold us in their arms."

In the second section, the now–18-year-old protagonist desires a mistress. He decides suddenly to visit a prostitute and states, "I felt dimly the oncoming of my season of heat. . . . I felt a need for sensual pleasure. . . . my passion overflowed." In his assignation with Marie, the young man provides the reader with his impressions before intercourse, as he watches "the shape of her breasts come and go in the motion of her breathing" and he marvels that "she had one of those splendid bosoms on which one would wish to die." The actual sexual experience is described in generalities:

> Her warm, tremulous flesh stretched beneath me, quivering. From head to foot I was all sensuality; my mouth pressed to hers, our fingers intertwined, shaken by one spasm, interlaced in one embrace.

Afterward, Marie tells the young man her story, and she begs him to love her. For some unexplained reason, however, he delays returning to her, by which time she has disappeared. He spends the rest of his life thinking of her and observes, "It was she that I pursued everywhere; in the beds of others I dreamed of her caresses."

CENSORSHIP HISTORY

November was completed in 1840, before Flaubert was 21 years old, but he refused to have it published during his lifetime. Although he avoided any explanation of his reticence, aside from references to the sexual content and the focus on the prostitute Marie, biographers have suggested that the intensely personal background to the narrative is a more likely reason. He claimed to have thought often of the model for Marie, Eulalie Foucaud, until the end of his life.

Thus, the first French publication of the novel did not occur until 1914, and the first English translation emerged in 1921 when Ernest Reichl published *November* as part of the Individual Library series of books of his Roman Press imprint. Reichl made these books available in attractive leather bindings with specially designed title pages. The following year, the novel was seized by United States Customs as "obscene," but it was released after being reviewed by literature experts of the Customs bureau.

In 1935, a bookseller named Herbert Miller was charged by John Sumner, secretary of the New York Society for the Suppression of Vice, with selling an obscene book, the Roman Press edition of *November*. Miller was taken to City Magistrates Court of New York City, Fourth District, Borough of Manhattan. Sumner charged that the work lacked "decency" and that it violated "contemporary public morals." In reaching a determination in *People on Complaint of Sumner v. Miller*, 279 N.Y.S. 583 (1935), City Magistrate Goldstein observed that

> the criterion of decency is fixed by time, place, geography and all the elements that make for a constantly changing world. A practice regarded as decent in one period may be indecent in another. . . . To change standards of morals is the task of the school and church; the task of the judge is to record the tides of public opinion, not to emulate King Canute in an effort to turn back the tide.

Magistrate Goldstein dismissed the complaint and discharged the defendant, after noting that there was not sufficient cause to hold the defendant for trial.

FURTHER READING

Kilpatrick, James J. *The Smut Peddlers*. New York: Doubleday, 1960.
Lottman, Herbert. *Flaubert: A Biography*. Boston: Little, Brown, 1989.
Troyat, Henri. *Flaubert*. Paris: Librairie Ernest Flammarion, 1988.

THE 120 DAYS OF SODOM (LES 120 JOURNÉES DE SODOME)

Author: Marquis de Sade
Original date and place of publication: 1904, Germany; 1962, France; 1966, United States
Original publisher: Fischer (Germany); Olympia Press (France); Grove Press (United States)
Type: Collection of tales

SUMMARY

The 120 Days of Sodom was a carefully planned work that de Sade completed while incarcerated, first in Vincennes, then in the Bastille. The work was written on both sides of numerous pieces of loose paper that the author then pasted end to end, rolled up and hid in his cell for safekeeping. When de Sade left the Bastille, the work remained. The manuscript was found in the cell in 1832 by a man named Arnoux de Saint-Maxim, who passed it on to the Villeneuve-Trans family, but it remained unpublished until the 20th century.

The author originally planned to illustrate through 600 examples all possible perversions. The premise for the book is that four wealthy and jaded men join forces and send their agents throughout France to kidnap the handsomest boys and the prettiest girls from the country's richest and most distinguished families. The children then are taken to the mountaintop castle of one of the men, where they are locked in with the men and four of the most experienced brothel mistresses in Paris. The entrances are all walled up, and the sole bridge that connects the castle to the outside world is removed. The voluptuaries have provided themselves with every necessity and every possible luxury and, secure from the prying eyes of the outside world, they embark on a continuous orgy.

The brothel mistresses are assigned the task of relating the experiences of their lives, in an assigned order and in graphic detail. The plan is that each woman will tell five stories each day of the most interesting sexual perversions possible, beginning with the "simple passions" in November and ending with the "murderous passions" in February. As Marchand notes, "there were to be 600 different tales of sexual profligacy, systematically ordered, and proceeding in the direction of ever greater and rarer perversions." While the tales are told, the boys and girls are kept close at hand so that the men can immediately gratify any sexual arousal that may occur.

Only 150 of the stories, the "simple passions," are completed. The remaining stories exist in outline form. The stories tell of "buggering," "frigging," "fucking" and devouring of excrement, all in repeated and graphic detail. The tales tend more toward the grotesque than the erotic, with their "discharges of spittle," the burying of hatpins and other sharp objects in flesh and the repeated episodes of pederasty.

CENSORSHIP HISTORY

The 120 Days of Sodom was banned from bookstores when it was first published in a limited edition in Germany, despite the learned notes to the text provided by psychiatrist Iwan [*sic*] Bloch, who had justified the publication by emphasizing its scientific importance. Authorities decried the pederasty and emphasis upon excrement throughout the work and the infliction of pain in the latter tales.

In 1966, Corgi Books in England planned to release the paperback edition of *The 120 Days of Sodom*, having already released the "complete and unexpurgated" edition of JUSTINE in 1965. Unfortunately for the publisher, the sensational Moors murder trial occurred in 1966 in England following the murders by Myra Hindley and Ian Brady of two children, aged 7 and 12, and one 17 year old between December 1964 and October 1965. They photographed and tape-recorded their torture and mutilation of the victims. In court, Brady told the judge that he had studied carefully de Sade's instructions, "Is murder a crime in the eyes of Nature? . . . Destruction is Nature's method of progress. . . . Murder is often necessary, never criminal and essential to tolerate in a republic." The public outcry stifled plans to reprint additional books by de Sade. As reviewer Ludovic Kennedy stated in an April 29, 1966, article in *The Spectator* regarding the Moors trial and books, "No respectable publisher would print a novel containing what is alleged." Because de Sade's novels contained scenes similar to what occurred in the Moors murders, thus, as Sutherland states, "no British publisher who valued his respectability should publish de Sade." The first English translation was published by Grove Press in 1966.

FURTHER READING

Hayman, Ronald *De Sade: A Critical Biography*. New York: Crowell, 1978.
Kendrick, Walter. *The Secret Museum: Pornography in Modern Culture*. Baltimore: Penguin, 1988.
Kennedy, Ludovic. "The Moors Murders and De Sade." *The Spectator* (April 29, 1966): 23–25.

Lever, Maurice. *Sade: A Biography*. Trans. by Arthur Goldhammer. New York: Farrar & Straus, 1993.

Marchand, Henry L. *The French Pornographers: Including a History of French Erotic Literature*. New York: Book Awards, 1965.

Sutherland, John. *Offensive Literature: Decensorship in Britain, 1960–1982*. London: Junction Books, 1982.

OUR LADY OF THE FLOWERS (NOTRE-DAME DES FLEURS)

Author: Jean Genet
Original date and place of publication: 1943, France; 1963, United States
Original publisher: L'Arbalete (France); Grove Press (United States)
Type: Novel

SUMMARY

Our Lady of the Flowers, written while Genet was serving a sentence in Fresnes prison in France, creates a world in which the author presents in a positive light every attribute despised by society and every crime. Sartre observed that the book is less an attempt at communication than it is "a willful perversion of the sexual act. . . . it is the epic of masturbation."

Throughout, Genet fantasizes in this highly autobiographical novel about past lovers, giving them such names as "Mimosa," "Darling," "First Communion" and "Divine," and he imagines himself making love to them. The name of "Our Lady of the Flowers" is given to the former butcher boy and brutal murderer, Adrien Baillon, who is on trial, while Darling is really a stereotypical muscleman, pimp and shoplifter; Divine is a transvestite male streetwalker once named Louis Culafroy, whose companions and fellow transvestites are Mimosa, First Communion and Lady Apple.

The novel does not contain a conventional plot. Rather, episodes are superimposed upon each other, moving from the beginning, which presents the funeral of Divine, through to the end, which is "her" death. At the funeral gather "the girl-queens and boy-queens, the aunties, fags, and nellies" who are part of Divine's circle. From that point, the novel returns to the past to explain how Louis Culafroy became Divine, then to recreate "her" life, affairs and drug use. She becomes involved with Darling, who becomes her pimp, and the two live together and attend Mass regularly. The novel mixes graphic sexual imagery with religious symbolism, most pointedly mimicked in the name "Our Lady of the Flowers." Repeated homosexual encounters are described, as if to prove the statement made by Darling that "a male that fucks another male is a double male." The novel ends with Darling in prison, sending a letter that contains a dotted line and the instructions to "kiss it." Genet explains that "the dotted line that Darling refers to is the outline of his prick."

CENSORSHIP HISTORY

Our Lady of the Flowers contains images and references that for two decades were considered too "obscene" to encourage any publisher to put out an English edition of the book, and the French version met with opposition in England. In 1957, the reference department of Birmingham Public Library in England ordered the two-volume French-language version of the work, but it was seized by British Customs and refused entry into England. Craig states that

> if the books had reached their destination, they could have been understood only by advanced students of the French language, and the librarian would have been responsible that they were issued only to responsible readers.

Birmingham authorities failed to support sufficiently their ordering of the book, sending a representative ignorant of the French language to the Custom and Excise Office in London, where he was persuaded to avoid challenging the seizure in the courts. Further, the chair of the Public Libraries Committee, also ignorant of the French language, was present and he "was dreadfully shocked at passages translated for their benefit which dealt with homosexual incidents."

The English version of *Our Lady of the Flowers*, published by Grove Press in 1963, was banned in Ireland on October 23, 1965. A prohibition order was published in the *Iris Oifigiuil*, "the only official source from which booksellers [and readers] might learn of a new prohibition order," in which all articles blacklisted by the Irish Board of Censors were listed. According to the Censorship of Publications Bill of 1928, "the notice in *Iris Oifigiuil* should be sufficient evidence in the courts of summary jurisdiction as to the character of the publication." The Irish Board of Censors found the novel "obscene" and "indecent," objecting particularly to the author's handling of the theme of homosexuality and brutal crime. The work was officially banned from sale in Ireland until the introduction of the Censorship Publications Bill in 1967 reduced to 12 years the duration of a prohibition order, and the work was among 5,000 titles released from the list of banned books.

FURTHER READING

Adams, Michael. *Censorship: The Irish Experience*. University: University of Alabama Press, 1968.

Craig, Alec. *Suppressed Books: A History of the Conception of Literary Obscenity*. New York: World Publishing, 1963.

Molz, Kathleen. "The Public Custody of the High Pornography." *American Scholar* (Winter 1966–1967): 93–103.

Perkins, Michael. *The Secret Record: Modern Erotic Literature*. New York: William Morrow and Company, 1976.

Sartre, Jean-Paul. *Saint Genet: Comedian and Martyr*. New York: Braziller, 1952.

White, Edmund. *Genet: A Biography*. New York: Knopf, 1994.

PAMELA, OR VIRTUE REWARDED

Author: Samuel Richardson
Original date and place of publication: 1740, England
Original publisher: Privately printed
Type: Epistolary novel

SUMMARY

Pamela is concerned with a domestic middle-class and predominantly feminine world of "domestic politeness." The novel grew out of a project that several booksellers commissioned of Richardson, a book of letters to be used as models by the less educated when they needed to write on special occasions. Among these models was a letter written by parents to their daughter, a servant whose master had tried to seduce her. Richardson's imagination was piqued by the idea and he expanded it into the series of letters that became *Pamela*.

The letters from Pamela to her parents dramatize her sexual ordeal, as she describes the manner in which Mr. B first attempts to seduce and then rape her. The story pits pure female innocence against ruthless and powerful male lust in letters that are frequently written by Pamela on the run, as she escapes one trap after another. Writing in her room, Pamela hears Mr. B at her door, so she hurriedly grabs her paper and pen and continues to scribble while slipping out through an open window. She runs from him, but not so quickly that he will not catch her.

Despite all protestations of innocence, Pamela provides her readers with detailed descriptions of her ravishment. Nearly swooning, she has the presence of mind to write, "he then put his hand in my bosom," before she "fainted away with terror." She repeatedly locks herself in a closet or her room but never takes any of the many opportunities to leave the estate. Finally, Mr. B. marries Pamela.

CENSORSHIP HISTORY

Pamela's behavior motivated both praise and censure for the novel. Although Richardson's proclaimed intention was to show the reward (marriage) to be gained when a girl preserves her virtue, his contemporaries were skeptical. Author Henry Fielding attacked in a parody named *Shamela* (1741) what he viewed as the facile opportunism of Pamela. His view was that, rather than an innocent victim, the servant girl was a coy temptress who, with bold calculation, constantly put herself in Mr. B's line of vision. Another contemporary, Charles Povey, blasted Richardson's "inflammatory novel" in his work *Virgin in Eden* (1741), stating, "What can youths and virgins learn from *Pamela*'s letters, more than lessons to tempt their chastity." The outraged moralist asserted that Pamela showed a lack of the very modesty for which Richardson had praised her when she exposed herself a second time to Mr. B's advances.

Pamela was condemned by the Roman Catholic Church in 1744 and was prohibited reading for Catholics. It appeared on the Index Librorum Prohibitorum mainly because it was a novel that related a suggestively romantic relationship, despite Richardson's pretense of presenting a moral. The work appears on the Index of Benedict XIV, issued in 1758, and the Indexes of Pope Leo XIII, issued in 1881 and 1900 and still in force in 1906. As Putnam observes, the selection of fiction that appears on various editions of the Index is "curiously disproportionate, and in fact almost haphazard in its character."

Both *Pamela* and Richardson's *Clarissa Harlowe* (1747) were published as long chapbooks in the United States in 1772, when Reverend Jonathan Edwards warned the young against reading both books more because they were fiction, "considered a sinful form of writing, than because of any intrinsic sin."

In 1893, the American Library Association created for the first time a 5,000-title book guide for small popular libraries and branches, claiming it to be a collection that "one could recommend to any trustee." *Pamela* and *Clarissa Harlowe* were omitted from the list, although works by Henry Fielding were included. When the ALA released its *Catalog* in 1904, *Pamela* and *Clarissa Harlowe* were still excluded from the list, leading to the implication of censorship via omission. Many individuals agreed with Corinne Bacon, first a librarian at the Newark (New Jersey) Public Library and later the editor of the H. W. Wilson *Fiction Catalog*, in criticizing the heroine who "held out for a 'higher price' (marriage), as more immoral than Hester Prynne of *The Scarlet Letter*."

FURTHER READING

Bacon, Corinne. "What Makes a Novel Immoral?" *Wisconsin Library Bulletin* 6 (August 1910): 83–95.

Geller, Evelyn. *Forbidden Books in American Public Libraries, 1876–1939*. Westport, Conn.: Greenwood, 1984.

Thomas, Donald. *A Long Time Burning: The History of Literary Censorship in England*. New York: Praeger, 1969.

PANSIES

Author: D. H. Lawrence
Original date and place of publication: 1929, England
Original publisher: Privately printed
Type: Poetry collection

SUMMARY

Pansies is a collection of poems, a play on the French term *pensees*, or simply thoughts, that Lawrence first published privately in its entirety.

As Lawrence states in the introduction to *Pansies*, "I should wish these *Pansies* to be taken as thoughts rather than anything else; casual thoughts that are true while they are true and irrelevant when the mood and circumstance changes." In essence, the poems do not form a manifesto for Lawrence, nor did he consider that he was making any sort of statement in their publication. Rather, he expressed his personal philosophy on a range of issues, from censors to love, in poems entitled "All I Ask," "Let Us Talk, Let Us Laugh," "Women Want Fighters for Their Lovers" and 225 others.

Censors were shocked by such verses as follow:

The fighting cock, the fighting cock—
have you got one, little blighters?
Let it crow then, like one o'clock!
    (from "Women Want Fighters for Their Lovers")

They say I wrote a naughty book
With perfectly awful things in it,
putting in all the impossible words
like b – – – – and f – – – and sh – – .
    (from "My Naughty Book")

CENSORSHIP HISTORY

Lawrence sent the manuscript of *Pansies* to agent Curtis Brown on January 7, 1929, and learned three weeks later that Brown had never received the package. Using powers granted by the Post Office Act of 1908, Home Secretary Sir William Joyson-Hicks ("Jix") had ordered the police to intercept and review all mail sent by Lawrence into England in the effort to locate copies of the Orioli edition of *Lady Chatterley's Lover*. The postal inspector who intercepted the *Pansies* manuscript "was disturbed" by it and sent it to Joyson-Hicks, who agreed that the poems were "indecent" and sent the manuscript to the director of public prosecutions.

The fanfare surrounding the seizure led to a debate in Parliament, when the Labour Party representative of West Leicester, F. W. Pethick-Lawrence, asked Home Secretary Joyson-Hicks

> if he will give the names and official positions of the persons on whose advice he causes books and manuscripts to be seized and banned; what are the qualifications of such persons for literary censorship; and whether, to assist authors and publishers, he will state what are the rules and regulations, the contravention of which causes a book to be seized and banned by his Department?

Joyson-Hicks attempted to circumvent accountability for the seizure by pointing out that Lord Campbell's act gave a metropolitan police magistrate or any two justices of the peace powers that "on sworn information" they might issue a search warrant. But Pethick-Lawrence pressed the issue and asked Joyson-Hicks what that had to do with the government's confiscation of materials in the mails. The home secretary then stated that, if a violation of rights had occurred, it was the responsibility of the police. However, he adamantly insisted that no violation had occurred because British postal laws decreed that the postmaster general should "refuse to take part in the conveyance of any indecent matter." In this case, Lawrence's manuscript was discovered "during a routine inspection of packages for concealed letters sent through the mails at lower than lawful postal rates." He added that the manuscript was then sent to his office and "by my directions forwarded to the Director of Public Prosecutions."

Pethick-Lawrence demanded to know who had determined the material to be "obscene." Joyson-Hicks responded that the postmaster general made the first determination, then sent it to him. He stated that in regard to the *Pansies* manuscript, "It is not a question of literary merit at all, and, if the honourable Member has any doubt, I will show him the book in question. It contains grossly indecent matter."

Publisher Martin Secker conceded that some of the poems "should be eliminated" and removed 14 poems—"The Noble Englishman," "Women Want Fighters for Their Lovers," "Ego-Bound Women," "There Is No Way Out," "My Naughty Book," "The Little Wowser," "The Young and Their Moral Guardians," "What Matters," "What Does She Want?," "Don't Look at Me!," "To Clarinda," "Demon Justice," "Be a Demon" and "The Jeune Fille"—before publishing the collection in 1931. Lawrence also authorized P. R. Stephenson to bring out an unexpurgated edition in collaboration with bookseller Charles Lahr. The government censorship made the poems more attractive to buyers and the collection sold well.

FURTHER READING

DeGrazia, Edward. *Girls Lean Back Everywhere: The Law of Obscenity and the Assault on Genius.* New York: Random House, 1992.

Lawrence, D. H. *Literature and Censorship.* Ed. by Harry T. Moore. New York: Viking, 1959.

Nehls, Edward, ed. *D. H. Lawrence: A Composite Biography.* Madison: University of Wisconsin Press, 1959.

Rolph, Cecil Hewitt. *Books in the Dock.* London: Deutsch, 1961.

THE PERFUMED GARDEN

Translator: Sir Richard Burton
Original date and place of publication: 1886, Switzerland; 1933, England
Original publisher: The Kama Shastra Society (Switzerland); Fortune Press (England)
Type: Sex manual

SUMMARY

The Perfumed Garden, attributed to the 15th-century Sheikh Nefzaoui, was first translated from Arabic into French by Isadore Liseux in 1885, then from French into English by Burton, who called it "a manual of erotology." In his notes to the translation, Burton questions, "What can be more important, in fact, than the study of principles upon which rest the happiness of man and woman, by reason of their mutual relations?" The work functions as a book of sexual etiquette and does not simply describe sexual positions. Rather, chapters contain instructions and illustrative stories that suggest ways of improving coition, dealing with praiseworthy men and women, dealing with men and women who are worthy of contempt, improving the act of generation, curing impotence, eliminating body odor, determining the sex of a fetus and dealing with deceitful spouses.

The work contains numerous Arabic words for male and female genitals, as well as definitions that are amusing and graphic but which avoid the clinical aspect of 20th-century sex manuals. Included are recipes to cure impotence ("a glassful of very thick honey, twenty almonds, and one hundred grains of the pine tree") and to effect abortion, although Burton points out that many of the latter could prove to be dangerous. The work also contains prescriptions for "increasing the dimensions of small members and for making them splendid." One such remedy consists in washing the member first in warm water, then rubbing it vigorously with a mixture containing pepper, lavender, galanga, and musk combined with honey and preserved ginger. Following is another remedy:

> wash the member in water until it becomes red, and enters into erection. Then take a piece of soft leather, upon which spread hot pitch, and envelop the member with it. It will not be long before the member raises its head, trembling with passion. The leather is to be left on until the pitch grows cold, and the member is again in a state of repose. This operation, several times repeated, will have the effect of making the member strong and thick.

CENSORSHIP HISTORY

Burton and his collaborators in the Kama Shastra Society anticipated attempts of censorship as they approached the publication of *The Perfumed Garden*. Their pretense was that the book was printed outside of England and that it was intended for scholars who wished to study "the great unknown literature of the East." Furthermore, by pricing the books at the equivalent in today's money of $200 each, the publishers also guaranteed that their readers had to be wealthy. The cover contained the words "For Private Circulation Only," and the place of publication was listed as Benares. Soon after the first copies appeared in 1886, pirated copies appeared in Paris, Brussels and the English Midlands.

The revised edition, which Burton called *The Scented Garden*, was nearly complete when he died, but his wife never approved of his preoccupation with erotic literature and had all of the notes to the revision destroyed within a fortnight of his death. Lady Isobel [*sic*] appointed William Coote, the secretary of the National Vigilance Association, as her husband's literary executor. Encouraged by the widow, Coote burned many of Burton's papers, including the complete translation of *The Perfumed Garden* from the original Arabic, with extensive notes and revisions, on which Burton had worked for 14 years.

The Perfumed Garden was not sold openly in England, but pirated copies did appear in the United States. After spending 60 days in jail in 1930 for distributing unexpurgated copies of ULYSSES, Samuel Roth turned to more profitable publications and produced editions of *The Perfumed Garden* and the KAMA SUTRA. Agents of the New York Society for the Suppression of Vice brought a complaint against Roth, who was prosecuted and sentenced to 90 days in jail for selling those books.

In 1930, a district attorney in Philadelphia authorized the raid of a bookshop and seizure of 300 books, among them *The Perfumed Garden*, FANNY HILL, LADY CHATTERLEY'S LOVER and *Lysistrata*. He announced that the raid marked the beginning of an extensive campaign to eliminate the sale of "obscene literature" in Philadelphia.

In 1933, Fortune Press in London was raided by police using the authority of Lord Campbell's Act, and among the works confiscated was a bowdlerized version of *The Perfumed Garden*. The case was heard in Westminster police court, where Magistrate Mr. A. Ronald Powell stated that it was not his role to consider whether a work was of literary or other merit and asserted that even "a classical author might lapse into obscenity." Ruling out expert evidence that would show the authors to be people of importance or classical authors in their own countries, the magistrate and the court showed the contempt of the law for a range of books, including historical and religious works as well as novels. Of the books seized, only *The Perfumed Garden* was recognized as conventionally pornographic.

FURTHER READING

Burton, Sir Richard, trans. "Introduction." In *The Perfumed Garden of Sheikh Nefzaoui*. New York: Lancer, 1964.

Craig, Alec. *Suppressed Books: A History of the Conception of Literary Obscenity*. New York: World Publishing, 1963.

Kilpatrick, James J. *The Smut Peddlers*. New York: Doubleday, 1960.

Rice, Edward. *Captain Sir Richard Francis Burton*. New York: Scribner's, 1990.

PEYTON PLACE

Author: Grace Metalious
Original date and place of publication: 1956, United States
Original publisher: Julian Messner
Type: Novel

SUMMARY

Peyton Place opens with some of the most provocative lines in literature: "Indian summer is like a woman. Ripe, hotly passionate, but fickle, she comes and goes as she pleases so that one is never sure whether she will come at all, nor for how long she will stay." The novel is devoid of blatantly sexual passages, except in one instance near the end, but the aura of illicit sexuality remains, as does the reminder that it is the book that "lifted the lid off a small New England town." At its most basic, *Peyton Place* is the melodramatic story of the greed, revenge, destructive pettiness and simmering sexuality that pervade many small towns. Neighbors spy on neighbors, people pry into each other's lives and townspeople try strenuously to hide their own faults and desires.

The story revolves around Allison MacKenzie, whose mother, Constance Standish, had left the town years before to make a career in New York City. Constance had returned with her infant daughter, fathered by a married man, and the story of having been married and widowed. Unaware of the circumstances of her birth, Allison dreams of similarly escaping from Peyton Place and its pettiness after high school graduation and becoming a writer in New York City. Selena Cross, the third main female character and a product of the poor neighborhood, is sexually victimized by her stepfather, but she becomes a strong and independent woman. The novel contains characters who engage in adultery and incest, and the women in the novel are among the first in popular fiction to seek sex rather than to act merely as pawns in sexual activity. Near the end of the novel, as Allison briefly becomes the lover of a married literary agent, she hesitates and states to him, "Then you think that sex between unmarried persons is excusable." Moments later, she is in his arms and "began to make moaning, animal sounds, and even then he continued his sensual touching and stroking and waited until she began the undulating movements of intercourse with her hips." She does not lose her virginity until 500 pages into the novel and seven pages before its end. Disappointed to learn that her lover is married, she returns to Peyton Place, no longer awed by its power over her.

CENSORSHIP HISTORY

Peyton Place created a sensation even before it was published; Allan Barnard, the editor at Dell Books, which bought the reprint rights in advance of publication, realized that publishing company head Frank Taylor might refuse to take a chance on the book so he told Taylor, "I have something I want to buy, but I don't want you to read it." Taylor agreed, but when he later asked about Barnard's earlier request, Barnard replied, "Because you wouldn't have let me buy it." The novel sold 3 million paperback copies in 1957, and more than 10 million paperback copies by 1967. Throughout years of enormous sales, the novel retained a notoriety that appeared to fuel sales.

In 1957, the city of Knoxville, Tennessee, activated a city ordinance that permitted the Knoxville City Board of Review to suppress any publication that it considered to be obscene. The target was *Peyton Place*; local dealers were forbidden to sell it. When one indignant newsstand owner tested the ordinance, it was ruled unconstitutional.

Peyton Place was banned in Ireland on May 6, 1958. A prohibition order was published in the *Iris Oifigiuil*, "the only official source from which booksellers [and readers] might learn of a new prohibition order," in which all articles blacklisted by the Irish Board of Censors were listed. According to the Censorship of Publications Bill of 1928, "the notice in *Iris Oifigiuil* should be sufficient evidence in the courts of summary jurisdiction as to the character of the publication," despite the acknowledgment by justices quoted in Adams's thorough study of Irish censorship laws that "this gazette is not a publication which booksellers are addicted to reading." The Irish Board of Censors found the work "obscene" and "indecent," objecting particularly to the author's handling of the characters' sexuality, acts of incest and "promiscuity." The work was officially banned from sale in Ireland until the introduction of the Censorship Publications Bill in 1967 reduced to 12 years the duration of a prohibition order, and the work was among 5,000 titles released from the list of banned books.

Also in 1958, a shipment containing copies of *Peyton Place* was confiscated by Canadian Customs officers and further copies of the book were refused entry. To determine if the novel was obscene, the Canadian Tariff Board held a hearing at which a professor of English and a former professor of history gave testimony on behalf of the book. Based on their testimony, the tariff board handed down a ruling that permitted the entry of *Peyton Place* into Canada. In its statement, the board observed that the statements of the witnesses give "a distinction between obscenity and realism in literature and an interpretation of modern fiction."

The novel was one of several paperback books considered objectionable for sale to youths under 18 in *State v. Settle*, 156 A.2d 921 (R.I. 1959). In 1959, the Rhode Island Commission to Encourage Morality in Youth brought action against Bantam and three other New York paperback publishers whose books were distributed throughout the state of Rhode Island by Max Silverstein & Sons. The commission notified Silverstein that the Bantam Books paperback editions of *Peyton Place* and *The Bramble Bush* were on their list of "objection-able" publications that they circulated to local police departments. Unwilling to risk court action, the distributor retrieved unsold copies of the books and returned them to the publishers, who appealed first to the Rhode Island Superior Court, which upheld the ban, then to the United States Supreme

Court, which reversed the decision. In rendering a decision, in *Bantam Books, Inc., et.al., v. Joseph A. Sullivan et al.*, Supreme Court Justice William J. Brennan stated that "informal censorship may sufficiently inhibit the circulation of publications to warrant injunctive relief . . . [but] criminal sanctions may only be applied after a determination of obscenity has been made in a criminal trial." Although the commission had no legal means of extracting compliance from Silverstein, their means of intimidation and the threats to institute criminal proceedings followed by police visits "plainly serve as instruments of regulation independent of the laws against obscenity." The Supreme Court reversed the lower court ruling.

FURTHER READING

Adams, Michael. *Censorship: The Irish Experience*. University: University of Alabama Press, 1968.

Beattie, A. M., and Frank A. Underhill. "Sense and Censorship: On Behalf of *Peyton Place*." *Canadian Library Association Bulletin* 15 (July 1958): 9–16.

Booth, Wayne C. "Censorship and the Values of Fiction." *English Journal* 53 (March 1964): 155–64.

Davis, Kenneth C. *Two-Bit Culture: The Paperbacking of America*. Boston: Houghton-Mifflin, 1984.

Ernst, Morris L., and Alan U. Schwartz. *Censorship: The Search for the Obscene*. New York: Macmillan, 1964.

Loth, David. *The Erotic in Literature*. New York: Dorset, 1961.

Pearce, Lillian. "Book Selection and Peyton Place." *Library Journal* 83 (March 1958): 712–13.

THE PHILANDERER

Author: Stanley Kauffmann
Original date and place of publication: 1952, United States; 1953, England
Original publisher: Simon & Schuster (United States); Secker & Warburg Ltd. (England)
Type: Novel

SUMMARY

The Philanderer was first published in the United States in 1952 under the title *The Tightrope*, and reviewers immediately compared it to James Joyce's *Portrait of the Artist as a Young Man* for its ability to excite the reader's feelings. In particular, although some critics lauded the author's ability to relate details that provided a realistic view of the protagonist, others such as the *New York Times* reviewer Richard Sullivan observed that "the effect of this kind of detail upon the reader gives rise to a pertinent question, that of simple propriety."

The novel provides a tawdry and maudlin view of life in which a 33-year-old man attempts to eliminate the desolation from his life by engaging in selfish and meaningless sexual affairs. The work provides an account of this man's extramarital affairs, as well as his thoughts regarding his wife and children and his unfathomable need to take revenge on the world. To avenge himself for wrongs that he never identifies, the main character decides to have an affair with every attractive woman whom he meets, viewing them as "the janes, the jazzy, jazzy janes" whose existence offers him a challenge. He is anxious, at first, in his mission of seduction, but he finds that the women whom he pursues offer little resistance. Seducing the wife of his boss almost costs the philanderer his job, but he manages to escape discovery and to continue with his seductions until he finds that no amount of illicit sex can fill the emptiness that he feels.

CENSORSHIP HISTORY

The Philanderer received strong reviews by critics who approvingly noted that it condemned the behavior that it portrayed. Walter Allen, writing in the April 25, 1953, issue of the *New Statesman*, observed that the novel provided "as devastating a criticism as any I've read of the consequences of the tradition of American adolescent competition in sexual experience that we have already had described for us by Dr. Margaret Mead and Mr. Gorer." Still, legal authorities on the Isle of Man had already condemned the novel after police received a complaint that a person could obtain the book at Boots' Library. The high bailiff had felt bound by existing law, however outmoded, to act in some manner, but he deprecatingly imposed a one-pound fine on the work and created for the novel a criminal record.

The trial of *The Philanderer* in London in 1954 was influential in changing the obscenity law in England, a move motivated largely by the summation of Mr. Justice Stable, who presided over the trial in the Queen's Bench Division in the Old Bailey. Defendants in the case were Secker & Warburg Ltd., the publisher, and Frederic Warburg, a director of the firm. The author was not in court.

Justice Stable opened the trial by telling the jury to take the novel home and "Read it as a *book*. Don't pick out the highlights. Read it through as a whole. And then we'll all come back here on Friday and proceed with the case." Before the court adjourned, both counsels gave opening arguments. The prosecutor, Mervyn Griffths-Jones, told the jury he expected that after reading the book they would say it had the "tendency to deprave and to corrupt those whose minds were open to such immoral influences and into whose hands it might fall." Rodger Winn, defense counsel, stated that such thinking was 150 years old and that the problem was to determine "whether the impact of certain passages on a Victorian mind would be the same as on a modern mind." The judge added that in 1909, when he was 21 years old, his parents had discussed seriously whether or not his mother could possibly attend a performance of

George Bernard Shaw's play *Pygmalion*. "When the lady in the play said 'Not bloody likely' it was the biggest social shock I can remember. If I had used that word when I was twenty-one, I would have been ordered out of any respectable house in England." By 1954, he added, that taboo was gone.

When the jury returned and the case resumed, no expert witnesses were called by either side. The judge's summation to the jury, strongly sympathetic to the defendants, ended with the caution to the jury that if criminal law were to be driven too far in the desire to stamp out the "bawdy muck," there existed the risk of a revolt, "a demand for a change in the law, so that the pendulum may swing too far the other way and allow to creep in things that at the moment we can keep out." The jury delivered the expected verdict of not guilty, and the defendants were discharged without court costs. Justice Stable's decision was not binding on future cases because it was not a court of appeals judgment, and Customs and postal authorities continued to seize books in transit while other magistrates prosecuted other publishers, but this case set the stage for change in English obscenity laws.

FURTHER READING

Kauffmann, Stanley. *The Philanderer*. 2d ed. London: Secker & Warburg, 1954.
Mackay, R. S. "Hidden Rule and Judicial Censorship." *Canadian Bar Review* 361 (March 1958): 1–24.
Rolph, Cecil Hewitt. *Books in the Dock*. London: Deutsch, 1969.
The Test of Obscenity. *Author* 65 (Autumn 1954): 1–5.
Warburg, Frederic. "A View of Obscenity." *New Yorker* 33 (April 20, 1957): 106–33.

POEMS AND BALLADS

Author: Algernon Charles Swinburne
Original date and place of publication: 1866, England
Original publisher: Moxon
Type: Collection of poetry

SUMMARY

Poems and Ballads shocked Victorian sensibilities with its sadomasochistic eroticism that is repeated throughout such poems as "Anactoria," "Laus Veneria," "Dolores," "Faustine" and "Feline." The language does not evoke the pleasures of sexuality as much as it emphasizes the pains of sexual love with its "violent delights" that "have violent ends." Although Swinburne sought deliberately to shock Victorian readers, his equally important goal was to accomplish what he saw accomplished in THE FLOWERS OF EVIL by Charles Baudelaire, who portrayed normally ugly objects and images as sources of beauty and desire and who represented the immoral as the moral.

Swinburne succeeded in creating images that had never before quite been heard in English poetry. The following lines appear in "Anactoria":

My life is bitter with thy love; thine eyes
Blind me, thy tresses burn me, thy sharp sighs
Divide my flesh and spirit with soft sound,
And my blood strengthens, and my veins abound.

Sexual passion is not portrayed in Swinburne's poems as sensuous and pleasurable; rather, bodies "crush" together and "bruise" each other:

I feel my blood against my blood: my pain
Pains thee, and lips bruise lips, and vein stings vein,
Let fruit be crushed on fruit, let flower on flower,
Breast kindle breast, and either burn one hour.

CENSORSHIP HISTORY

Soon after publication of *Poems and Ballads*, in 1866, rumors arose that the *Times* was going to publish a review of the work by Eneas Sweetland Dallas and include a demand that the publisher be prosecuted. Moxon, the publisher, became frightened and withdrew the book from sale without consulting Swinburne. Copies that remained on the market commanded prices of upwards of five guineas (nearly $12 in current value). An unexpurgated version of the book was then published by John Camden Hotten, an English publisher of mainly flagellent pornography. Although reviewers and public opinion widely attacked the book, no legal action was brought. Public opinion did, however, influence Mudie's Library to withdraw the book from its shelves, thus removing a major source of sales for the publisher.

In August 1866, Swinburne wrote to Charles Augustus Howell, "I got an anonymous note today threatening to 'cut off my stones' within six weeks if my poems are not withdrawn."

FURTHER READING

Greenberg, Robert A. "'Anactoria,' and the Sapphic Passion." *Victorian Poetry* 29 (Spring 1991): 79–87.

Mordell, Albert, ed. *Notorious Literary Attacks.* New York: Boni & Liveright, 1926.

Swinburne, Algernon Charles. *Letters of Algernon Charles Swinburne.* Vol. 1. Ed. by C. Y. Lang, 173–74. New Haven, Conn.: Yale University Press, 1959.

Thomas, Donald. *A Long Time Burning: The History of Literary Censorship in England.* New York: Praeger, 1969.

Wagner-Lawlor, Jennifer. "Metaphorical 'Indiscretion' and Literary Survival in Swinburne's 'Anactoria.'" *Studies in English Literature, 1500–1900* 36 (Autumn 1996): 917–34.

POINT COUNTER POINT

Author: Aldous Huxley
Original date and place of publication: 1928, United States
Original publisher: Harper & Row
Type: Novel

SUMMARY

Point Counter Point presents a satiric portrayal of the members of English society and of the London intellectual set in the 1920s. The novel is dated by the frequent references to contemporary British politics, but numerous allusions are also made to literature, painting, music and scientific information of the time. Elaborately constructed, the novel is supposedly based on Bach's Suite No. 2 in B Minor in the intricacy of its interrelationships. Philip Quarles, a major character in the novel, is writing a novel, thus creating a novel-within-the-novel structure that creates echoes or "counterpoints" between the two. Further complicating *Point Counter Point* is Huxley's admission that he patterned his characters after real literary figures. Thus, Mark and Mary Rampion are idealized portrayals of D. H. and Frieda Lawrence; the diabolical, sexually depraved Spandrell is based on Charles Baudelaire; and Everard Webley, assassinated by Spandrell, is based on Sir Oswald Mosley, leader of the British Fascist movement. J. Middleton Murry and Katherine Mansfield are portrayed in the characters Denis Burlap and Beatrice Gilray. Quarles is Huxley.

For the most part, the long and complicated novel with its numerous characters concerns the broken marriages, adulterous affairs and other interactions of this group. Their behavior is irreverent in regard to traditional social behavior, and their sexual proclivities are tolerated more within the group than they would be by the greater society.

CENSORSHIP HISTORY

Point Counter Point was one of numerous novels that were banned in Boston due to the efforts of the Watch and Ward Society. In 1928, the society placed the novel on its list of "unacceptable" books, then circulated the list to Boston booksellers, suggesting that it was in their best interests not to display advertising for the books nor to sell the books that appeared on their list. Booksellers adhered to this "gentleman's agreement" and effectively, if unofficially, sales of the novel were banned in Boston.

In 1930, librarian Margery Quigley withdrew *Point Counter Point* from the Montclair (New Jersey) Public Library because she felt that, given its apparent approval of extramarital sex, "she had no moral right to distribute it from the library." She returned the novel to the shelves a few days later when a group of her most conservative clubwomen assigned it as a book for discussion.

Point Counter Point was banned in Ireland on May 13, 1930, for containing "immoral matter." A prohibition order was published in the *Iris Oifigiuil*, "the only official source from which booksellers [and readers] might learn of a new prohibition order," in which all articles blacklisted by the Irish Board of Censors were listed. According to the Censorship of Publications Bill of 1928, "the notice in *Iris Oifigiuil* should be sufficient evidence in the courts of summary jurisdiction as to the character of the publication," despite the acknowledgment by justices quoted in Adams's thorough study of Irish censorship laws that "this gazette is not a publication which booksellers are addicted to reading." The Irish Board of Censors found the novel to be "obscene" and "indecent." The ban against *Point Counter Point* was not revoked until 1970.

FURTHER READING

Adams, Michael. *Censorship: The Irish Experience.* University: University of Alabama Press, 1968.

Lewis, Felice Flanery. *Literature, Obscenity and the Law.* Carbondale: Southern Illinois University, 1976.

Quigley, Margery. "Books in Suburbia—The Suburban Library's Book-Buying Problems." *Library Journal* 55 (April 1, 1930): 303.

RABBIT, RUN

Author: John Updike
Original date and place of publication: 1960, United States
Original publisher: Alfred A. Knopf
Type: Novel

SUMMARY

Rabbit, Run relates the story of onetime high school basketball star Harry "Rabbit" Angstrom, 26, who impulsively deserts his pregnant wife. The novel is set in the small town of Mt. Judge, a "suburb of the city of Brewer, fifth largest city in Pennsylvania," in the spring of 1959. Rabbit feels trapped in his life as a lower-middle-class family man who now demonstrates "a penny's worth of tin called a friggin' MagiPeeler in five-and-dime stores." His wife, Janice, pregnant with their second child, spends her days in an alcoholic stupor, watching television. Despite his contempt for her, Rabbit sometimes finds wisdom in the "Mickey Mouse Club," especially in the daily advice offered by head Mouseketeer, Jimmy.

Little in Rabbit's life is what it appears to be. The fame and success of his high school basketball career have left him with an idealized view of those years that extends to his old coach, Marty Tothero, now unemployed and living in a tenement. As Rabbit tries to recapture some of the order and certainty of his earlier life, he realizes that Tothero is only a broken old man with a penchant for being beaten by his stern lover, Margaret, who refers to him as "an old bloated bastard." The young minister, Jack Eccles, sent to find Rabbit and return with him to Janice and her family, is ineffective. Unable to make Rabbit return, Eccles suggests that they play golf sometime. When Rabbit arrives at the Eccles' house and finds the minister's young wife in tight orange shorts, he cannot resist slapping "her sassy ass," then ruminating on its firmness. When Rabbit eats in a Chinese restaurant, the waiters speak in heavily accented English as they take his order but speak in perfect English once he leaves.

Throughout the novel, Rabbit remains constantly aware of his sexuality. When he first runs off, he thinks of finding "hard-bodied laughers" in West Virginia and remembers the "young whores in Texas," whom he frequented when in the army. Through Tothero, Rabbit meets Ruth, a warmhearted, voluptuous prostitute into whose apartment he moves. He rhapsodizes about her body and their sexual relationship in specific detail at various points in the novel.

When Janice goes into labor, Rabbit moves home, but he moves out again when Janice rejects his sexual advances as signs of "his whore's filthiness." She accidentally drowns their baby while drunk. The day of his baby's funeral, Rabbit sees "two teenage girls in snug shorts" and is unable to resist ogling "their perky butts and expectant sex." After the funeral, Rabbit returns to Ruth, pregnant with his child, but she refuses to resume their relationship unless he chooses between his wife and her. The novel ends with the panicked Rabbit running blindly down the street.

CENSORSHIP HISTORY

Rabbit, Run was banned in Ireland on February 20, 1962. A prohibition order was published in the *Iris Oifigiuil*, "the only official source from which book-sellers [and readers] might learn of a new prohibition order," in which all articles blacklisted by the Irish Board of Censors were listed. According to the Censorship of Publications Bill of 1928, "the notice in *Iris Oifigiuil* should be sufficient evidence in the courts of summary jurisdiction as to the character of the publication," despite the acknowledgment by justices quoted in Adams's thorough study of Irish censorship laws that "this gazette is not a publication which booksellers are addicted to reading." The Irish Board of Censors found the work "obscene" and "indecent," objecting particularly to the author's handling of the characters' sexuality, the "explicit sex acts" and "promiscuity." The work was officially banned from sale in Ireland until the introduction of the revised Censorship Publications Bill in 1967.

In 1976, parents of students in six community high schools in Aroostock County, Maine, challenged the inclusion of *Rabbit, Run* in the high school libraries because of its references to sex and to an extramarital affair. Parents cited as one of several objectionable scenes Rabbit's first sexual encounter with

Ruth, in which Updike first describes Rabbit caressing her breasts, then provides a detailed description of them having sex:

> He kneels in a kind of sickness between her spread legs. With her help their blind loins fit. . . . she reaches her hand down and touches their mixed fur and her breathing snags on something sharp. Her thighs throw open wide and clamp his sides and throw open again so wide it frightens him. . . . His sea of seed buckles, and sobs into a still channel. At each shudder her mouth smiles in his and her legs, locked at his back, bear down.

They also raised objections to Rabbit's constant fantasizing about sexual experiences with most of the women he meets and the language in which he expresses such desires. His two-month affair with Ruth, after he leaves Janice for the first time, motivated further objections because the book "seems to make his wife at fault for the affair."

The county school board established a review committee to consider the complaints and recommended that the book be retained. In making the final decision on the book, the school board voted 8 to 6 against banning the book from the libraries but determined that some restriction was required. In a vote of 7 to 6, with one abstention, the board decided that the novel should be placed on the reserved shelf in each of the six county high school libraries and only charged out to students who brought signed permission slips from their parents.

In 1986, the novel was removed from the required reading list for the high school English classes at Medicine Bow, Wyoming, because of the sexual descriptions and profanity in the book. In their complaint to the school board, parents cited Rabbit's cursing, including "shit," "bastard" and "son of a bitch," and Tothero's use of the word "cunt." They also identified the sexually explicit passages between Ruth and Rabbit and his "sexually explicit fantasies."

FURTHER READING

Adams, Michael. *Censorship: The Irish Experience.* University: University of Alabama Press, 1968.

Galloway, David D. *The Absurd Hero in American Fiction*: 21-50. Rev. ed. Austin: University of Texas Press, 1970.

Hunt, George W. *John Updike and the Three Great Secret Things: Sex, Religion, and Art.* Grand Rapids, Mich.: Eerdmans, 1980.

Markle, Joyce. *Fighters and Lovers: Theme in the Novels of John Updike.* New York: New York University Press, 1973.

Newsletter on Intellectual Freedom (March 1977): 36; (March 1987): 55.

Updike, John. "The Plight of the American Writer." *Change* 9 (April 1978): 36–41.

Wright, Derek. "Mapless Motion: Form and Space in Updike's *Rabbit, Run.*" *Modern Fiction Studies* 37 (Spring 1991): 35–44.

THE RAINBOW

Author: D. H. Lawrence
Original date and place of publication: 1915, England; 1915, United States
Original publisher: Methuen and Company (England); B. W. Huebsch (United States)
Type: Novel

SUMMARY

The Rainbow spans three generations of the Brangwen family, moving from the beginning of the English industrial revolution in 1840 through the first decade of the 20th century. Lawrence shows the destruction of the traditional way of life and the ways in which the Brangwen family must accommodate themselves to their changing lives. The early Brangwens farm the land and live in harmony with their surroundings, but the second generation of Brangwens move into the industrial town of Beldover, where the seasonal cycle is replaced by a manmade calendar. Will and Anna no longer participate in the rhythms of nature, and their relationship suffers. They fall into a fixed domestic routine, and Anna begins to live through her children.

Ursula, daughter of Will and Anna, represents the modern woman, becoming the first Brangwen female to support herself and to enter a profession. She also rejects the traditional expectations of her family, such as religion, marriage and love, becoming involved in unsatisfying relationships with fellow teacher Winifred Inger and shallow aristocrat Anton Skrebensky. She becomes pregnant by Skrebensky but takes ill with pneumonia and miscarries. The novel ends on a hopeful note as Ursula awakens one morning and sees a rainbow, "as if a new day had come on the earth."

CENSORSHIP HISTORY

The Rainbow contains several passages that have aroused challenges. Lawrence believed that the passage in the book that prosecutors found most offensive was likely one in which the pregnant Anna dances naked in her bedroom:

> She would not have had any one know. She danced in secret, and her soul rose in bliss. She danced in secret before the Creator, she took off her clothes and danced in the pride of her bigness. . . . She stood with the firelight on her ankles and feet, naked in the shadowy, late afternoon, fastening up her hair.

Other passages that generated numerous complaints by editors at Methuen were scenes that were characterized in editorial notes as "lesbian" incidents. In one beach scene, Winifred suggests that she carry Ursula into the water, and in another the two are caught in the rain and "after a while the rain came down on their flushed, hot limbs, startling, delicious." B.W. Huebsch, the publisher of the first American edition of *The Rainbow*, deleted these two passages and a third that had "generated the most complaints" from reviewers about the Methuen edition:

> Ursula lay still in her mistress's arms, her forehead against the beloved, maddening breast.
> "I shall put you in," said Winifred.
> —But Ursula twined her body about her mistress.

The Rainbow was censored by Lawrence before publication after editors at Methuen and Company sent the manuscript back to the author's agent, J. B. Pinker, "for alteration." Lawrence made cuts, but the altered manuscript was still unacceptable, and the editor again returned the work with portions marked for cutting. Lawrence refused to make further cuts, writing in a letter to Pinker, "I have cut out as I said I would, all the *phrases* objected to. The passages and paragraphs marked I cannot alter." The publisher recognized that the 13 passages the author refused to cut were likely to cause trouble. As soon as the novel was published, book reviewers alerted circulating libraries and legal authorities, calling it "an orgy of sexiness," "windy, tedious, boring and nauseating" and "a monstrous wilderness of phallicism."

The novel was condemned in 1915 after a private citizen complained to the London police. They, in turn, acquired a copy of the novel and took it to Sir John Dickinson, a Bow Street magistrate who issued a warrant under the Obscene Publications Act of 1857. The warrant called for the seizure of the 1,000 copies of the novel found on the publisher's premises. Dickinson also issued a summons that was served on Methuen, requiring that the publisher "show cause why the said books should not be destroyed." The police solicitor charged that the obscenity was so extensively distributed throughout the book that "I am at a loss, Sir, to understand how Messrs. Methuen came to lend their name to its publication."

Methuen claimed that they had asked Lawrence twice to modify the language of the manuscript but he had refused, so they published as it stood. A destruction order was granted by the court under Lord Campbell's Act of 1857 to legal authorities without prosecution "or, therefore, any chance of its adequate defence." Thus, the police action against *The Rainbow* was not a criminal proceeding that would result in a jail term. The benefit to such a proceeding for the legitimate publisher was that it carried no risk of being stigmatized by the government nor did the publisher face fines or imprisonment.

The magistrate ordered all 1,000 copies to be destroyed and chided the publisher that he was sorry "that a firm of such high repute should have allowed their reputation to be soiled as it has been by the publication of this work." As publisher Algernon Methuen stated, "The [Scotland Yard] solicitors, in consideration of the reputation of our firm, kindly suggested that we might prefer to hand over the books rather than submit to actual search, and this we did." Aside from the loss of book stock, the publisher paid costs that amounted to 10 guineas, about $30 in contemporary currency. Methuen then requested that Lawrence return the advance they had paid him for the work, but he refused and they dropped their request. The novel was not available in an unexpurgated edition again until 1949, when Penguin Books published an edition.

In the United States, B. W. Huebsch published the novel in 1915, using the corrected proofs from Methuen and deleting the 13 "offensive" passages without obtaining permission from the author for the expurgations.

FURTHER READING

Ben-Ephraim, Gavriel. *The Moon's Dominion: Narrative Dichotomy and Female Dominance in Lawrence's Earlier Novels*. Rutherford, N.J.: Fairleigh Dickinson University Press, 1989.

DeGrazia, Edward. *Girls Lean Back Everywhere: The Law of Obscenity and the Assault on Genius*. New York: Random House, 1992.

Doherty, Gerald. "The Art of Appropriation: The Rhetoric of Sexuality in D. H. Lawrence." *Style* 30 (Summer 1996): 289–308.

Geller, Evelyn. *Forbidden Books in American Public Libraries, 1876–1939: A Study in Cultural Change*. Westport, Conn.: Greenwood, 1984.

Lawrence, D. H. *The Quest for Rananim: D. H. Lawrence's Letters to S. S. Koteliansky, 1914–1930*. Ed. and intro. by George J. Zytaruk. Montreal: McGill-Queen's University Press, 1970.

Rolph, Cecil Hewitt. *Books in the Dock*. London: Deutsch, 1961.

REPLENISHING JESSICA

Author: Max Bodenheim
Original date and place of publication: 1925, United States
Original publisher: Horace Liveright
Type: Novel

SUMMARY

Replenishing Jessica contributed to the reputation of the author as a libertine, yet the publisher and author both asserted that it was an essentially moral book. Although the main character displays erotic rebellion as her weapon against society, Bodenheim shows that she is essentially corrupted by her behavior and her life is shown to decline in a distasteful manner. Although she attempts to separate her sex life from the rest of her existence, Jessica's sexual adventures with more than a dozen men on two continents, and from all social levels, eventually harden and degrade her.

Although the very wealthy Jessica is worth $4 million, the novel does not make money the reason for her intense promiscuity. After a sexually adventurous existence, she marries Ted Purrel, an aggressive upstart who combines an acquisitive mentality with brutal sexuality. He earns a substantial salary, but he views Jessica as a property, an object whose acquisition will make him the envy of others. Although she is not in love with Purrel, she "finally agreed to marry Purrel because he had become much less aggressive and blatant, and because she had determined to narrow most of her life to sexual pleasures."

Soon after, they both take up love affairs, but Purrel desires that Jessica remain faithful to him while he does as he pleases. One evening, returning after they have been separated for a while, Purrel beats Jessica so that her face becomes bruised and discolored. After the bruises heal, she sells her house, arranges a divorce, then spends two years running around with a variety of men, one of whom introduces her to heroin use. When that man dies of an overdose and another whom she dates commits suicide, Jessica reevaluates her life and decides to become useful to society. She works with a children's group at a settlement house and, while on a trip to the art museum with them, meets a "tall, bony, crippled man" whose left side of the torso is paralyzed, left arm is doubled up and left hand droops in a twisted fashion "while his left leg was a little shorter than his right." She becomes close to him and eventually asks him to marry her, for he is the only man who can replenish her emotionally.

CENSORSHIP HISTORY

Early in the 1920s, publisher Horace Liveright had paid the author $1,000 for a still-unwritten novel. When the novel was delivered, Liveright found it to be "filthy," despite his own permissive standards. After bitter discussions with Bodenheim, the publisher and author reached an agreement to rewrite portions of the book, a task that fell to editor T. R. Smith. After the most glaringly offensive passages were modified or removed, the book was published in 1925 as *Replenishing Jessica*. Liveright's expurgation did not go far enough, and the New York Society for the Suppression of Vice, led by John Sumner, obtained a grand jury obscenity indictment against Liveright for the book. The publisher retained as defense attorney Arthur Garfield Hays, who proclaimed the novel to be a "highly moral" work, written by "a great author and poet."

When the case was heard in general sessions court in March 1928, the judge ordered the entire 272 "smoldering pages" of the book read to the jury. Newspapers reported that jurors slept through the supposedly "juicy passages." Mayor Jimmy Walker commented, "No girl has ever been seduced by reading a book." Despite Sumner's presentation of damaging testimony regarding Liveright's earlier private opinion of the book, the jury took only 15 minutes to return a verdict of not guilty and to acquit Liveright. Despite the victory, Bodenheim was upset by the trial because he had wanted to testify. Instead, the defense thought it wiser that he leave town during the trial rather than risk his possibly disruptive testimony.

FURTHER READING

Boyer, Paul S. *Purity in Print: The Vice-Society Movement and Book Censorship in America.* New York: Scribner's, 1968.
Gilmer, Frank Walker. *Horace Liveright: Publisher of the Twenties.* New York: Lewis, 1970.
Moore, Jack B. *Maxwell Bodenheim.* New York: Twayne, 1970.

SANCTUARY

Author: William Faulkner
Original date and place of publication: 1931, United States
Original publisher: Cape & Smith
Type: Novel

SUMMARY

In brief, *Sanctuary* tells the story of sexually provocative 17-year-old Temple Drake, a socially prominent judge's daughter and college student, who accidentally becomes a witness to murder, then falls victim to a sadistic rape. Taken to the isolated house of ex-convict Lee Goodwin and his common-law wife, Ruby, one evening by her date, Gowan Stevens, after the two have had too much to drink, Stevens wants to buy bootlegged liquor. While there, he remains drunk for three days. When he finally sobers up and realizes that he is outnumbered he runs off and leaves Temple. Temple is sexually harassed, then raped with a corncob by an impotent bootlegger named Popeye, who also kills Tommy, a mentally retarded gang member who witnessed the act. Afterward, Popeye confines Temple in a Memphis brothel, where she is forced to engage in sexual acts with a stranger named Red while Popeye watches. When Temple begins to enjoy her involvement with Red, Popeye shoots him, then disappears.

Temple is located at the brothel by the lawyer assigned to defend Goodwin on the charge of murdering Tommy, but she falsely identifies him as the killer to protect her reputation. Both she and her prominent father want to hide her sexual involvement with Red and her experiences at the brothel, so they guarantee that her testimony and the trial will be over quickly by implicating Goodwin. Without remorse, Temple is escorted from the courtroom after testifying and leaves for vacation in Luxembourg. The innocent Goodwin is burned to death by a lynch mob.

Despite the persistent sexual undercurrent of much of the novel, none of the sexual acts is described in detail. Even the rape by corncob is referred to and only Temple's bleeding afterward is described. Throughout, anatomical references are limited to the thighs or the loins. The erotic passages emerge in images of Temple's appearance, with her short dress that reveals "fleet revelations of flank and thigh," and the voyeurism in the brothel. Popeye's advances are detailed: "Then it touched me, that nasty little cold hand, fiddling around inside the coat where I was naked. . . . his hand was going inside the top of my knickers." Later in the novel, after becoming eroticized by Red, Temple sits "in a floating swoon of agonized sorrow and erotic longing, thinking of Red's body," then begs him to have sex with her: "Please. Please Please. Don't make me wait. I'm burning up." The novel was unusual for its time in its topics of rape and voyeurism as well as for the brothel setting, in which a major part of the action takes place.

CENSORSHIP HISTORY

William Faulkner's sixth novel, *Sanctuary*, gained notoriety as much for its erotic passages and inclusion of rape, voyeurism and prostitution as for the author's claim in his introduction to the 1932 Modern Library edition that he had written about these topics for financial rather than artistic reasons.

In 1948, *Sanctuary* was one of nine novels identified as obscene in criminal proceedings in the Court of Quarter sessions in Philadelphia County, Pennsylvania. (See GOD'S LITTLE ACRE for a complete discussion of the case.) Indictments were brought by the state district attorney, John H. Maurer, against five booksellers who were charged with possessing and intending to sell the books. The other allegedly obscene novels were Harold Robbins's *Never Love a Stranger*, James Farrell's STUDS LONIGAN TRILOGY (*Young Lonigan*, *The Young Manhood of Studs Lonigan* and *Judgment Day*), Farrell's *A World I Never Made*, Erskine Caldwell's GOD'S LITTLE ACRE, Calder Willingham's *End as a Man* and Faulkner's *WILD PALMS*.

In his March 18, 1949, decision in *Commonwealth v. Gordon*, 66 D. & C. 101 (1949) that *Sanctuary* is not obscene, Judge Curtis Bok stated: "There are no vulgar Saxon words in the book, but the situations are stark and unrelieved. It makes one shudder to think of what can happen by misadventure." Bok refused to declare *Sanctuary* "obscene" because the definition in cases that he cited in his decision restricted the meaning of the term "to that of sexual impurity, and with those cases that have made erotic allurement the test of its effect." The work also failed to meet Bok's definition of sexual impurity in literature, which he defined "as any writing whose dominant purpose and effect is erotic allurement—that is to say, a calculated and effective incitement to sexual desire."

Faulkner was awarded the Nobel Prize for literature in 1950. Although *Sanctuary* did not go to court again, by 1954, it was again condemned as obscene by numerous local censorship groups throughout the United States, and the National Organization for Decent Literature placed it on the disapproved list. Also in 1954, Ireland banned *Sanctuary*, along with most of the author's other works, because of the language such as "son of a bitch," "whore," "slut" and "bastard" combined with the brutal violence of the story. Irish and U.S.

censors also objected to the character Ruby, who prostituted herself to obtain money to free her common-law husband from jail, to obtain legal fees and to pay their expenses. Changes in society have removed most objections to the book, although scattered local censorship continues throughout the United States.

FURTHER READING

Gladstein, Mimi. *The Indestructible Woman in Faulkner, Hemingway, and Steinbeck*. Ann Arbor, Mich.: UMI Research Press, 1986.

Heller, Terry. "Mirrored Worlds and the Gothic in Faulkner's *Sanctuary*." *Mississippi Quarterly* 42 (Summer 1989): 247–59.

Loe, Mary Hong. "Case Studies in Censorship: William Faulkner's *Sanctuary*." *Reference Services Review* 23 (Spring 1995): 71–84.

Page, Sally R. *Faulkner's Women: Characterization and Meaning*. De Land, Fla.: Everett/Edwards, 1972.

Tanner, Laura E. "Reading Rape: *Sanctuary* and the Women of *Brewster Place*." *American Literature* 62 (December 1990): 559–82.

Williams, David. *Faulkner's Women: The Myth and the Muse*. Montreal: McGill-Queen's University Press, 1977.

Wilson, Andrew J. "The Corruption in Looking: William Faulkner's *Sanctuary* as a Detective Novel." *Mississippi Quarterly* 47 (Summer 1994): 441–60.

THE SATYRICON

Author: Gaius Petronius Arbiter
Original date and place of publication: c. A.D. 60, Rome; 1918, United States
Original publisher: Privately published (Rome); Boni & Liveright (United States)
Type: Satire

SUMMARY

The original version of *The Satyricon* consisted of prose interspersed with verse, but no complete text of the work remains, nor are historians certain by whom the work was actually written. Instead, because the text contains clues that it was written in the first century A.D., researchers have ascribed it to a member of the emperor Nero's court, Petronius, who lost favor with the emperor and was driven to suicide. Over centuries, anonymous forgers have pieced together the remaining fragments to present an irreverent and frequently racy account of the picaresque adventures of two witty and erudite rogues, Encolpius and Ascyltos, who wander with their young male companion, Giton, on the fringes of society and survive through petty thievery and trickery. The themes of the work champion the enjoyment of life at any cost and ridicule the fickleness of men and women and the absurdity of pretentiousness. Exaggerated, humorous and ironic in their behavior, the characters avoid as far as possible contact with the usual social virtues of honesty, integrity, discretion and dependability, preferring to indulge in a range of libidinal adventures, both heterosexual and homosexual.

The narrator, Encolpius, is sexually involved with the young boy, Giton, and the two engage in numerous other sexual encounters with both men and women. Their relationship forms the chief motif of the work, as Ascyltos and others try to lure Giton away from Encolpius. The sex acts are briefly mentioned, more often suggestive rather than explicit, but licentiousness does punctuate the narrative. In the one extended sensual scene, the work depicts an orgy in the court of the priestess, Quartilla, during which a catamite (a boy used in pederasty) is led in who, "One minute . . . nearly gored us to death with his writhing, and the next, he befouled us . . . with his stinking kisses."

In another scene, Giton is placed in a room with a seven-year-old girl and the two are encouraged to engage in sexual exploration while Encolpius watches through a keyhole. In another extended scene, the trio are guests of the coarse and crude Trimalchio, modeled on Nero, who makes rude noises and speaks repeatedly of the "evacuation" of the body. The end of the work places Encolpius at home, criticized by servants and acquaintances for seeming to be sedentary and showing no sense of enterprise.

CENSORSHIP HISTORY

In 1921, John Sumner and the New York Society for the Suppression of Vice went to court against publishers Boni & Liveright for publishing *The Satyricon*. Their edition contained two volumes, sold for $20 and was limited to 1,200 sets. The case was dismissed by Magistrate Charles A. Oberwager in Magistrate's Court on September 27, 1922, in a decision that contained extensive quoting from the works of literary authorities, encyclopedias and higher-court decisions. Oberwager established that, despite lewd passages, *The Satyricon* was a recognized classic and a significant historical document, and he pointed out that the obscenity statute was not meant "to anathematize all historical manners and morals different from our own, or to close the treasure house of the past." He also sharply reprimanded the society and warned that "no individual or private organization should be permitted to exercise general powers of censorship over literary works."

On October 1922, the New York district attorney reopened the case at the insistence of Sumner, who asserted in testimony that "the *Decameron* was a Sunday School book beside *Satyricon*. It is so bad that if it can be published, there is nothing which can be prevented." Chief City Magistrate William G. McAdoo, who was assigned the case, refused to take it. Instead, he warned Sumner that such attacks on "inert publications, which are . . . at once historic, classical, and erotogenic" were eroding the influence of both Sumner and the society. Unwilling to accept defeat, Sumner sought a grand jury indictment of the publisher with the help of District Attorney Joab A. Banton. The jurors, faced with having to read the entire two-volume *Satyricon*, quickly turned down the request for an indictment. As a result, *The Satyricon* was never banned, but printers remained cautious for many decades. To evade censors, those who reprinted the work usually set the potentially objectionable passages of the book in Latin. In 1927, Liveright published a one-volume, highly expurgated edition of the work that contained little to which even the vice society could object.

FURTHER READING

Boyer, Paul S. *Purity in Print: The Vice-Society Movement and Book Censorship in America.* New York: Scribner's, 1968.
"Judge as Literary Critic." *Catholic World* 116 (December 1922): 392–99.
Schmeling, Gareth. "*The Satyricon*: Forms in Search of a Genre." *Classical Bulletin* 47 (1970): 49–53.

SEPTEMBER IN QUINZE

Author: Vivian Connell
Original date and place of publication: 1952, United States; 1954 (England)
Original publisher: The Dial Press (United States); Hutchinson Publishing, England
Type: Novel

SUMMARY

September in Quinze was written at the Gallia Palace Hotel at Cannes, and the author expresses his appreciation to the director and concierge in a note preceding the story. The title is a pun on the name Cannes (Quinze). The novel relates the love affairs and tragedies of a collection of disaffected individuals, including a Russian countess married to an opium addict and a Middle Eastern potentate who has settled in Quinze and dedicated himself to the pursuit of self-indulgence. Although aristocrats proliferate, the main focus is on Pietro Salvadori, a young Italian man who lost his family when Americans bombed his village during World War II. He serves as an insightful observer of the emptiness of others' lives.

Quinze is a city of lonely decadence, where "the whores sat at the bar" in the casino in which millions of francs are lost in single bets. King Sadook, ruler of an unnamed Middle Eastern nation, brags, "I've had a couple of hundred of women in bed," but feels "hungry in his loins" for "a woman with hair under her arms and sweat on her belly." Heloise, the cool and elegant Countess Saignor, attracts admiring glances, but she is dead inside and can feel no passion. Her opium-addicted husband Raymond, who has passed off the poetry of Baudelaire as his own, haunts her, and they both eventually commit suicide. Manuelo is born in Spain and Harvard educated, but his passion is kindled by the young American Sara when he learns that her father is a wealthy business-man with European ties that can further his semi-legal enterprises. The French Marcel is a pimp, and he bemoans September in Quinze because business is slow. American Homer Barton seems to be the typical loud and obnoxious tourist until he receives word of his only son's death in the Korean War, which makes him evaluate his own wasted existence and seek love and happiness rather than material success.

Pietro also bears the scars of his family's deaths, and he appears to have no direction at the outset of the novel. To make food money, he walks poodles for the fashionable ladies, taking the dogs to the Poodle Club, where they are placed on cushions, given yellow tea and pampered. He wins a million francs in one try at the roulette wheel with a coin acquired from a dead man, then proceeds to sort out his life, eventually finding true love with a woman of similar background.

The novel contains several sexual scenes in which people "ached for love," "stripped" and the body of one or another "became an animal." Sadook disguises himself as a commoner and shares a night of lust with a woman who "wanted him because he savaged her with his manhood in the forest of hair and roared like a wild stallion." Pietro initiates a sexual experience as "he ripped off her skirt and imprisoned her with an angry hand and pulled the silk off her breasts. They glowed like gourds of love in the moonlight and Pietro stooped and smothered his face in her bosom." Other characters engage in sexual activity with varying degrees of explicitness in the novel.

CENSORSHIP HISTORY

September in Quinze was banned in Ireland on August 1, 1952, after the Irish Board of Censors found the novel "obscene" and "indecent." A prohibition order was published in the *Iris Oifigiuil*, "the only official source from which booksellers [and readers] might learn of a new prohibition order," in which all materials blacklisted by the Irish Board of Censors were listed. According to the Censorship of Publications Bill of 1928, "the notice in *Iris Oifigiuil* should be sufficient evidence in the courts of summary jurisdiction as to the character of the publication." The work was officially banned from sale in Ireland until the introduction of the Censorship Publications Bill in 1967 reduced to 12 years the duration of a prohibition order, and the work was among 5,000 titles released from the list of banned books.

In 1954, *September in Quinze* became the subject of litigation after Treasury Counsel examined the novel and determined it was "obscene." Both the government and Hutchinson Publishing wanted the case dealt with by the Marlborough Street magistrate, but Magistrate Mr. Frank Milton insisted on committing the case for trial at the Old Bailey. In preliminary hearings,

Magistrate Milton allowed the defense to include supporting criticisms and reviews of the book, but these were later disallowed when the case was heard at the Old Bailey. Sir Gerald Dodson, the presiding judge in the case and also the recorder of London, determined that the novel did not meet his standard that all books must be suitable reading for "a callow youth, or a girl just budding into womanhood." Hutchinson Publishing and its director, Katherine Webb, were each fined 500 pounds. In his summing up, Sir Dodson stated,

> I should have thought any reader, however inexperienced, would have been repelled by a book of this sort, which is repugnant to every decent emotion which ever concerned man or woman. It is a very comforting thought that juries from time to time take a very solid stand against this sort of thing, and realise how important it is for the youth of this country to be protected and that the fountain of our national blood should not be polluted at its source.

FURTHER READING

Adams, Michael. *Censorship: The Irish Experience*. University: University of Alabama Press, 1968.

Craig, Alec. *Suppressed Books: A History of the Conception of Literary Obscenity*. New York: World Publishing, 1963.

Rolph, Cecil Hewitt. *Books in the Dock*. London: Deutsch, 1961.

SERENADE

Author: James M. Cain
Original date and place of publication: 1937, United States
Original publisher: Alfred A. Knopf
Type: Novel

SUMMARY

Serenade is the story of John Howard Sharp, a concert singer who has landed fundless in Mexico City because his voice has failed him. He meets Juana Montes, a "three-peso whore," who appears to be receptive to his advances until she hears him sing. She changes her mind because she hears a wooden quality in his voice that she associates with homosexuals. The two decide to join forces, nonetheless, and open a house of prostitution in Acapulco. On the way, they are caught in a rainstorm and take refuge in a church, where John rapes Juana. He justifies his action by saying, "Yes, it was rape, but only technically, brother, only technically. Above the waist, maybe she worried about the *sacrilegio*, but from the waist down she wanted me bad."

They live together, indulging frequently in such sex play as "smearing her nipples with soup." After a run-in with a Mexican official, the two move to California, where John regains his voice. When conductor Winston Hawes reenters John's life, their strong physical attraction to each other is evident. Desperate to "save" John from his homosexual feelings, Juana kills Winston and must escape from the United States into Mexico. John follows her, but Juana runs away from him only to be reunited as she is about to die at the hands of the official who originally forced them to flee Mexico.

CENSORSHIP HISTORY

Serenade was not the object of attempted censorship until a decade after publication. In 1949, after receiving complaints from patrons of the Free Public Library in Worcester, Massachusetts, the state attorney general ordered that copies of *Serenade* and GOD'S LITTLE ACRE be removed from the library shelves. The case appeared before the Superior Court of Suffolk County, Massachusetts, which judged the book "not obscene." The attorney general filed an appeal with the Supreme Judicial Court where, in September 1950, *Serenade* was again cleared in a 4 to 3 decision in *Attorney General v. Book Named "Serenade"*, 326 Mass. 324, 94 N.E.2d 259 (1950). In presenting the majority decision, Judge Spalding wrote that the sexual episodes in *Serenade* were "not portrayed in a manner that would have a 'substantial tendency to deprave or corrupt readers by inciting lascivious thoughts or arousing lustful desires.'"

FURTHER READING

DeVoto, Bernard. "The Easy Chair: Liberal Decisions in Massachusetts." *Harper's Magazine* 199 (July 1949): 62–65.
Frohock, W. M. *The Novel of Violence in America*. Dallas, Tex.: Southern Methodist University, 1950.
"Worcester Library Directors Support Their Librarian." *Library Journal* 74 (April 15, 1949): 649.

SEXUS

Author: Henry Miller
Original date and place of publication: 1949, France; 1965, United States; 1969, England
Original publisher: Obelisk Press (France); Grove Press (United States); Calder & Boyars (England)
Type: Novel

SUMMARY

Sexus is the first of three volumes in a series that Miller called *The Rosy Crucifixion*. The second volume is *Plexus*, published in 1953 by Olympia Press in Paris, in 1963 by Weidenfeld & Nicolson in London and in 1965 by Grove Press. *Nexus*, the third volume, was published in 1960 by Obelisk Press, in 1964 by Weidenfeld & Nicolson and in 1965 by Grove Press. *Sexus* is largely autobiographical, and it provides graphic details of the promiscuous behavior of its principal characters.

The novel, which began as custom-written erotica for a wealthy individual collector, contains two themes that run simultaneously throughout the novel. The first theme relates the narrator's affair with a woman for whom he has left his wife and child, and the second theme recounts his beginnings as a writer and the frustrations that he faces in his boring job that provides financial survival. The novel contains numerous unadorned sex scenes, many recounted in flashback, that are simple physical couplings in bushes or on bare and dirty slum floors. The novel also contains several homosexual episodes, one incident in which the narrator has consecutive sex with two female partners in one bed and many instances of fellatio, cunnilingus and mutual masturbation. Sex plays a major role in the book, and the author never raises any questions of morality, but he does discuss the ills of society as well as the cures for these ills.

CENSORSHIP HISTORY

Sexus accidentally became involved in an obscenity trial in Norway in 1959, the first in 70 years in that nation. The prosecutor in Oslo decided to test whether the national law against obscene literature still had meaning and brought charges against a Norwegian novel called *The Song of the Red Ruby*. The defense claimed that there were many other more pornographic books being sold undisturbed in Norway and named *Sexus* as the best example. The novel had been translated into Danish in 1957, and the similarity of the languages meant that the book was also sold in Norway.

The prosecutor ordered the several hundred copies in Danish and a few of the English version confiscated for being "obscene writing" and brought proceedings against two Oslo booksellers in the Oslo Town Court. They were found guilty the following year, but an appeal of the case to the Norwegian Supreme Court resulted in a reversal of the decision against the two booksellers. In a letter in defense of the novel, Miller stated,

> It is not something evil, not something poisonous, which this book Sexus offers the Norwegian reader. It is a dose of life which I administered to myself first, and which I not only survived but thrived on. Certainly, I would not offer it to infants, but then neither would I offer a child a bottle of *aqua vitae*. I can say one thing for it unblushingly—compared to the atom bomb it is full of lifegiving qualities.

Despite his efforts, the ban on *Sexus* remained.

FURTHER READING

Loth, David. *The Erotic in Literature*. New York: Dorset, 1961.
Miller, Henry. "Defense of the Freedom to Read—A Letter to the Supreme Court of Norway in Connection with the Ban on *Sexus* (*The Rosy Crucifixion*)." In *Versions of*

Censorship: Anthology, ed. by John McCormick and Mairi MacInnes, 223–30. Garden City, N.Y.: Doubleday, 1962.

Sutherland, John. *Offensive Literature: Decensorship in Britain, 1960–1982*. Totowa, N.J.: Barnes & Noble, 1982.

SIMON CALLED PETER

Author: Robert Keable
Original date and place of publication: 1921, United States
Original publisher: E. P. Dutton and Company
Type: Novel

SUMMARY

Simon Called Peter is the story of Peter Graham, an Anglican chaplain serving in France during World War I, who struggles to deal with what he views as the lax standards of those around him. As the months of the war drag out, Graham becomes close to those whose behavior he disdained earlier and he struggles with the growing awareness that he is much less effectual than he has hoped to be. As his standards of personal behavior become increasingly lower, Graham learns to feel compassion for others around him and for prostitutes, one of whom, Louise, becomes his friend. As his self-image deteriorates and he becomes discouraged and angry with himself, Graham turns to Louise in a moment of temptation and begs her to have sex with him:

> "That's just it, Louise," he cried. "I am a wild beast tonight. I can't stand it any longer. Kiss me."
> He put his arms around her, and bent her head back, studying her French and rather inscrutable eyes, her dark lashes, her mobile mouth, her long white throat. He put his hand caressingly upon it, and slid his fingers beneath the loose lace that the open wrap exposed. "Dear," he said, "I want you tonight."
> "Tonight, cherie?" she questioned.
> "Yes, now," he said hotly. "And why not? You give to other men—why not to me, Louise? . . . I've a body, like other men."

Although Graham passionately demands that Louise have sex with him, she refuses, knowing that he would only regret the experience.

Continuing to struggle with his duties and with his growing desires, Graham later falls in love with Julie, an unconventional young woman with whom he plans marriage. Toward the end of the novel, the two spend a few passionate days in a London hotel without any expression of hesitation or guilt regarding their behavior. Obsessed by Julie, Graham proclaims, "I believe I'd rather have you than—than God!" To Graham, "she was his bride, his wife, coming to him consecrate—not by any State convention, not by any ceremony of man-made religion, but by the pure passion of human love, virginal, clean."

In spite of their proclamations of love and desire, the two decide that they should not marry because Graham's allegiance is to his church. As the novel ends, he concludes that "the things of the spirit were, after all, so much greater than the things of the flesh."

CENSORSHIP HISTORY

Simon Called Peter aroused the ire of censors because it portrays a cleric who exhibits no guilt when he breaks the moral code by engaging in a premarital sexual relationship. Although the view of the main character is that sincere emotion is sufficient sanctification for his sexual relationship, it was not enough for those who wanted the novel banned.

In October 1922, *Simon Called Peter* became the center of attention of the Boston Watch and Ward Society. The public demand for the novel became "irresistible" after newspapers reported that the novel had been favorite reading of the victims in the sensational double murder of Mrs. James Mills and her minister-lover Reverend Edward Hall in September 1922 in New Jersey. The Boston Watch and Ward Society brought charges against Edith Law of Arlington, Massachusetts, the owner of a Boston rental library, who was convicted in the Cambridge District Court in October 1922 and fined $100 by Judge Arthur Stone for stocking *Simon Called Peter* in her rental library. In an appeal, Judge Stone suspended the fine but warned Law that she faced a jail sentence if she were ever again convicted in an obscenity case. The case drew particular attention because the novel had been a best-seller for more than a year.

In New York City, John Sumner, secretary of the New York Society for the Suppression of Vice, tried without success to have the book banned, but the courts refused to hear the complaint. Nonetheless, a second conviction for the sale of *Simon Called Peter* occurred in 1923, brought by the Boston Watch and Ward Society against Morris Honigbaum of Boston's Modern Bookshop. Despite continuing strong sales of *Simon Called Peter* in other areas of the country, Honigbaum was fined $100 for selling the novel.

FURTHER READING

"Boston Clean Book Case." *Publishers Weekly* (January 26, 1924): 240.

Boyer, Paul S. *Purity in Print: The Vice-Society Movement and Book Censorship in America.* New York: Scribner's, 1968.

"Finds Keable Book Obscene." *New York Times* (October 19, 1922): 2.

Fuller, Richard F. "How Boston Handles Problems." *Publishers Weekly* 103 (May 26, 1923): 1,624–25.

"Sumner Denounces Book in Hall Case." *New York Times* (October 20, 1922): 3.

1601—A FIRESIDE CONVERSATION IN YE TIME OF QUEEN ELIZABETH

Author: Mark Twain (Samuel Langhorne Clemens)
Original date and place of publication: 1876, United States
Original publisher: Privately printed
Type: Satire

SUMMARY

1601—A Fireside Conversation in Ye Time of Queen Elizabeth is Mark Twain's underground classic, and one of his few attempts at erotica. Regarding the work, he stated, "If there is a decent word in it, it is because I overlooked it." Written after having just completed *The Adventures of Tom Sawyer* and before starting *The Adventures of Huckleberry Finn*, the work is as highly crafted as his most popular works. Despite its extensive use of language usually labelled "obscene," the author claimed to have put great care into the writing of *1601* and once stated, "I built a conversation which *could* have happened—I used words such as were used at that time—1601."

Twain set the work in the court of Queen Elizabeth I and gathers to her fireside such contemporary luminaries as William Shakespeare, Sir Walter Raleigh, Ben Johnson and a number of imaginary women who are identified as ladies of the queen's household. The imagined conversation is related by the queen's cupbearer, who relates that the flatulation of one of those present motivates the queen to question all present to identify the culprit, then to state, "I have not heard the fellow [admit] to this fart."

In the conversation that follows, each individual present speaks in the style and manner expected—the learned and pompous Bacon, the poetic Shakespeare and Jonson and the sharp and arrogant queen. The talk moves quickly to tales of sexual prowess and sexual misconduct. Participants recount the story of one king (unnamed) who could claim having deflowered 10 virgins in one night, while his wife "serviced" twice as many young men in the same time period. References are made to the custom of a "far-off land" in which widows wear phallic symbols in their hair, prompting the queen to tartly state that English widows use them, too, but "prefer them between their thighs." When the ladies of the court appear to enjoy too heartily the accounts of others' adventures, they must bear with a discussion of their own sexual adventures.

CENSORSHIP HISTORY

Twain wrote *1601* in 1876 for his friend, the Reverend Joseph Twitchell, with the proclaimed purpose of disclosing "the picturesqueness of parlor conversation in Elizabeth's time." In 1880, Secretary of State John Hay received a copy, then sent it to his friend, Alexander Gunn, in Cleveland. Gunn wrote Hay that he intended to print the book, to which Hay protested that he could not condone doing this. However, he added that if Gunn was willing to go ahead with the printing without Hay's consent, he would like for Gunn to save him a copy. C. E. S. Wood, a West Point lieutenant, is also said to have had a finely made edition printed on the West Point presses—one that was circulated among "popes and kings and such people," Twain wrote. Some of these copies were taken abroad and, as a result of Twain's large international reputation, many limited-run editions in both English and translation appeared in Europe, some with expensive illustrations. In 1900, higher-quality editions of the book were worth 20 guineas in England. Ernst and Schwartz have called the work "one of the outstanding American examples of high literary pornography," but the author's self-banning of the work and the surreptitious manner in which pirated copies were circulated kept the work out of the sight of official book banners.

In 1962, *1601* appeared in Volume 1, Number 4 of *Eros*, a deluxe hardbound quarterly magazine published by Ralph Ginzburg that became the subject of an obscenity trial in *Ginzburg v. United States*, 383 U.S. 463 (1966). Its existence went unmentioned in the company of a story entitled "Madame Tellier's Brothel," photographs of male prostitutes, French postcards with buxom women nude from the waist up and a photographic essay of an African-American male having sex with a Caucasian female. Edward De Grazia, an author and attorney who defended in many such trials, states that the Department of the United States Post Office had received more than 35,000 complaints against Ginzburg's use of the mails "to peddle his 'sex and love' publications," but Attorney Robert Kennedy remained reluctant to prosecute because he feared that people "will blame it on my Catholicism." He waited until prosecution was initiated by a U.S. attorney in Philadelphia. When the case appeared before the Supreme Court, Ginzburg was sentenced to serve five years in prison for "pandering," but the appeals filed by defense attorneys kept Ginzburg free on bail for eight years. When Ginzburg again faced the Supreme Court, his sentence was lowered to eight months and the charges of "commercial exploitation," "pandering" and "titillation" remained.

FURTHER READING

Ernst, Morris L., and Alan U. Schwartz. *Censorship: The Search for the Obscene*. New York: Macmillan, 1964.

De Grazia, Edward. *Girls Lean Back Everywhere: The Law of Obscenity and the Assault on Genius*. New York: Random House, 1992.

Lewis, Felice Flanery. *Literature, Obscenity, & Law*. Carbondale: Southern Illinois University Press, 1976.

Loth, David. *The Erotic in Literature*. New York: Dorset, 1961.

SLEEVELESS ERRAND

Author: Norah C. James
Original date and place of publication: 1929, England

Original publisher: Scholartis Press
Type: Novel

SUMMARY

Sleeveless Errand, written by the publicity and advertising manager of publishing house Jonathan Cape, is a novel about two members of the post–World War I Lost Generation typical in the 1920s. The young man and woman have become so disillusioned in both life and love that they form a suicide pact. Covering two days in their lives, the novel relates their continuous conversation using the stream-of-consciousness technique, in a manner similar to that of James Joyce in ULYSSES.

The characters reveal their most intimate thoughts, desires and fears. In doing so, they use language that appears natural to the segment of the population they represent. They use such expressions as "balls," "bloody" and "poor little bugger." In discussing an adulterous friend, they offer no condemnation. The terms God and Christ offhandedly pepper their speech, and, in an instance to which the prosecution pointed as an example of the "shocking depravity" of the book, one character demands, "For Christ's sake give me a drink."

CENSORSHIP HISTORY

Sleeveless Errand was banned soon after publication, in proceedings that started when a reviewer sent his copy of the novel to British Home Secretary Sir William Joyson-Hicks. Known as "Jix," the home secretary was a staunch conservative who had made sex his target in the censorship of bookshops and the theater, and his policemen had been sent on repeated raids to confiscate "obscene" books and to close down "immoral" productions. He sent the case to Director of Public Prosecution Sir Archibald Bodkin, who ordered that police seize copies at the premises of Scholartis Press, the publishing house. Publisher Eric Partridge was summoned and ordered to show cause why the book should not be destroyed. Bodkin also ordered that the case be heard in front of the Bow Street magistrate on March 3, 1929, and applied for a destruction order for the book, which he claimed "tolerated and even advocated adultery." The prosecution cited the "obscene" language used by the characters as evidence of its "shocking depravity."

The defense asserted that the intent of the author had been "to portray and condemn the mode of life and language of a certain section of the community" and that the book merely reflected life as it was in that community. The magistrate ruled in favor of the prosecution and granted the destruction order, stating that the novel suggested "thoughts of the most impure character" to readers of all ages.

FURTHER READING

Elliott, Desmond. "Field Day for the Righteous." *Books and Bookmen* 5 (December 1959): 17.

MacCarthy, Desmond. "Literary Trends." *Life and Letters* 1 (October 1928): 329–41.

Partridge, Eric. *The First Three Years*. London: Scholartis, 1930.

A STORY TELLER'S HOLIDAY

Author: George Moore
Original date and place of publication: 1918, England
Original publisher: Henry Vizitelly
Type: Collection of tales

SUMMARY

A Story Teller's Holiday is a rambling 500-page work that contains dozens of Irish folk stories and legends, many relating amorous activities in convents and monasteries. Written in a carefree and flowing style, the work offers a light-hearted commentary on human behavior, although critics have complained that the dialogue in many of the tales is somewhat contrived. The stories are highly suggestive, but the language is delicate and restrained, allowing little explicit description of these sexual goings-on to emerge. The story of Adam and Eve is typical:

> In spite of her silence, perhaps because of it, he [Adam] began to speak once more of Iahveh's providence and his design, saying: "Eve, if it be within his design that we beget children the secret how we shall beget them will not be withheld from us." "Adam," she answered, "I cannot talk any more," and fell back amid the mosses, and his joy was so great that he could not get a word past his teeth, and when relief came they lay side by side, enchanted lovers, listening to the breeze that raised the leaves of the fig-tree, letting the moonlight through.

Overall, although the stories are drawn from folktales and legends, they present carefully detailed depictions of human behavior that revealed the vices and follies of society in Moore's time.

CENSORSHIP HISTORY

In 1929, the United States Customs seized an inscribed first edition copy of *A Story Teller's Holiday* when noted book collector Paul Hyde attempted to import a copy, because the book was on the Customs banned list. The ban was appealed to the United States Customs court, and prominent bookmen, including John Macrae, Sr., Donald Friede and Arthur Krock, appeared in the U.S. Customs court to testify on behalf of *A Story Teller's Holiday*. In May 1930, the court upheld the ban. The United States Customs court declared *A Story Teller's*

Holiday to be "obscene within any fair meaning of the word." In rendering judgment, the court referred to the following formulation of the Hicklin rule: "What is [the] probable, reasonable effect [of this book] on the sense of decency, purity and chastity of society extending to the family made up of men and women, young boys and girls—the family, which is the common nursery of mankind?" The application of this standard established for the court that Moore's novel was unfit and the novel was banned.

Three years later, the United States Department of the Treasury reversed the ban, using its so-called classics option that existed in the newly recon-structed Section 305 of the *Fordney-McCumber Tariff of 1922*, which governed seizures by Customs.

A Story Teller's Holiday was banned in Ireland on January 20, 1933. A prohibition order was published in the *Iris Oifigiuil*, "the only official source from which booksellers [and readers] might learn of a new prohibition order," in which all articles blacklisted by the Irish Board of Censors were listed. According to the Censorship of Publications Bill of 1928, "the notice in *Iris Oifigiuil* should be sufficient evidence in the courts of summary jurisdiction as to the character of the publication," despite the acknowledgment by justices quoted in Adams's thorough study of Irish censorship laws that "this gazette is not a publication which booksellers are addicted to reading." The Irish Board of Censors found the novel to be "obscene" and "indecent." In 1944, a Council of Action, composed of individuals representing literary and civil liberties groups, examined the incidence of censorship in Ireland in the years 1930 to 1943. The ban against the work remained in force until the 1970s, when it was among the many books removed from the banned list.

FURTHER READING

Adams, Michael. *Censorship: The Irish Experience*. University: University of Alabama Press, 1968.
Boyer, Paul S. *Purity in Print: The Vice-Society Movement and Book Censorship in America*. New York: Scribner's, 1968.
Paul, James C. N., and Murray L. Schwartz. *Federal Censorship: Obscenity in the Mail*. New York: Free Press, 1961.

STUDS LONIGAN: A TRILOGY

Author: James T. Farrell
Original date and place of publication: 1935, United States 1932, United States (*Young Lonigan*); 1934, United States (*The Young Manhood of Studs Lonigan*); 1935, United States (*Judgment Day*)
Original publisher: Vanguard Press (all)
Type: Novel

SUMMARY

Studs Lonigan: A Trilogy consists of three independently titled volumes that trace the physical and moral disintegration of a young Chicago man of Irish descent in the period from 1916 to 1933. The story begins with Studs Lonigan's graduation from a parochial school and ends with his death. For most of the 1920s, Studs and his family enjoy financial prosperity, leading them to whole-heartedly embrace the myth that democratic capitalism guaranteed success to anyone with sufficient ambition and ability. The economic devastation brought by the Great Depression reverses this optimism, destroying the economic and spiritual foundations of the Lonigan family. Studs dies at the end of *Judgment Day*, his ill health caused by excessive consumption of cheap bootleg liquor that he used as an escape from the bleakness of his life.

Young Lonigan takes place in 1916 and follows the 15-year-old Studs in the year after he graduates from parochial school. Studs spends most of his time on the streets with his friends, smoking, fighting, stealing small items and bragging about sexual exploits. He believes that to be a man means being tough and his language is peppered with such terms as *goddam*, *son of a bitch* and *whore*, as well as terms censored in the text by Farrell such as *s—t* and *kiss my —*. Studs's sexual arousal by girls, even his 13-year-old sister, is described at many points in the novel. When his sister accidentally brushes her breast against him, "Dirty thoughts rushed to his head like hot blood. He told himself he was a bastard because—she was his sister." Farrell describes Studs's first sexual experience, his involvement in a "gang-shag" with a girl named Iris.

Characters mention "show parties," in which younger children disrobe and exhibit their genitals. When his friend Helen Shires tells him that Weary Reilley "tried to do that to me," Studs thinks about mothers and fathers "doing it." He also considers the appearances of girls in detail, determining that "if they had good legs they were supposed to be good for you-know, and if they didn't they weren't; and to notice their boobs, if they were big enough to bounce."

The Young Manhood of Studs Lonigan takes place over 12 years, from 1917 through 1929. Studs cuts high school and he drinks heavily and brawls in the streets, having detailed sexual fantasies and trading graphic stories of sexual conquests with his friends. Although he eventually takes a job and seems to begin planning for a future, his drinking blurs his judgment. On New Year's Eve, 1929, Studs reaches his lowest point when he and his friends host a wild party that gets out of hand after several of the women they have invited refuse to have sex. Studs dances with one girl and vows that "he was going to give it to her like she'd never gotten it before." His friend Weary later knocks Studs out then rapes the girl after beating her severely. The volume ends with the unconscious Stud lying drunk in his own vomit on a sidewalk, his clothes bloody and torn.

In *Judgment Day*, Studs and his remaining friends recall the many men of their group who have died after destroying their health by drinking. They look forward to changing their former ways of being "drunk and whoring all the time, with no ambition." Studs is aware that he has wasted numerous opportunities in life, and he regrets his choices. As he plans to marry Catherine, who is pregnant with his child, Studs learns that he has a serious heart condition. Soon after, he develops pneumonia and dies, leaving Catherine destitute.

CENSORSHIP HISTORY

Young Lonigan was published in 1932 with a note warning that its buyers were "limited to physicians, social workers, teachers, and other persons having a professional interest in the psychology of adolescence."

In 1942, the trilogy was dropped by the American Library Association as being among the list of books identified as immoral and damaging in their efforts to portray American lifestyles. As a result, British publishers Constable & Co. were refused a permit to import the American printings, which amounted to a ban in England because there was insufficient paper there to print it. After two years, paper stock was made available, and 5,000 copies of the book were printed. That same year, the trilogy was banned from entry into Canada when Canadian Customs officials labeled the book as being of "an indecent and immoral character."

In 1948, the three novels of the *Studs Lonigan Trilogy* were among nine novels identified as obscene in criminal proceedings in the Court of Quarter sessions in Philadelphia County, Pennsylvania. (See GOD'S LITTLE ACRE for a complete discussion of the case.) Indictments were brought by the state district attorney, John H. Maurer, against five booksellers who were charged with possessing and intending to sell the books. The other allegedly obscene novels were Harold Robbins's *Never Love a Stranger*, Farrell's *A World I Never Made*, Erskine Caldwell's GOD'S LITTLE ACRE, Calder Willingham's *End as a Man* and William Faulkner's SANCTUARY and THE WILD PALMS.

In his March 18, 1949, decision in *Commonwealth v. Gordon*, 66 D. & C. 101 (1949) that the trilogy was not obscene, Judge Curtis Bok stated:

> It is not a pleasant story, nor are the characters gentle and refined. There is rape and dissipation and lust in these books, expressed in matching language, but they do not strike me as out of proportion. The books as a whole create a sustained arc of a man's life and era, and the obvious effort of the author is to be faithful to the scene he depicts.
>
> No one would want to be Studs Lonigan.

Bok refused to declare *Studs Lonigan: A Trilogy* "obscene" because in cases cited in his decision the definition restricted the meaning of the term "to that of sexual impurity, and with those cases that have made erotic allurement the test of its effect." The work also failed to meet Bok's definition of sexual impurity in literature, which he defined "as any writing whose dominant purpose and effect is erotic allurement—that is to say, a calculated and effective incitement to sexual desire."

The Select Committee on Current Pornographic Materials, in hearings authorized by the United States House of Representatives in 1953, recommended that the trilogy be removed from sale because of its "indecent" content. The National Organization for Decent Literature (NODL) also placed the trilogy on its blacklist and the work was banned from sale in St. Cloud, Minnesota, the result of efforts by local NODL members. The novel was banned in Ireland that same year because of its "excessive sexuality" and discussion of abortion.

In 1957, the United States Information Agency banned the trilogy from its overseas libraries because it portrayed "brutality" and sexual content.

FURTHER READING

Elliott, Desmond. "Scandal over Studs (Trial over James Farrell's *Studs Lonigan*)." *Books and Bookmen* 5 (November 1959): 23–26.

Farrell, James T. "The Author as Plaintiff: Testimony in a Censorship Case." In Farrell's *Reflection at Fifty and Other Essays*: 188–223. New York: Vanguard, 1954.

———. "Lonigan, Lonergan, and New York's Finest." *Nation* 158 (March 18, 1944): 338.

Huntington, Henry S. "The Philadelphia Book Seizures." *Elation* 167 (August 21, 1948): 205–7.

Smith, Gene. "The Lonigan Curse." *American Heritage* 46 (April 1995): 150–51.

SUSAN LENOX: HER FALL AND RISE

Author: David Graham Phillips
Original date and place of publication: 1917, United States
Original publisher: D. Appleton Company
Type: Novel

SUMMARY

Susan Lenox is the story of a small-town girl of illegitimate birth who lives with her uncle and aunt after her mother dies giving birth to her. Viewed by her family and townspeople as bound to "suffer for her mother's sins," she is blamed when her cousin's boyfriend falls in love with her. Branded a "loose" woman, she is quickly married off to a coarse local farmer who terrifies her on their wedding night: "He crushed her. He kissed her with great slobbering smacks and gnawed at the flesh of her neck with teeth that craved to bite."

With the help of journalist Rod Spenser, Susan runs away, assumes a new name and begins a career as a singer on a riverboat. When the boat is wrecked and her manager-lover contracts typhoid, she becomes a prostitute to support them, but he dies. Susan then works in a sweatshop for a time, but she discovers that life as a streetwalker is more lucrative. Spenser reenters her life, reforms her and takes her with him to New York City, where he hopes to have a career as a playwright, but Susan soon leaves him after his friends tell her that she is hampering Spenser's career. As a model in the garment district, Susan must often have sex with business owners to keep her job, so she returns to streetwalking. When she becomes addicted to opium and alcohol, she lands in a brothel for a time, then escapes and ponders "abandoning her body to abominations beyond belief at the hands of degenerate oriental sailors." Spenser also sinks into drug addiciton.

Susan meets Spenser once again, and they become each other's salvation. She becomes a successful actress and inherits the estate of a bachelor director, thus achieving emancipation. As the novel closes, Susan, finally financially secure, realizes: "Yes, she has learned to live. But—she has paid the price." Spenser rebuilds his career as a journalist.

Both the main character's lifestyle and her philosophy of life were sources of criticism when the novel first appeared. At one point in the novel, a girl who works for the Salvation Army calls out, "The wages of sin is death [sic]." Susan responds, "The wages of weakness is death . . . but the wages of sin—well, it's sometimes a house on Fifth Avenue."

CENSORSHIP HISTORY

The novel, inspired by the "white slave" furor in New York City in the 1890s, was completed at the author's death in 1911 but did not appear in publication until 1917, when *Hearst's Magazine* took advantage of a renewed public interest in prostitution and published the novel in serialized form. When the book was first published, the *New York Times* branded the story "essentially false" and "profoundly immoral." The New York Society for the Suppression of Vice brought charges against the magazine for printing "obscene" material, but the case was promptly dismissed. When D. Appleton Company published the entire novel in 1917, John Sumner and the New York Society for the Suppression of Vice threatened the company with legal action.

Joseph H. Sears, president of Appleton, was not intimidated and responded to Sumner that the novel had been published "to awaken the American people to a high moral sense, in order that the terrible evils going on daily about them might be eliminated." Sears defiantly promoted the book, and the society initiated proceedings. The author's sister intervened and persuaded Sears to establish a compromise so that "this last product of her brother's genius [would] reach as wide an audience as possible." Appleton agreed to withdraw the first edition of *Susan Lenox* and to publish an expurgated version. Mollified, the society withdrew its complaint and scored a partial victory.

FURTHER READING

Filler, Louis. *Voice of Democracy: David Graham Phillips*. University Park: Pennsylvania State University, 1968.

Goldman, Eric F. "David Graham Phillips, Victorian Critic of Victorianism." In *The Lives of Eighteen from Princeton*. Ed. by Willard Thorp, 118–153. Princeton, N.J.: Princeton University Press, 1946.

Marcosson, Isaac F. *David Graham Phillips and His Times*. New York: Dodd, Mead, 1932.

Ravitz, Abe C. *David Graham Phillips*. New York: Twayne, 1966.

SWEETER THAN LIFE

Author: Mark Tryon (pseud.)[1]
Original date and place of publication: 1958, United States
Original publisher: Vixen Press
Type: Novel

SUMMARY

Sweeter Than Life, a forerunner of the sexually oriented pulp novels that were so numerous in the 1960s, contains a prominent lesbian theme. The novel relates the life and death of Nym Bardolph, a young woman who lives in Okeechee, Florida. After an unhappy marriage, her mother, Lucy, teaches Nym to hate all men and inadvertently introduces her daughter to lesbian lovemaking when Nym finds her mother and the red-haired schoolteacher on the couch. Both are completely naked, the teacher's face is "a mask of frantic ecstasy" and "deep-throated hoarse animal groans poured from the little redhead."

Nym is not so much traumatized by the incident as she is liberated to seduce both men and women. Nym's adventures with her future husband, Sean Bardolph, are described in highly suggestive but not explicit language. She manipulates his libido,

> arousing him, helping him remove his clothes and then letting her educated fingers and hands roam over his trembling body, their search and skillful stimulation growing gradually in intimacy, only to stop her little game short when his face contorted with the painful ecstasy of the ultimate moment.

Determined to gain control over a valuable plot of land, she needs Bardolph to aid her so she willingly fulfills "his wildest dreams of blissful satiety in her arms." The task is aided by "her breasts quivering with the most apparent physical desire, . . . her mouth a moist cavern of accomplishment." When

---

[1] The Library of Congress catalog indicates that this name is a pseudonym and lists no other books by this author. An extensive search of diverse sources has not revealed the author's true identity.

Bardolph's ardor cools, she seduces Johnny Martel in scenes that contain the same long passages of undressing, nudity and foreplay.

The change of pace in this novel occurs when Nym seduces Lynn, the young girl who works in Bardolph's real estate office. The action starts as a rape, with Lynn "straining to push Nym away" and Nym clinging tightly as "with one hand she held the girl down and . . . stripped the dress from Lynn." After a detailed description of Lynn's underwear, "Nym's hand found the nubile breasts, molding and caressing until she felt the tips harden." Nym's breasts are also described, "so full that they seemed swollen, their great dark eyes gleaming dully against the white flesh"; then "there were no sounds in the office but the sounds of love."

CENSORSHIP HISTORY

Sweeter Than Life was a distinct departure from earlier works that had been condemned for erotic content. As Lewis observes, "that novel contains numerous long, sensual passages which, since they contribute little to plot or characterization, might be termed 'dirt for dirt's sake'." Edward De Grazia, a prominent defense attorney in such high profile censorship cases as those involving Aristophanes' *Lysistrata*, William Burroughs's *Naked Lunch*, Henry Miller's TROPIC OF CANCER and the Swedish film *I Am Curious—Yellow*, states that *Sweeter Than Life* "seems to have had no appreciable literary value." Supreme Court Justice Felix Frankfurter told his law clerk, Paul Bender, that the book was "horrible filthy junk!" Yet all agreed that the defendant's constitutional right to due process of law had been violated in the lower court decisions involving the book.

In 1958, bookseller Eleazar Smith was charged with "disseminating obscene matter" and ordered to appear in municipal court where Judge James H. Pope declared Smith guilty of the charge. The bookseller appealed the conviction to the appellate department of the Los Angeles Superior Court, which upheld the prior decision in *People v. Smith*, 161 Cal. App. 2d 860, 327 P.2d 636 (1958), but Judge David did not discuss the nature of the novel or the criteria that led to his decision. Under the California obscenity statute, knowledge of the obscene nature of the book was required before the court could establish guilt. Thus, when the decision was appealed to the United States Supreme Court, in *Smith v. California*, 361 U.S. 147 (1959), the court reversed the decisions of the lower courts. Smith claimed that, even though the book might be "obscene," he never read the books in his stock and should be immune from prosecution. His attorney persuaded the Supreme Court that his client was innocent of "disseminating obscene matter," even though the book might be labeled "obscene" under prevailing standards.

Justice William J. Brennan delivered the opinion of the court that it was unconstitutional for the California legislature to punish a bookseller for selling a book called *Sweeter Than Life*, found by a judge to be obscene, without proof that the bookseller knew of the sexually oriented content of the book. "Every bookseller would be placed under an obligation to make himself aware of the contents of every book in his shop. It would be altogether unreasonable to demand so near an approach to omniscience." Thus, the decision in the case was based on the legality of the municipal ordinance rather than on the content of the novel.

FURTHER READING

De Grazia, Edward. *Censorship Landmarks*. New York: Bowker, 1969.
———. *Girls Lean Back Everywhere: The Law of Obscenity and the Assault on Genius*. New York: Random House, 1992.
Lewis, Felice Flanery. *Literature, Obscenity, and the Law*. Carbondale: Southern Illinois University Press, 1976.

TEN NORTH FREDERICK

Author: John O'Hara
Original date and place of publication: 1955, United States
Original publisher: Random House
Type: Novel

SUMMARY

Ten North Frederick opens with the funeral of prominent Gibbsville resident Joseph B. Chapin, then examines the circumstances that shaped him and eventually led to his death. The novel offers an unadorned view of the "real" man hidden behind the apparently successful attorney, as it also uncovers the social structure, codes and values of Gibbsville.

Yale graduate Chapin grows up with a domineering mother who smothers him and expresses ambitions that create in him an exaggerated sense of his own importance. Chapin's subservience to his mother influences his choice of wife, the ambitious, cold, shrewd and tough Edith Stokes, who wants to own Joe. Mrs. Chapin thoroughly approves of Edith, for "no girl with a face as plain as Edith's could inspire a love or even a passion that would cause a son to reject his mother." The couple move in with Joe's parents, beginning their married life at 10 North Frederick Street. The scene depicting their wedding night reveals Edith's demanding nature, and it is also one of the passages cited in efforts to ban the novel:

> He put his knee between her legs and she made a sound like a moan. . . . He felt her breasts and she pulled up her nightgown.
> "Do it to me, do it to me," she said. "Hurry." She made it difficult for him to find her; she was already in the rhythm of the act and could not stop. "For God's sake," she said. "For God's sake."

"I'm trying, dearest."

"*Do* it then," she said angrily.

The moment he entered her she had her climax, with a loud cry. His own climax followed and immediately she wanted him again.

Between the obsessions of his wife and mother, Chapin becomes dispirited and allows himself to be manipulated by them and by others. Chapin lives in an emotional straitjacket and lacks vitality for much of the novel. Stagnated by the desire to maintain appearances as Gibbsville aristocracy, Chapin and his wife ruin their daughter's marriage to an amiable Italian musician, whom she truly loves, and force her to have an abortion. They also try to stop their son from dropping out of Yale and becoming a jazz pianist.

Edith and other characters in the novel are involved in extramarital relationships, but most of the sexual acts are implied rather than described explicitly. When Chapin falls deeply in love with his daughter's New York roommate, Kate, they spend one night together that is only referred to but not described. Kate loves Chapin but refuses to talk of marriage and the future, knowing fully that the 50-year-old man would be miserable if he were to give up his friends, home and family for her. She sends him away and he returns to 10 North Frederick Street, Gibbsville, Pennsylvania, where he begins to drink heavily and dies of cirrhosis of the liver.

CENSORSHIP HISTORY

Between 1956 and 1958, *Ten North Frederick* was the object of a series of local bans and seizures in Port Huron, Michigan; Detroit, Michigan; and Albany, New York, despite its continued steady sales in other parts of the nation. Law enforcement officials applied local obscenity standards, threatened prosecution, then raided booksellers to remove the "obscene" novel.

In 1956, the prosecuting attorney in Port Huron, St. Clair County, Michigan, ordered booksellers and distributors to cease displaying and selling all books that appeared on the disapproved list of the National Organization for Decent Literature, a Catholic censorship group founded in 1938. The complaining organization cited the few erotic passages in the novel as the basis for identifying as "objectionable" *Ten North Frederick*, along with other novels such as James Jones's FROM HERE TO ETERNITY, Bud Schulberg's *On the Waterfront*, Ernest Hemingway's *To Have and Have Not* and John Steinbeck's WAYWARD BUS. The ban was lifted after Bantam Books, paperback publisher of *Ten North Frederick*, joined with other publishers and obtained a federal district court injunction against the prosecution for "going beyond legal authority."

In 1957, a year after winning the National Book Award for fiction, the novel was banned in the paperback edition in Detroit, Michigan, by Police Commissioner Piggins, who applied a Michigan obscenity statute. The hardcover edition of the novel, available in the public library and sold for a year in Detroit bookstores, was also banned. The following year, Random House, publisher of the hardcover edition, and Bantam Books, publisher of the paperback edition, jointly obtained a permanent injunction against the ban. The Detroit police commissioner attempted to circumvent the injunction and was cited for contempt of court. Local authorities later dropped the case, and censorship of the novel ended in Detroit.

One year later, a local censorship group in Albany, New York, gained an indictment in the Albany County Supreme Court against Bantam Books, John O'Hara and the distributors of the novel "for conspiring to publish and distribute an obscene book." Lawyers for the defendants reviewed the testimony and argued that only specific passages had been read to the grand jury rather than the entire work. This challenge represented the first time following the decision in *Roth v. United States*, 354 U.S. 476 (1957) that an indictment involving a charge of obscenity had been argued on the basis that the entire work had not been read to or by the grand jury. The publishers successfully defended their position and the ban was lifted.

FURTHER READING

Hempl, William J., and Patrick M. Wall. "Extralegal Censorship of Literature." In *Issues of Our Time*, ed. by Herbert W. Hildebrandt, 130–43. New York: Macmillan, 1963.
Oboler, Eli M. *The Fear of the Word: Censorship and Sex*. Metuchen, N.J.: Scarecrow, 1974.
Tuttleton, James. *The Novel of Manners in America*. New York: Norton, 1972.

TESS OF THE D'URBERVILLES

Author: Thomas Hardy
Original date and place of publication: 1891, England; 1892, United States
Original publisher: Osgood, McIlvaine (England); Harper (United States)
Type: Novel

SUMMARY

Tess of the D'Urbervilles was subtitled "A Pure Woman Faithfully Presented," and Hardy intended to portray a woman whose intentions had been good throughout despite eventually becoming a mistress and a murderess. The novel opens as John Durbeyfield learns that he is the last descendant of one of England's oldest and most powerful families. A poor and powerless working man and a heavy drinker, Durbeyfield sends his eldest daughter, Tess, to the still-wealthy branch of the D'Urbervilles at their estate at Trantridge to claim kinship.

They are really wealthy people named Stokes who have taken the unused ancestral title as their own, and innocent Tess is unaware that Alec D'Urberville is not her cousin. He gives Tess a job caring for his mother's chickens to keep her nearby and rapes her one night in the woods. She stays with him for a few weeks, then returns home pregnant. Their child dies soon after birth.

Grieving for her child and disgraced, Tess takes a job on a distant farm, where she meets Angel Clare, who claims to follow the spirit but not the letter of the Bible. They fall in love, and, on their wedding night, Tess and Angel confess to each other. Angel tells of a brief affair, and Tess forgives him. She then tells him about Alec, and Angel rejects her.

Angel leaves for Brazil, and Tess returns briefly to her family before taking a job at another dairy at Flintcomb-Ash, where she again meets Alec, now a fire-and-brimstone preacher. He wants her back, but she is still married to Angel and does not love Alec. When Tess' father dies the family loses its home, and Alec steps in, promising to educate her brothers and sisters and to protect her mother if only Tess will live with him. She resists Alec and sets up camp with her family at the ancient D'Urberville burial vaults. Alec reappears, and a disheartened Tess relents, because her letters to Angel have gone unanswered.

Angel returns, ready to forgive Tess, and finds her at the luxurious sea resort of Sandbourne, where he begs her forgiveness. She tells him about Alec and orders him to leave. He refuses, and Tess loses control of her senses. She murders Alec, the source of her unhappiness, then runs away with Angel, whom she believes will now truly forgive her because she has eliminated the root of their problems. They hide in a deserted mansion, then move on to Stonehenge, where Tess falls asleep on a sacrificial altar. The police arrive and arrest her, and Tess is tried for murder. Before she is hanged, Tess asks Angel to care for and to marry her innocent younger sister 'Liza-Lu. The novel ends as Angel and 'Liza-Lu watch the hanging, then walk off together, hand in hand.

CENSORSHIP HISTORY

Hardy consented to the bowdlerization of many of his works before they reached the public just to get them published, and his experience with *Tess of the D'Urbervilles* was no exception. Hardy had great difficulty finding a publisher for the novel and magazines demanded radical revisions before serializing it. Tillotson and Son, a Lancashire newspaper syndicate, contracted with Hardy in 1889 to serialize the novel, but their suggestions that he make changes in the scene in which Tess is seduced and in the improvised baptism of her dying baby alienated the author. He refused to agree to their suggestions and, instead, asked the publishers to cancel the contract. Hardy then took the still incomplete work to *Murray's Magazine*, whose editor, Edward Arnold, rejected the piece because the magazine "preferred girls to grow up in ignorance of sexual hazards." Mowbray Morris, editor of *Macmillan's Magazine*, rejected the novel because he was "profoundly upset by the book's sexuality."

Before offering the novel to another magazine, Hardy revised the work to produce a version that would not cause offense. In November 1890, Hardy agreed to terms with *Graphic* to begin serialization in July 1891 and for serialization in *Harper's New Monthly* in the United States soon after. Several passages were excised from the novel. Hardy had to remove the seduction scene and the improvised baptism. He was also forced to include a mock marriage staged by Alec to make Tess believe that she was actually his legal wife. The illegitimate baby was also omitted.

In addition to objections to the illicit relationship between Tess and Alec, Hardy was accused of taking a "low" view of women. His sensuous descriptions of Tess were labeled "French" and critics said that it was "degrading" to see women portrayed as in the following example from the novel:

> She had stretched one arm so high above her coiled-up cable of hair that he could see its delicacy above the sunburn; her face was flushed with sleep and her eyelids hung heavy over their pupils. The brimfulness of her nature breathed from her. It was a moment when a woman's soul is more incarnate than at any other time; when the most spiritual beauty inclines to the corporeal; and sex takes the outside place in her presence.

In 1891, the novel was banned by Mudie's and Smith's circulating libraries, leading to a virtual censorship over popular reading in England. The popular circulating libraries had significant influence on book sales during the second half of the 19th century. Novels were expensive and authors made little money in sales unless the circulating libraries accepted their books. That same year, the novel was also the object of banning by the Watch and Ward Society in Boston, which charged that the novel contained illicit sexuality and immorality. The society forced Boston booksellers to agree that they would not advertise or sell *Tess of the D'Urbervilles*, and most adhered to the request.

While attempting to find a publisher for *Tess*, Hardy published in 1890 in *New Review* an essay called "Candour in English Fiction," in which he noted that "the novels which most conduce to moral profit are likely to be among those written without a moral purpose." Hardy, far in advance of the court decisions in such novels as James Joyce's ULYSSES, D. H. Lawrence's LADY CHATTERLEY'S LOVER, Henry Miller's TROPIC OF CANCER and others, recognized the need to portray life honestly; "the passions ought to be proportioned as in the world itself." Viewing life as a "physiological fact," he felt that life's "honest portrayal must be largely concerned with, for one thing, the relations of the sexes, and the substitution for catastrophes as favor the false coloring best expressed by the regulation finish that 'they married and were happy ever after,' of catastrophes based upon sexual relationship as it is. To this expansion English society opposes a well-nigh insuperable bar." He concedes that satisfying "the prudery of censorship" is "the fearful price that he has to pay for the privilege of writing in the English language—no less a price than the complete extinction, in the mind of every mature and penetrating reader, of sympathetic belief in his personages."

FURTHER READING

Cowley, Malcolm. *After the Genteel Tradition*. Rev. ed. Carbondale: Southern Illinois University, 1964.
Hardy, Thomas. "Candour in Fiction." In *Thomas Hardy's Personal Writings: Prefaces, Literary Opinions, Reminiscences*. Ed. by Harold Orel, 89-108. Lawrence, KS: University of Kansas Press, 1966.
Pinion, F.B. *Thomas Hardy: His Life and Friends*. New York: St. Martin's, 1992.
Seymour-Smith, Martin. *Hardy: A Biography*. New York: St. Martin's, 1994.

THEN AGAIN, MAYBE I WON'T

Author: Judy Blume
Original date and place of publication: 1971, United States
Original publisher: Bradbury Press
Type: Young adult novel

SUMMARY

Then Again, Maybe I Won't focuses on a few years in the life of Tony Miglione, beginning when he is 13 years old. The adolescent is growing up in Jersey City, New Jersey, in a two-family home that also contains his father, mother, grandmother, older brother, Ralph, and Ralph's wife. Tony's father is an electrician, his mother is a clerk in a department store and his grandmother does the family housekeeping. Ralph is a teacher, a profession that his father hopes Tony will also enter. The novel examines the manner in which each generation deals with its specific needs and concerns as the family encounters increasing financial burdens.

The family's difficulties begin after Tony's father becomes the manager of an electronics plant in Queens and the family moves to an upper-middle-class suburb on Long Island. Once there, the Migliones are caught up in the competition of keeping up with the neighbors. Tony's father trades in his pickup truck for a fancy car, and his mother hires a live-in housekeeper, which leaves his grandmother with nothing to do except watch television alone. The changes place the family in financial jeopardy, and Tony experiences continuing and severe stomach pains.

In addition to all of this change, Tony awakens sexually and becomes strongly attracted to 16-year-old Lisa, the daughter of the snobbish family living next door. Each night, he watches from his bedroom window as she undresses, even though he feels guilt and shame as his sexual awareness grows.

He becomes even more upset after he has several wet dreams, and he fears that his parents know when his father unexpectedly decides to have a "man-to-man" talk about sex. Given a pair of binoculars for Christmas, Tony uses them to take closer looks at Lisa, which makes his guilt feelings increase. Tony begins to suffer severe gastric attacks as the result of the combined anxieties of family financial problems, his sexual urges and fears that he will be implicated in his friend Joel's shoplifting. He is hospitalized for 10 days of tests and observation, after which the doctors conclude that his problems are psychological, and Tony begins treatment by a psychiatrist. By the end of the novel, he has learned to control his fears and resolves to act more responsibly. He surmises that he might even stop watching Lisa undress at night; "then again, maybe I won't."

CENSORSHIP HISTORY

Then Again, Maybe I Won't has been challenged in many schools because of its references to masturbation, nocturnal emissions, erections and other "immorality and voyeurism." In 1980, the novel was removed from the Gilbert, Arizona, elementary school libraries and the school board ordered that students who wanted to check out the book from the junior high school library could only do so if they had written parental consent. In 1982, the book was challenged in the Tuscaloosa, Alabama, Orlando, Florida, and Harford County, Maryland, school systems for being "sexually offensive." In 1983, the Elk River, Minnesota, school board responded to parent complaints about the book and decided to restrict the title to students who had written parental permission. Several parents who supported the book contacted the Minnesota Civil Liberties Union, which sued the school board, forcing it to reverse the decision later in the same year.

In 1984, the novel was removed from all of the school libraries in the St. Tammany Parish, Louisiana, school district, after parents complained that its "treatment of immorality and voyeurism does not provide for the growth of desirable attitudes." The book was later reinstated. In Peoria, Illinois, that same year, parents complained that the book contained "strong sexual content" and "vulgar" language and alleged that the book lacked social or literary value. The school board voted to remove the book from all libraries in the school district, but the decision was later changed to restrict the book to students who brought written parental permission.

A year later, the book was challenged as being "profane, immoral, and offensive," but after consideration the school board decided to retain the book in the school district libraries. In 1988, parents complained that "sexual content" made the book unsuitable to be included in the Des Moines, Iowa, elementary school libraries, but the district officials rejected the challenge. In 1989, a group of parents of student attending elementary and middle schools in the Salem-Keizer, Oregon, school district complained that the book is a "dismal tale of a young boy's inability to cope and his very inappropriate responses to the changes taking place in his life." They asked the school board to remove the book from the school district libraries, but the move was rejected.

In 1990, parents in Tyrone, Pennsylvania, challenged the inclusion of the novel in the elementary school libraries, claiming that the main character is a voyeur and that the book deals with masturbation and alcohol abuse. The school board considered their complaint and in a 6 to 2 vote retained the book. The same group of parents then objected to the appearance of the novel on the suggested reading list, and the school board agreed to form a committee to review the policy and guidelines for creating reading lists. The book was retained on the reading list. In 1991, a parent in Hartford, Wisconsin, asked that the school board remove the novel from the elementary school library, charging that it contained "profanity" and "promoted shoplifting and voyeurism." The board-appointed school review committee voted to retain the book.

FURTHER READING

Donelson, Kenneth L., and Alleen Pace Nilsen. *Literature for Today's Young Adults.* Glenview, Ill.: Scott Foresman, 1989.

Foerstel, Herbert N. *Banned in the U.S.A.: A Reference Guide to Book Censorship in Schools and Public Libraries.* Westport, Conn.: Greenwood, 1994.

Newsletter on Intellectual Freedom (July 1982): 124; (September 1982): 155–56; (May 1983): 71; (September 1983): 153; (May 1984): 69; (July 1984): 121; (January 1985): 8; (March 1985): 33, 42, 58; (July 1985): 112; (January 1990): 4–5; (July 1990): 127; (March 1991): 62.

THE THIEF'S JOURNAL

Author: Jean Genet
Original date and place of publication: 1954, France; 1964, United States
Original publisher: Olympia Press (France): Grove Press (United States)
Type: Novel

SUMMARY

The Thief's Journal is a semiautobiographical novel in which the author relates his life from his birth as the illegitimate child of parents who abandon him, through the years spent as a vagabond. Raised by foster parents whom he robbed, Genet was incarcerated in a juvenile facility, then spent years in a series of correctional institutions. He gives detailed accounts of his imprisonments for theft and dope smuggling or peddling, as well as of his homosexual relations with other prisoners and with a French police detective and British soldiers at Gibraltar. The work also details his wanderings as a beggar and tramp from one end of Europe to the other.

At turns philosophical, Genet repudiates good throughout all of his accounts, often reversing accepted moral values and embracing the evil he encounters. He purports to find God in the places that traditional, middle-class society has abandoned—"the dark corners of crime, vice and shame." He unabashedly speaks openly of one of his lovers Stilitano, a notorious criminal and pimp.

Throughout, Genet purports to function for the good of others. One example of such thinking is his sexual encounter, with a "coast guard" [sic] stationed on the shores of Spain, that keeps the man occupied when he should be on duty. As Genet sleeps in a shack near the sea, the man stumbles in, looking for fishermen and sailors who are smuggling goods between Morocco and Spain. The thirtyish guard shares supper with Genet, who is several years younger; "then he began to caress me. . . . He knew he ought to leave, but my caresses grew more artful. He couldn't bear to tear himself away; the smugglers must have landed peacefully." He perceives of himself as "the favorite mistress who, beneath a starry sky, soothes the conqueror" and grants the man "the loveliest of my nights" as the sounds of smugglers' boats landing can be heard through an open window.

CENSORSHIP HISTORY

The Thief's Journal was banned in Ireland on December 21, 1961. A prohibition order was published in the *Iris Oifigiuil*, "the only official source from which booksellers [and readers] might learn of a new prohibition order," in which all articles blacklisted by the Irish Board of Censors were listed. According to the Censorship of Publications Bill of 1928, "the notice in *Iris Oifigiuil* should be sufficient evidence in the courts of summary jurisdiction as to the character of the publication," despite the acknowledgment by justices quoted in Adams's thorough study of Irish censorship laws that "this gazette is not a publication which booksellers are addicted to reading." The Irish Board of Censors found the novel "obscene" and "indecent," objecting particularly to the author's handling of the theme of homosexuality and the poetic treatment of crime. The work was officially banned from sale in Ireland until the introduction of the Censorship Publications Bill in 1967 reduced to 12 years the duration of a prohibition order, and the work was among 5,000 titles released from the list of banned books.

FURTHER READING

Adams, Michael. *Censorship: The Irish Experience*. University: University of Alabama Press, 1968.

Kronhausen, Eberhard, and Phyllis Kronhausen. *Pornography and the Law*. New York: Ballantine, 1959.

White, Edmund. *Genet: A Biography*. New York: Knopf, 1994.

THREE WEEKS

Author: Elinor Glyn
Original date and place of publication: 1907, England; 1907, United States
Original publisher: Gerald Duckworth (England); Duffield & Co. (United States)
Type: Novel

SUMMARY

Three Weeks tells the simple and dramatic story of Paul Verdayne, a handsome and wealthy English nobleman in his early twenties, sent by his parents first to France, then Switzerland after he is caught embracing the parson's daughter, Isabella Waring. Once in Switzerland, Verdayne pines for the earthy Isabella until he sees a beautiful older woman, in her thirties, who is dressed in black and has a face "like a magnolia bloom." After several days of smoldering glances, Paul and the Lady (as she is referred to throughout the novel) meet, and she boldly asks him to visit her in her suite. Rich in the exotic decor of sumptuous silks, satins and brocades, the Lady's suite also contains a huge tiger skin draped over her couch, upon which she reclines provocatively, "while between her red lips was a rose not redder than they—an almost scarlet rose.... the whole picture was barbaric."

The two begin a passionate sexual relationship that lasts only three weeks, during which the Lady is repeatedly described as "undulating" on the tiger skin and whispering such lines as "This is our souls' wedding." The Lady reads Apuleius in Latin to Paul and sings as she plucks the strings of a guitar, but reviewers did not criticize the novel for these incidents. Rather, criticism emerged because of the numerous times in which Paul and the Lady "melted into one another's arms" and "the spirit of their natures melted as One." The Lady is fierce in her passion and tireless in her lovemaking, and the physicality of the descriptions shocked many reviewers.

Paul learns that the Lady is really the queen of a small (unnamed) Balkan kingdom and that her husband is abusive. When she vanishes after three weeks have passed, Paul becomes physically ill, and his father takes him home to England. Nine months later, Paul receives a letter from the Lady informing him that she has given birth to their son. Through his father's efforts, Paul learns her identity but she is murdered by her husband before they reunite. Overcome by grief, Paul roams the world for five years, then arranges to see his son.

CENSORSHIP HISTORY

Three Weeks was viewed by critics of the time as one of many novels written in England by women in 1907 containing what *Publishers Weekly* viewed as "questionable morality" and "morbid or abnormal conditions." Many were

193

unremittingly hostile to what amounted to an illicit love affair. Even Glyn's friends in society professed to be scandalized by the book; her grandson recounts in his biography of her that "among her friends in society she was abused and reviled, called an immoral woman and a glorifier of adultery." The novel was banned at Eton, and the headmaster, Dr. Edward Lyttleton, informed Glyn of the ban. The author assumed that he had not yet read the book, so she sent him a copy. After reading it, he wrote to her and stated that he had enjoyed the book and admitted to having been misled by its reputation. The ban, however, remained in place.

Although the book raised an uproar among reviewers in the United States, the lurid eroticism of the novel fascinated American readers, selling 50,000 copies in the first three weeks after publication in the United States, then averaging 2,000 sales daily for the three months following. The novel also served to create a new standard in sexual content in novels.

In 1908, the Boston Watch and Ward Society placed pressure on booksellers to agree to withhold the novel from sale, thus effectively banning the work in Boston. Backed by the New York publisher of the novel, Duffield & Company, Joseph E. Buckley deliberately incited a confrontation with legal authorities by selling a copy of the novel to Inspector McCarr of the Boston police. Buckley was indicted and charged with "selling a certain printed book entitled *Three Weeks*, containing in and upon certain pages certain obscene, indecent and impure language, manifestly tending to corrupt the morals of youth."

In the case that followed, *Commonwealth v. Buckley*, 200 Mass. 346, 86 N.E. 910 (1909), the grand jury asserted that the language of the offending sections of the book could not be included in the transcript of the proceedings, because it was too "improper to be placed upon the court records and offensive to the court." The jury in the Superior Court of Suffolk County case declared the book "obscene" and the court fined Buckley $100. Duffield & Company appealed the decision, but the Supreme Judicial Court of Massachusetts upheld the Superior Court decision. The ruling became an important guide for judicial interpretation of the obscenity laws of Massachusetts for decades to come.

In the appeal, the publisher questioned whether the presiding Superior Court judge had properly instructed the jury in the term *obscene* and regarding the author's purpose. In writing the Supreme Judicial Court opinion, Judge Hammond asserted that terms such as *obscene* and *impure* were not technical terms and, therefore, need not be explained to a jury. The judge further asserted that the author's purpose need not be considered in judging the effect of a book. More specifically, Judge Hammond observed:

> An author who has disclosed so much of the details of the way to the adulterous bed as the author of this book has and who has kept the curtains raised in the way that she has kept them, can find no fault if the jury says that not the spiritual

but the animal, not the pure but the impure, is what the general reader will find as the most conspicuous thought suggested to him as he reads.

Writing about the case a few years later, conservative literary critic Brander Matthews, usually a strong supporter of the Watch and Ward Society, condemned the court action. He observed that *Three Weeks* was "a cheap tale of superficial cleverness" that would have sunk "swiftly beneath the waters of oblivion" without the publicity generated by the trials. Instead, sales of the novel became even stronger throughout the United States and stimulated sales in England as well.

The Watch and Ward Society savored its victory and achieved increased power as a result of the case. Sporadic bannings, similar to that imposed by the Society, occurred throughout the nation but without litigation. Massachusetts booksellers, unwilling to risk more arrests and losses in court, joined forces with the Watch and Ward Society in a "gentleman's agreement" to keep much of modern fiction out of Commonwealth bookstores for more than a decade, until H. L. Mencken challenged the Society's edict in 1926 by selling a copy of *American Mercury* on Boston Common and was cleared by a municipal judge.

Three Weeks remained scandalous for a long while. As late as 1932, a Mickey Mouse cartoon was banned from publication in Ohio newspapers because it depicted a cow reclining in a field, reading *Three Weeks*.

FURTHER READING

Etherington-Smith, Meredith, and Jeremy Pilcher. *The "It" Girls: Elinor Glyn, Novelist and Her Sister Lucile, Couturiere*. New York: Harcourt Brace Jovanovich, 1986.

Glyn, Anthony. *Elinor Glyn*. Garden City, New York: Doubleday, 1955.

Grant, Sidney S., and S. E. Angoff. "Censorship in Boston." *Boston University Law Review* 10 (January 1930): 36–60.

Matthews, Brander. "Books That Are Barred." *Munsey's Magazine* 50 (December 1913): 493–97.

McCoy, Ralph E. *Banned in Boston: The Development of Literary Censorship in Massachusetts*. Urbana: University of Illinois, 1956.

Rolph, Cecil Hewitt. *Books in the Dock*. London: Deutsch, 1961.

TOBACCO ROAD

Author: Erskine Caldwell
Original date and place of publication: 1932, United States
Original publisher: Charles Scribner's Sons
Type: Novel

SUMMARY

Tobacco Road presents an unflinching look at the Lester family, a rural family whose grim experiences living on the edge of starvation jolt readers into an awareness of the plight of the rural poor. The novel is filled with acts of brutality and the hopeless futility felt by the derelict family living on a barren and poverty-ridden Georgia tobacco farm.

Amoral rather than immoral in behavior, patriarch Jeeter Lester boasts of his potency, having fathered 17 children by his wife, Ada, and untold numbers of children with women living on area farms. He and Ada abuse Jeeter's elderly mother, denying her food, ignoring her and, finally, refusing to go to her aid when Jeeter's son Dude backs over her with a car and leaves her lying facedown in the dust. Hours later, when Jeeter does turn his attention to his mother, she has stopped bleeding and makes no sound although "she ain't stiff yet, but I don't reckon she'll live." While neighbor Lov Bensey is around to help, Jeeter takes her out to the field, digs a ditch and buries her without worrying if she is dead yet.

Jeeter gives his 12-year-old daughter Pearl in marriage to Lov Bensey in trade for "some quilts, nearly a gallon of cylinder oil and, besides giving him all of a week's pay, which was seven dollars." He attempts to marry off his hare-lipped daughter, Ellie May, but settles for sending her to comfort Lov after Pearl runs away, with the demand that Ellie May return the following morning with food and some of Lov's clothes. His son, Dude, marries Bessie, an older woman and self-styled preacher whom the women call a "hussy" because of her affinity for men. Jeeter tries to climb into bed with Dude and Bessie, "a right smart piece to live with," when the three stay at a hotel after a trip to Augusta to sell firewood. He is foiled in his attempt when the manager knocks at their door and tells them that he has another room available, but Bessie is the one who leaves. The next morning, she is sleepy and tired, reports that she had been asked to move from bed to bed and concludes that "there sure is a lot of men staying there."

The final tragedy of the novel occurs because years of agricultural misman-agement have left the fields barren, and the Lesters are too poor to buy needed fertilizer to grow anything. In desperation, Jeeter follows an old tradition of burning the broom sedge off the fields, but he and Ada burn to death when their cabin catches fire. He could have left the farm and worked in the cotton mills, but he stubbornly clung to the land as his ancestors had.

CENSORSHIP HISTORY

The novel escaped extensive attempts at censorship in part because major efforts were directed at the stage version, closely adapted from the novel. In 1935, Chicago mayor Edward J. Kelly banned performances of the play, backed by expert witnesses including a former governor, a circuit judge and members of the bar who claimed that the play "offered more obscenity than Chicagoans wished to tolerate." The ban was upheld by the Seventh Circuit Court of Appeals, which determined Kelly's assessment of community standards to be accurate justification. The stage version was also banned in Detroit, Michigan; St. Paul, Minnesota; Minneapolis, Minnesota; Utica, New York; and Tulsa, Oklahoma. Also in 1935, a member of the House of Representatives from Georgia appealed to Congress to forbid staging of the novel, because it presented an "infamous, wicked, and untrue portrait" of his district. Six assistant district attorneys viewed the play to address the charge, after which they refused the representative's request.

Attempts to ban the novel also occurred in several instances. In 1934, several faculty members at Columbia University condemned *Tobacco Road* and Caldwell's GOD'S LITTLE ACRE as "indecent and tending to corrupt" and demanded the withdrawal of both books from the Teachers College library. The action was taken even though both books were on required reading lists of several university English courses. In 1941, the novel was barred from the mails by the postmaster general, who claimed that the book was "indecent and immoral." At the same time, the novel continued to be sold in bookstores. In 1953, *Tobacco Road* was banned from import and sale by the Irish government, which claimed that the novel was "obscene."

FURTHER READING

Caldwell, Erskine. "My Twenty-Five Years of Censorship." *Esquire* 50 (October 1958): 176–78.

Caldwell, Erskine. "Protest against Columbia University's Ban on *Tobacco Road* and *God's Little Acre*." *New Republic* 79 (June 1934): 184–85.

Haskins, Doug. "The Many Faces of Censorship." *Canadian Forum* 33 (June 1953): 57–58.

Klevar, Harvey L. *Erskine Caldwell: A Biography*. Knoxville: University of Tennessee Press, 1993.

Mikva, Abner J. "Chicago: Citadel of Censorship." *Focus/Midwest* 2 (March–April 1963): 16–17.

Miller, Dan B. *The Journey from Tobacco Road: A Biography*. New York: Knopf, 1994.

TRAGIC GROUND

Author: Erskine Caldwell
Original date and place of publication: 1944, United States
Original publisher: Grosset & Dunlap
Type: Novel

SUMMARY

Tragic Ground relates the existence of the Douthits, a Georgia family who relocated from their rural surroundings to an urban industrialized area on the

Gulf Coast to take advantage of the work opportunities in a munitions factory during World War II. The end of the war brings a closing of the factory, leaving the family destitute and unable to cope with their impoverished life in the city. The efforts of social workers to assist the family are ineffective, so patriarch Spence Douthit decides to solve their problems by finding a rich husband for his 13-year-old daughter, Mavis. Much of the comedy, and most of the erotic references, emerge from this quest and from the inability of the family to cope with precarious urban life. Nonetheless, Caldwell makes an important statement about the fate of the illiterate and transient workers who are unprepared to survive in what becomes an alien environment once their source of income—jobs at the munitions factory—ends.

As Spence pursues his mission, he speaks of young girls becoming prostitutes and refers freely to the genitals of both males and females. In one incident, he is lured by a prostitute into a hotel room, where he is beaten and robbed of his money. Finding his older daughter, Libby, in bed with her boyfriend, who has just returned from the war, he expresses surprise rather than anger because of all the Douthits, Libby is the one who usually follows social rules.

In describing the manner in which recruiters for the munitions jobs persuade rural wives to withhold sex until their husbands agree to take the jobs, Spence says that he felt "like a rabbit with his balls caught in a sewing machine." He tells a sexily dressed prostitute in a nightclub, "Your tits are showing." In efforts to interest a man in marrying Mavis, he states, "She keeps me pricked up around the house." His wife is similarly blunt, pointing out when she feels threatened by the attractiveness of the social worker, "If I had my looks back . . . I could go out and get sported, too. . . . I'd hist [sic] my skirt and have the men poking hards at me all over this part of the world. . . . You've worked my region to a frazzle."

CENSORSHIP HISTORY

Tragic Ground was one of eight works by American authors that became the subject of obscenity cases between 1934 and 1944, after the ban against importation of erotic classics was eased by the 1930 amendment of the Tariff Act and censors turned their attention to American works. Other works that suffered in this period were Lillian Hellman's *Children's Hour*, Jim Tully's LADIES IN THE PARLOR, James T. Farrell's WORLD I NEVER MADE, William Faulkner's WILD PALMS, James M. Cain's SERENADE, Lillian Smith's STRANGE FRUIT and Kathleen Winsor's FOREVER AMBER. Three of these novels—TRAGIC GROUND, STRANGE FRUIT and FOREVER AMBER—became bestsellers after their challenges in court.

The language of *Tragic Ground*, natural to the characters, raised objections among critics when the novel appeared. In the same year that the novel was published, members of the Boston Watch and Ward Society lodged a complaint with the police, claiming the novel was "obscene" and dealt with "low life matters." Acting on the complaint, a detective purchased a copy of the book from Miss E. Margaret Anderson of the Dartmouth Book Stall in Boston, then arrested her for "distributing obscene material." The case went to municipal court, in a hearing presided over by Municipal Judge Elijah Adlow, who ridiculed the obscenity charge and stated, "I'm not interested in these crusades against literature, and I'm getting tired of books being banned." When the arresting detective pointed out that one scene in the book depicted a woman and man together, the man naked to the waist, the judge asked, "Do you think anybody would be astounded to hear that?"

In delivering a ruling, Judge Adlow observed to the police, "It's not for me or for you to try to establish literary tastes of the community." He stated that he had found *Tragic Ground* to be "dull," but concluded that "the judges of the Municipal Court and the members of the Police Department were not qualified to pass on the literary value of books."

FURTHER READINGS

Burgum, Edwin Berry. "Erskine Caldwell and His Jeeters." *New York Times Book Review* (October 15, 1944): 46.

Caldwell, Erskine. "My Twenty-Five Years of Censorship." *Esquire* 50 (October 1958): 176–78.

"Caldwell Novel Cleared as 'Dull'." *New York Times* (December 29, 1944): 13.

Daniels, Jonathan. "American Lower Depths." *Saturday Review of Literature* (October 14, 1944): 6.

Miller, Daniel B. *The Journey from 'Tobacco Road.'* New York: Knopf, 1995.

TRILBY

Author: George du Maurier
Original date and place of publication: 1894, United States
Original publisher: Harper & Brothers
Type: Novel

SUMMARY

Trilby introduced Americans to the common romantic conception of artistic and bohemian Paris in the 19th century. Despite its relative lack of prestige as a literary classic, the novel is deserving of mention because it introduced the concept of Svengali to the American idiom. Written in French, then translated by the author before publication, the novel is set in the Parisian Latin Quarter, a glamorous, gay and free place where parties and activities were spontaneous and continuous. To give his setting authority, du Maurier used concrete details and names of real places and people.

Combining elements of the Gothic romance with the sentimental seduction novel, *Trilby* offers readers a sinister villain who, despite being mysterious, impressive, extremely intelligent and talented, also happens to possess strange and seemingly diabolical powers. His strong personality and mysterious powers overcome the personality of a mediocre singer named Trilby, mesmerizing her and turning her into a major European singing star. "He seemed to her a dread, powerful demon, who . . . oppressed and weighed on her like an incubus." For five years, they tour the world capitals, with Trilby referred to as Madame Svengali and La Svengali, although others voice doubts that the two are actually married.

When Svengali dies of apoplexy during a performance by Trilby, she regains control over her personality but has no recollection of the previous five years, nor can she remember her many peformances. Svengali's influence exerts itself from beyond the grave, and he returns via a mysterious photograph to claim Trilby's life.

CENSORSHIP HISTORY

In 1894, *Trilby*, one of the literary crazes of the 1890s and one of the most widely read books ever published in America to that date, became the target of censors in Philadelphia, who demanded that the board of education and the city council remove the novel from the public library in the 21st ward. The request was made by three district residents, two of them clergymen. The objections centered on the doubtful marriage between Trilby and Svengali, as well as the diabolical hold that Svengali had upon his protégée.

The board created a committee to consider the request, but they were unable to come to a decision. One committee member illogically suggested that the problem might be due to the translation, noting that "Many a book that may appear perfectly harmless in French becomes harmful when read here in a translation." This was unlikely because the author created his own translation for Harper & Brothers. The committee chairman disagreed and asserted that the book would probably have to be removed, because the board had already been forced to remove many books from the shelves. After the decision was moved to the library committee of the Philadelphia Board of Education, they chose to retain the book, considering that hundreds of thousands of Americans were already reading it.

FURTHER READING

Haney, Robert W. *Comstockery in America: Patterns of Censorship and Control.* Boston: Beacon, 1960.
Tebbel, John. *A History of Book Publishing in the United States.* New York: Bowker, 1975.

THE TRIUMPH OF DEATH

Author: Gabriele D'Annunzio
Original date and place of publication: 1889, Italy; 1896, United States

Original publisher: Da Palmo (Italy); George H. Richmond & Co. (United States)
Type: Novel

SUMMARY

The Triumph of Death is an autobiographical novel that relates the fatal romantic infatuation of a young man that closely parallels D'Annunzio's love affair with Elvira Leoni. Tindall characterizes the novel as "artificial, morbid, without simplicity or sanity," and the work does provide numerous scenes of depression and long introspective passages that far outnumber the erotic scenes. Although the novel details the orgiastic abandon of characters George and Hippolyte, many nonerotic passages convey the feelings of George toward his mother and father and toward the beloved uncle, Demetrius, who commits suicide, as well as his thoughts regarding music and religion.

George's intellect remains at war with his sensuality, and he comprehends "that he would in no way succeed in realizing the type of exuberant life . . that his intellectual and moral faculties, too disproportioned, would never succeed in finding their equilibrium and their model." He also experiences the frustration of knowing that he can never fully possess his ideal woman Hippolyte, who is married, and he can never be fully sure of her love nor can he control his desire for her.

The sexual attraction between George and Hippolyte is evident in the novel, but the descriptions are not explicit. Traveling by train together, "they spoke in low tones, communicating the ardor of their blood, exchanging burning promises. . . . Their desire grew. . . . They united their lips." Although this description is the reader's introduction to the coming stolen week of love, no explicit erotic activity is presented. The most erotic scene in the novel occurs when George thinks in detail about Hippolyte's physical beauty, belaboring his description of her body. Beyond an adoring mention of her "serpentine elegance" and "the narrowness of her thigh," George describes her "sterile abdomen" with its "virginal purity," her "alabaster" skin and the graceful curve of her back. He turns his most specific attention to her breasts, "firm and small, as if sculptured in very delicate alabaster, and the points of her extraordinarily erect breasts [which] were of a rose-violet hue."

The lovers' downfall is George's fascination with death, which emerges after they learn of a suicide that leads George to exclaim, "Happy are the dead! They have no more doubts!" As George's feelings of insecurity in his love for Hippolyte increase, he thinks of being released from his torment through death—hers or his own. At the end of the novel, George causes the death of both of them.

CENSORSHIP HISTORY

The *Triumph of Death* captured the attention of the New York Society for the Suppression of Vice and its secretary Anthony Comstock in 1897. Comstock purchased a copy of the book, then brought charges against the clerk who sold him the book, George H. Richmond, Jr., and Richmond's father, who was both a reputable book dealer and the American publisher of the novel. The defendants appeared for arraignment before Magistrate Leroy B. Crane in a New York City court on March 4, 1897, before which the Richmonds were held on $500 bail.

When the case went to court on March 25, 1897, Judges Hinsdale, Jerome and Jacob of the Court of Special Sessions presided. A number of literary critics and literature professors were present, ready to testify to the critical value of the book, but the court refused to permit expert testimony. The judges refused to assess the book simply based on passages pointed out by Comstock and, instead, admitted the whole book into evidence. On April 5, 1897, the judges acquitted the Richmonds of all charges. In response, George Richmond threatened to sue Magistrate Crane for saying at the end of the arraignment hearing, "If a man were to put that book into the hands of my daughter I should not wait for the law; I would shoot him."

The publicity surrounding the arraignment of the Richmonds increased sales of the novel, making it suddenly popular. When Comstock made efforts to ban the novel in Asbury Park, New Jersey, the *New York Times* published an article about the effort and ridiculed his activities, noting that

> until that illustrious maker of reputations took the matter in hand the Italian's books were a drug in the market. The make-believe decadents and the like who "wrote them up" in weekly journals of small circulation found them hopeless as a topic. Now Mr. COMSTOCK has taken one of them up and is pushing its circulation beyond that of a penny newspaper with plenty of crude pictures of ladies' footwear.

In 1898, the Boston Watch and Ward Society attempted to acquire the cooperation of city book dealers to repress sales and advertising of the novel. The society was unsuccessful because sales of the book had already been so numerous as to convince booksellers that the book should remain. The ensuing publicity further increased sales.

FURTHER READING

"D'Annunzio at Asbury Park." *New York Times* (July 24, 1897): 6.

De Grazia, Edward. *Girls Lean Back Everywhere: The Law of Obscenity and the Assault on Genius*. New York: Random House, 1992.

"Offended at the Magistrate." *New York Times* (April 16, 1897): 5.

Tindall, William York. *Forces in Modern British Literature, 1885–1956*. 2d ed. New York: Vintage, 1956.

"*Triumph of Death* Exonerated." *New York Times* (April 6, 1897): 5.

TROPIC OF CANCER

Author: Henry Miller
Original date and place of publication: 1934, France; 1961, United States
Original publisher: Obelisk Press (France); Grove Press (United States)
Type: Novel

TROPIC OF CAPRICORN

Author: Henry Miller
Original date and place of publication: 1939, France; 1962, United States
Original publisher: Obelisk Press (France); Grove Press (United States)
Type: Novel

SUMMARY

Tropic of Cancer relates the loneliness, futility, shallow pleasure-seeking, degradation and squalor of one American's life in France in the early 1930s. Begun as Miller's autobiography and written in the form of a diary, with a main character named for the author, the novel relates Miller's life in Paris and includes portraits of his many friends and acquaintances there. Despite the link to his life, the novel is neither chronologically organized nor specific as to dates and places. Rather, Miller uses a technique of free association in recalling events and creates an impressionistic rather than reportorial interior monologue.

An American expatriate in Paris who depends upon his friends for meals and lodging, the main character enjoys sexual adventures with a diverse number of women. His erotic life is graphically described, although the frequent use of exaggeration turns the seemingly erotic material into outlandish situations that point up the absurdity of human existence more than they arouse.

The sexual imagery and the language used to relate Miller's views are blunt throughout the novel, as the following passage that appears early in the novel illustrates:

> O Tania, where now is that warm cunt of yours, those fat, heavy garters, those soft, bulging thighs? There is a bone in my prick six inches long. I will ream out every wrinkle in your cunt, Tania, big with seed. I will send you home to your Sylvester with an ache in your belly and your womb turned inside out. Your Sylvester! Yes, he knows how to build a fire, but I know how to inflame a cunt. . . . I am fucking you, Tania, so that you'll stay fucked. And if you are afraid of being fucked publicly I will fuck you privately. I will tear off a few hairs from your cunt. . . . I will bite into your clitoris and spit out two franc pieces.

Miller also includes numerous emetic references in the work. In one instance, he describes the continuous droning speech of a dinner companion as feeling "exactly as if he had taken out that circumcised dick of his and was peeing on us." In another instance, he offers social criticism and notes, "for a hundred years or more the world, *our* world has been dying. And not one man, in these last hundred years or so, has been crazy enough to put a bomb up the asshole of creation and set it off."

Tropic of Capricorn is also semiautobiographical. The novel covers the years from 1920 to 1924 in Miller's life, before he left America for Europe. During this period, he worked for Western Union, called the Cosmodemonic Telegraph Company of North America in the work. Once again, as in the earlier novel, Miller recounts his agony in trying to "find" himself and to be true to himself despite the pressures to conform brought on artists by an industrial society. Although he was married to his first wife during the years covered by *Tropic of Capricorn*, Miller relates a series of sexual adventures with prostitutes, the wives and sisters of friends, and casual acquaintances.

Strewn throughout the novel are numerous "four-letter" words, not only relating to sexual and emetic incidents but also infused in casually related incidents. At one point, he states, "I had a good time because, as I said before, I really didn't give a fuck about anything." In another section, he notes, "I wasn't a good ass licker." He criticizes America in equally blunt language: "I think of all the streets in America combined as forming a huge cesspool, a cesspool of the spirit in which everything is sucked down and drained away to everlasting shit. . . . In the belly of the trombone lies the American soul farting its contented heart out."

As in *Tropic of Cancer*, Miller uses exceedingly frank language in this novel in referring to bizarre sexual activity with "Mona," who represents his second wife. After spying on Mona, who is masturbating in the bathroom, Miller approaches her:

> She just stood there quietly and as I slid my hand up her legs she moved one foot a little to open her crotch a bit more. I don't think I ever put my hand into such a juicy crotch in my life. . . . I had my whole four fingers inside her, whipping it up to a froth. Her mouth was stuffed full and the juice pouring down her legs. Not a word out of us, as I say. Just a couple of quiet maniacs working away in the dark like gravediggers. It was a fucking Paradise and I knew it, and I was ready and willing to fuck my brains away if necessary. She was probably the best fuck I ever had.

Despite the blunt language, sexual descriptions and emetic references, Miller manages to impart to readers the absurdity of the human condition.

CENSORSHIP HISTORY

Tropic of Cancer was first published in Paris in 1934 and remained officially banned from the United States for three decades, but college students smuggled thousands of copies into the United States in that time until Grove Press published the novel in the United States. Of nearly 2 million copies of the book distributed, nearly three-quarters of a million were returned to the publisher. The book was involved in at least 40 criminal cases against wholesalers and booksellers, even after the federal government refused to ban the book. An untold number of civil suits to suppress the book have also occurred, as have "voluntary" withdrawals from sale after local intimidation.

In 1950, Ernest Besig, the director of the American Civil Liberties Union in San Francisco, attempted to import both *Tropic of Cancer* and *Tropic of Capricorn* into the United States and initiated the first court case involving the novels. Citing Section 1305 of the United States Code, Customs department officials held the books and Besig sued the government. Before the case went to trial, Besig requested a motion to admit 19 depositions from literary critics testifying to the literary value of the novels and to Miller's stature as a serious writer. The motion was denied by Judge Louis A. Goodman, who stated bluntly:

> In my opinion the dominant effect of the two respondent books is obscene. Both books are replete with long passages that are filthy and revolting and that tend to excite lustful thoughts and desires. While the books also have passages, and indeed chapters, that may be said to have literary merit, the obscene portions have no literary value; they are directly, completely and wholly filthy and obscene and have no reasonable relation to any literary concept inherent in the books' theme.

The case went to trial without a jury in 1951 with Judge Goodman presiding. Despite the presentation by Besig of literary reviews of Miller's work and the statements from critics describing the literary merits of the books, the judge condemned the books and declared them obscene. In closing statements, Judge Goodman wrote,

> The many long filthy descriptions of sexual experiences, practices and organs are of themselves admitted to be lewd. . . . It is sufficient to say that the many obscene passages in the books have such an evil stench that to include them here in footnotes would make this opinion pornographic. . . . There are several passages where the female sexual organ and its function are described and referred to in such detailed and vulgar language as to create nausea in the reader. If this be importable literature, then the dignity of the human person and the stability of the family unit, which are the cornerstones of society, are lost to us.

Besig appealed the decision to the Ninth Circuit Court of Appeals, and on October 23, 1953, the novels were again declared "obscene" by a unanimous decision in *Besig v. United States*, 208 F. 2d 142 (9th Cir. 1953). In his written decision, Circuit Judge Albert Lee Stephens characterized the books as being the "unprintable word of the debased and morally bankrupt" and claimed that, even taken as a whole, they lacked literary merit. He stated:

Practically everything that the world loosely regards as sin is detailed in the vivid, lurid, salacious language of smut, prostitution, and dirt. And all of it is related without the slightest expressed idea of its abandon. Consistent with the general tenor of the books, even human excrement is dwelt upon in the dirtiest words possible.

The 1961 Grove Press edition of *Tropic of Cancer* attracted numerous later legal actions because no test case had been heard by the Supreme Court, as there had been in the case of LADY CHATTERLEY'S LOVER. Grove Press delayed appealing the earliest cases to the Supreme Court, and the delay in securing a definitive judgment proved costly because the publishing firm committed itself to assisting every bookseller prosecuted. Five state courts declared the novel "obscene" in *State v. Huntington*, no. 24657, Super. Ct., Hartford County, Conn. (1962) (Connecticut); *Grove Press, Inc. v. Florida*, 156 So. 2d 537 (Fla. Dist. Ct. App. 1963) (Florida); *Haiman v. Morris*, Ill. Sup. Ct., June 18, 1964 (opinion not printed; later withdrawn) (Illinois); *Commonwealth v. Robin*, no. 3177, C.P. Phila. Co. Penn. (1962) (Pennsylvania); and *People v. Fritch*, 13 N.Y.2d 119, 192 N.E.2d 713 (1963) (4–3 decision) (New York). Within the same period, California, Massachusetts and Wisconsin declared the novel "not obscene" in *Zeitlin v. Arnebergh*, 31 Cal. 800, 383 P.2d 152 (1963) (unanimous); *Attorney General v. Book Named "Tropic of Cancer,"* 345 Mass. 11, 184 N.E.2d 328 (1962) (4–3 decision); and *McCauley v. Tropic of Cancer*, 20 Wisc. 2d 134, 121 N.W.2d 545 (1963) (4–3 decision).

On June 22, 1964, in a 5 to 4 decision in *Grove Press, Inc. v. Gerstein*, 378 U.S. 577 (1964), the United States Supreme Court reversed the Florida decision of *Grove Press, Inc. v. Florida*, 156 So. 2d 537 (Fla. Dist. Ct. App. 1963). The judgment was reversed by a *per curiam* order in which Justice William J. Brennan, Jr., declared that "material dealing with sex in a manner that advocates ideas, or that has literary or scientific or artistic value or any other form of social importance, may not be branded as obscenity and denied the constitutional protection."

Grove Press vigorously defended *Tropic of Cancer* in numerous jurisdictions, but the publisher was forced to issue a statement that it did not have the financial means to defend booksellers in cases regarding Miller's *Tropic of Capricorn*.

FURTHER READING

"Another Furor over Books." *Ohio State University Monthly* 55 (December 1963): 8–12.

Ciardi, John. *"Tropic of Cancer." Saturday Review* 45 (June 1962): 13.

De Grazia, Edward. *Girls Lean Back Everywhere: The Law of Obscenity and the Assault on Genius*. New York: Random House, 1992.

Hutchison, E. R. *Tropic of Cancer on Trial*. New York: Grove, 1968.

Kilpatrick, James J. *The Smut Peddlers*. New York: Doubleday, 1960.

Kincaid, Larry, and Grove Koger. "*Tropic of Cancer* and the Censors: A Case Study and Bibliographic Guide to the Literature." *Reference Services Review* 25 (Spring 1997): 31–38, 46.

Kuh, Richard H. *Foolish Figleaves? Pornography In and Out of Court.* New York: Macmillan, 1967.

Moore, Everett T. "*Tropic of Cancer*" (Second Phase). *ALA Bulletin* 56 (February 1962): 81–84.

"Obscenity-Evidence Admission of Contemporary Critical Evaluation of Libeled Book." *Minnesota Law Review* 35 (February 1951): 326–30.

Roeburt, John. *The Wicked and the Banned.* New York: Macfadden, 1963.

Smith, Roger H. "Cops, Counselors and *Tropic of Cancer.*" *Publishers Weekly* 180 (October 23, 1961): 35.

United States President's Commission on Obscenity and Pornography. *The Report of the Commission on Obscenity and Pornography.* New York: Random House, 1970.

ULYSSES

Author: James Joyce
Original date and place of publication: 1918, England; 1933, United States
Original publisher: Sylvia Beach's Shakespeare & Co. (England); Random House (United States)
Type: Novel

SUMMARY

Written in the stream-of-consciousness style, *Ulysses* takes place on one day, June 16, 1904, and relates the thoughts, feelings, words and actions of Leopold Bloom, his wife, Molly, and Stephen Dedalus. The novel was severely criticized because it explicitly describes physical and sensual pleasures, makes emetic references and depicts sexual incidents in frank terms. In addition, complaints were made about the language, which contains numerous uses of "fuck," as well as frequent genital references such as "vagina," "scrotum," "penis," "hymen," and euphemisms for the genitals.

Most of the erotic references emerge through the characters of Bloom and Molly. Wandering through the city of Dublin and stopping at various bars throughout the day, Bloom reflects the journey of the epic hero Ulysses, who wandered 10 years before reaching his home and family. Bloom, who is obsessed with physical and sensual pleasures, recalls his sexual experiences while on his daylong journey, remembering one instance in which "Wildly I lay on her, kissed her; eyes, her lips, her stretch neck, beating, woman's breasts full . . . fat nipples upright." He is also explicit in emetic references, describing in detail a bowel movement in the outhouse and relating the physical sensations produced. He enjoys eating "grilled mutton kidneys which gave to his palate a fine tang of faintly scented urine."

Molly is equally concerned with emetic matter and sex. When she has run out of a skin cosmetic, she thinks, "I suppose Ill [*sic*] only have to wash in my piss." She thinks of sex with her lover, Blazes Boylan, noting, "I think he made them a bit firmer sucking them like that so long he made me thirsty titties he calls them I had to laugh yes this one anyhow stiff the nipple gets for the least thing Ill [*sic*] get him to keep that up." Molly describes the male sexual organ as a "tremendous big red brute of a thing" and "some kind of a thick crowbar" as she prepares to have sex near the end of the novel. In rhapsodizing about the encounter, she describes taking off her clothes and experiencing "one the size of that to make you feel full up . . . like a stallion driving it up into you. . . . I made him pull it out and do it on me considering how big it is so much the better in case any of it wasnt [*sic*] washed out properly the last time I let him finish it in me." The sexual references are numerous, but the descriptions emerge in a fragmentary manner, most appearing as interior monologues of the characters.

CENSORSHIP HISTORY

In 1922, the United States Department of the Post Office burned 500 copies of the novel when an attempt was made to import the book and court decisions ruled against the book. The first court trial of the book, however, actually occurred in 1921, when John Sumner, the secretary for the New York Society for the Suppression of Vice, and his followers seized an issue of the *Little Review*, which contained one chapter of the serialized version of the novel. The trial took place in the court of general sessions with magazine editors Margaret Head and Jane Heap as defendants. Author John Cowper Powys and play-wright Philip Moeller, called as witnesses, testified that Joyce's style was too obscure to be understood by most people, but the court ruled against the *Little Review* and the novel.

Bowdlerized and bootlegged copies of the novel appeared, but no further action occurred until 1932, when the collector of Customs seized a copy of the book sent to Random House and declared it obscene under the Tariff Law of 1930. Random House intervened in the case because the publisher was, at that time, producing copies of the book with the intent to distribute it to the American reading public. The publisher demanded the court hearing required by the tariff law and asked for exculpation of the work. In pleas to the Federal Court of New York, Random House asked that the book be read in its entirety and that the passages declared to contain "the dirtiest language" be viewed in the context of the whole. In *United States v. One Book Entitled "Ulysses"*, 5 F. Supp. 182 (S.D.N.Y. 1933), later affirmed in *United States v. One Book Entitled "Ulysses"*, 72 F.2d 705 (2d Cir. 1934), Judge John M. Woolsey rejected the claims of obscenity, stating that despite the "unusual frankness" of the novel, "I do not anywhere detect the leer of the sensualist. I hold, therefore, that it is not pornographic." He further observed that he viewed the language and actions to be entirely consistent with the types of people whom Joyce describes. As to "the recurrent emergence of the theme of sex in the minds of his characters, it must always be remembered that his locale was Celtic and his season Spring." Judge Woolsey ruled that the book was not obscene when judged by its effect on the average man, *l'homme moyen sensuel*. He stated the following:

> In many places it seems to be disgusting, but although it contains, as I have mentioned above, many words usually considered dirty, I have not found anything that I consider to be dirt for dirt's sake. Each word of the book contributes like a bit of mosaic to the detail of the picture which Joyce is seeking to construct for his readers.

The government appealed the decision in the circuit court of appeals where, in *United States v. One Book Called "Ulysses"*, Judge Augustus Hand and Judge Learned Hand upheld the earlier decision. In the majority decision, they noted, "We think that *Ulysses* is a book of originality and sincerity of treatment, and that it has not the effect of promoting lust." The government chose not to appeal to the Supreme Court, and thus ended a decade-long struggle with the United States government and local censorship groups. It also provided a step toward freedom in the struggle between the moralists and publishers. In essence, the court ruled that the harm of an "obscene" book must be judged not from reading select passages but as a result of the whole book. Therefore, if the book as a whole had merit and the allegedly obscene parts were germane to the purpose of the book, then the book could not be viewed as obscene. In summing up the new interpretation of the law, Judge Augustus Hand stated:

> We believe that the proper test of whether a given book is obscene is its dominant effect. (I.e., is promotion of lust the dominant effect of reading the whole book?) In applying this test, relevancy of the objectionable parts to the theme, the established reputation of the work in the estimation of approved critics, if the book is modern, and the verdict of the past, if it is ancient, are persuasive pieces of evidence; for works of art are not likely to sustain a high position with no better warrant for their existence than their obscene content.

A significant result of the verdict was that it led judges and prosecutors to examine a book in its entirety rather than according to isolated passages. The decision also admitted the novel into the United States.

FURTHER READING

"Another Repeal: Joyce's *Ulysses* Is Legal at Last." *Nation* 137 (December 20, 1933): 693.

Arnold, Bruce. *The Scandal of "Ulysses": The Sensational Life of a Twentieth-Century Masterpiece*. New York: St. Martin's, 1994.

Bryer, J. R. "Joyce, *Ulysses* and the *Little Review*." *South Atlantic Quarterly* 66 (Spring 1967): 148–64.

Ernst, Morris L., and Alan U. Schwartz. *Censorship: The Search for the Obscene*. New York: Macmillan, 1964.

Marcuse, Ludwig. *The History of an Indignation*. London: MacGibbon & Key, 1965.

Paul, James C. N., and Murray L. Schwartz. *Federal Censorship: Obscenity in the Mail*. New York: Free Press, 1961.

St. John-Stevas, Norman. *Obscenity and the Law*. London: Secker & Warburg, 1956.

United States President's Commission on Obscenity and Pornography. *The Report of the Commission on Obscenity and Pornography*. New York: Random House, 1970.

VENUS AND TANNHAUSER (UNDER THE HILL)

Author: Aubrey Beardsley
Original date and place of publication: 1903, United States; 1904, England
Original publisher: Dodd, Mead and Company (United States); John Lane Company (England)
Type: Novel

SUMMARY

Venus and Tannhauser contains constant references to the sensuality of Venus and her court, including homosexual practices, orgies and such perversions as bestiality. The tone of the work is fantasy, and the literary style and the minute descriptions of the characters, as well as what they wear and say, provide a mocking air that blunts the sexual tone of the work.

Beardsley appeared to have consciously sought to shock his readers, as he has Venus, the queen of his fantasy empire, engage in sexual play with her tame unicorn named Adolphe. In one incident, Venus tries mightily to please her pet:

> Poor Adolphe! How happy he was, touching the Queen's breasts with his quick tongue-tip. . . . After the first charming interchange of affectionate delicacies was over, the unicorn lay down upon his side and, closing his eyes, beat his stomach wildly with the mark of manhood.
>
> Venus caught that stunning member in her hands and laid her cheek along it; but few touches were wanted to consummate the creature's pleasure.

Other passages that have been identified as offensive contain emetic references:

> Felix always attended Venus upon her little latrinal excursions, holding her, serving her, and making much of all she did. To undo her things, lift her skirts, to wait and watch the coming, to dip a lip or finger in the royal output, to stain himself deliciously with it, to lie beneath her as her favours fell, to carry off the crumpled, crotted paper—these were the pleasures of that young man's life.

Passages of both types were expurgated when the work first appeared.

CENSORSHIP HISTORY

Venus and Tannhauser was not published in unexpurgated form until 1959, when Grove Press published the novel under the title *Under the Hill*. The work first appeared in heavily expurgated form in the January 1897 and April 1898 issues of *The Savoy*, and publisher Arthur Symons hailed it as reflecting "undoubted, singular, literary ability." In 1903, Dodd, Mead and Company published an equally heavily expurgated version that was later "mutilated" further when John Lane published another version in 1904.

In 1954, Samuel Roth, denounced by the post office as the "leading smut king" in America, was charged with 26 indictments of obscenity. Among these counts was the charge that the fragment of *Venus and Tannhauser* included in volume three of Roth's quarterly magazine *American Aphrodite* was obscene. The government obtained the needed evidence when a post office inspector, using the pseudonym of Archie Lovejoy, ordered and received that issue of the magazine through the mails. Roth was convicted on 22 counts of distributing "obscene materials," sentenced to five years in jail and fined $5,000. The conviction was upheld in *Roth v. United States*, 237 F.2d 796 (2d Cir. 1956) in the United States Court of Appeals, Second Circuit, on September 18, 1956. Roth then appealed the decision to the United States Supreme Court, which ruled on the constitutionality of the statute under which Roth was convicted. In a decision in *Roth v. United States*, 354 U.S. 476 (1957), the Supreme Court voted 6 to 3 to uphold Roth's sentence.

FURTHER READING

Ernst, Morris L., and Alan U. Schwartz. *Censorship: The Search for the Obscene*. New York: Macmillan, 1964.

De Grazia, Edward. *Girls Lean Back Everywhere: The Law of Obscenity and the Assault on Genius*. New York: Random House, 1992.

Lewis, Felice Flanery. *Literature, Obscenity, & Law*. Carbondale: Southern Illinois University Press, 1976.

Magrath, C. Peter. "The Obscenity Cases: Grapes of Roth." *Supreme Court Review* 139 (1966): 9–13.

THE WILD PALMS

Author: William Faulkner
Original date and place of publication: 1939, United States
Original publisher: Random House
Type: Novel

SUMMARY

The Wild Palms counterpoints two stories, each containing a male character who is forced into a relationship with a woman who eventually becomes the inadvertent destroyer of the man. In "The Wild Palms," medical student Harry Wilbourne falls in love with Charlotte Rittenmeyer, married and the mother of two children. The two run away together to find the romantic love that Charlotte craves, but Wilbourne's inability to support them adequately places the couple in an increasingly perilous financial situation. When Charlotte becomes pregnant and demands that Wilbourne perform an abortion, he resists at first, then gives in to her demands.

Charlotte dies of the complications, feeling angered and betrayed. Yet, before dying, she makes her husband promise that he will not prosecute Wilbourne. Rittenmeyer, however, does prosecute, then offers Wilbourne cyanide as an alternative to life imprisonment. Recalling Charlotte's motto, "Between grief and nothing I will take grief," Wilbourne refuses and prepares to spend his life in prison.

"Old Man," the second story, parallels the first but reverses the situation. A convict, imprisoned after committing a robbery to obtain gifts for his girlfriend who soon marries another man, is on a work gang when a flood arises. He is sent to rescue a pregnant woman from a tree, which he does, but their boat rushes off course, stranding them for seven weeks on an island. In that time, the woman gives birth to a son with the help of the convict, who uses a tin-can lid to cut the umbilical cord.

He protects the woman and her child until they can return home, where he is promptly imprisoned and given 10 additional years in jail for attempting to escape. Rather than protest, he takes his punishment, viewing prison as a sanctuary. He lands in the same prison as Wilbourne. The irony of the two stories is that the apparently unheroic convict, a man who fears women, has acted heroically for the lady while the romantic Wilbourne has failed in his effort to play the role of hero.

The stories are relatively free of graphic sexuality, but censors objected to the discussion of abortion and the graphic description of Charlotte's pregnancy in "The Wild Palms." In one scene in that story, Charlotte and Wilbourne share a room with another couple and hear a "stallion-like surge from the other bed, the violent blanket-muffled motion ceasing into the woman's panting moans and at times a series of pure screams tumbling over one another." This is followed by "fierce breathing, the panting and shuddering woman moans." Also objectionable were the references to the birth of the baby in "Old Man" and the cutting of the cord.

CENSORSHIP HISTORY

The Wild Palms received complimentary critical reviews when it was first published, and no protests arose regarding its content until nearly a decade later. In 1948, *The Wild Palms* was one of nine works identified as obscene in criminal proceedings in the Court of Quarter Sessions in Philadelphia County, Pennsylvania. (See GOD'S LITTLE ACRE for a complete discussion of the case.) Indictments were brought by State District Attorney John H. Maurer against five booksellers who were charged with possessing and intending to sell *The Wild Palms* and other allegedly obscene works, including Erskine Caldwell's GOD'S LITTLE ACRE, Harold Robbins's *Never Love a Stranger*, James Farrell's STUDS LONIGAN TRILOGY (*Young Lonigan, The Young Manhood of Studs Lonigan* and *Judgment Day*) and *A WORLD I NEVER MADE*, Calder Willingham's END AS A MAN and Faulkner's SANCTUARY.

Judge Curtis Bok, who presided in *Commonwealth v. Gordon et al.*, 66 D.&C. 101 (1949), stated in his decision that "the redeeming feature of this tale ['The Wild Palms'] is that an acid loneliness comes through, the awful loneliness that pervades lost people, even in company. No one could envy these two miserable creatures." He discussed at length the concern whether in censoring obscenity the court were contravening the principles of freedom of speech and of the press. Judge Bok concluded, "I hold that the books before me are not sexually impure and pornographic, and are therefore not obscene, lewd, lascivious, filthy, indecent, or disgusting."

The Wild Palms was banned in Ireland on April 16, 1954. A prohibition order was published in the *Iris Oifigiuil*, "the only official source from which booksellers [and readers] might learn of a new prohibition order," in which all articles blacklisted by the Irish Board of Censors were listed. Based on tenets established in the Censorship of Publications Bill of 1928, the Irish Board of Censors found the novel "obscene" and filled with "indecency." The work was officially banned from sale in Ireland until the introduction of the Censorship Publications Bill in 1967 reduced to 12 years the duration of a prohibition order, and the work was among 5,000 banned titles released.

FURTHER READING

Adams, Michael. *Censorship: The Irish Experience*. University: University of Alabama Press, 1968.
McHaney, Thomas L. *William Faulkner's "The Wild Palms": A Study*. Jackson: University of Mississippi, 1975.
Page, Sally R. *Faulkner's Women: Characterization and Meaning*. De Land, Fla.: Everett/Edwards, 1972.

WOMEN IN LOVE

Author: D. H. Lawrence
Original date and place of publication: 1920, United States
Original publisher: Thomas Seltzer
Type: Novel

SUMMARY

Women in Love deals with the psychological explorations and the interrelationships of sisters Ursula and Gudrun Brangwen as they deal with love and life in a small English mining town. Alike in many respects, the sisters mirror the goals and desires of other modern young women of the early 19th century in their reservations about marriage and having children, as well as in their hatred of their middle-class origins. Ursula, however, is different from Gudrun in her ability to respond both spiritually and physically to Rupert Birken, although the two struggle mightily before Ursula and Rupert reach an understanding in which "He wanted sex to revert to the level of the other appetites, to be regarded as a functional process, not as a fulfillment." When they do consummate their relationship, Lawrence blends the physical passion with a spiritual bonding.

> They threw off their clothes, and he gathered her to him, and found her, found the pure lambent reality of her forever invisible flesh. Quenched, inhuman, his fingers upon her unrevealed nudity were the fingers of silence upon silence. . . . She had her desire fulfilled. He had his desire fulfilled.

In another segment of the novel, their sexual interaction is more fully revealed as "Kneeling on the hearth-rug before him, she put her arms around his loins, and put her face against his thighs."

Gudrun, on the other hand, and her lover Gerald are too self-absorbed to establish any true communication, and references to their sexual relationship are brief.

Beyond the sensual passages between Ursula and Rupert, critics have objected to Rupert's desire for intimacy with Gerald Crich. Rupert believes that men are capable of establishing an intimate friendship that a man can never attain with a woman. At one point in the novel when the two men wrestle in the nude, Rupert believes that he and Gerald are about to reach a plateau of trust and understanding, but Gerald appears unable to surrender his feelings entirely to anyone.

CENSORSHIP HISTORY

Overall, although *Women in Love* does not contain language that is usually identified as "obscene," nor are passages graphically sexual, the sexual relationship between Ursula and Rupert and the homoerotic relationship of Rupert and Gerald evoked strong objections from critics. The novel first appeared in 1920 in a limited edition of 1,250, marked "for subscribers only." The title page omitted Seltzer's imprint and carried, instead, the phrase "Privately Printed" to protect the company from attacks by censors. That move alone might have signaled to would-be censors that even the publisher thought the book too erotic to be published as part of the company's usual list. Two years later, Seltzer published the novel in a regular trade edition with the company imprint.

In 1922, the limited edition of *Women in Love* became one of three titles, published by Thomas Seltzer, that were involved in a well-publicized censorship case. The other two were Arthur Schnitzler's CASANOVA'S HOMECOMING and the anonymous YOUNG GIRL'S DIARY. The magistrate's court ruled in favor of the publisher. (See CASANOVA'S HOMECOMING.)

In 1923, Supreme Court Justice John Ford tried to suppress *Women in Love* after his daughter brought the book home from the circulating library that had recommended it to her. Ford founded the Clean Books League and worked with John Sumner, secretary of the New York Society for the Suppression of Vice, to achieve the passage of a "clean books" bill in the New York legislature. He also favored upholding and strengthening existing obscenity laws. Incensed by the action, Lawrence sent Ford a telegram from Taos, quoted on page 580 of the February 24, 1923, issue of *Publishers Weekly*:

> Let Judge John Ford confine his judgment to courts of law, and not try to perch in seats that are too high for him. Also let him take away the circulating library tickets from Miss Ford, lest worse befall her. She evidently needs an account at a candy shop, because, of course, 'Women in Love' wasn't written for the Ford family. . . . Father and mother and daughter should all leave the tree of knowledge alone. The Judge won't succeed in chopping it down, with his horrified hatchet. Many better men have tried and failed.

FURTHER READING

Boyer, Paul S. *Purity in Print: The Vice-Society Movement and Book Censorship in America.* New York: Scribner's, 1968.
"Censorship Beaten in New York Case." *Publishers Weekly* 102 (September 16, 1922): 801–904.
De Grazia, Edward. *Girls Lean Back Everywhere: The Law of Obscenity and the Assault on Genius.* New York: Random House, 1992.
Ford, John. *Criminal Obscenity, a Plea for Its Suppression.* New York: Revell, 1926.
Lawrence, D. H. "On Obscenity." *Publishers Weekly* (February 23, 1923): 580.
Loth, David. *The Erotic in Literature.* New York: Dorset, 1961.

A YOUNG GIRL'S DIARY

Author: Anonymous
Original date and place of publication: 1919, Switzerland; 1921, England; 1921, United States
Original publisher: Internationaler Psychoanalytischer Verlag (Switzerland); George Allen & Unwin (England); Thomas Seltzer (United States)
Type: Journal

SUMMARY

The anonymously written *A Young Girl's Diary* contains a preface by Sigmund Freud, who proclaimed the diary to be a "gem" that was the first work "enabling us to see so clearly into the soul of a young girl, belonging to our social and cultural stratum, during the years of puberal development." The work is a diary written by the pseudonymous Grete Lanier, an adolescent Viennese girl of the upper class who writes without self-consciousness about her reflections on sex.

The work is divided into four parts, each covering a year in Grete's life from the ages of 11 through 14 1/2, when her father dies of a stroke. Now orphaned, she and her sister are sent to live with relatives in a provincial city. In one passage, the writer observes that her friend told her that "when one is dark under the eyes one has *it* and that when one gets a baby then one doesn't have it any more until one gets another." She also reflects that her friend Bertha "told us how one gets it, but I didn't really believe what she said. . . . She said it must happen every night, for if not they don't have a baby. . . . That's why they have their beds so close together. People call them *marriage beds*!!" The final part of the journal contains the author's excited and hazy impression of what she observes while watching the young couple living next door to her engaged in sexual intercourse.

CENSORSHIP HISTORY

In 1921, Sir Archibald Bodkin, director of public prosecutions in England, summoned publisher Stanley Unwin to his office and shouted loudly that *A Young Girl's Diary*, published recently by Allen & Unwin, was "Filth, my dear Sir, filth." Ready to refute the charge, Unwin pointed out that each invoice for the book carried a label that stated, "This psychological study is intended for the use of members of the educational, medical and legal professions only." Bodkin retorted that one of his policemen had purchased a copy, then warned Unwin that "in the future you must obtain the name, address and occupation of the bookseller's customer before supplying the book." Bodkin pressed Unwin "to eliminate the objectionable passages and then distribute it" but backed down when Unwin asked him to identify specifically the "objectionable" passages. In reply to Unwin's request for specificity, Bodkin wrote,

> I must make it quite clear to you that to adopt any such suggestion would place me in the position of acting as a censor, a position I entirely decline to fill and one which would be contrary to my duty to fill.

In 1922, the limited edition of *A Young Girl's Diary*, translated from German by Eden and Cedar Paul, became one of three titles published by Thomas Seltzer, involved in a well-publicized censorship case with two other Seltzer titles: Arthur Schnitzler's CASANOVA'S HOMECOMING and D. H. Lawrence's WOMEN IN LOVE. John Sumner, secretary of the New York Society for the Suppression of Vice, led raids that seized copies of the books from the publisher's office and took stock of *A Young Girl's Diary* from shelves at Brentano's bookstore. The society also arrested Mary H. Marks, a clerk at Womrath's circulating library chain, for lending *A Young Girl's Diary* to a borrower, and they also removed stock of the three books from store shelves. The magistrate's court ruled in favor of the publisher, and Mary Marks, who had been made a codefendant in the trial, was also cleared. (See CASANOVA'S HOMECOMING.)

One year later, Sumner again secured a grand jury indictment against *A Young Girl's Diary* and CASANOVA'S HOMECOMING. In this case, the presiding judge declared immaterial the fact that the judge in the previous case had allowed experts to testify regarding the merits of the books. Instead, without testimony from experts, the books were found to be obscene. Faced with financial difficulties that prevented the expense of further litigation, Seltzer withdrew the books from circulation and agreed to destroy the plates. The criminal case was withdrawn but Seltzer's firm never recovered.

FURTHER READING

Boyer, Paul S. *Purity in Print: The Vice-Society Movement and Book Censorship in America.* New York: Scribner's, 1968.

"Censorship Beaten in New York Court." *Publishers Weekly* 20 (September 16, 1922): 801–4.

Gunn, Daniel, and Patrick Guyomard. "Introduction." In *A Young Girl's Diary*. Ed. by Daniel Gunn and Patrick Guyomard. New York: Doubleday, 1990.

"The Law and the Censor." *New York Times* (September 14, 1922): 21.

Tanselle, G. Thomas. "The Thomas Seltzer Imprint." *Papers of the Bibliographic Society of America* 58 (Fourth Quarter 1964): 380–416.

Unwin, Sir Stanley. *The Truth About Publishing*. London: Allen & Unwin, 1960.

APPENDIX I

BIOGRAPHICAL PROFILES

APOLLINAIRE, GUILLAUME (1880–1918)

Born Wilhelm Apollinaris de Kostrowitzki in Rome, Italy, the French poet, theorist and art critic was a major force in the avant-garde movements of early 20-century art. Among his noteworthy contributions were a famed analysis and defense of cubism and his creation of the term *surrealism*. He also wrote fiction, including the highly controversial THE MEMOIRES OF A YOUNG RAKEHELL and *The Debauched Hospadar.*

ARBITER, GAIUS PETRONIUS (d. A.D. 66)

Born in Rome, Italy, at an undetermined date, the prose and verse author left no historical evidence of his life, aside from mentions of him in the 16th book of the *Annals* of Tacitus. *The Satyricon* (A.D. 60) was censored in 1921 for its openly sexual descriptions.

ATWOOD, MARGARET (1939–)

Born in Ottawa, Ontario, the Canadian poet and novelist is also a political activist. Recurrent themes in her work revolve around the interlocked issues of power and language and the struggle of individuals, particularly women, to persevere in an indifferent society. All these elements come together in THE HANDMAID'S TALE (1986), a hotly debated novel about state control of reproduction in a totalitarian state.

AUEL, JEAN (1936–)

Born in Chicago, Illinois, the former technical writer, circuit board designer and credit manager first conceived of THE CLAN OF THE CAVE BEAR (1980) as a short story. After developing the story into the controversial 450,000-word novel, she followed with two sequels, *The Valley of Horses* (1982) and *The Mammoth Hunters* (1985).

BALZAC, HONORÉ DE (1799–1850)

Born in Tours, France, the novelist and short story writer was a founder of the realistic school and faithfully depicted ordinary and undistinguished lives. *Droll Stories (Contes Drolatiques)* (1832), a departure from realism, attracted the attention of censors for its excretory references and graphic sexual descriptions.

BAUDELAIRE, CHARLES (1821–67)

Born in Paris, France, the poet, critic and translator was a key member of the French Symbolist movement. He introduced the works of Edgar Allan Poe to Europe through his translations, making them French classics. THE FLOWERS OF EVIL (LES FLEURS DU MAL) (1857), the only volume of poetry published in Baudelaire's lifetime, was the object of a highly publicized censorship trial and later banned for its sexual and lesbian references.

BEARDSLEY, AUBREY (1872–98)

Born in Brighton, England, the artist and illustrator was a representative of the English aesthetic movement of the 1890s. Known for his black-and-white drawings on erotic and fabled subjects, he was one of the most important illustrators of his day. His few efforts at fiction were collected as VENUS AND TANNHAUSER (UNDER THE HILL) (1904), a work censored for its sexual and emetic imagery.

BLUME, JUDY (1938–)

Born in Elizabeth, New Jersey, the author writes romantic books for young people and has earned a reputation for dealing candidly with problems of early adolescence that traditional children's literature ignores. Most of her more than a dozen books have ignited challenges as to their appropriateness for school libraries and classrooms due to their language, religious references and sexual content, especially THEN AGAIN, MAYBE I WON'T (1971), *Blubber* (1974) and FOREVER (1975).

BOCCACCIO, GIOVANNI (1313–75)

Born in Uffizi, Florence, and acknowledged as the father of Italian prose style, the pastoral allegorist, epic poet and novella writer is also viewed by critics as one of the first Renaissance humanists. His work influenced the writings of Geoffrey Chaucer and William Shakespeare, despite the notoriety that the 100 tales of THE DECAMERON have engendered over the centuries.

BODENHEIM, MAXWELL (1893–1954)

Born in Clinton, Mississippi, the poet, novelist and playwright was influenced in his early work by the Romantic and Imagist movements. His notoriously bohemian life ended when he and his third wife were found murdered in a dingy, heatless room. REPLENISHING JESSICA (1927) became the target of censors and the subject of a widely publicized trial because of its sexual content.

BURNS, ROBERT (1759–96)

Born in Alloway, Ayreshire, Scotland, the poet is best known for his lyrical poems on the subjects of nature, love, patriotism and peasant life. His fascination with old Scottish airs led to the compilation of the posthumously published THE MERRY MUSES OF CALEDONIA (1800), censored for its bawdy language and frank sexuality.

BURTON, SIR RICHARD FRANCIS (1821–90)

Born in Torquay, Devonshire, England, the explorer, linguist and translator became in 1858 the first white person in modern times to view Lake Tanganyika in Africa. In addition to his travels, he produced books on swordsmanship and falconry; he is widely remembered for his translation of the TALES OF THE ARABIAN NIGHTS, as well as a number of sexually frank Eastern erotic manuals, including THE KAMA SUTRA, that aroused the interest of censors. His widow burned his papers and unpublished translations.

CABELL, JAMES BRANCH (1879–1958)

The American author wrote more than 50 works of fiction, essays and reminiscences, using his novels to attack modern orthodoxies. His best-known work, JURGEN (1919), whose symbolism was persistently sexual, earned him a popularity that faded when the elegant, sophisticated style he used passed from fashion. Among the best of his allegorical and fantastical novels are *The Cream of the Jest* (1917), *Figures of the Earth* (1921) and *The High Place* (1923).

CAIN, JAMES M. (1892–1977)

Born in Annapolis, Maryland, the newspaperman, novelist and playwright was a member of the hard-boiled school of writers, publishing such novels as *The Postman Always Rings Twice* (1934), SERENADE (1937) and *Mildred Pierce* (1941). The candidly sexual SERENADE was censored in 1949 in Massachusetts.

CALDWELL, ERSKINE (1903–87)

Born in Moreland, Georgia, the American author chronicled rural southern life and values in his major works. Among his best-known novels are TOBACCO ROAD (1932), GOD'S LITTLE ACRE (1933) and TRAGIC GROUND (1944), all of which drew the complaints of censors. The 1933 stage version of TOBACCO ROAD excited controversy and set Broadway records with its run of seven years.

CASANOVA DE SEINGALT, GIOVANNI JACOPO (1725–98)

Born in Venice, Italy, the gambler and adventurer made a name for himself as a prodigious lover throughout Europe. His sole literary contribution is the 12-volume compilation of his MEMOIRES (1826), which was not completely translated into English until 1966. MEMOIRES was banned because of the graphic descriptions of Casanova's sexual exploits.

CLELAND, JOHN (1710–89)

Born in Kingston-upon-Thames, Surrey, England, the novelist, playwright and essayist is best known as the author of FANNY HILL, OR MEMOIRS OF A WOMAN OF PLEASURE (1748). The novel has been censored repeatedly for its multiple sexual pairings and graphic sexual description.

CONNELL, VIVIAN (1905–)

Born in Cork County, Ireland, the playwright and novelist has lived most of his life in France. He published six novels and three plays; his most successful works, THE CHINESE ROOM (1942) and SEPTEMBER IN QUINZE (1952), were both objects of censors for their celebration of sexual openness.

D'ANNUNZIO, GABRIELE (1836–1938)

Born in Abruzzi, Italy, the novelist, poet, dramatist and soldier typified the fin de siècle decadence that defied bourgeois ethics. His works omit any concern for morality or conscience and profess, instead, that meaning in life comes from the pleasures of the senses. THE TRIUMPH OF DEATH (1894) was attacked by American censors who were offended by the decadence of the novel.

DEFOE, DANIEL (1660–1731)

Born Daniel Foe in London, England, the pamphleteer, journalist, political agent and novelist wrote frank and dramatically realistic fiction. His novel MOLL FLANDERS (1922) was heartily received upon publication, but late-19th-century censors found its frank sexuality immoral.

DELL, FLOYD (1887–1969)

Born in Barry, Illinois, the celebrated novelist, playwright, critic, editor and poet became one of the brightest lights in American avant-garde and Greenwich Village bohemianism in the early years of the 20th century. A major member of the Chicago Literary Renaissance of the early 1920s, Dell moved to New York City where, in the late 1920s and the 1930s, this proponent of free love and champion of feminism, socialism and Freudianism flourished as a writer. His novel JANET MARCH created a controversy in 1923 with its portrayal of a sexually active modern young woman.

DONLEAVY, JAMES PATRICK (1926–)

Born in Brooklyn, New York, the novelist and short story writer has lived mostly in Ireland, which figures prominently in his work. THE GINGER MAN (1955), an autobiographical novel, is his most celebrated and most censored book. An unexpurgated version did not appear in the United States until 1965.

DREISER, THEODORE (1871–1945)

Born in Terre Haute, Indiana, the American journalist, magazine editor, playwright and prolific novelist pioneered the literary movement known as naturalism. Dreiser depicted the lives of common people in such novels as *Sister Carrie* (1900) and AN AMERICAN TRAGEDY (1925). *Sister Carrie* was attacked and heavily censored as an immoral treatment of a scandalous woman's rise to success. He also suffered failure due to censorship of THE GENIUS (1915), an autobiographical novel about power and sex that was labeled "pornography" and attacked by moralists. In 1925, Dreiser published *An American Tragedy*, widely regarded as his finest achievement. Critics labeled it "immoral," and the novel became the subject of a notorious trial.

DU MAURIER, GEORGE (1834–96)

Born in Paris, France, the novelist and illustrator was famous for his caricatures in *Punch* before achieving success through his novels. TRILBY (1894), censored in Philadelphia, incorporates memories of his days as an art student in Paris.

FARRELL, JAMES THOMAS (1904–79)

Born in Chicago, the poet, critic, journalist and novelist often depicted in his fiction the lives of Irish-Americans in Chicago from 1900 through the Great Depression of the 1930s. His best- known novels make up the STUDS LONIGAN trilogy, which, with *A World I Never Made* (1936), were repeatedly subjected to banning attempts for their language and sexual situations. Farrell's fiction is a part of the tradition of naturalistic writing.

FAULKNER, WILLIAM (1897–1962)

Born in Oxford, Mississippi, this major figure of contemporary American literature and one of America's most innovative novelists depicted ordinary society in terms of ageless human dramas. In 1949, Faulkner won the Nobel Prize for literature. He repeatedly explored the question of human freedom and the obstacles to it—racism, regimentation, shame, fear, pride and overly abstract principles—infusing his novels with this honesty. Such works as *I Lay Dying* (1930), SANCTUARY (1931) and THE WILD PALMS (1939) have been attacked as being "vulgar" and "immoral" precisely because they depict realistically how people think, speak and feel.

FIELDING, HENRY (1707–54)

Born in Sharpham Park, Glastonbury, Somerset, England, the lawyer, playwright and novelist contributed significantly to the development of the English novel. He became London's first police magistrate and organized the "Bow Street runners," the first paid police force. Fielding's THE HISTORY OF TOM JONES, A FOUNDLING (1749) stirred controversy upon publication and suffered censorship for nearly two centuries.

FLAUBERT, GUSTAVE (1821–80)

Born at Rouen in Normandy, France, the novelist aimed to create reality through exactness, accuracy of detail and careful portrayal of object and event. Typical of his realistic method is MADAME BOVARY (1856), censored because of its suggestions of sexual activity and theme of adultery.

GAUTIER, THÉOPHILE (1811–72)

Born in Tarbes, France, the poet, novelist, journalist, travel writer and critic became the leader of France's "art for art's sake" movement. His first important novel, MADEMOISELLE DE MAUPIN (1835), epitomized the movement and was banned after motivating controversy. Gautier's sensitivity to beauty and insistence on formal perfection inspired Charles Baudelaire and the Parnassian movement.

GENET, JEAN (1910–86)

Born in Paris, France, the dramatist and novelist was the son of a prostitute and spent many years after the age of 10 in jail. He was released from a life sentence in 1947 through the intervention of Jean-Paul Sartre, after writing OUR LADY OF THE FLOWERS (NOTRE-DAME DES FLEURS) (1943), an autobiographical account of life in the criminal underworld. The novel was censored because it contained graphic descriptions of heterosexual and homosexual acts.

GIDE, ANDRÉ (1869–1951)

Born in Paris, the novelist, critic and dramatist addressed in his work the problems of personal freedom within the confines of conventional moral and ethical codes. Through such works as the controversial autobiography IF IT DIE (1920), he defended the right of each person to choose and to change his or her mind. Gide won the Nobel Prize for literature in 1947.

GLYN, ELINOR (1864–1943)

Born in Ottawa, Canada, but raised in England, the writer of romantic novels enjoyed shocking the public with a lifestyle replete with tiger skin rugs and stories of her violent passions. She defined "it" for film audiences, when the movie based on her novel *It* (1927) became a box office hit starring Clara Bow. Considered scandalous, THREE WEEKS (1909) became a best-seller because of efforts to ban it.

GOODMAN, DANIEL CARSON (1883–1957)

Born in Chicago, Illinois, the physician, film company executive, novelist and playwright only practiced medicine for 12 years before turning to writing full time. He served as the executive officer of the International Films Corporation from 1922 to 1924. *Hagar Revelly* (1913) created a controversy with its depiction of a young woman who resorts to prostitution to support herself and her baby.

GORHAM, CHARLES O. (1911–75)

Born in Philadelphia, Pennsylvania, the novelist and nonfiction writer produced five novels and two biographical studies. THE GILDED HEARSE (1948), his first novel, is about the advertising industry and was written while the author was a publicity director for Doubleday Publishing Company. The ensuing sensationalism over sexual content produced enormous sales.

GRIFFIN, JOHN HOWARD (1920–80)

Born in Dallas, Texas, the author worked as a photographer, lecturer and journalist before publishing nine books, including THE DEVIL RIDES OUTSIDE (1952), banned for its frank sexuality, and *Black Like Me* (1961), for which

Griffin is best known. The Caucasian author used chemicals and ultraviolet light to darken his skin, then traveled throughout the South as a black man. The resulting realism was disturbing to society.

HANLEY, JAMES (1901–85)

Born in Dublin, Ireland, the novelist, short story writer, playwright and biographer was prolific in his literary output and sometimes used the pseudonym Patric Shone in his writing. BOY (1931), his second and most acclaimed novel, was impounded under British obscenity laws for its graphic violence and brutal sexuality, becoming a cause celebre and securing the author's literary reputation.

HARDY, THOMAS (1840–1928)

Born in Upper Bockhampton, Dorset, the novelist, short story writer and poet introduced the concept of fatalism into Victorian literature. His final two of 15 novels, TESS OF THE D'URBERVILLES (1891), and JUDE THE OBSCURE (1895), explored the classic conflict between human passions and an indifferent universe, creating controversy and motivating efforts to ban them because of their treatment of sexuality and marriage. The outrage of the puritanical Victorian public over these books made Hardy stop writing fiction and return to his first artistic love, poetry, for the final 30 years of his life.

HARRIS, JAMES THOMAS "FRANK" (1856–1931)

Born in Galway, Ireland, the journalist, biographer and playwright was one of the most controversial authors of the early 20th century. He won considerable acclaim through his fictionalized biographies of Oscar Wilde, William Shakespeare and George Bernard Shaw, but he is best remembered for his frequently censored autobiography, MY LIFE AND LOVES (1923-27), which describes his sexual adventures and his early life in America.

HOFFENBERG, MASON (1922–86)

The avant garde poet was born in New York City but lived mainly in Paris after World War II. He wrote erotica for Olympia Press under such pseudonyms as Chamberlain Drake and Faustine Perez, as well as poetry under the pseudonym of Maxwell Kent. The author claimed in interviews given soon after the publication of *Candy* (1964) that coauthor Terry Southern had conceived of the book and began writing it alone. When Southern ran into difficulties in 1957, he called upon Hoffenberg to help complete it.

HUXLEY, ALDOUS LEONARD (1894–1963)

Born in Goldaming, Surrey, England, the novelist, essayist and critic is best known for his witty and humorous satiric portraits of early 20-century upper-class British society in *Antic Hay* (1923) and POINT COUNTER POINT (1928), as well as for his scathing indictment of oppressive government and the dangers of technology in *Brave New World* (1932). All three works have been subject to censorship attempts. His disillusionment led him toward mysticism and the use of hallucinatory drugs and to write such works as the novel *Eyeless in Gaza* (1936) and *The Doors of Perception* (1954) and *Heaven and Hell* (1956), in which he describes the use of mescaline to induce visionary states.

JAMES, NORAH C. (1902–87)

Born Norah Cordher in London, England, the novelist and short story author was working as the advertising and publicity manager for publisher Jonathan Cape, Ltd., when her sensational best-seller, *Sleeveless Errand*, appeared in 1929. It became the most famous of her more than 40 novels, most of them romances.

JONES, JAMES (1921–77)

Born in Robinson, Illinois, the novelist used his five-year army career as background for his writing. FROM HERE TO ETERNITY (1951), a brutal depiction of the army life, attracted censors because of its graphic sexuality and theme of adultery.

JOYCE, JAMES (1882–1941)

Born in Dublin, the short story writer, novelist and poet is known for his extensive use of interior monologue, as well as other technical innovations. Dublin is the subject matter of all his writing, including DUBLINERS (1914) and ULYSSES (1922), which were pirated by publishers and banned by censors.

KAUFFMANN, STANLEY (1916–)

Born in New York City, the writer, editor, actor and director is also a well-respected theater and film critic. THE PHILANDERER (1952) became Kauffmann's best-known novel after attempts to censor it led to a well-publicized London trial.

KEABLE, ROBERT (1887–1927)

Born in Bedfordshire, England, the novelist used his experiences as an Anglican chaplain during World War I as the basis for the controversial SIMON CALLED PETER, the most successful of his 13 novels. His financial success allowed the author to move to Tahiti, where he continued to write and rebel against prudery and convention.

KENTON, MAXWELL (*See* SOUTHERN, TERRY and HOFFENBERG, MASON

KEYES, DANIEL (1927–)

Born in Brooklyn, New York, the novelist has written several works that focus on psychological themes. FLOWERS FOR ALGERNON (1966), the best-known of Keyes's works, has been banned because of the sexually related thoughts and actions of the developmentally slow main character.

KING, STEPHEN (1947–)

Born in Portland, Maine, the writer of suspense and horror novels and stories is one of America's best-selling authors, under his own name and the pseudonym Richard Bachman, whose works have gained both critical acclaim and popular success. At the same time, many of his better-known works, among them *Carrie* (1974), *The Shining* (1977), *Cujo* (1981), CHRISTINE (1983), *Pet Sematary* (1983) and *The Stand* (1990), have been singled out by censors who have sought to remove these novels and, in some cases, all of King's works from school and public libraries.

LAWRENCE, DAVID HERBERT ("D. H.") (1885–1930)

Born in Nottinghamshire, England, the novelist, poet, critic, travel writer and social commentator is best remembered for such controversial novels as THE RAINBOW (1915), WOMEN IN LOVE (1920) and LADY CHATTERLEY'S LOVER (1928), banned because of Lawrence's candid portrayal of sexuality. His regard of sexual relations as the decisive element in human behavior shocked readers and became an integral part of his crusade against the constricting and sterile values of modern civilization.

MAILER, NORMAN (1923–)

Born in Long Branch, New Jersey, the novelist, journalist, essayist and political candidate is known for his brash politics and controversial views. His first novel, *The Naked and the Dead* (1948), based on his World War II combat experience in the Pacific, is viewed by critics as the finest of the modern war novels. Ensuing works such as THE DEER PARK (1955) and *An American Dream* (1965) continued this vision. All three books have been the targets of censors because of the author's blunt language and sexual imagery. Mailer won the National Book Award for *The Armies of the Night* (1968), his personal account of the 1967 peace march on the Pentagon. Mailer has also ignited controversy for *Oswald's Tale* (1995), which reviews the life of Lee Harvey Oswald and ponders his involvement in the death of President Kennedy.

MCCARTHY, MARY THERESA (1912–89)

Born in Seattle, Washington, the novelist, critic and short story writer scrutinized the fads that influenced women's lives in the 1930s and 1940s in her best-selling novel *The Group* (1963), which also drew the attention of censors for its sexual content. In other novels and nonfiction, McCarthy examined national politics, United States policy in Southeast Asia, the Nixon administration scandals and terrorism. McCarthy was married to novelist Edmund Wilson, with whom she worked on *The Partisan Review* and whose *Memoirs of Hecate County* was also banned.

METALIOUS, GRACE (1924–64)

Born Grace De Repentigny in Manchester, New Hampshire, she wrote only four novels, but PEYTON PLACE (1956) made her a literary celebrity. Highly critical of the small town in which she and her educator husband lived, the book resulted in the author and her family being shunned by local residents and led to her self-isolation.

MILLER, HENRY (1891–1980)

Born in New York City, the novelist lived for nine years in France, where he produced several major novels. His writing was mainly autobiographical, detailing his sexual misadventures and his compulsion to acknowledge the body. TROPIC OF CANCER (1934), TROPIC OF CAPRICORN (1939) and SEXUS (1949) were banned for many years because of their sexual content and language.

MOORE, GEORGE (1852–1933)

Born in County Mayo, Ireland, the novelist and playwright was active in the Irish Literary Renaissance of the early 1900s. His best-known novel, *Esther Waters* (1894), relates the story of a religious young woman with an illegitimate son. The novel was attacked for sexual content and banned, as were *A Modern Lover* (1883) and A STORY TELLER'S HOLIDAY (1918), a collection of short stories.

MORRISON, TONI (1931–   )

Born in Lorain, Ohio, the editor, novelist, educator and playwright proudly embraces her designation as "a black woman writer." Her novels focus on the struggles of female characters faced with the difficulties of growing up in a predominantly white society. *The Bluest Eye* (1970) was the target of censors for its sexual violence and theme of incest.

NABOKOV, VLADIMIR (1899–1977)

Born in St. Petersburg, Russia, the novelist, poet, short story writer and expert on butterflies first received international recognition with LOLITA (1955), a highly successful as well as controversial novel. He was noted for his superb control of language and plot and for his satire of American morés in fiction and nonfiction.

NAVARRE, MARGUERITE D'ANGOULÊME DE (QUEEN MARGARET OF NAVARRE) (1492–1549)

Born in Angouleme, France, the author became queen when she married Henry d'Albret, king of Navarre. Although highly religious, her work THE HEPTAMERON (1558) was a bawdy collection of tales patterned after Boccaccio's DECAMERON. The work did not arouse the interest of censors until the end of the 19th century.

NEVILLE, HENRY (c. 17th century)

ISLE OF PINES was written by a British author about whom no information is available, which leads literary historians to assume that this is a pseudonym. The work was the first to be censored in the United States for containing sexual content.

O'HARA, JOHN (1905–70)

Born in Pottsville, Pennsylvania, the novelist and short story writer is one of the best-selling writers of the 20th century. His ear for irony and acute powers of observation made his first novel, *Appointment in Samarra* (1934) a great success, and many later novels, including *Butterfield 8* (1935), *A Rage to Live* (1955), TEN NORTH FREDERICK (1955) and *From the Terrace* (1958) became popular films. He set most of his novels in the fictitious community of Gibbsville, Pennsylvania, and infused the works with realistic portrayals of the American upper-middle class, including its sex and drinking patterns. *Appointment in Samarra* and TEN NORTH FREDERICK both shocked reviewers and motivated censors who complained of the "vulgarity" in the novels and the sexual suggestiveness.

OVID (PUBLIUS OVIDIUS NASO) (43 B.C.–A.D. 17)

Born in Rome, the poet, dramatic monologuist and historian, hailed as the successor to Virgil, is considered the greatest poet of his age. His *The Art of Love* (*Ars Amatoria*) (c. A.D. 1) was an instant success, establishing him as the leading interpreter of upper-class Roman society of his day. The suggestiveness and psychological content of the poems were enjoyed for many centuries, but the poems became the object of censors in the late 19th and early 20th centuries.

PEPYS, SAMUEL (1633–1703)

Born in London, the government employee and one-time secretary of the admiralty did not have literary ambitions. His DIARY (1660–69) was written in shorthand that was not deciphered until 1824. In addition to providing an accurate view of the age, the diary also offers an uninhibited view of the author's personal life, which led to its suppression until the 19th century.

PHILLIPS, DAVID GRAHAM (1867–1911)

Born in Madison, Indiana, the journalist and novelist earned a reputation as a fierce crusader for the lower classes early in his career. He boldly attacked the United States Senate as being corrupt, earning from President Theodore Roosevelt the label of the "Man with the Muck Rake." The posthumously published SUSAN LENOX (1917) attracted the greatest notoriety for its sexually liberal heroine.

PRZYBYSKZEWSKI, STANISLAW ("STANLEY") (1868–1927)

Born in Kujawy, Poland, the dramatist, novelist, essayist, editor and poet was one of the most influential writers in Polish literature. His work emphasized sexual instinct as the primary force in human life, an element that led to the banning of his novel HOMO SAPIENS (1898).

RICHARDSON, SAMUEL (1689–1761)

Born in Derbyshire, England, the printer and novelist expanded the novel form to include psychological aspects of character and a highly emotional tone. PAMELA, OR VIRTUE (1740) was meant to be a manual on letter writing, but the provocative behavior of the main female character led to censorship in the 19th century.

ROBBINS, HAROLD (1916–1997)

Born in New York City, the novelist has produced a large number of financially successful novels that have been derided by critics for being sensationalist and poorly constructed. His autobiographical first novel, *Never Love a Stranger* (1948), was the target of censors for its frank language and references to sexuality, and THE CARPETBAGGERS (1961) suffered attempts at suppression for its blatant portrayal of sexual activity. Changing mores have prevented further censorship of Robbins's increasingly sexually explicit novels.

ROUSSEAU, JEAN JACQUES (1712–78)

Born in Geneva, Switzerland, the French philosopher and essayist motivated controversy in his emphasis upon individual liberty in such writings as his major political treatise, *The Social Contract* (1762), and his work on education, *Emile* (1762). The graphic accounts of his sexual activities included in his posthumously published CONFESSIONS (1884) led to their frequent banning.

SADE, MARQUIS DE (1740–1814)

Born Donatien-Alphonse-François in Paris, France, the author and libertine spent nearly 27 years in prison, after his first imprisonment in 1768 for mistreating a prostitute. He died in the insane asylum of Charenton. JUSTINE; OR, THE MISFORTUNES OF VIRTUE (1791), which chronicles the sexual mal-treatment of a young girl, is the best-known novel by de Sade, from whose name the word for the psychopathic behavior *sadism* is derived. The posthumously published THE 120 DAYS OF SODOM (1904) became an underground pornographic classic in the early 20th century.

SCHNITZLER, ARTHUR (1862–1931)

Born in Vienna, Austria, the dramatist and novelist was a physician before turning to writing. His works often delved into psychological themes related to sexuality and marriage that are evident in both his drama and such novels as the controversial CASANOVA'S HOMECOMING (1918).

SMITH, WALLACE (1888–1937)

Born in Chicago, Illinois, the novelist, short story writer and newspaper reporter was a veteran of four Mexican military campaigns before writing screenplays for the early Hollywood "talkies." BESSIE COTTER (1934) was his most serious novel, and the one in which he returned to his Chicago roots to explore his realistic theme.

SOUTHERN, TERRY (1924–95)

Born in Alvarado, Texas, the novelist, humorist and screenwriter blended black humor, parody and satire in his fiction, which includes *The Magic Christian* (1960); CANDY (1964), his parody of an erotic novel; and *Red-Dirt Marijuana and Other Tastes* (1967). The controversy over CANDY arose because censors did not realize that Southern and coauthor Mason Hoffenberg were parodying pornographic novels in the work and meant the exaggerated graphic sexuality to be funny.

SWINBURNE, ALGERNON CHARLES (1837–1909)

Born in London, England, the poet exhibited in his work rebellion against Victorian manners and morals and sympathies with the political movements of his time. POEMS AND BALLADS (1866) contained lyrics that dealt mainly with sensual love, leading censors to call for suppression of the work.

TOLSTOY, COUNT LEO (1828–1910)

Born at the family estate, Yasnaya Polyana (Clear Glade), a few miles south of Moscow, the Russian novelist and philosopher displayed in his work a genius for description and psychological acuity. Today famous for writing *War and Peace* (1865–69) and *Anna Karenina* (1875–77), Tolstoy achieved notoriety when censors banned THE KREUTZER SONATA (1890), in which he explored the conflict between sexual passion and morality.

TRYON, MARK (n.d.)

The Library of Congress catalog lists the author of SWEETER THAN LIFE (1958) as a pseudonym, with no further information.

TULLY, JIM (1891–1947)

Born in St. Mary's, Ohio, the prize fighter, publicity man and writer spent several years as a publicist for film star Charlie Chaplin. LADIES IN THE PARLOUR (1935) was censored for its theme of prostitution and one sexually graphic scene.

TWAIN, MARK (1835–1910)

Born Samuel Langhorne Clemens in Florida, Missouri, the humorist, novelist, journalist, lecturer and travel writer took his pseudonym from a phrase meaning "two fathoms deep" used by Mississippi river boatmen. He is largely associated with life on the Mississippi River because of the literary successes of *The Adventures of Tom Sawyer* (1876), *1601—A Fireside Conversation in Ye Time of Queen Elizabeth* (1876), *Life on the Mississippi* (1883) and *The Adventures of Huckleberry Finn* (1884–85), although he chronicled his journeys to the West and experiences in California, as well as adventures abroad in *Innocents Abroad* (1869), *Roughing It* (1872) and others. Two of Twain's most popular works are also among the most frequently banned or censored in the United States: *The Adventures of Tom Sawyer* and *The Adventures of Huckleberry Finn*.

UPDIKE, JOHN (1932–   )

Born in Shillington, Pennsylvania, the novelist, short story writer and poet often explores the conflict between mundane existence and the possibility of higher purpose in his writing. His novels examine middle-class manners from every possible perspective, exhibiting the flaws behind the finely created facade. *Rabbit, Run* (1960), typical of Updike's novels, aroused the interest of censors because of the sexual relationships among the characters and the graphic descriptions of sexual activity.

VOLTAIRE (1694–1778)

Born François Marie Arouet in Paris, France, the novelist, dramatist and philosopher also wrote histories, essays, reformist tracts, poetry and satirical tales such as CANDIDE (1759) and THE MAID OF ORLEANS (1762), which were banned for their sexual content. A fighter for reform, Voltaire violently denounced intolerance and injustice, often aiding victims. He mercilessly satirized social, political and religious figures and ideas of his time.

WILSON, EDMUND (1895–1972)

Born in Red Bank, New Jersey, the critic, novelist, short story writer, playwright and poet was a highly respected literary critic as well as a writer. MEMOIRS OF HECATE COUNTY (1946) was banned after publication because of the candid sexuality of one of the stories. Wilson was married to novelist Mary McCarthy, with whom he worked on *The Partisan Review* and whose novel *The Group* was also banned.

WINSOR, KATHLEEN (1919–)

Born in Olivia, Minnesota, the novelist and former newspaper reporter is best known for her Restoration romance, FOREVER AMBER (1944). The novel created controversy when it first appeared, which led to its being banned in Boston and other cities.

ZOLA, ÉMILE (1840–1902)

Born in Aix-en-Provence, France, the journalist and novelist used his fiction to campaign for social reform and justice and became the major proponent of literary naturalism. Zola created a cycle of 20 novels called collectively *Les Rougon Macquart*, which were criticized for their gratuitous brutality and obscenity. Today they are valued as fictionalized sociology. Of particular interest are NANA (1880) and LA TERRE, the latter translated variously as THE EARTH and THE SOIL (1887). In later years, Zola gained further notoriety for his celebrated campaign and notorious "J'accuse" letter to defend Captain Alfred Dreyfus.

BIBLIOGRAPHY

BOOKS

Acts and Laws, Passed by the Great and General Court or Assembly of the Province of the Massachusetts-Bay in New-England, from 1692 to 1719. London: John Baskett, 1724.

Adams, Michael. *Censorship: The Irish Experience.* University: University of Alabama Press, 1968.

Alkon, Paul. *Defoe and Fictional Time.* Athens: University of Georgia Press, 1979.

Arnold, Bruce. *The Scandal of "Ulysses": The Sensational Life of a Twentieth-Century Masterpiece.* New York: St. Martin's, 1994.

Ayer, Alfred Jules. *Voltaire.* New York: Random House, 1986.

Balzac, Honoré de. *Correspondence.* Ed. by Roger Pierrot. Paris: Barnier, 1969.

Ben-Ephraim, Gavriel. *The Moon's Dominion: Narrative Dichotomy and Female Dominance in Lawrence's Earlier Novels.* Rutherford, N.J.: Fairleigh Dickinson University Press, 1989.

Bercovici, Alfred. *That Blackguard Burton!* Indianapolis, Ind.: Bobbs-Merrill Co., 1962.

Besterman, Theodore. *Voltaire.* New York: Harcourt Brace & World, 1969.

*Boyer, Paul S. *Purity in Print: The Vice-Society Movement and Book Censorship in America.* New York: Scribner's, 1968.

Brightman, Carol. *Writing Dangerously: Mary McCarthy and Her World.* New York: Clarkson Potter, 1992.

Brodie, Fawn M. *The Devil Drives: A Life of Sir Richard Burton.* New York: Norton, 1967.

Brooks, Van Wyck. *The Confident Years: 1885–1915.* New York: Dutton, 1952.

Broun, Heywood, and Margaret Leech. *Anthony Comstock.* New York: Albert and Charles Boni, 1927.

Bryant, Arthur. *Samuel Pepys: The Man in the Making.* London: Cambridge University Press, 1943.

Burton, Sir Richard, trans. "Introduction." In *The Perfumed Garden of Sheikh Nefzaoui.* New York: Lancer, 1964.

Butler-Evans, Elliott. *Race, Gender and Desire: Narrative Strategies in the Fiction of Toni Cade Bambara and Toni Morrison.* Philadelphia: Temple University Press, 1989.

Campbell, Jeff H. *John Howard Griffin.* Austin, Tex.: Steck-Vaughn, 1970.

Clayton, Douglas. *Floyd Dell: The Life and Times of an American Rebel.* Chicago: Ivan R. Dee, 1994.

Colum, Padraic, and Margaret Freeman Cabell, eds. *Between Friends: Letters of James Branch Cabell and Others.* New York: Harcourt, Brace & World, 1962.

Cowley, Malcolm. *After the Genteel Tradition.* Rev. ed. Carbondale: Southern Illinois University, 1964.

*Craig, Alec. *Suppressed Books: A History of the Conception of Literary Obscenity.* New York: World Publishing, 1963.

Cranston, Maurice. *The Noble Savage: Jean-Jacques Rousseau.* Chicago: University of Chicago, 1991.

Davis, Kenneth C. *Two-Bit Culture: The Paperbacking of America.* Boston: Houghton Mifflin, 1984.

*De Grazia, Edward. *Censorship Landmarks.* New York: Bowker, 1969.

*———. *Girls Lean Back Everywhere: The Law of Obscenity and the Assault on Genius.* New York: Random House, 1992.

---

* Key sources

Donelson, Kenneth L., and Alleen Pace Nilsen. *Literature for Today's Young Adults.* Glenview, Ill.: Scott Foresman, 1989.

Donleavy, J. P. *The History of the Ginger Man.* Boston: Houghton-Mifflin, 1994.

Dudley, Dorothy. *Forgotten Frontiers: Dreiser and the Land of the Free.* New York: Smith & Haas, 1932.

Egerton, John. *A Mind to Stay Here: Profiles from the South.* New York: Macmillan, 1970.

*Ernst, Morris L., and Alan U. Schwartz. *Censorship: The Search for the Obscene.* New York: Macmillan, 1964.

Farrell, James T. "The Author as Plaintiff: Testimony in a Censorship Case." In Farrell's *Reflection at Fifty and Other Essays.* New York: Vanguard Press, 1954.

Filler, Louis. *Voice of Democracy: David Graham Phillips.* University Park: Pennsylvania State University, 1968.

*Foerstel, Herbert N. *Banned in the U.S.A.: A Reference Guide to Book Censorship in Schools and Public Libraries.* Westport, Conn.: Greenwood, 1994.

Ford, John. *Criminal Obscenity, A Plea for Its Suppression.* New York: Revell, 1926.

Ford, Worthington Chauncey. *The Isle of Pines 1668: An Essay in Bibliography.* Boston: The Club of Odd Volumes, 1920.

Forster, E. M. *Abinger Harvest.* New York: Harcourt, Brace, 1936.

Foxon, David. *Libertine Literature in England, 1600–1745.* New Hyde Park, N.Y.: University Books, 1965.

Frohock, W. M. *The Novel of Violence in America.* Dallas, Tex.: Southern Methodist University, 1950.

Galloway, David D. *The Absurd Hero in American Fiction.* Rev. ed. Austin, Tex.: University of Texas Press, 1970.

Gelderman, Carol. *Mary McCarthy: A Life.* New York: St. Martin's, 1988.

*Geller, Evelyn. *Forbidden Books in American Public Libraries, 1876–1939.* Westport, Conn.: Greenwood, 1984.

Gerber, Albert B. *Sex, Pornography and Justice.* New York: Lyle Stuart, 1965.

Gerson, Noel B. *The Prodigal Genius.* Garden City, N.Y.: Doubleday, 1972.

Gilmer, Frank Walker. *Horace Liveright: Publisher of the Twenties.* New York: Lewis, 1970.

Girodias, Maurice. "Introduction." *The Olympia Reader.* New York: Grove, 1965.

Gladstein, Mimi. *The Indestructible Woman in Faulkner, Hemingway, and Steinbeck.* Ann Arbor, Mich.: Research Press, 1986.

Glyn, Anthony. *Elinor Glyn.* Garden City, N.Y.: Doubleday, 1955.

Goldman, Eric F. "David Graham Phillips, Victorian Critic of Victorianism." In *The Lives of Eighteen from Princeton.* Ed. by Willard Thorp. Princeton, N.J.: Princeton University Press, 1946.

Green, Virginia M. *Heroic Virtue, Comic Infidelity: Reassessing Marguerite de Navarre's Heptameron.* Amherst, Mass.: Hestia Press, 1993.

Gunn, Daniel, and Patrick Guyomard. "Introduction." In *A Young Girl's Diary.* Ed. by Daniel Gunn and Patrick Guyomard. New York: Doubleday, 1990.

Gustafson, Richard F. *Leo Tolstoy, Resident and Stranger: A Study in Fiction and Theology.* Princeton, N.J.: Princeton University Press, 1986.

Haney, Robert W. *Comstockery in America: Patterns of Censorship and Control.* Boston: Beacon, 1960.

---

* Key sources

Hardy, Thomas. "Candour in Fiction." In *Thomas Hardy's Personal Writings: Prefaces, Literary Opinions, Reminiscences.* Ed. by Harold Orel. Lawrence: University of Kansas Press, 1966.

Harris, Frank. "Foreword." In *My Life and Loves.* New York: Grove, 1963.

Etherington-Smith, Meredith, and Jeremy Pilcher. *The "It" Girls: Elinor Glyn, Novelist and Her Sister Lucile, Couturiere.* New York: Harcourt Brace Jovanovich, 1986.

Hart, John E. *Floyd Dell.* New York: Twayne, 1971.

Hayman, Ronald. *De Sade: A Critical Biography.* New York: Crowell, 1978.

Hemmings, F. W. J. *The Life and Times of Emile Zola.* New York: Scribner's, 1977.

Hempl, William J., and Patrick M. Wall. "Extralegal Censorship of Literature." In *Issues of Our Time.* Ed. by Herbert W. Hildebrandt. New York: Macmillan, 1963.

Holt, Guy, ed. *Jurgen and the Law: A Statement with Exhibits, Including the Court's Opinion and the Brief of the Defendants on Motion to Direct an Acquittal.* New York: Robert M. McBride, 1923.

Huizinga, J. H. *Rousseau: The Self-Made Saint.* New York: Grossman, 1976.

Hunt, George W. *John Updike and the Three Great Secret Things: Sex, Religion, and Art.* Grand Rapids, Mich.: Eerdmans, 1980.

*Hurwitz, Leon. *Historical Dictionary of Censorship in the United States.* Westport, Conn.: Greenwood, 1985.

Hutchison, E. R. *Tropic of Cancer on Trial.* New York: Grove Press, 1968.

Josephson, Matthew. *Zola and His Time.* Garden City, N.Y.: Garden City Publishers, 1928.

Katz, Jonathan. *Gay/Lesbian Almanac.* New York: Carroll & Graf, 1994.

Kauffmann, Stanley. "Introduction." *The Philanderer.* 2d ed. London: Secker & Warburg, 1954.

*Kearney, Patrick J. *A History of Erotic Literature.* Hong Kong: Parragon, 1982.

*Kendrick, Walter. *The Secret Museum: Pornography in Modern Culture.* Baltimore: Penguin, 1988.

*Kilpatrick, James J. *The Smut Peddlers.* New York: Doubleday, 1960.

King, Stephen. "Banned Books and Other Concerns: The Virginia Beach Lecture." In *The Stephen King Companion.* Ed. by George Beahm. Kansas City, Mo.: Andrews & McMeel, 1989.

Klevar, Harvey L. *Erskine Caldwell: A Biography.* Knoxville: University of Tennessee Press, 1993.

*Kronhausen, Eberhard, and Phyllis Kronhausen. *Pornography and the Law: The Psychology of Erotic Realism.* New York: Ballantine, 1959.

*Kuh, Richard H. *Foolish Figleaves? Pornography In and Out of Court.* New York: Macmillan, 1967.

Lawrence, D. H. *The Quest for Rananim: D. H. Lawrence's Letters to S. S. Koteliansky, 1914–1930.* Ed. and intro. by George J. Zytaruk. Montreal: McGill-Queen's University Press, 1970.

Legman, George, ed. "Introduction." *The Merry Muses of Caledonia: Collected and Written in Part by Robert Burns.* New Hyde Park, N.Y.: University Books, 1965.

Lever, Maurice. *Sade: A Biography.* Trans. by Arthur Goldhammer. New York: Farrar & Straus, 1993.

---

* Key sources

*Lewis, Felice Flanery. *Literature, Obscenity, & Law*. Carbondale: Southern Illinois University Press, 1976.

*Loth, David. *The Erotic in Literature*. New York: Dorset, 1961.

Lottman, Herbert. *Flaubert: A Biography*. Boston: Little, Brown, 1989.

MacCarthy, Desmond. *Criticism*. London: Dent, 1932.

Maddox, Brenda. *D. H. Lawrence: The Story of a Marriage*. New York: Simon & Schuster, 1993.

Mancuso, Ludwig. *The Obscene: The History of an Indignation*. London: MacGibbon & Key, 1965.

Manso, Peter. *Mailer: His Life and Times*. New York: Simon & Schuster, 1985.

*Marchand, Henry. *The French Pornographers: Including a History of French Erotic Literature*. New York: Book Awards, 1965.

Marcosson, Isaac F. *David Graham Phillips and His Times*. New York: Dodd, Mead, 1932.

*Marcus, Stephen. *The Other Victorians*. New York: Basic, 1966.

Marcuse, Ludwig. *The History of an Indignation*. London: MacGibbon & Key, 1965.

Markle, Joyce. *Fighters and Lovers: Theme in the Novels of John Updike*. New York: New York University Press, 1973.

Markmann, Charles L. *The Noblest Cry: A History of the American Civil Liberties Union*. New York: St. Martin's, 1965.

*McCoy, Ralph E. *Banned in Boston: The Development of Literary Censorship in Massachusetts*. Urbana: University of Illinois, 1956.

McHaney, Thomas L. *William Faulkner's "The Wild Palms": A Study*. Jackson: University of Mississippi, 1975.

Miller, Daniel B. *The Journey from 'Tobacco Road.'* New York: Knopf, 1995.

Miller, Henry. "Defense of the Freedom to Read—A Letter to the Supreme Court of Norway in Connection with the Ban on *Sexus* (*The Rosy Crucifixion*)." In *Versions of Censorship: An Anthology*. Ed. by John McCormick and Mairi MacInnes. Garden City, N.Y.: Doubleday, 1962.

Mills, Hillary. *Mailer: A Biography*. New York: Empire, 1982.

Moore, Jack B. *Maxwell Bodenheim*. New York: Twayne, 1970.

Moore, John R. *Daniel Defoe: Citizen of the Modern World*. Chicago: University of Chicago Press, 1958.

Mordell, Albert, ed. *Notorious Literary Attacks*. New York: Boni & Liveright, 1926.

Morgan, Edwin. *Flowers of Evil: A Life of Charles Baudelaire*. Freeport, N.Y.: Books for Libraries Press, 1943.

Newman, M. W. *The Smut Hunters*. Los Angeles: All American Distributors, 1964.

Oboler, Eli M. *The Fear of the Word: Censorship and Sex*. Metuchen, N.J.: The Scarecrow Press, 1974.

Page, Sally R. *Faulkner's Women: Characterization and Meaning*. De Land, Fla.: Everett/Edwards, 1972.

Partridge, Eric. *The First Three Years*. London: Scholartis, 1930.

Paul, James C. N., and Murray L. Schwartz. *Federal Censorship: Obscenity in the Mail*. New York: Free Press, 1961.

*Perkins, Michael. *The Secret Record: Modern Erotic Literature*. New York: Morrow, 1976.

---

* Key sources

*Perrin, Noel. *Dr. Bowdler's Legacy: A History of Expurgated Books in England and America.* Boston: Godine, 1992.

*Perry, Stuart. *The Indecent Publications Tribunal: A Social Experiment.* London: Whitcombe and Tombs, 1965.

Pichois, Claude. *Baudelaire.* London: Hamish Hamilton, 1989.

Pinion, F. B. *Thomas Hardy: His Life and Friends.* New York: St. Martin's, 1992.

Putnam, George Haven. *The Censorship of the Church of Rome and Its Influence upon the Production and Distribution of Literature.* Vol. II. New York: Putnam's, 1906.

Ravitz, Abe C. *David Graham Phillips.* New York: Twayne Publishing, 1966.

Rembar, Charles. *The End of Obscenity: The Trials of "Lady Chatterley's Lover," "Tropic of Cancer" & "Fanny Hill" by the Lawyer Who Defended Them.* New York: Random House, 1968.

Rice, Edward. *Captain Sir Richard Francis Burton.* New York: Scribner's, 1990.

Robb, Graham. *Balzac: A Biography.* New York: Norton, 1994.

Roeburt, John. *The Wicked and the Banned.* New York: Macfadden, 1963.

Rollyson, Carl. *The Lives of Norman Mailer.* New York: Paragon House, 1991.

Rolph, Cecil Hewitt. *Books in the Dock.* London: Deutsch, 1961.

Sartre, Jean-Paul. *Saint Genet: Comedian and Martyr.* New York: George Brazillier, 1952.

Schom, Alan. *Emile Zola: A Biography.* New York: Holt, 1987.

Seymour-Smith, Martin. *Hardy: A Biography.* New York: St. Martin's, 1994.

Steegmuller, Francis. *Flaubert and Madame Bovary.* Boston: Houghton Mifflin, 1970.

St. John-Stevas, Norman. *Obscenity and the Law.* London: Secker & Warburg, 1956.

*Stuart, Perry. *The Indecent Publications Tribunal: A Social Experiment.* Christchurch, New Zealand: Whitcombe and Tombs, 1965.

Sutherland, James. *Defoe.* Philadelphia: Lippincott, 1938.

*Sutherland, John. *Offensive Literature: Decensorship in Britain, 1960–1982.* London: Junction, 1982.

Swinburne, Algernon Charles. *Letters of Algernon Charles Swinburne.* Vol. I. Ed. by C. Y. Lang. New Haven, Conn.: Yale University Press, 1959.

Tebbel, John. *A History of Book Publishing in the United States.* Vol. II. New York: Bowker, 1975.

*Thomas, Donald. *A Long Time Burning: The History of Literary Censorship in England.* New York: Praeger, 1969.

Thomas, Donald Serrell. *The Marquis de Sade.* Boston: New York Graphic Society, 1976.

Tindall, William York. *Forces in Modern British Literature, 1885–1956.* 2d ed. New York: Vintage, 1956.

Tjader, Marguerite. *Theodore Dreiser: A New Dimension.* Norwalk, Conn.: Silvermine, 1965.

Tobin, A. I., and Elmer Gertz. *Frank Harris: A Study in Black and White.* Chicago: Madelaine Mendelsohn, 1931.

Troyat, Henri. *Flaubert.* Paris: Librairie Ernest Flammarion, 1988.

Tully, Jim. *A Dozen and One.* Hollywood: Murray & Gee, 1943.

Tuttleton, James. *The Novel of Manners in America.* New York: Norton, 1972.

* Key sources

*United States President's Commission on Obscenity and Pornography. *The Report of the Commission on Obscenity and Pornography*. New York: Random House, 1970.

Unwin, Sir Stanley. *The Truth about Publishing*. London: Allen & Unwin, 1960.

Vizitelly, Ernest A. *Emile Zola, Novelist and Reformer: An Account of His Life and Work*. London: Lane, 1904.

Wainhouse, Austryn. "Foreword." *The Marquis de Sade: Juliette*. New York: Grove, 1968.

Weinstein, Philip M. *What Else but Love? The Ordeal of Race in Faulkner and Morrison*. New York: Columbia University Press, 1996.

Wellek, Rene and Austin Warren. *Theory of Literature*. 3rd ed. New York: Harcourt, Brace & World, 1956.

White, Edmund. *Genet: A Biography*. New York: Knopf, 1994.

Williams, David. *Faulkner's Women: The Myth and the Muse*. Montreal: McGill-Queen's University Press, 1977.

Wilson, Sharon Rose. *Margaret Atwood's Fairy-Tale Sexual Politics*. Jackson: University of Mississippi, 1993.

Zweig, Stefan. *Balzac*. London: Cassell, 1970.

PERIODICALS

"Again the Literary Censor." *Nation* 3 (September 25, 1920): 343.

"Another Furor over Books." *Ohio State University Monthly* 55 (December 1963): 8–12.

"Another Repeal: Joyce's *Ulysses* Is Legal at Last." *Nation* 137 (December 20, 1933): 693.

"Anthony Comstock Overruled." *Publishers Weekly* 45 (June 30, 1894): 942–43.

Auerbach, Joseph S. "Authorship and Liberty." *North American Review* 207 (July 1918): 902–17.

Bacon, Corinne. "What Makes a Novel Immoral?" *Wisconsin Library Bulletin* 6 (August 1910): 83–95.

Baker, George. "*Lolita*: Literature or Pornography." *Saturday Review* 40 (June 22, 1957): 18.

Balbert, Peter. "From *Lady Chatterley's Lover* to *The Deer Park*: Lawrence, Mailer, and the Dialectic of Erotic Risk." *Studies in the Novel* 22 (Spring 1990): 67–81.

Barlow, Samuel L. M. "The Censor of Art." *North American Review* 213 (March 1921): 346–50.

Bates, Ralph. "Mr. Wilson's Visit to Suburbia." *New York Times Book Review* (March 31, 1946): 7, 16.

"Battling the Wolves." *Christian Century* 48 (April 8, 1931): 470–71.

Beattie, A. M., and Frank A. Underhill. "Sense and Censorship: On Behalf of *Peyton Place*." *Canadian Library Association Bulletin* 15 (July 1958): 9–16.

Benhuniak-Long, Susan. "Feminism and Reproductive Technology." *Choice* 29 (October 1991): 243.

Bergeron, Katherine. "The Echo, the Cry, the Death of Lovers." *Nineteenth Century Music* 18 (Fall 1994): 136–51.

Booth, Wayne C. "Censorship and the Values of Fiction." *English Journal* 53 (March 1964): 155–64.

"Boston Clean Book Case." *Publishers Weekly* (January 26, 1924): 240.

---

* Key sources

Boyer, Paul S. "Boston Book Censorship in the Twenties." *American Quarterly* 15 (Spring 1930): 3–24.

Broun, Heywood. "Heywood Broun Comes to the Rescue of Immoral Books." *Current Opinion* 67 (December 1919): 315–16.

Bryer, J. R. "Joyce, *Ulysses* and the *Little Review.*" *South Atlantic Quarterly* 66 (Spring 1967): 148–64.

Bullard, F. Lauriston. "Boston's Ban Likely to Live Long." *New York Times* (April 28, 1929): Sec. 3: 1, 7.

Burgum, Edwin Berry. "Erskine Caldwell and His Jeeters." *New York Times Book Review* (October 15, 1944): 46.

Caldwell, Erskine. "My Twenty-Five Years of Censorship." *Esquire* 50 (October 1958): 176–78.

"Protest Against Columbia University's Ban on *Tobacco Road* and *God's Little Acre.*" *New Republic* 79 (June 27, 1934): 184–85.

"Caldwell Novel Cleared as 'Dull'." *New York Times* (December 29, 1944): 13.

"Censorship Beaten in New York Court." *Publishers Weekly* 20 (September 16, 1922): 801–4.

Centerwall, Brandon S. "Hiding in Plain Sight: Nabokov and Pedophilia." *Texas Studies in Literature & Language* 32 (Fall 1990): 468–84.

Champion, Laurie. "Jones's *From Here to Eternity.*" *Explicator* 54 (Summer 1996): 242–44.

"Chicago Bookseller Wins Case." *Publishers Weekly* 119 (April 4, 1931): 1,790.

Ciardi, John. "The Marquis de Sade II." *Saturday Review* 48 (October 2, 1965): 36.

———. "*Tropic of Cancer.*" *Saturday Review* 45 (June 1962): 13.

Clancy, Ambrose. "Wild Irish Rogue." *Gentleman's Quarterly* 61 (June 1991): 60–68.

Cohen, Emily Jane. "Mud into Gold: Baudelaire and the Alchemy of Public Hygiene." *Romantic Review* 87 (March 1996): 239–55.

Cook Bruce. "Candy Comes to Chicago." *Nation* 199 (September 14, 1964): 125–26.

Cooper, Morton. "Fanny Hill vs. the Constitution." *Pageant* 14 (June 1964): 14–20.

Cooper, Pamela. "Sexual Surveillance and Medical Authority in Two Versions of *The Handmaid's Tale.*" *Journal of Popular Culture* 28 (Spring 1995): 49–66.

"Court Bans Tully Book." *New York Times* (November 1, 1935): 19.

Cusseres, Benjamin de. "Case of Prudery against Literature: Attack on Gautier's Novel Brings to Mind Many Historical Examples of Law's Moral Censorship of Books." *New York Times* (May 23, 1920): Sec. 7: 3.

Dangerfield, George. "Invisible Censorship." *North American Review* 244 (Winter 1937–1938): 334–48.

Daniels, Jonathan. "American Lower Depths." *Saturday Review of Literature* (October 14, 1944): 6.

"D'Annunzio at Asbury Park." *New York Times* (July 24, 1897): 6.

"Defoe's Works Banned." *Publishers Weekly* 116 (October 19, 1929): 1,938.

DeVoto, Bernard. "The Easy Chair: Liberal Decisions in Massachusetts." *Harper's Magazine* 199 (July 1949): 62–65.

Doherty, Gerald. "The Art of Appropriation: The Rhetoric of Sexuality in D. H. Lawrence." *Style* 30 (Summer 1996): 289–308.

Dupee, F. W. "*Lolita* in America." *Encounter* 12 (February 1959): 30–35.

Durham, Frank M. "Mencken as Missionary." *American Literature* 29 (January 1958): 478–83.

"The Editor Recommends—." *The Bookman* 57 (February 1924): 459.

Elliott, Desmond. "The Book That Shocked Paris: The Strange Story of *Madame Bovary*." *Books and Bookmen* 5 (June 1960): 11, 46.

———. "Field Day for the Righteous." *Books and Bookmen* 5 (December 1959): 17.

———. "Scandal over Studs (Trial over James Farrell's *Studs Lonigan*)." *Books and Bookmen* 5 (November 1959): 23–26.

Ernst, Morris L., and Alexander Lindey. "The Censor Marches On. . . ." *Esquire* 11 (June 1939): 174–77.

"Evil in Our Time." *Time* 48 (March 25, 1946): 102.

Farrell, James T. "Lonigan, Lonergan, and New York's Finest." *Nation* 158 (March 18, 1944): 338.

Farriman, Milton. "Bookseller Victorious in Chicago Reformer's Campaign." *Publishers Weekly* 117 (February 1, 1930): 566–68.

Feeney, Ann. "*Lolita* and Censorship: A Case Study." *References Services Review* 21 (Winter 1993): 67–74, 90.

Ferns, Chris. "The Values of Dystopia: *The Handmaid's Tale* and the Anti-Utopian Tradition." *Dalhousie Review* 69 (Fall 1989): 373–82.

"Finds Keable Book Obscene." *New York Times* (October 19, 1922): 2.

Flower, Benjamin O. "Conservatism and Sensualism: An Unhallowed Alliance." *Arena* 3 (December 1890): 126–28.

———. "The Postmaster-General and the Censorship of Morals." *Arena* 2 (October 1890): 540–52.

Forman, Jack. "Young Adult Books: 'Watch Out for #1'." *Horn Book* 61 (January–February 1985): 85.

Foxon, David F. "John Cleland and the Publication of *Memoirs of a Woman of Pleasure*." *Book Collector* 12 (Winter 1963): 476–87.

Fuller, Richard F. "How Boston Handles Problems." *Publishers Weekly* 103 (May 26, 1923): 1,624–1,625.

Gilloti, Chris F. "Book Censorship in Massachusetts: The Search for a Test of Obscenity." *Boston University Law Review* 42 (Fall 1962): 476–91.

"Gottschalk Fined for Obscene Book Sale." *Publishers Weekly* 111 (March 8, 1924): 834.

Grant, Sidney S., and S. E. Angoff. "Censorship in Boston." *Boston University Law Review* 10 (January 1930): 36–60.

———. "Recent Developments in Censorship." *Boston University Law Review* 10 (November 1930): 488–509.

Green, Samuel S. "Sensational Fiction in Public Libraries." *Library Journal* 4 (September–October 1879): 349–52.

Greenberg, Robert A. "'Anactoria,' and the Sapphic Passion." *Victorian Poetry* 29 (Spring 1991): 79–87.

Haskins, Doug. "The Many Faces of Censorship." *Canadian Forum* 33 (June 1953): 57–58.

Heller, Terry. "Mirrored Worlds and the Gothic in Faulkner's *Sanctuary*." *Mississippi Quarterly* 42 (Summer 1989): 247–59.

Henderson, R. W. "The Devil Rides Outside." *Library Journal* (November 1, 1952): 77.

Hicks, Granville. "Lolita and Her Problems." *Saturday Review* 41 (16 August 1958): 12, 38.

Hohne, Karen A. "The Power of the Spoken Word in the Works of Stephen King." *Journal of Popular Culture* 28 (Fall 1994): 93–103.

"*Homo Sapiens*: A Review." *The Little Review* 2 (December 1915): 25–27.

Huntington, Henry S. "The Philadelphia Book Seizures." *Elation* 167 (August 21, 1948): 205–7.

"In Brief: *The Chinese Room*." *The Nation* 156 (January 9, 1943): 67.

Johnson, B. S. "Pi Printers." *Censorship* 3 (Summer 1965): 43–45.

Joyce, James. "A Curious History." *Egoist* 1 (January 5, 1914): 26–27.

"Judge as Literary Critic." *Catholic World* 116 (December 1922): 392–99.

Kallen, Horace M. "Protean Censorship." *Freeman* 3 (June 29, 1921): 370–72.

Kauffman, Stanley. "God's Belittled Acre." *New Republic* 138 (June 30, 1958): 21.

Kaun, Alexander S. "The Ecstasy of Pain." *The Little Review* 2 (December 1915): 16–23.

Kennedy, Ludovic. "The Moors Murders and De Sade." *The Spectator* (April 29, 1966): 23–25.

Kincaid, Larry, and Grove Koger. "*Tropic of Cancer* and the Censors: A Case Study and Bibliographic Guide to the Literature." *Reference Services Review* 25 (Spring 1997): 31–38, 46.

"*Kreutzer Sonata*." *American Law Review* 25 (January–February 1891): 102–4.

Kuenz, Jane. "*The Bluest Eye*: Notes on History, Community and Black Female Subjectivity." *African American Review* 27 (Fall 1993): 421–31.

Lambert, Robert. "Charley: Metamorphosis by Media." *Media and Methods* 5 (February 1969): 29–31.

"The Law and the Censor." *New York Times* (September 14, 1922): 21.

Lawrence, D. H. "On Obscenity." *Publishers Weekly* (February 23, 1923): 580.

Levin, Bernard. "Why All the Fuss?" *Spectator* 202 (January 9, 1959): 32–33.

Lockhart, William B., and Robert C. McClure. "Censorship of Obscenity: The Developing Constitutional Standards." *Minnesota Law Review* 45 (November 1960): 19.

Lockhart, William B., and Robert C. McClure. "Literature, the Law of Obscenity, and the Constitution." *Minnesota Law Review* 38 (March 1954): 295–395.

Loe, Mary Hong. "Case Studies in Censorship: William Faulkner's *Sanctuary*." *Reference Services Review* 23 (Spring 1995): 71–84.

"Lolita in the Dock." *New Zealand Libraries* 23 (August 1960): 180–83.

Lucey, Michael. "The Consequences of Being Explicit: Watching Sex in Gide's *Si le grain ne meurt*." *Yale Journal of Criticism* 4 (1990): 174–92.

MacCarthy, Desmond. "Literary Trends." *Life and Letters* 1 (October 1928): 329–41.

Mackay, R. S. "Hidden Rule and Judicial Censorship." *Canadian Bar Review* 361 (March 1958): 1–24.

Magrath, C. Peter. "The Obscenity Cases: Grapes of Roth." *Supreme Court Review* 139 (1966): 9–13.

Matthews, Brander. "Books That Are Barred." *Munsey's Magazine* 50 (December 1913): 493–97.

Maynard, Joyce. "Coming of Age with Judy Blume." *New York Times Magazine* (December 3, 1978): 80+.

Mikva, Abner J. "Chicago: Citadel of Censorship." *Focus/Midwest* 2 (March-April 1963): 16–17.

Molz, Kathleen. "The Public Custody of the High Pornography." *American Scholar* (Winter 1966–1967): 93–103.

Moore, Everett T. "*Tropic of Cancer* (Second Phase). *ALA Bulletin* 56 (February 1962): 81–84.

"More of the Same: Massachusetts Supreme Court and Dreiser's *American Tragedy*." *Outlook* 155 (June 11, 1930): 214.

Morse, J. M. "*Forever Amber*: Defendant at Trial in Suffolk County Superior Court, Boston." *New Republic* (January 6, 1947): 39–40.

Moskin, Morton. "Inadequacy of Present Tests as to What Constitutes Obscene Literature." *Cornell Law Quarterly* 34 (Spring 1949): 442–47.

Murray, D. M. "Candy Christian as a Pop-Art Daisy Miller." *Journal of Popular Culture* 5 (1971): 340–48.

"Neither Censorship nor Puritanism Involved." *Christian Century* 47 (March 19, 1930): 357–58.

Nelson, Hilda. "Theophile Gautier: The Invisible and Impalpable World." *French Review* 45 (June 1972): 819–30.

Newsletter on Intellectual Freedom. Judith F. Krug, ed. Chicago, Ill.: American Library Association, Intellectual Freedom Committee. Numerous issues from July 1976 through March 1995.

"Obscenity-Evidence Admission of Contemporary Critical Evaluation of Libeled Book." *Minnesota Law Review* 35 (February 1951): 326–30.

"Offended at the Magistrate." *New York Times* (April 16, 1897): 5.

Patnoe, Elizabeth. "Lolita Misrepresented, Lolita Reclaimed: Disclosing the Doubles." *College Literature* 22 (June 1995): 81–104.

Pearce, Lillian. "Book Selection and Peyton Place." *Library Journal* 83 (March 1958): 712–13.

Podhoretz, Norman, and Brian O'Doherty. "The Present and Future of Pornography." *Show* 4 (June 1964): 54-55+.

"Pound of Waltzing Mice." *Time* 48 (December 9, 1946): 24–25.

Pringle, Henry F. "Comstock the Less." *The American Mercury* 10 (January 1927): 56–63.

"Publishing's Past Fifty Years, a Balance Sheet—II." *Saturday Review* 47 (November 28, 1964): 17–19, 69.

Quigley, Margery. "Books in Suburbia—The Suburban Library's Book-Buying Problems." *Library Journal* 55 (April 1, 1930): 303.

Ramazani, Vaheed K. "Writing in Pain: Baudelaire, Benjamin, Haussmann." *Boundary 2* 23 (Summer 1996): 199–224.

"A Reader's List: *The Chinese Room*." *The New Republic* 107 (November 9, 1942): 618.

Redman, B. R. "The Devil Rides Outside." *Saturday Review* (November 1, 1952): 16.

Rigolet, François. "Magdalen's Skull: Allegory and Iconography in *The Heptameron*." *Renaissance Quarterly* 47 (Spring 1994): 57–73.

Robbins, Harold. "Master Harold." *Advocate: The National Gay and Lesbian Newsmagazine* (August 22, 1995): 38-43.

Sachs, Ed. "I Want *Candy*." *Focus/Midwest* 3 (February 1964): 11–13, 23-24.

"School's Purchase of Four Books Ignites a Furor in Waterloo." *Des Moines Register* (April 15, 1992): M2.

Schmeling, Gareth. "*The Satyricon*: Forms in Search of a Genre." *Classical Bulletin* 47 (1970): 49–53.

Schriftgiesser, Karl. "Boston Stays Pure." *New Republic* 58 (May 8, 1929): 327–29.

Scott, W. J. "The *Lolita* Case." *Landfall* 58 (June 1961): 134–38.

Sebastian, Raymond F. "Obscenity and the Supreme Court: Nine Years of Confusion." *Stanford Law Review* 19 (November 1966): 167–89.

Shugert, Diane P. "Rationales for Commonly 'Challenged' Taught Books." *Connecticut English Journal* 15 (Fall 1983): 145–46.

Silva, Edward T. "From *Candide* to *Candy*: Love's Labor Lost." *Journal of Popular Culture* 8 (1974): 783–91.

Smith, Gene. "The Lonigan Curse." *American Heritage* 46 (April 1995): 150–51.

Smith, Harrison. "Practitioners of Culture." *Saturday Review of Literature* (February 28, 1948): 13.

Smith, Roger H. "Cops, Counselors and *Tropic of Cancer*." *Publishers Weekly* 180 (October 23, 1961): 35.

Stein, Karen. "Margaret Atwood's Modest Proposal: *The Handmaid's Tale*." *Canadian Literature* 23 (Spring 1996): 57–73.

St. John-Stevas, Norman. "Art, Morality and Censorship." *Ramparts* 2 (May 1963): 40–48.

"Sumner Denounces Book in Hall Case." *New York Times* (October 20, 1992): 3.

Tait, Sue, and Christy Tyson. "Paperbacks for Young Adults." *Emergency Librarian* 16 (October 1988): 53–54.

Tanner, Laura E. "Reading Rape: *Sanctuary* and the Women of *Brewster Place*." *American Literature* 62 (December 1990): 559–82.

Tanselle, G. Thomas. "The Thomas Seltzer Imprint." *Papers of the Bibliographic Society of America* 58 (Fourth Quarter 1964): 380–416.

"The Test of Obscenity." *Author* 65 (Autumn 1954): 1–5.

Thompson, Susan. "Images of Adolescence: Part I." *Signal* 34 (1981): 57–59.

Tirrell, Lynne. "Storytelling and Moral Agency." *Journal of Aesthetics & Art Criticism* 48 (Spring 1990): 115–26.

Traubel, Horace L. "Freedom to Write and to Print." *Poet-Lore* 2 (October 1890): 529–31.

"*Triumph of Death* Exonerated." *New York Times* (April 6, 1897): 5.

"Two Booksellers Arrested on Sumner Complaint." *Publishers Weekly* 110 (December 23, 1923): 1,974.

Updike, John. "The Plight of the American Writer." *Change* 9 (April 1978): 36–41.

Wagner-Lawlor, Jennifer. "Metaphorical 'Indiscretion' and Literary Survival in Swinburne's 'Anactoria.'" *Studies in English Literature, 1500–1900* 36 (Autumn 1996): 917–34.

Wald, Emil W. "Obscene Literature Standards Re-Examined." *South Carolina Law Review* 18 (Spring 1966): 497–503.

Warburg, Frederic. "A View of Obscenity." *New Yorker* 33 (April 20, 1957): 106–33.

Watson, Jay. "The Rhetoric of Exhaustion and the Exhaustion of Rhetoric: Erskine Caldwell in the Thirties." *Mississippi Quarterly* 46 (Spring 1993): 215–29.

Weightman, John. "Andre Gide and the Homosexual Debate." *American Scholar* 59 (Autumn 1990): 591–601.

Wilcox, Clyde. "The Not-So-Failed Feminism of Jean Auel." *Journal of Popular Culture* 28 (Winter 1994): 63–70.

Wilson, Andrew J. "The Corruption in Looking: William Faulkner's *Sanctuary* as a Detective Novel." *Mississippi Quarterly* 47 (Summer 1994): 441–60.

Woodward, Frances. "*Forever Amber*." *Atlantic* (December 1944): 137.

"Worcester Library Directors Support Their Librarian." *Library Journal* 74 (April 15, 1949): 649.

Wright, Derek. "Mapless Motion: Form and Space in Updike's *Rabbit, Run*." *Modern Fiction Studies* 37 (Spring 1991): 35–44.

Yevish, I.A. "Attack on *Jude the Obscure*: A Reappraisal Some Seventy Years After." *Journal of General Education* 18 (January 1967): 239–48.

WORKS DISCUSSED IN THE OTHER VOLUMES OF THIS SERIES

AREOPAGITICA
John Milton

BLACK BOY
Richard Wright

*BLOODS: AN ORAL HISTORY OF THE VIETNAM WAR
BY BLACK VETERANS*
Wallace Terry

BORN ON THE FOURTH OF JULY
Ron Kovic

BOSS: RICHARD J. DALEY OF CHICAGO
Mike Royko

BURGHER'S DAUGHTER
Nadine Gordimer

BURY MY HEART AT WOUNDED KNEE
Dee Brown

*BY WAY OF DECEPTION: THE MAKING AND UNMAKING
OF A MOSSAD OFFICER*
Victor Ostrovsky and Claire Hoy

CANCER WARD
Aleksandr Solzhenitsyn

THE CASE FOR INDIA
Will Durant

CAT'S CRADLE
Kurt Vonnegut Jr.

CHILD OF ALL NATIONS
Pramoedya Ananta Toer

THE CHINA LOBBY IN AMERICAN POLITICS
Ross Y. Koen

THE CIA AND THE CULT OF INTELLIGENCE
Victor Marchetti and John D. Marks

CITIZEN TOM PAINE
Howard Fast

THE COMMERCIAL RESTRAINTS OF IRELAND CONSIDERED
John Hely Hutchinson

COMPARATIVE POLITICS TODAY: A WORLD VIEW
Gabriel A. Almond, general ed.

CRY AMANDLA!
June Goodwin

DAS KAPITAL
Karl Marx

DAUGHTER OF EARTH
Agnes Smedley

THE DAY THEY CAME TO ARREST THE BOOK
Nat Hentoff

DECENT INTERVAL: AN INSIDER'S ACCOUNT OF SAIGON'S INDECENT END
Frank Snepp

DOCTOR ZHIVAGO
Boris Pasternak

THE DRAPIER'S LETTERS
Jonathan Swift

A DRY WHITE SEASON
André Brink

DU PONT: BEHIND THE NYLON CURTAIN
Gerald Colby Zilg

EL SEÑOR PRESIDENTE
Miguel Angel Asturias

FAIL-SAFE
Eugene Burdick and Harvey Wheeler

FIELDS OF FIRE
James Webb

A FLEET IN BEING: NOTES OF TWO TRIPS WITH THE CHANNEL SQUADRON
Rudyard Kipling

THE FRAGILE FLAG
Jane Langton

THE FUGITIVE
Pramoedya Ananta Toer

A GLOBAL HISTORY OF MAN
Leften S. Stavrianos

THE GRAPES OF WRATH
John Steinbeck

THE GREEN POPE
Miguel Angel Asturias

THE GULAG ARCHIPELAGO 1918–1956
Aleksandr Solzhenitsyn

GULLIVER'S TRAVELS
Jonathan Swift

HANDBOOK FOR CONSCIENTIOUS OBJECTORS
Robert A. Seeley, ed.

A HERO ON A DONKEY
Miodrag Bulatovic

THE HOAX OF THE TWENTIETH CENTURY
Arthur R. Butz

I AM THE CHEESE
Robert Cormier

INSIDE RUSSIA TODAY
John Gunther

INSIDE THE COMPANY: CIA Diary
Philip Agee

IN THE SPIRIT OF CRAZY HORSE
Peter Matthiessen

AN INTRODUCTION TO PROBLEMS OF AMERICAN CULTURE
Harold O. Rugg

THE INVISIBLE GOVERNMENT
David Wise and Thomas B. Ross

IT CAN'T HAPPEN HERE
Sinclair Lewis

JOHNNY GOT HIS GUN
Dalton Trumbo

A JOURNEY FROM ST. PETERSBURG TO MOSCOW
Aleksandr Nikolaevich Radishchev

JULIE OF THE WOLVES
Jean Craighead George

THE JUNGLE
Upton Sinclair

KEEPING FAITH: MEMOIRS OF A PRESIDENT
Jimmy Carter

THE LAND AND PEOPLE OF CUBA
Victoria Ortiz

LAND OF THE FREE: A HISTORY OF THE UNITED STATES
John W. Caughey, John Hope Franklin and Ernest R. May

LAUGHING BOY
Oliver LaFarge

LES MISÉRABLES
Victor Hugo

MANIFESTO OF THE COMMUNIST PARTY
Karl Marx and Friedrich Engels

MARXISM VERSUS SOCIALISM
Vladimir G. Simkhovitch

MEIN KAMPF
Adolf Hitler

MEN AND NATIONS
Anatole G. Mazour and John M. Peoples

MY BROTHER SAM IS DEAD
James Lincoln Collier and Christopher Collier

MY NAME IS ASHER LEV
Chaim Potok

MY PEOPLE: THE STORY OF THE JEWS
Abba Eban

NELSON AND WINNIE MANDELA
Dorothy Hoobler and Thomas Hoobler

NINETEEN EIGHTY-FOUR
George Orwell

NOVEL WITHOUT A NAME
Duong Thu Huong

OIL!
Upton Sinclair

ONE DAY IN THE LIFE OF IVAN DENISOVICH
Aleksandr Solzhenitsyn

ONE PEOPLE, ONE DESTINY: THE CARIBBEAN
AND CENTRAL AMERICA TODAY
Don Rojas

OUR LAND, OUR TIME
Joseph Robert Conlin

PARADISE OF THE BLIND
Duong Thu Huong

THE PRINCE
Niccolò Machiavelli

PRINCIPLES OF NATURE
Elihu Palmer

PROMISE OF AMERICA
Larry Cuban and Philip Roden

RED STAR OVER CUBA
Nathaniel Weyl

REPORT OF THE SIBERIAN DELEGATION
Leon Trotsky

THE RIGHTS OF MAN
Thomas Paine

RUSSIA
Vernon Ives

SECRECY AND DEMOCRACY: THE CIA IN TRANSITION
Stansfield Turner

SLAUGHTERHOUSE-FIVE OR THE CHILDREN'S CRUSADE
Kurt Vonnegut Jr.

SPYCATCHER
Peter Wright

THE STATE AND REVOLUTION
Vladimir I. Lenin

STRONG WIND
Miguel Angel Asturias

THE STRUGGLE IS MY LIFE
Nelson Mandela

A SUMMARY VIEW OF THE RIGHTS OF BRITISH AMERICA
Thomas Jefferson

SYLVESTER AND THE MAGIC PEBBLE
William Steig

TEN DAYS THAT SHOOK THE WORLD
John Reed

THE THINGS THEY CARRIED
Tim O'Brien

THIS EARTH OF MANKIND
Pramoedya Ananta Toer

365 DAYS
Ronald J. Glasser

TODAY'S ISMS: COMMUNISM, FASCISM, CAPITALISM, SOCIALISM
William Ebenstein

THE UGLY AMERICAN
William J. Lederer and Eugene Burdick

UNCLE TOM'S CABIN
Harriet Beecher Stowe

UNITED STATES VIETNAM RELATIONS, 1945–67 ("THE PENTAGON PAPERS")
U.S. Department of Defense

WHY ARE WE IN VIETNAM?
Norman Mailer

WORDS OF CONSCIENCE: RELIGIOUS STATEMENTS OF CONSCIENTIOUS OBJECTORS
Shawn Perry, ed.

WORKS DISCUSSED IN BANNED BOOKS: LITERATURE SUPPRESSED ON RELIGIOUS GROUNDS BY MARGARET BALD

ADDRESS TO THE CHRISTIAN NOBILITY OF THE GERMAN NATION
Martin Luther

THE ADVANCEMENT OF LEARNING
Francis Bacon

THE AGE OF REASON
Thomas Paine

ALCIPHRON, OR THE MINUTE PHILOSOPHER
George Berkeley

THE ANALECTS
Confucius

ARCANA COELESTIA
Emanuel Swedenborg

THE BABYLONIAN CAPTIVITY OF THE CHURCH
Martin Luther

THE BIBLE

THE BLOUDY TENENT OF PERSECUTION
Roger Williams

THE BOOK OF COMMON PRAYER
Thomas Cranmer and others

CHILDREN OF THE ALLEY
Naguib Mahfouz

THE CHRISTIAN COMMONWEALTH
John Eliot

CHRISTIANITY NOT MYSTERIOUS
John Toland

CHRISTIANITY RESTORED
Michael Servetus

*CHURCH: CHARISM AND POWER: LIBERATION THEOLOGY
AND THE INSTITUTIONAL CHURCH*
Leonardo Boff

COLLOQUIES
Desiderius Erasmus

COMMENTARIES
Averroës (Ibn Rushd)

COMPENDIUM REVELATIONUM
Girolamo Savonarola

CONCERNING HERETICS
Sebastian Castellio

THE COURSE OF POSITIVE PHILOSOPHY
Auguste Comte

CREATIVE EVOLUTION
Henri Bergson

THE CRITIQUE OF PURE REASON
Immanuel Kant

DE ECCLESIA
John Hus

DE INVENTORIBUS RERUM
Polydore Vergil

DE L'ESPRIT
Claude Adrien Helvétius

DIALOGUE CONCERNING THE TWO CHIEF WORLD SYSTEMS
Galileo Galilei

DIALOGUES CONCERNING NATURAL RELIGION
David Hume

DISCOURSE ON METHOD
René Descartes

DON QUIXOTE
Miguel de Cervantes Saavedra

DRAGONWINGS
Laurence Yep

ÉMILE
Jean-Jacques Rousseau

ENCYCLOPÉDIE
Denis Diderot and Jean d'Alembert, eds.

AN ESSAY CONCERNING HUMAN UNDERSTANDING
John Locke

ESSAYS
Michel de Montaigne

ETHICS
Baruch (Benedict) Spinoza

THE FABLE OF THE BEES
Bernard Mandeville

THE GUIDE OF THE PERPLEXED
Moses Maimonides

THE HIDDEN FACE OF EVE: WOMEN IN THE ARAB WORLD
Nawal El Saadawi

HISTORICAL AND CRITICAL DICTIONARY
Pierre Bayle

HISTORY OF THE CONFLICT BETWEEN RELIGION AND SCIENCE
John William Draper

HISTORY OF THE DECLINE AND FALL OF THE ROMAN EMPIRE
Edward Gibbon

INFALLIBLE? AN INQUIRY
Hans Küng

AN INQUIRY CONCERNING HUMAN UNDERSTANDING
David Hume

INSTITUTES OF THE CHRISTIAN RELIGION
John Calvin

INTRODUCTION TO THEOLOGY
Peter Abelard

*AN INTRODUCTION TO THE PRINCIPLES OF
MORALS AND LEGISLATION*
Jeremy Bentham

INTRODUCTORY LECTURES ON PSYCHOANALYSIS
Sigmund Freud

THE KORAN

LAJJA (SHAME)
Taslima Nasrin

THE LAST TEMPTATION OF CHRIST
Nikos Kazantzakis

LETTER ON THE BLIND
Denis Diderot

LETTERS CONCERNING THE ENGLISH NATION
Voltaire (François Marie Arouet)

LEVIATHAN
Thomas Hobbes

THE LIFE OF JESUS
Ernest Renan

MEDITATIONS ON FIRST PHILOSOPHY
René Descartes

THE MERITORIOUS PRICE OF OUR REDEMPTION
William Pynchon

THE METAPHYSICS
Aristotle

THE NEW ASTRONOMY
Johannes Kepler

THE NEW TESTAMENT
William Tyndale, trans.

NINETY-FIVE THESES
Martin Luther

OF THE VANITIE AND UNCERTAINTIE OF ARTES AND SCIENCES
Henricus Cornelius Agrippa

OLIVER TWIST
Charles Dickens

ON CIVIL LORDSHIP
John Wycliff

ON JUSTICE IN THE REVOLUTION AND IN THE CHURCH
Pierre-Joseph Proudhon

ON MONARCHY
Dante Alighieri

ON THE INFINITE UNIVERSE AND WORLDS
Giordano Bruno

ON THE LAW OF WAR AND PEACE
Hugo Grotius

ON THE ORIGIN OF SPECIES
Charles Darwin

ON THE REVOLUTION OF HEAVENLY SPHERES
Nicholas Copernicus

OPUS MAIUS
Roger Bacon

PENGUIN ISLAND
Anatole France (Jacques Anatole Thibault)

THE PERSIAN LETTERS (1721)
Charles-Louis de Secondat de Montesquieu

PHILOSOPHICAL DICTIONARY
Voltaire (François Marie Arouet)

THE POLITICAL HISTORY OF THE DEVIL
Daniel Defoe

POPOL VUH

THE POWER AND THE GLORY
Graham Greene

THE PRAISE OF FOLLY
Desiderius Erasmus

PRINCIPLES OF POLITICAL ECONOMY
John Stuart Mill

THE PROVINCIAL LETTERS
Blaise Pascal

THE RAPE OF SITA
Lindsey Collen

THE RED AND THE BLACK
Stendhal (Marie Henri Beyle)

RELIGIO MEDICI
Sir Thomas Browne

RELIGION WITHIN THE LIMITS OF REASON ALONE
Immanuel Kant

THE RIGHTS OF THE CHRISTIAN CHURCH ASSERTED
Matthew Tindal

THE SANDY FOUNDATION SHAKEN
William Penn

THE SATANIC VERSES
Salman Rushdie

A SHORT DECLARATION OF THE MISTERY OF INIQUITY
Thomas Helwys

THE SHORTEST WAY WITH THE DISSENTERS
Daniel Defoe

THE SOCIAL CONTRACT
Jean-Jacques Rousseau

THE SORROWS OF YOUNG WERTHER
Johann Wolfgang von Goethe

THE SPIRIT OF LAWS
Charles-Louis de Secondat de Montesquieu

SPIRITS REBELLIOUS
Khalil Gibran

THE STORY OF ZAHRA
Hanan al-Shaykh

A TALE OF A TUB
Jonathan Swift

THE TALMUD

THEOLOGICAL-POLITICAL TREATISE
Baruch (Benedict) Spinoza

THREE-PART WORK
Meister Eckhart

THE VEIL AND THE MALE ELITE: A FEMINIST INTERPRETATION OF WOMEN'S RIGHTS IN ISLAM
Fatima Mernissi

VOYAGES TO THE MOON AND THE SUN
Savinien Cyrano de Bergerac

ZOONOMIA
Erasmus Darwin

WORKS DISCUSSED IN BANNED BOOKS: LITERATURE SUPPRESSED ON SOCIAL GROUNDS BY DAWN SOVA

THE ADVENTURES OF HUCKLEBERRY FINN
Mark Twain

THE ADVENTURES OF SHERLOCK HOLMES
Sir Arthur Conan Doyle

THE ADVENTURES OF TOM SAWYER
Mark Twain

ALICE'S ADVENTURES IN WONDERLAND
Lewis Carroll

THE AMBOY DUKES
Irving Shulman

AMERICAN HERITAGE DICTIONARY

AND STILL I RISE
Maya Angelou

ANNE FRANK: THE DIARY OF A YOUNG GIRL
Anne Frank

ANNIE ON MY MIND
Nancy Garden

ANOTHER COUNTRY
James Baldwin

APHRODITE
PierreLouÿs

APPOINTMENT IN SAMARRA
John O'Hara

AS I LAY DYING
William Faulkner

THE AUTOBIOGRAPHY OF BENJAMIN FRANKLIN
Benjamin Franklin

THE AUTOBIOGRAPHY OF MALCOLM X
Malcolm X, with Alex Haley

THE AUTOBIOGRAPHY OF MISS JANE PITMAN
Ernest J. Gaines

BEING THERE
Jerzy Kosinski

THE BELL JAR
Sylvia Plath

THE BEST SHORT STORIES BY NEGRO WRITERS
Langston Hughes, ed.

BLACK LIKE ME
John Howard Griffin

BLESS THE BEASTS AND CHILDREN
Glendon Swarthout

BLUBBER
Judy Blume

BRAVE NEW WORLD
Aldous Huxley

BRIDGE TO TERABITHIA
Katherine Paterson

CAIN'S BOOK
Alexander Trocchi

CAMILLE
Alexander Dumas Jr.

THE CANTERBURY TALES
Geoffrey Chaucer

CATCH-22
Joseph Heller

THE CATCHER IN THE RYE
J. D. Salinger

THE CHOCOLATE WAR
Robert Cormier

A CLOCKWORK ORANGE
Anthony Burgess

THE COLOR PURPLE
Alice Walker

CUJO
Stephen King

DADDY'S ROOMMATE
Michael Willhoite

A DAY NO PIGS WOULD DIE
Robert Newton Peck

DELIVERANCE
James Dickey

A DICTIONARY OF AMERICAN SLANG
Harold Wentworth

DICTIONARY OF SLANG AND UNCONVENTIONAL ENGLISH
Eric Partridge

DOCTOR DOLITTLE
Hugh John Lofting

DOG DAY AFTERNOON
Patrick Mann

DOWN THESE MEAN STREETS
Piri Thomas

DRACULA
Bram Stoker

EAST OF EDEN
John Steinbeck

ELMER GANTRY
Sinclair Lewis

END AS A MAN
Calder Willingham

ESTHER WATERS
George Moore

FAHRENHEIT 451
Ray Bradbury

A FAREWELL TO ARMS
Ernest Hemingway

THE FIXER
Bernard Malamud

FRUITS OF PHILOSOPHY
Charles Knowlton

GARGANTUA AND PANTAGRUEL
François Rabelais

GO ASK ALICE
Anonymous

GONE WITH THE WIND
Margaret Mitchell

GORILLAS IN THE MIST
Dian Fossey

GO TELL IT ON THE MOUNTAIN
James Baldwin

GRENDEL
John Gardner

HEATHER HAS TWO MOMMIES
Leslea Newman

A HERO AIN'T NOTHIN' BUT A SANDWICH
Alice Childress

HOWL AND OTHER POEMS
Allen Ginsberg

I KNOW WHY THE CAGED BIRD SINGS
Maya Angelou

IN THE NIGHT KITCHEN
Maurice Sendak

INVISIBLE MAN
Ralph Ellison

JAMES AND THE GIANT PEACH
Roald Dahl

JAWS
Peter Benchley

JUNKY
William S. Burroughs

KINGSBLOOD ROYAL
Sinclair Lewis

LAST EXIT TO BROOKLYN
Hubert Selby Jr.

LEAVES OF GRASS
Walt Whitman

LITTLE BLACK SAMBO
Helen Bannerman

LITTLE HOUSE ON THE PRAIRIE
Laura Ingalls Wilder

LITTLE RED RIDING HOOD
Charles Perrault

LORD OF THE FLIES
William Golding

MANCHILD IN THE PROMISED LAND
Claude Brown

MARRIED LOVE
Marie Stopes

MY HOUSE
Nikki Giovanni

THE NAKED APE
Desmond Morris

NAKED LUNCH
William S. Burroughs

NANA
Émile Zola

NEVER LOVE A STRANGER
Harold Robbins

NEW DICTIONARY OF AMERICAN SLANG
Robert Chapman

OF MICE AND MEN
John Steinbeck

OF TIME AND THE RIVER
Thomas Wolfe

ONE FLEW OVER THE CUCKOO'S NEST
Ken Kesey

ORDINARY PEOPLE
Judith Guest

THE OX-BOW INCIDENT
Walter Clark

THE RED PONY
John Steinbeck

THE SCARLET LETTER
Nathaniel Hawthorne

A SEPARATE PEACE
John Knowles

SISTER CARRIE
Theodore Dreiser

SOUL ON ICE
Eldridge Cleaver

STEPPENWOLF
Hermann Hesse

STRANGE FRUIT
Lillian Smith

STRANGER IN A STRANGE LAND
Robert A. Heinlein

THE SUN ALSO RISES
Ernest Hemingway

TO HAVE AND HAVE NOT
Ernest Hemingway

TO KILL A MOCKINGBIRD
Harper Lee

WELCOME TO THE MONKEY HOUSE
Kurt Vonnegut Jr.

THE WELL OF LONELINESS
Radclyffe Hall

WOMAN IN THE MISTS
Farley Mowat

WORKING
Studs Terkel

A WORLD I NEVER MADE
James T. Farrell

Index

Boldface numbers indicate major treatment of a topic.